From Traitor to Zealot

What makes a neo-Nazi become a convinced anti-fascist or a radical left-winger become a devout Salafist? How do they manage to fit into their new environment and gain acceptance as a former enemy? The people featured in this book made highly puzzling journeys, first venturing into extremist milieus and then deciding to switch to the opposite side. By using their extraordinary life stories and their own narratives, this book provides the first in-depth analysis of how and why people move between seemingly opposing extremist environments that can sometimes overlap and influence each other. It aims to understand how these extremists manage to convince their new group that they can be trusted, which also allows us to dive deep into the psychology of extremism and terrorism. This fascinating work will be of immense value to those studying radicalization and counter-radicalization in terrorism studies, social psychology, and political science.

DANIEL KOEHLER is Founding Director of the German Institute on Radicalization and De-radicalization Studies (GIRDS) and a leading expert on terrorism, violent extremism, radicalization, and deradicalization. He is member of the editorial board of the International Centre for Counter-Terrorism in The Hague and a research fellow at the Polarization and Extremism Research and Innovation Lab of the American University in Washington, DC.

From Traitor to Zealot

Exploring the Phenomenon of Side-Switching in Extremism and Terrorism

Daniel Koehler

German Institute on Radicalization and De-radicalization Studies (GIRDS)

CAMBRIDGE
UNIVERSITY PRESS

CAMBRIDGE
UNIVERSITY PRESS

Shaftesbury Road, Cambridge CB2 8EA, United Kingdom

One Liberty Plaza, 20th Floor, New York, NY 10006, USA

477 Williamstown Road, Port Melbourne, VIC 3207, Australia

314–321, 3rd Floor, Plot 3, Splendor Forum, Jasola District Centre, New Delhi – 110025, India

103 Penang Road, #05–06/07, Visioncrest Commercial, Singapore 238467

Cambridge University Press is part of Cambridge University Press & Assessment, a department of the University of Cambridge.

We share the University's mission to contribute to society through the pursuit of education, learning and research at the highest international levels of excellence.

www.cambridge.org
Information on this title: www.cambridge.org/9781108825085

DOI: 10.1017/9781108918626

First published 2022
First paperback edition 2023

A catalogue record for this publication is available from the British Library

Library of Congress Cataloging-in-Publication data
Names: Koehler, Daniel, author.
Title: From traitor to zealot : exploring the phenomenon of side-switching in extremism and terrorism / Daniel Koehler, German Institute on Radicalization and De-Radicalization Studies (GIRDS).
Description: Cambridge, United Kingdom ; New York, NY : Cambridge University Press, 2022. | Includes bibliographical references and index.
Identifiers: LCCN 2021030279 (print) | LCCN 2021030280 (ebook) | ISBN 9781108842945 (hardback) | ISBN 9781108825085 (paperback) | ISBN 9781108918626 (epub)
Subjects: LCSH: Radicalism–Psychological aspects. | Radicalization–Psychological aspects. | BISAC: PSYCHOLOGY / Social Psychology
Classification: LCC HN49.R33 K64 2021 (print) | LCC HN49.R33 (ebook) | DDC 303.48/4–dc23
LC record available at https://lccn.loc.gov/2021030279
LC ebook record available at https://lccn.loc.gov/2021030280

ISBN   978-1-108-84294-5   Hardback
ISBN   978-1-108-82508-5   Paperback

This book is dedicated to all victims of violent extremism and terrorism, as well as to those who show the strength and courage to make right on previous mistakes in their lives.

Contents

Tables

Foreword

Spoiler alert – becoming involved in terrorism involves significant risk. Despite the allure of adventure, excitement, belonging to, and serving a cause and community bigger than oneself, it is fraught with danger. Even if recruits are allowed to join (or encouraged to act on their own), success is set at a very high bar indeed. Terrorist attacks constitute effective psychological warfare in the short term, but they rarely accomplish long-term goals. For its participants, involvement in terrorism likely ends in capture, conviction, and detention. It often ends in death. Now these realities are not unknown to the prospective recruit. In fact, terrorist organizations and their recruiters are keen to point out that this life isn't for everyone. But they do so for very particular reasons. It is often the very promise of danger, of righteous suffering in the face of insurmountable odds against an enemy and ideology, that to a certain mindset is an irresistible allure. As even casual observers of terrorism know, there is no shortage of prospects willing to risk seeing if the reality can match the fantasy. And yet, even for the most ardent of true believers, reality can bite hard. The day-to-day grind of clandestine groups, the stress, fear, paranoia, exhaustion, and countless other group pressures can be suffocating. Most members of terrorist groups, and extremist groups more broadly, struggle to cope with such strain. More often than not, disillusionment sets in. Yet even then, some thrive under these conditions while watching others buckle around them. For some, disillusionment is temporary, just one more step on a rocky road, another obstacle to test one's commitment and faith. For others, disillusionment is a wake-up call, a warning to get out, and get out now before it's too late. For those that do get out, some leave with their views intact. They may no longer be involved and engaged in terrorist activity but remain as committed and radical as ever. Others, however, not only leave but disavow the very beliefs, ideals, and core principles they once seemed ready to risk death for – they not only disengage, but they *deradicalize*.

To those who study such things, Daniel Koehler is a household name. A true scientist-practitioner, Daniel is one of the few in the field who talks the talk and walks the walk. In 2016, his book, *Understanding Deradicalization: Methods, Tools and Programs for Countering Violent Extremism* provided us a richly detailed guide to designing programs aimed at facilitating that process. That book was nothing less than a revelation. He provided theoretical insights for those seeking to conceptualize and design such programs and real-world practical advice to those tasked with building, running, and evaluating them. In the four years that followed, Daniel's work catapulted him to the front lines of deradicalization programs worldwide, where his input and advice is routinely solicited by those who take deradicalization seriously. As if all that wasn't enough, now, barely five years later, he has once again given us something extraordinary.

Building on his knowledge of how, why, and when people leave terrorist groups, Daniel turns his attention to those who defect by *switching sides*. When he told me he was writing a book on this topic, I stopped in my tracks. The questions came thick and fast. *Wow. Do we even know anything about this? Why would someone do that? How can they do it without being killed?* If being involved in extremist and terrorist groups was not already risky enough, Daniel found that there are some (just how many we don't know, and he freely acknowledges this) that seek out the opportunity to migrate to *other* extremist groups. Not only that, but they also sometimes switch over to those at the complete *opposite* end of their ideological spectrum – Daniel found cases of members of far-left extremist groups moving to the far right, and vice versa. Elsewhere, he uncovered cases of people once deeply committed to far-right or far-left groups who ended up switching over to Islamic extremist groups. To put it mildly, these cases are head-scratchers. Why on earth would someone commit the time, effort, and risk involved in developing commitment to one ideological extremist group, and entertain the astronomical risk that entails, to then not just turn *against* their group, but in doing so move toward their once-mortal enemy in order to gain *their* trust and serve *their* cause? Who would do that? Why would they do that? How can they not only perform the requisite mental gymnastics to switch ideologies but, as Daniel asks, in the process of successfully switching sides, to somehow gain the trust of a group made up entirely of one's former enemies instead of being killed on sight?

The background to this book can be traced to an article of Daniel's, published in the academic journal *Political Psychology*. In that paper he highlighted four case studies of people who had switched sides. During his research for the piece, Daniel found that side-switching was virtually ignored by researchers of terrorism and political violence. Sure, there was a little recognition here and there in the literature about the existence of some extremists holding certain ideologies prior to their involvement in different extremist groups, but, he found, existing data sets either didn't provide enough information or, worse still, they simply failed to see the significance of it. As a result, Daniel has given us this wonderful book.

From Traitor to Zealot: Exploring the Phenomenon of Side-Switching in Extremism and Terrorism is profoundly important. It is a serious attempt to address a deeply neglected, and admittedly fascinating, puzzle. It is a rare book indeed that reads both as thriller, with rich historical illustrations of side-switching, combined with nuanced theoretical analysis of how side-switching in today's extremist and terrorist milieu can be understood via perspectives from academic disciplines. The book is illustrated with dozens of real-life accounts of testimonies from those involved. In doing so, Daniel identifies the similarities in side-switcher pathways, life cycles, and experiences. The existing research on violent extremism can only take us so far; Daniel acknowledges this point while masterfully anchoring his arguments in concepts from criminology, psychology, sociology, history, and philosophy. That he does so with such ease highlights his own capacity to side-switch perspectives, theories, and conceptual frameworks in a way that most terrorism researchers would find challenging (and for which we both admire Koehler and are envious of him). Even the process of mapping defector life cycles, let alone uncovering the mystery of what motivates side-switchers, constitutes complex, difficult problems. To fully understand these processes requires not just a close examination of how they navigate such pathways, but how they cope with the realities of the day-to-day internal conflict that so often defines such groups. On its surface, side-switching seems to defy explanation. To ally oneself against an ideology one previously rallied against so vehemently appears at odds with a key requisite to being an effective extremist – remaining steadfastly committed to core principles. How then can we reconcile mental rigidity with ideological flexibility? If the questions seem complex, it can hardly be surprising that answers do not easily reveal themselves. Yet this doesn't deter Daniel. On the contrary, he effortlessly weaves painstaking historical research, with insights from research on terrorism, extremism, civil wars, and ideologies and so much more.

Yet despite all of this, what always shines through Daniel Koehler's work is an unwavering sense of optimism. He carefully and meticulously identifies lessons from these storylines for preventing and countering violent extremism. What do we do with people who don't just want to get out of an extremist group, but in doing so want to "re-up" with alternative extremist group? Can anything be done to divert side-switchers, to steer them toward an off-ramp headed back to conventional society instead of onward into new extremist territory? To learn more, you simply have to turn these pages. If this area represents, in Daniel's words, uncharted territory, then Koehler is its cartographer, navigator, captain, and sailor.

John Horgan, PhD
Distinguished University Professor
Department of Psychology
Georgia State University

Preface

On Sunday, June 28, 1914, in the city of Sarajevo, today's capital of Bosnia and Herzegovina, the 19-year-old Bosnian-Serb Nedeljko Čabrinović, member of a seven-men-strong hit squad, hurled a hand grenade at a procession of six cars that passed by the central police station. He aimed at the third car with a rolled back top that exposed to the public the Archduke Franz Ferdinand of Austria, the heir presumptive to the throne of Austria-Hungary, on his way to an opening ceremony of a hospital. The bomb exploded under the wheel of the following fourth car after the driver of the targeted vehicle had spotted the attack and accelerated to avoid being hit. After Čabrinović had missed the Archduke's car, he swallowed a cyanide capsule to escape arrest and jumped into the River Miljacka. A few seconds later, however, he was hauled back out and detained. The cyanide pill had failed to kill him. Franz Ferdinand and his wife Sophie, Duchess of Hohenberg, decided to visit the victims of the bomb attack at the local hospital. By pure chance, Gavrilo Princip, another assassin of the ultra-nationalist "Black Hand" secret military society to which Čabrinović belonged as well, sat in a café nearby. He immediately seized the opportunity, walked across the street, and shot the royal couple, thereby setting in motion a chain of events that led to the outbreak of the First World War.

Over eight years later in Rome, on October 28, 1922, leaders of the Italian Fascist Party had planned a coup d'état. On that day, between 25,000 and 30,000 troops of the so-called Blackshirts entered the city and directly threatened a violent takeover of state power from King Victor Emmanuel III. Even though the Italian Prime Minister Luigi Facta initially wanted to declare a state of siege, the king gave in to the Fascist's demands and yielded power without resistance, fearing the outbreak of civil war. Fascist propaganda subsequently celebrated the event as the "March on Rome" and idolized it as a revolutionary seizure of the government even though the truth was far from it. Nevertheless, this pivotal moment in Italian and European history brought to power 39-year-old Benito Mussolini, nicknamed "Il Duce" ("The Leader"), who was appointed prime minister of Italy by the king one day after the "March." Through this act, state power was handed over to him and his

"National Fascist Party" (Partito Nazionale Fascista, or PNF) without large-scale armed conflict. Under Mussolini's reign, Fascist Italy would rise to a significant military power and directly inspire neighboring political movements ideologically aligned with Fascism. In Germany, for example, the young National Socialist movement led by the so far mostly unknown Adolf Hitler would see the Italian success in taking over the government through demonstrative show of force as a proof of concept, and emulate it with the failed November 8–9, 1923, "Hitler-Ludendorff" coup d'état against the Weimar Republic (Alcalde, 2018). In this way, the Italian "March on Rome" precipitated a course of events that led to Hitler's imprisonment and had a significant impact on his political strategies. The botched National Socialist march on Berlin, commonly referred to as the "Beer Hall Putsch," would become a galvanizing moment for the Nazi movement and give rise to a martyr cult acting as one of their key recruiting narratives afterward (Gordon, 2015).

On February 22, 1945, an Allied Forces combat aircraft attacked a car on the road between the small southern German towns of Mainau and Sigmaringen. The incident left dead 46-year-old Jacques Doriot, a member of the German Waffen-SS and head of the "Fascist French Populist Party" (Parti Populaire Français, or PPF). Doriot had come to Germany in December 1943 to join the exiled pro-German government of Vichy France, which had been installed by the Nazis to control the non-occupied part of the country between 1940 and 1944. With the death of its chairman, the PPF was dissolved and the most collaborationist French Fascist party that had helped to round up and hand over members of the Jewish community to the Nazis came to an end. Although by the time of its demise the PPF had lost virtually all political relevance, it nevertheless played an important role in the mobilization of French volunteers for the German SS. Doriot himself had created the "French Volunteer Legion against Bolshevism" (Légion des volontaires français contre le bolchévisme, or LVF), which became an official unit in the Wehrmacht and saw action on the Eastern Front. During his time in and around Sigmaringen, Doriot, together with the PPF, created their own French newspaper and radio station designed to spread pro-Nazi propaganda among their fellow countrymen and sow disunity. The organization was also involved in conducting guerrilla and sabotage operations in the liberated parts of France against the Allied Forces, for example, by parachuting operatives behind enemy lines (Brunet, 1986; Kestel, 2012).

At first sight, these three historical events seem to have little in common, except that they all involve convinced extremists, violence, and partially wide repercussions on a national and even global scale. All three events had profound and immediate impacts on the societies around them and contemporary observers who were attuned enough with public affairs to pay attention to them. But this is not the reason why I chose to begin this book with those three incidents and the three individuals at their core. Indeed, the common thread between these events is not the violence per se, nor the form of violent extremism or the potential national and global impact, but the biographical pathways of the three persons whose own lives and by extension those of hundreds, thousands, and even millions of others have directly or indirectly changed as a consequence of their involvement in these incidents. All three, Nedeljko Čabrinović, Benito Mussolini, and Jacques Doriot, held very different political views at one point of their lives before they acted upon (and became infamous for) an ideology so opposed to their previously held opinions that these can only be described as hostile to each other. All three began their political and radical careers with a movement and ideology that aimed to eradicate those groups they later joined and helped to succeed. In short, all three are examples of extremist side-switchers, which one side might call traitors and the other newborn converts who rid themselves of the erroneous ways in their past.

Nedeljko Čabrinović was a convicted socialist before joining the ultra-nationalist and militaristic "Black Hand" group. Fascinatingly, the organization was ideologically diverse and included also some members who held anarchist views. During the interrogation, Čabrinović later explained his ideological shift. At the age of 14 he worked in a socialist printing press, which also produced an anarchist journal. Hence, members of anarchist groups regularly came to the office, where Čabrinović engaged in conversations with them: " ... and I argued with them frequently. I was a socialist and as such I fought their ideas as much as I could. Finally, I was defeated by their ideas and became a convinced anarchist. Every evening I came to their lectures and stayed until ... the night" (original in German, translated by author, Kohler, 1918, p. 4). Once he had joined the anarchists, Čabrinović was expelled from the socialist party, lost his job, and was attacked as a traitor. He later met one of the coconspirators, whom he noted to be a nationalist with opposing views to his own at that point but continued to develop his own ideology. Asked about his own conviction in the interrogation, Čabrinović replied: "anarchist with a nationalist blend" (original in German, translated by author, Kohler, 1918, p. 6).

Benito Mussolini had taken over the secretary position of the Socialist Party in Trent (which was Austrian at the time) in 1909 and became the editor in chief of the newspaper *Avanti!* in December 1910, the main outlet of the "Italian Socialist Party" (Partito Socialista Italiano, or PSI), before he evolved into one of the world's most infamous ultra-nationalist extremists under the banner of Fascism. Jaques Doriot was a leading member of the French Communist Party, which he had joined in 1920. Two years later, he became a member of the Presidium of the Executive Committee of the Comintern, and in 1923 Doriot was made the secretary of the French Federation of Young

Communists. In 1934, he was expelled from the Communist Party for advocating an alliance with the socialists. At the time, Doriot was the mayor in Saint Denis. His views changed drastically toward nationalism and in 1936 he founded the PPF and oriented the party toward Nazi Germany and Fascist Italy. The PPF attracted many far-left defectors and its leadership circle, calling itself "politburo" after the executive committee in communist parties, for example, included Henri Barbé (1902–1966, former member of the French Communist Party's leadership) and Paul Marion (1899–1954, journalist and former member of the central committee of the French Communist Party) (Allardyce, 1966; Brunet, 1986).

These three individuals have shown remarkable ideological flexibility over their life courses, which enabled them to shift between positions so fundamentally opposed that most observers struggle to fathom how this is even possible psychologically and physically. Naturally, the easiest way to explain this behavior is to dismiss it as mere opportunism by people who look to gain power and status with complete disregard for actual political values, goals, and ideals. Also, it might be tempting to see side-switching as proof that "all extremist groups are alike" and the ideology truly does not matter. Whether this is the case or not (I will attempt to show it is not), these perspectives do not help to explain how such side-switchers actually manage to convince themselves and more importantly the new group they defect to, that they are indeed not simple and untrustworthy opportunists but instead real believers in the (now) true cause. Imagine the substantial risks involved in approaching a violent extremist milieu from the camp of its ideological mortal enemies and it becomes obvious that you better have a good and credible narrative at hand, because in all likelihood, there will be a lot of explaining to be done. Strikingly, the three cases I chose to introduce us to the phenomenon of side-switching in extremism and many of those we will encounter in the following study have not only successfully managed to defect from one extremist milieu to another (hostile) one, they oftentimes also reached significant and exalted position with much influence, status, and respect from their new extremist peers. Could it be that this ideological flexibility and whatever else makes those side-switchers survive the transition mentally and physically becomes a unique strength and decisive push factor in their extremist careers?

When I began to research extremist and terrorist side-switching in early 2019 for an article published in the journal *Political Psychology* (Koehler, 2019b), I initially focused on four well-known cases of extremist side-switchers from Germany who had become fairly exposed due to their uncompromising and outspoken extremist views in public and their (partially) violent actions. At that point, I assumed that this phenomenon would be extremely rare and linked to exceptional personal and contextual circumstances. Contrary to my expectations, however, I discovered more and more cases of extremist side-switchers from many different backgrounds and countries who had successfully managed the transition and lived to tell the story throughout the decades. My curiosity began to grow even more after I looked into various fields of research and found that the migration between hostile groups is mostly untreated not only in terrorism and radicalization research, but in wider social psychology and many adjacent disciplines as well. Something undoubtedly significant happened in the lives and radical careers of some, maybe even many, extremists and terrorists seemingly overlooked by academics and most observers.

How widely spread is the phenomenon of side-switching in extremist radicalization pathways? Are we looking at a rare curiosity that is clearly the exception to the rule or is it a piece in the puzzle of explaining large portions of radicalization processes we have missed so far? No one really knows at this point. Since the issue of extremist side-switching has received so little academic attention until now, it would be fair to speak of an unchartered territory. Usually, researchers are only interested in the extremist milieu a person ended up in or was lastly active in. Of course, many scholars have attempted to profile individual risk factors and biographical trajectories that led to that violent engagement but stunningly, previous contrary political convictions were either so rare that they did not end up being reported as significant or never caught the attention of those scholars.

Naturally, side-switching depends a lot on the historical and political context we look at. Defectors switching sides to the enemy have always been part of wars and violent conflicts, for example. Even between highly ideologicalized combatant parties defections occur. In the Second World War, for example, the Soviet Union supported the "National Committee Free Germany" (Nationalkomitee Freies Deutschland, or NKFD), which was founded in 1943 by German prisoners of war and communist emigrants. The NKFD was used to produce German-language counterpropaganda that called upon German soldiers and officers to defect and it even fielded combat units to fight the Nazis. One could argue that unpolitical soldiers taken prisoner could be easily persuaded to become active against their former comrades in exchange for better treatment and status, but the NFKD was led by numerous former high ranking officers and members of the Nazi party "National Socialist German Workers Party" (Nationalsozialistische Deutsche Arbeiterpartei, or NSDAP) (Scheurig, 1993; Ueberschär, 1996).

To name only one example, Major Heinrich Homann was born in 1911 and became a member of the NSDAP in 1933. Commanding an artillery regiment, he was taken prisoner during the battle of Stalingrad in 1943, after which he became one of the founding members of the NKFD. After the war, he achieved high-ranking political positions in the socialist German Democratic Republic (GDR). To facilitate ideological defection of Nazi prisoners of war, the Soviets ran numerous so-called anti-fascist front schools led by the NKFD. These schools had the primary goal of ideologically turning around Nazi officers and soldiers in three- to four-months–long rehabilitation courses (Scheurig, 1993; Ueberschär, 1996). This also worked the other way.

Russian Red Army general Andrey Andreyevich Vlasov, for example, was born in 1901 and joined the Communist Party in 1930. Hailed as a hero of the Soviet Republic for his actions during the battle for Moscow between October 1941 and January 1942, he was awarded the Order of the Red Banner on January 24, 1942. During the battle for Leningrad, his unit was encircled and eventually destroyed by the Wehrmacht. He refused to be flown out and hid for ten days in German-occupied territory before he was taken prisoner on July 12, 1942. Vlasov then defected to collaborate with Nazi Germany and publicly claimed to have come to realize during his ten-day hiding that Josef Stalin was the greatest enemy of the Russian people. With German support, he then created the "Russian Liberation Army," which fielded combat units including those Russian prisoners of war who were willing to fight against their former comrades. Vlasov and eleven other senior officers were executed for high treason in August 1946 (Andreyev, 1989; Lyth, 1989). Transitions between the Nazi movement and communists in Germany before the Second World War were not uncommon at all as both sides tried to appeal to the same target group with similar arguments, in part (Timothy Scott Brown, 2009).

Take for example the case of Herbert Crüger (1911–2003), a resistance fighter against the Nazis and leading member of the German Communist Party. Crüger's story is not only fascinating because he began his political career as a member of the Nazi Hitler Youth (Hitler Jugend, or HJ), which he joined in 1931 and quickly rose to be a leading figure in a Berlin section of the organization. In his memoirs, Crüger describes his early motivations for this step as a deep commitment to social justice, anti-capitalism, and a national revolution. Since the social democrats had signed the treaty of Versailles in 1919, he deemed the left-wing socialists to be traitors to the national cause and well-being (Crüger, 1998, pp. 76–77). At this time, leading Nazis clashed over the importance of key ideological concepts within the movement, such as anti-capitalism, nationalism, anti-Semitism, or racism. Most notably Otto Strasser, a highly prominent leader of the Nazi Stormtroopers (Sturmabteilung, or SA), split off from the rest of the party and created his own organization (for a more detailed discussion of Strasser and the conflict within the highest Nazi ranks, see Section B2.2 in the Bonus Chapter, on Richard Scheringer). Crüger and most of his HJ comrades followed Strasser into an ideological position closer to socialism and communism, but still very much based in ultra-nationalism (a hybrid he himself called "National Communism"). This development allowed for better contacts with fully committed German communists, for example, during debates over ideological and philosophical topics (Crüger, 1998, pp.

81–89). Through gradually increasing his study of Communist literature and exchanges with communists, Crüger realized that for him only a full commitment to a proletarian revolution on the side of the working class made sense. Hence, he completely moved over to the Communist Party via ideological intermediate hybrid steps. This, however, was not the end of his side-switching storyline. Herbert Crüger was recruited by the underground communist intelligence bureau to re-infiltrate the Nazi SA and spread anti-Nazi propaganda within it, which he incredibly was able to do before being detected and arrested in 1934 (Crüger, 1998, pp. 132–143).

As for a modern-era context with a focus on extremist movements in Western countries, the only currently available rough indication of how common or uncommon side-switching might be is hidden in the "Profiles of Individual Radicalization in the United States" (PIRUS) database compiled and administrated by the National Consortium for the Study of Terrorism and Responses to Terrorism (START) at the University of Maryland. This groundbreaking collection of biographical data for the currently 2,226 violent extremists and terrorists who were active in the USA between 1948 and 2019 fortunately includes the variable "Other Ideologies" in the "Mindset Prior to Radicalization" section. Since the data set includes four different kinds of violent extremist ideologies (far right, far left, "Islamist," and single issue), we can assume that one of these ideologies was visible first before turning to another one. Unfortunately, the researchers who collected this treasure trove of data did not go into detail here and merely checked "yes" or "no" if "prior to their date of exposure" there is "evidence that the individual adhered to another ideology or movement besides the one in which he/she became radicalized" (START, 2018, p. 46).

What the PIRUS database shows is that a total of 65 individuals were coded positive for other prior ideologies (8 unknown and 2.153 negative), meaning that within the PIRUS sample merely around 2.9 percent can be considered side-switchers. Only three of them are women, which means that only 4.6 percent of the side-switchers compared to 10.1 percent of the non-switchers are female. It appears that transitioning between hostile milieus is a predominantly male phenomenon, even more so then activism in extremist environments already is (see Section 5.8). Next, we can figure out which groups and ideologies the switchers transitioned to up to the date of data collection: 18 (27.7 percent) side-switchers turned to "Islamism" (compared to 22.9 percent of non-switchers who are classified as "Islamists"); 25 (38.5 percent) side-switchers turned to far-right ideologies (compared to 43.9 percent of non-switchers who are classified as far-right extremists); 17 (26.2 percent) side-switchers turned to the far left (compared to 16.6 percent of non-switchers who are classified as far-left extremists); and 5 (7.7 percent) side-switchers turned to single-issue extremism (compared to 16.6 percent of their comparison group of single-issue extremists among non-switchers). One might quickly jump to the conclusion that these descriptive statistics indicate strong and significant patterns. Obviously, more side-switchers join far-right ideologies than other extremist ideologies but only the far-left and single-issue groups are over-represented (in the case of the far left) or underrepresented (in the case of single issue extremism). Statistical tools designed to differentiate between seemingly clear patterns and random distribution (in this case the so-called Mann-Whitney-U-Test) show us that gender and direction of ideological transition are not statistically significant, unfortunately.

Of course, there are many more variables (e.g., mental health issues, involvement in violent plots, severity of criminal acts, status in extremist group) that we could look at to identify potential links to the side-switcher subsample. The biggest problem with interpreting the PIRUS data in this context lies in the lack of information regarding when exactly the side-switching took place and how the coded individual's other variables changed with the shift in ideologies. This creates significant problems if one wants to understand side-switching across extremist milieus.

To give an example: One can group different mental health variables from PIRUS into a single index (i.e., child abuse, adult abuse, psychological issues, and trauma) because it is possible to suspect that a person with severe mental health problems could be more susceptible to outside influence or look for ways to achieve a higher status. Indeed, the sample shows us that 41.5 percent of side-switchers (27 out of 65) rank positive for at least one of these mental health variables, whereas only 18.6 percent of non-switchers rank positive for at least one variable. Mental health problems appear to be somehow connected to side-switching. However, since we do not know if the trauma or abuse happened before or after the side-switching, we have no way to explain this relation. A person could be more open to defection due to a certain mental health condition or the trauma could have happened years after the transition and be completely unrelated. We simply cannot tell and that is why further statistical analyses to describe the strength and significance of the relationship between side-switching and other variables in the PIRUS database cannot be conducted. Stunningly, the researchers behind PIRUS took notice of this phenomenon and hence included it in their data set, but they did not venture to explore it in any more detail. Still, by the PIRUS account moving between hostile extremist milieus is indeed a rarity. Those 3 percent, however, should not be dismissed easily. They could have had significant careers and lasting impact in the groups they joined, if one of the key assumptions of my work holds some truth: In order to mitigate the risks of extremist side-switching, defectors need to prove to their new group that they can be trusted and that they are now more convinced of the ideological cause than before. This might push them much further in their radicalization processes and lead to more influential positions, crimes, violence, or recruitment.

When I revisited the original article that kindled my interest in this particular phenomenon, I realized that many more case studies of extremist side-switchers exist but not in an equally distributed way. It seems that transitions between these ideologies and their attached milieus do not work in every direction with the same ease, if one can speak of "easy" side-switching at all. Hence, I began to speculate if those narratives of defectors could reveal more information about ideological connections or tunnels of sort between them that might work in distinct directions. In continuation of my initial research, I wanted to learn more about those questions that kept coming back to me: *How are acts of extremist side-switching across hostile groups possible? How is it, that these individuals not only manage to shift between groups that are actively fighting each other, but also to successfully enter the new group, gain trust of the group's members and even rise to fame and power within them? How is it that they are not branded as traitors, unreliable opportunists, or potential spies? Why are side-switchers between certain milieus and into certain ideological directions seemingly more common than others and what does this reveal about the ideological connections between them? In short, how and why do they do it?* Ultimately, I also came to realize that side-switchers could provide us with a unique peek at the ideological "road map" between extremist ideologies, which might help us to differentiate between mutual "highways" or "one-way" streets.

It is not surprising that extremist and terrorist milieus are difficult to penetrate for researchers. Those groups typically do not welcome outsiders if they have no intention to join their cause or promise to hold some kind of benefit for them. In an ideal (academic) world, it would be possible to observe side-switching while it occurs and develops from both sides, interview all the involved persons, receive fully honest and truthful answers, and study its impact over the course of years. Few things are further from reality, as many of my fellow researchers know and have painstakingly pondered about for ages, trying to find alternative ways to collect viable data with such hard-to-reach milieus. This book aims to place the personal accounts and stories of side-switchers at the center of the analysis. I will attempt to let the life stories and narratives of the defectors themselves form the basis of our attempt to explore these radical shifts. Therefore, I searched widely for existing interviews, self-written articles, court statements, and autobiographies authored by defectors that mention and possibly even recount the events that led to switching sides, as well as what happened afterward. Sometimes, these accounts have been passed on by other observers who spoke with the side-switchers or had access to their peers. The cases presented here are by no means an exhaustive list of side-switchers nor can I draw any generally representative claims about them from the sample. I will discuss the methodological constraints and focus of my research in the Chapter 1 in detail, but it can be said here that I wanted to let the side-switcher storylines speak for themselves as much as possible.

Of course, I do not mean to claim that their narratives are factually truthful accounts. Especially when side-switchers tell the story of their defection while still being an active member of their newfound (extremist) group, it is certainly not a good idea to say anything positive about their membership in the hostile previous environment. Naturally, defectors have a strong interest in painting the group they ended up with in the most coaxing way and the group of origin in the most deprecatory terms. I am interested in analyzing how side-switchers present these radical shifts in their own lives and through their own words. In short, when I began my research on extremist side-switchers, I wanted to understand what narrative strategies they use to convince their new group to accept them. The benefit of assessing such self-narratives in this light was pointed out by Altier, Horgan, and Thoroughgood (2012, pp. 89–90) in much wiser words than I could hope to produce here: "By letting the terrorists and former terrorists 'speak for themselves,' the approach increases the likelihood that the data one obtains are valid and meaningful representations of the attitudes, perceptions, and experiences of those involved in terrorism, and that they are reliable reflections of the mindset of participants at that particular point in their developmental trajectory ... However ... these primary source materials are ... often more revealing than the author necessarily intends." By using these accounts provided by violent extremists and terrorists themselves, researchers might learn to "understand how terrorists construct their social realities, interpret their environments, and make critical life decisions," which are "shaped by their unique cognitive interpretations of the world" (Altier et al., 2012, p. 90).

With this book I therefore aim to contribute the theoretical basis for understanding extremist side-switching and its implications to the study of radicalization, extremism, terrorism, and deradicalization. Beyond the individual level analysis, to explore defections among extremist milieus also provides us with a unique and rare opportunity to catch a glimpse at the mutual interaction between extremist groups and their members. We can study the strategies of coping with internal conflict and the psychological as well as ideological relationships between hostile movements. This might allow us to learn about failed (on the side of the abandoned group) and successful (on the side of the joined group) "human resource management" in extremism and terrorism. This in turn holds the promise of producing significant insights that might prove immensely valuable in preventing and fighting terrorism, extremism, and violent radicalization.

The book explores extremist side-switching through the life stories of individual defectors in the following seven chapters. Chapter 1 mainly dives into existing research on anything related to extremist side-switching; the development and change of political attitudes; the psychology of migration between social groups and disengagement from terrorism; as well as civil wars, where, it seems, so-called fratricidal flipping is not uncommon. This chapter also discusses the main assumptions of the book and briefly introduces us to the main concepts and theories I use for the analysis to follow, for example, Social Identity Theory (SIT), the Five Stage Model (FSM), the Choice Blindness paradigm, and sacred values. We will also learn how I understand the key terms used throughout this study, such as "extremism," the "far right," or "radicalization," as well as which methodology I used to translate accounts and life stories into meaningful analysis.

Chapter 2 then looks at biographical accounts of individuals who joined the far-right milieu, all of whom were previously active in far-left environments. In Chapter 3, I will turn the perspective around and introduce us to several storylines by persons who joined extreme left groups and milieus, coming from neo-Nazi or other far-right backgrounds. In Chapter 4, I will focus on those who decided to convert to Islam and join Islamic extremist or jihadist groups during their personal development. Here we will see a dominance of individuals coming from far-right groups but also, in one case, from left-wing terrorism. This chapter includes a discussion about the peculiarities of extremist side-switching processes that overlap with religious conversion and a potential explanation of why so few cases of defectors from Islamic extremist milieus to one of the other two exist.

Chapter 5 will bring the main findings of the book together and formulate key components of a theory of cross-ideological extremist side-switching, which also involves a discussion of the role of the group versus the individual, the impact of gender, and specific ideological "highways" between extremist environments. Finally, before the conclusion, Chapter 6 will apply what we have learned about extremist side-switching to the field of preventing and countering extremism, which also includes disengagement and deradicalization, to better understand what makes defectors different from those who exit extremism completely, and how this could help us to improve existing programs and strategies to counter the threat of extremism and terrorism around the world.

During the process of collecting and researching side-switching accounts for this book, I came along so many fascinating and stunning biographies that it was impossible to include them all here. Thanks to Cambridge University Press, some of these most interesting cases will be available in an online-only Bonus Chapter, downloadable for free at www.cambridge.org/koehler. The Bonus Chapter, to which I will refer here occasionally, mainly extends the focus of the book to (German) intellectual defectors from the extreme left who joined the extreme right on the one hand, as well as additional historical and court case studies on the other. Those intellectual side-switchers provide examples of highly ideological group and milieu transition, as they mostly (but not entirely) refrained from criminal activities. Nevertheless, they changed their ideological positions fundamentally while always clearly remaining "extremist" and lending their intellectual support to a violent cause. The Bonus Chapter also takes an in-depth look at the biographies of Benito Mussolini and German army officer Richard Scheringer, who both switched sides in the era between the two World Wars. Finally, the Bonus Chapter presents two additional court cases from the United States (Joseph Brice and Nicholas Young), who changed their main ideological affiliation from the extreme right to jihadist.

Acknowledgments

Writing a book even in the most ordinary of times is always a challenge and an exceptional exercise in perseverance. How to find the mental focus to consistently put the words on paper every minute, hour, day, or week in a row until they (hopefully) form meaningful sentences, paragraphs, and chapters has been an enigma for many authors. If one actually reads the acknowledgment sections of academic books in particular, we learn about at least one secret ingredient for productive (and healthy) writing: the reliance on friends and colleagues who provide a stable, encouraging, and supportive social environment. Indeed, I have found this to be true and invaluable for the books I have written before. But this one was different. I started to work on it in March 2020, right when the world was entering the first stage of a global pandemic, hard lockdowns, and widespread uncertainty about the duration and consequences of this rapidly spreading disease named COVID-19. In times like these when the world appears to be going up in flames (and in no small part due to some deliberately pouring gasoline on it), social networks the way we knew them are shattered, putting us all to the test to accomplish even the basic day-to-day tasks. Too many lost their loved ones, their jobs, or indeed their lives. How can anyone expect friends and colleagues to provide emotional or professional support for a book in such exceptional times when we were all strained to the limit?

I have found that, albeit invaluable as it is, direct support from friends and colleagues through feedback, exchange, or the occasional distraction to get back on track is not the only gift to be thankful for when it comes to acknowledging those who contributed in one way or the other. More than ever, I felt inspired by those academic and nonacademic heroes of mine, who master their own everyday challenges with dignity, respect, love, compassion, and commitment to their families, their responsibilities, and the world around them.

Among those who I continue to admire for their brilliant work and seemingly never-ending amicability to the field and academia in general are John Horgan, Cynthia Miller-Idriss, Kurt Braddock, Graham Macklin, Paul Gill,

Jacob Ravndal, Mick Williams, Ryan Scrivens, Bart Schuurman, Mary Beth Altier, Aaron Zelin, Julie Hwang, Maura Conway, Gordon Clubb, and many more. You might not all have provided feedback on this manuscript, but your work and professionalism nevertheless has had a great influence and inspired me (again) to write the best book I could. I am deeply grateful for that.

There are also those at Cambridge University Press who believed in this project from the start and kept it alive by being encouraging and supportive at all times. My sincere thanks go to the wonderful Janka Romero, Ilaria Tassistro, and Emily Watton, an absolute publishing dream team any author can only wish for.

Last but not least, especially when it all seems to hit you at once, there are family and friends, those who stick with you no matter what. My accomplishments are always yours as well: Mom, Dad, Stephan, Andreas, Daniel, and Albrecht.

Through this book I have learned (yet again), that there are no psychological and physical barriers too high, no changes too fundamental, and no supposedly eternal enmity too existential for human beings to overcome. For some, this human ability to adapt and literally jump right over one's own shadow leads further down the path to their personal purgatory. For others, it becomes their lifesaver.

To paraphrase a wise popular culture character: I firmly believe that we all have to face the truth and choose. Give off light, or darkness. Be a candle, or the night.

Abbreviations

AFA	Anti-Fascist Action
AFD	Alternative für Deutschland ("Alternative for Germany")
AIMS	Anti-Immigration Society
AIZ	Antiimperialistische Zellen ("Anti-Imperialist Cells")
AMEF	Ansar al-Mujahideen English Forum
APO	Außerparlamentarische Opposition ("Extra-Parliamentary Opposition")
AR	Antipodean Resistance
AWD	Atomwaffen Division
BDP	British Democratic Party
BfV	Bundesamt für Verfassungsschutz ("Federal Office for the Protection of the Constitution")
BM	British Movement
BNF	British National Front
BNP	British National Party
CDU	Christlich Demokratische Union ("Christian Democrat Union")
CSU	Christlich Soziale Union ("Christian Social Union")
CT	counterterrorism
DAT	Devoted Actor Theory
DKP	Deutsche Kommunistische Partei ("German Communist Party")
DGB	Deutscher Gewerkschaftsbund ("German Union Federation")
DTM	Deutsche Taliban Mujahideen ("German Taliban Mujahideen")
DVU	Deutsche Volksunion ("German People's Union")
ETA	Euskadi Ta Askatasuna ("Basque Homeland and Liberty")
FAZ	Frankfurter Allgemeine Zeitung
FDP	Freiheitlich Demokratische Partei Deutschlands ("Free Democrat Party of Germany")
FF	Fascist Forge

FKD	Feuerkrieg Division
FN	Front National
FPÖ	Freiheitliche Partei Österreichs ("Freedom Party of Austria")
FRG	Federal Republic of Germany
FSM	Five Stage Model
GDR	German Democratic Republic
HJ	Hitler Jugend (Hitler Youth)
HNG	Hilfsgemeinschaft für nationale politische Gefangene und deren Angehörige ("Aid Community for National Political Prisoners and Their Relatives")
HNP	Herstigte National Party
HuT	Hizb ut-Tahrir
IdM	Identitarian Movement
IED	improvised explosive device
IM	IronMarch
IRA	Irish Republican Army
ISIS	Islamic State of Iraq and al-Sham
KB	Kommunistischer Bund ("Communist Federation")
KDS	Kampfbund deutscher Sozialisten ("Combat Federation of German Socialists")
KGB	Komitet Gosudarstvennoy Bezopasnosti ("Committee for State Security")
KGRNS	Kampfbund revolutionärer Nationalsozialisten ("Combat Federation of Revolutionary National Socialists")
KPD	Kommunistische Partei Deutschlands ("Communist Party of Germany")
KPD/ML	Kommunistische Partei Deutschlands/Marxisten-Leninisten ("Communist Party of Germany/Marxists-Leninists")
LVF	Légion des volontaires français contre le bolchévisme ("French Volunteer Legion against Bolshevism")
MB	Muslim Brotherhood
MfS	Ministerium für Staatssicherheit ("Ministry for State Security")
MFT	Moral Foundations Theory
NF	National Front
NKFD	Nationalkomitee Freies Deutschland ("National Commitee Free Germany")
NPD	Nationaldemokratische Partei Deutschlands ("National Democratic Party of Germany")
NRAF	Nationalrevolutionäre Arbeiterfront ("National Revolutionary Workers Front")
NRM	Ugandan National Resistance Movement

NS	National Socialism
NSDAP	Nationalsozialistische Deutsche Arbeiterpartei ("National Socialist German Workers Party")
NSDAP/AO	Nationalsozialistische Deutsche Arbeiterpartei/Aufbau- und Auslandsorganisation ("NSDAP Development and Foreing Organization")
NSM	National Socialist Movement
NSU	Nationalsozialistischer Untergrund ("National Socialist Underground")
P/CVE	Preventing/Countering Violent Extremism
PIM	Pro-integration Model
PIRUS	Profiles of Individual Radicalization in the United States
PLF	Palestinian Liberation Front
PLO	Palestinian Liberation Organization
PNF	Partito Nazionale Fascista ("National Fascist Party")
PPF	Parti Populaire Français ("Fascist French Populist Party")
PSI	Partito Socialista Italiano ("Italian Socialist Party")
PVV	Partij voor de Vrijheid ("Party for Freedom")
RAF	Rote Armee Fraktion ("Red Army Faction")
RH	Rote Hilfe ("Red Help")
RNF	Ring Nationaler Frauen ("Circle of Nationalist Women")
RPS	Racial Preservation Society
SA	Sturmabteilung
SAK	Sozialistisches Anwaltskollektiv ("Socialist Lawyers Collective")
SANF	South African National Party
SDS	Sozialistischer Deutscher Studentenbund ("Socialist German Student Union")
SIT	Social Identity Theory
SPD	Sozialdemokratische Partei Deutschlands ("Social Democrat Party of Germany")
SPLC	Southern Poverty Law Center
SS	Schutzstaffel
STEM	science, technology, engineering, mathematics
TWP	Traditionalist Workers Party
UNOSAA	United Nations Office of the Special Adviser on Africa
USSR	Union of Soviet Socialist Republics
VUS	Vereinigung Unabhäniger Sozialisten ("Association of Independent Socialists")
WSG	Wehrsportgruppe Hoffmann ("Military Sports Group Hoffmann")
ZOG	Zionist Occupied Government

1 Betraying the Cause?

Side-Switching and Violent Extremism

In November 2011, two German neo-Nazis conducted a successful bank robbery in the small town of Eisenach and – as they had done many times before – began waiting out the manhunt by the police in a rental caravan parked nearby. By coincidence, Uwe Böhnhardt (1977–2011) and Uwe Mundlos (1973–2011) were observed loading their mountain bikes into the caravan and soon after a police patrol closed in on the duo to investigate the situation. By monitoring police radio, Mundlos and Böhnhardt knew that they were cornered and before the officers could enter the vehicle, they set fire to the caravan and committed suicide. Roughly at the same time a third person, Beate Zschäpe, began pouring out a combustible liquid in her apartment in the town of Jena, about 100 kilometers away. After igniting the material, an explosion rocked and destroyed large parts of the building. In the debris of the caravan and the apartment, investigators quickly discovered cash and multiple weapons, one of which could be tied to an attack on two police officers in April 2007, leaving one officer dead. Zschäpe was on the run, seemingly aimless, and mailed out copies of a DVD-video to different journalists, politicians, and one extreme-right company.

It took the authorities a couple of days to understand the importance of these connected events, leading to a shattering of the German security infrastructure that was called "our September 11" (FAZ, 2012) by then–Federal Prosecutor General Harald Range. On the video Zschäpe sent out, a group calling itself the "National Socialist Underground" (Nationalsozialistischer Untergrund, or NSU) claimed responsibility for the murders of nine shopkeepers with Turkish and Greek background, as well as one police officer. The NSU had financed itself through bank robberies (15 in total) and not only assassinated victims by shooting them at point blank range but the group also conducted at least three bomb attacks targeting neighborhoods with a large percentage of minorities. Forming the core of the NSU, the trio had been living underground and pursuing its terrorist agenda since 1998, and at no point did the authorities manage to even suspect their involvement in the murders and bombings, which happened across Germany. Because of this grave failure to detect the group, a wave of shock and outrage swept across the country. Until July 2013, six directors or deputy directors of various intelligence agencies resigned or were removed from their posts. A total of nine parliamentary inquiry commissions (one on the federal and eight on the state level) investigating the reasons for this counterterrorism failure were set up and began their years-long work (Koehler, 2016a). On November 8, 2011, Beate Zschäpe was arrested after turning herself in and charged exactly one year later. She, too, is a side-switcher into the far-right environment.

Between May 2013 and July 2018, the longest trial in post–Second World War German history led to a guilty verdict for Beate Zschäpe, who had been charged with four coconspirators, on the counts of 10 murders, 32 attempted murders, and membership in a terrorist organization (among other charges). Her role in the core cell is still debated, as her claim to not have been involved in the attacks of the other two, now deceased, members is disputable. Still, Zschäpe never was present at any of the attack sites and her involvement seems to have been maintaining group solidarity and logistics. As the trial has produced extensive evidence about her life and radicalization process, it is comparatively easy to trace her steps into the terrorist underground.

Born in January 1975 in Jena, the only daughter of her mother, Zschäpe was mainly raised by her grandmother and never knew her father, a Rumanian student. He had met Zschäpe's mother during her university studies in dental medicine. Beate Zschäpe experienced two divorces and moved six times during her childhood until the age of 15, accounting for a quite unsteady life (Baumgärtner & Böttcher, 2012; Fuchs & Goetz, 2012). In 1991, she left school and finished her vocational training as a gardener between 1992 and 1996. Her involvement in politically extremist and violent youth gangs had started at the age of 14, around 1989, in the turmoil of the German Democratic Republic's (the socialist East German state, or GDR) demise and the country's reunification. In those years, much of the social infrastructure in the East (e.g., youth clubs, sports associations) were disbanded and state authorities largely withdrew from the public realm for a couple of years. This left a vacuum for many extremist entrepreneurs to form new groups, mostly youth gangs, across the territory of the former GDR. Even though dominated by far-right skinhead subculture, there were also forms of left-wing activism. Many teenagers found themselves without a perspective and looking for direction.

Zschäpe joined an openly far-left punker group called "The Ticks" (Die Zecken), a reference to a widely used slur by right-wing skinheads against their left opponents. Even though Zschäpe's group also included unpolitical teenagers simply looking to have fun with peers, she actively participated in planning and conducting an attack against a youth club known for harboring neo-Nazi skinheads. In those early years of her political activism, she was described as thirsty for experiencing life, frequenting left-wing alternative discotheques and enjoying reggae and ska music (Fuchs, 2012; Fuchs &

Goetz, 2012, p. 59). Being an alternative leftist adolescent in these years was risky in many parts of Germany. A wave of far-right violence swept over the country in the first years after the reunification in 1990. Neo-Nazi skinheads regularly attacked left-wing youths, often with unrestricted and sometimes fatal violence.

Zschäpe had found a boyfriend in her first youth group, a left-wing punker, with whom she engaged in acts of petty crime. At the age of 16, in late 1991, she met Uwe Mundlos and the two fell in love. Together they broke into a far-right youth club and stole money, as well as cigarettes. Mundlos, who would later become one of the three core members in the NSU trio, also considered himself to be a left-wing skinhead for some years. Asked in school about why he was a neo-Nazi, Mundlos reportedly answered: "I am not right, I am left – my combat boots have red laces in it!" (original in German, translated by author, as cited in Fuchs & Goetz, 2012, p. 68). However, it appears that Mundlos was mainly driven by a desire for provocation and rebellion, as he also expressed his anger against the socialist system and the Soviet Union by drawing swastikas into schoolboards when he began his involvement in the skinhead milieu around 1988 – two years before the reunification (Fuchs & Goetz, 2012, pp. 67–68).

In the last years of the East German GDR, youth subcultures deemed antisocial by the regime began to appear en masse. While the far-left-oriented groups based their rebellion against the system on defying social norms regarding work, education, and so-called proper appearance, the far right hit the nerve of the legally mandated anti-fascist state by showing open allegiance with National Socialism and Fascism (Ross, 2000). Zschäpe and Mundlos got engaged before he served in the Germany army as part of the mandatory conscription between April 1994 and March 1995. The couple had by then become integrated into the local neo-Nazi environment, especially by regularly visiting a youth club heavily frequented by the far right. It was there the trio came into existence, by meeting the third later terrorist Uwe Böhnhardt. While Mundlos was away in the military, Zschäpe broke up with him and began a relationship with his best friend, Böhnhardt.

Circling back a few years to Zschäpe's story, she had entered the local neo-Nazi movement between 1991 and 1992. Her integration into the far-right milieu was swift and facilitated by her new boyfriend Mundlos, who by that time had already become a right-wing extremist. Breaking into the far-right youth club with Zschäpe might be seen as an attempt to impress her with his uncompromising search for rebellion and adventure. Soon, Zschäpe partici-pated in and even organized some neo-Nazi rallies. Her violent crimes increased rapidly and were mostly directed against left-wing activists and minorities. However, she also was not a stereotypical right-wing extremist, as her heavy use of drugs was noted by intelligence operatives who probed to recruit her as a potential informant (Jüttner, 2013). Upon the return of her former future husband from the military in 1995, the trio was complete again and significantly radicalized in the following months and years.

Mundlos had evolved into a fully committed National Socialist. His goal was to educate and harden the small group ideologically. At first, Mundlos was furious about the relationship between Zschäpe and Böhnhardt but friends from that time recount his unwillingness to abandon the two, arguably out of still very strong feelings for his former fiancée (Fuchs & Goetz, 2012, pp. 106–107). The trio became inseparable and gradually stepped up their violence and preparations for serious attacks. In October 1996, for example, the group was responsible for depositing a fake bomb with a swastika painted on it on a sports field, not the first of its kind. In November 1996, the trio, together with other neo-Nazis, visited the Buchenwald concentration camp memorial wearing uniforms mimicking Nazi storm troopers. In early 1997, they began mailing out nonfunctional letter bombs, which contained small amounts of explosives but no ignition mechanism. Zschäpe had rented a small garage, which the three used to store their bomb-making equipment and prepare the explosives. After a police search in January 1998, which turned up several pipe bombs and TNT explosives, the trio went underground and began their new life as an organized clandestine far-right terror cell until their detection by accident 13 years later.

From what is known, Beate Zschäpe and Uwe Mundlos were not fully committed and convinced far-left activists. Both rather looked for community, social status, adventure, and rebellion. Zschäpe appears to have been more interested in enjoying the lifestyle with the occasional thrill of breaking the law. Her anchor in the left-wing group was comprised of friendships and her romantic relationship with another member. Mundlos on the other hand is described by many former friends and bystanders as intelligent but having been driven toward constant provocation and conflict. His transition to the far right was much more fluent and it is questionable whether he ever truly considered himself to be a left-wing skinhead. It should not be discounted too quickly, however, that Zschäpe was part of a group in constant fear of being attacked by neo-Nazis. Her participation in the violent raid on the far-right youth club was likely both joining in on the action with her peers and returning some of the terror inflicted upon alternative youths by their omnipresent enemies: right-wing skinheads.

The biographies of Zschäpe and to some degree Mundlos lead us to a different form of side-switching with grave consequences. Commitment and integration into an extremist milieu do not automatically have to be based on ideological convictions. It can be, and arguably even more often is, fueled by the desire to belong to a group, for social status and recognition, friendships, fun, and adventure instead of following the doctrines set by the underlying ideology. Naturally, this is more likely the case with youth groups, which might claim a crude politically connotated collective identity, but are usually more focused on addressing the everyday needs of their members. Nevertheless, the ideological conviction can develop either in the original milieu or the one after the defection. Beate Zschäpe's radical career neatly alerts us to some of the many complex and overlapping factors we need to understand when studying violent and nonviolent extremism, radicalization, and defection processes, as well as the development and change of political attitudes. By using these terms, I am very conscious that I tap into questions about human nature and behavior, which are immensely controversial and heatedly debated, for example, among academics and policy makers. Hence, clarification about how I understand the key terms and concepts I will use throughout this book is warranted. This chapter will also introduce the body of research from different academic fields, such as social psychology, terrorism, and civil war studies, which formed the basis of my attempt to make sense of extremist side-switching.

1.1 Extremism

Naturally, "extremism" is one of the most fundamental terms of this book, which after all focuses explicitly on those persons switching between hostile extremist and terrorist groups. The term is widely used to describe specific ideologies defining themselves through a maximum degree of opposition to a certain mainstream or political center. That meaning is already attached to its epistemology with the combination of the Latin root *extremus*, meaning "situated at the end, edge, or tip; occurring at the end (of a period of time), last; or something extreme in degree," with the suffix "ism" signaling a specific practice, system, or philosophy. In that sense, extremism is a relational concept reflecting ideological distance and dependency at the same time (Vermeulen & Bovenkerk, 2012, p. 48). Logically, this means that any opposition to the mainstream center would be extremism, regardless of the moral justification behind its actions or ideological positions. This has led to some more specific definitions of extremism containing the opposition against pluralism, rule of law and self-determination by a population (Backes, 2009), or the curtailment of individual liberties justified by a total will to power (Midlarsky, 2011).

Provocatively turning this argument around: Anything other than a Western concept of democracy can be called extremism, which is a criticism fielded against this term by scholars, activists, politicians, and social movements alike who see themselves criminalized and stigmatized as "extremists" in the name of moral judgments against nondemocratic political philosophies. Furthermore, "extremism" is also the main concept interlocked with the term "radicalization," providing the ideological core to the latter. These two characteristics of how the term "extremism" is used most widely establish its thoroughly negative and condemning effects. On a more differentiated level, extremism is typically discussed along two qualifying lines: violent vs. nonviolent manifestations on the one hand and attitudes vs. behavior on the other. Nevertheless, most casual, and nonacademic applications of the term go hand in hand with equaling violent extremism to terrorism explicitly, leaving aside the fact that variations occur and not all extremists are violent, for example.

To avoid a potentially endless circle of debates focusing on the legitimacy of specific political concepts and forms of government as the core of what is extremist and what is not, I will follow Berger's (2018) most valuable alternative approach to the term. His understanding of "extremism" essentially focuses on the importance of in-group bias and hostility toward a defined other or enemy: "Extremism refers to the belief that an in-group's success or survival can never be separated from the need for hostile action against an out-group. The hostile action must be part of the in-group's definition of success. Hostile acts can range from verbal attacks and diminishment to discriminatory behavior, violence, and even genocide" (Berger, 2018, p. 44). Extremist milieus require an "unwavering commitment" (Berger, 2018, p. 33) to that out-group hostility as the group could not exist or be triumphant without it. It is therefore the inseparability of that enmity against outsiders from the very nature of what the underlying ideology is all about that characterizes extremism. As I will show with the many biographical case studies of extremist side-switchers throughout this book, it is most often that fiery hostility to a very specific out-group shared by various extremist groups, even among those interlocked in direct opposition to each other, that creates a basis for successful defection narratives.

In this book I will often use "extremist" and "terrorist" as a pair. Of course, I am aware that "extremism" and "terrorism" are two very different phenomena; the first being a thought system and the latter a tactic. In addition, many of the individual side-switchers I will look at have not been involved in terrorist activities or even violence. In my perspective, I see a dynamic and fluent escalation between being a radical, a nonviolent extremist, a violent extremist, and a terrorist. However, only a minority of radicals will turn out to be extremists and only a minority of them will move to violence and terrorism in their radicalization processes. Luckily, the majority either remains at a nonviolent stage or quits before turning to violence. Nevertheless, I want to include violent and nonviolent forms of extremism in my account of side-switching, as I regard the common psychological element to be the inseparability of hostility toward an out-group from the collective and individual identities of the defectors and their milieus.

1.2   Radicalization, Radicalism, and Being a Radical

The controversial term "radicalization" fully entered the academic and public discourses after the London terror attacks on July 7, 2005 (Sedgwick, 2010), replacing "root causes" of terrorism (Neumann, 2008, p. 4). Usually, the concept describes a "process by which an individual adopts an extremist ideology" (Braddock, 2014, p. 62). Whether or not the use of violence is a key aspect of radicalization remains contested. The European Commission for example sees radicalization as a process of "embracing opinions, views and ideas which could lead to acts of terrorism" (Reinares et al., 2008, p. 5). Similarly focusing on the aspect of violence, Bosi et al. understand it as "a process forming through strategy, structure, and conjuncture, and involving the adoption and sustained use of violent means to achieve articulated political goals" (Bosi, Demetriou & Malthaner, 2014, p. 2).

Other scholars have argued that we must differentiate between violent and nonviolent forms of radicalization (Bartlett & Miller, 2012; Jaskoski, Wilson & Lazareno, 2017) and even recognize that benevolent forms of this phenomenon exist (Reidy, 2018). Therefore, nonviolent radicalization can be seen as "the social and psychological process of incrementally experienced commitment to extremist political or religious ideology" (Horgan & Braddock, 2010, p. 152). This means that: "radicalization may not necessarily lead to violence, but is one of several risk factors required for this" (Horgan & Braddock, 2010, p. 152). Alternatively, some scholars have argued to speak of "cognitive" (focusing on extremist beliefs) and "behavioral" radicalization (focusing on extremist actions) (Neumann, 2013).

In the decades after the September 11 attacks, an almost unmanageable amount of research has been conducted on the potential causes of radicalization, its phases and steps, potential risk factors, or links with mental health issues. Numerous meta-studies have attempted to summarize the state of the academic discourse at various times (e.g., Borum, 2011a, 2011b; Christmann, 2012; Dalgaard-Nielsen, 2008a, 2008b, 2010; Horgan, 2008; Reinares et al., 2008), but a particularly useful one was provided by Gøtzsche-Astrup (2018), focusing on the empirical validity within radicalization research. In his perspective, strong empirical evidence points to radicalization as a normal psychological mechanism rather than psychopathology. He also sees enough support in the literature to focus on motivational processes rather than instrumental calculations of risk and reward, as well as negative life experiences that put the individual in flux in terms of fundamental questions. Experiences of fundamental uncertainty or loss of meaning or significance, shift in social identity toward a single social group rather than many, and small-group dynamics driving the process to behavioral extremes are equally key to understanding the term and its underlying process. Finally, Gøtzsche-Astrup highlights a heightened dispositional anxiety, aggression and impulsivity, and the role of "sacred values" in developing extremist attitudes and action.

One way to define the core of radicalization beyond the use of violence is the individual's motive to fundamentally alter the surrounding environment. In this regard, Moskalenko and McCauley (2009) have suggested introducing the concept of "activism" as the legal counterpart to illegal "radicalism." Echoing this notion, Dalgaard-Nielsen defines "radicalization" as "a growing readiness to pursue and support far-reaching changes in society that conflict with, or pose a direct threat to, the existing order" (Dalgaard-Nielsen, 2010, p. 798). As noted by Pisoiu (2011, p. 12), most definitions actually describe a result, rather than the process or mechanism of radicalization as such, suggesting that one should understand "radicalism" as a "political ideology with the objective of inducing sweeping change based on fundamental or 'root' principles" (Pisoiu, 2011, p. 23). This means, that being radical implies a twofold state of mind: on the one hand a growing desire for (fundamental) change and on the other an increasing importance of "root" or fundamental principles, which is already indicated in the word's Latin origin: *radix* meaning "root" or "base." Furthermore, numerous process models of radicalization trajectories have been developed to show the different phases and motivational mechanisms in each step (for an overview see Christmann, 2012). All these models point to the fact that individual radicalization pathways are gradual processes spanning over a certain time period that involve different cognitive and behavioral steps one must take toward an end state that could be classified as extremist.

My own conceptualization of radicalization (Koehler, 2016b, pp. 65–94) understands the phenomenon as a process of individual de-pluralization of political concepts and values (e.g., justice, freedom, honor, violence, democracy) on the one hand, and an increase in ideological urgency to act against an individual or collective problem on the other. With a higher degree of individual internalization of the notion that no other alternative interpretations of the (individually prioritized) political concepts and values exist (or are relevant), one can show (e.g., in syntax, language, and behavior) the progression of the radicalization process toward a mindset that is fully exclusive and relies on existential conflict for social and individual identity as laid out in the extremism concept by Berger (2018). This internalization of ideologically framed political concepts and problems can be emotional and/or intellectual as I will also describe in detail in the following discussion of the term "ideology."

1.3   Ideology

The third most important and contested term I am using in this book is "ideology." This comes as a necessity, since I am interested in those side-switchers crossing between groups I define as mutually exclusive and hostile on an ideological basis. The term is extensively used, for example, in political theory, political psychology, terrorism, or historical research to differentiate between different types of terrorist groups and political movements. Most often, "ideology" is equaled to something like a set of mobilizing beliefs and worldviews structuring attitudes and behaviors (e.g., Feldman, 2013; Hoffman, 2006; Kalmoe, 2020; Sageman, 2004; Snow, 2004). This functionalist approach to ideology assumes that these beliefs contain consciously or unconsciously held values, understandings, interpretations, myths, or preferences in regard to political action and processes used to formulate a rationale for political action (for the roots of this understanding see Hamilton, 1987; W. A. Mullins, 1972).

Ideology also tends to create an association with a movement, party, or group. As a much discussed and criticized concept in social movement research, one suggestion to define the term is as a "variable phenomenon that ranges on a continuum from a tightly and rigidly connected set of values and beliefs at one end to a loosely coupled set of values and beliefs on the other end, and that can function, in either case, as both a constraint on and a resource for the kind of sense-making, interpretive work associated with framing" (Snow, 2004, p. 400). I argue that this understanding of ideology is too shallow and too much focused on an intellectual reflection and awareness of those "beliefs" forming a system somehow. Most importantly, it almost completely ignores the emotional side of ideology and does not help us understand why and how some ideologies are mutually exclusive or even toxic to each other.

In my studies of extremism, terrorism, radicalization, and deradicalization, I have found the seminal work of Michael Freeden (e.g., 1994, 1996) in establishing a morphological study of ideologies to be an exceptionally valuable way of looking at the term. Freeden describes ideologies as "an organizing frame of reference for action-oriented political thinking" and "thought-edifices which serve to organize their perceptions of their political environments, to direct them towards certain types of political conduct, and to provide or support plans of action for public political institutions" (Freeden, 1994, p. 140). He adds to this an understanding of ideologies as "particular patterned clusters and configurations of political concepts. An ideology is hence none other than the macroscopic structural arrangement that attributes meaning to a range of mutually defining political concepts" (Freeden, 1994, p. 141).

These political concepts are "complex entities that inject order and meaning into observed sets of political phenomena and hold together an assortment of connected ideas ... their mode of employment is subject only to the test of acceptability to significant numbers of their users" (Freeden, 1994, p. 141) and, for example, take the form of words like "justice," "freedom," "power," "rights," "equality," or "democracy." Such concepts can be found at the core of every ideology but are characteristically organized and clustered, creating something like an ideological fingerprint, consisting not only of the cluster of political concepts, but also of those concepts culturally and logical adjacent to it. Naturally, these political concepts are not static but very much fluid and allow for a variety of linguistic and cultural meanings to be attached to them (Freeden, 1994, p. 154).

A major function of an ideology is to "cement the word–concept relationship" and to "attach a single meaning to a political term" (Freeden, 1994, p. 156). Thus, every ideology strives to decontest the range of meanings that can possibly be attached to central political concepts. "Decontestation" is of course not only a function of extremist but of every ideology, thus making it possible to recognize what competing ideologies actually are: "struggles over the legitimate meanings of political concepts and the sustaining arrangements they form" (Freeden, 1994, p. 156). Following what we have seen about the nature of "extremism" and "radicalization," namely that they include by definition almost completely exclusive definitions of central political concepts, we can now recognize that these extremist milieus and their followers are engaged in ideological struggles about the meaning of fundamental aspects of human life. The mutual exclusivity of extremist ideologies is defined here as the inherent incompatibility of each ideology's core concepts with the opposing one. For an example, one central feature of many far-right extremist ideologies is the claim that racial differences between human beings account for their cultural and biological value; mixing of races automatically leads to conflicts and deterioration of societies. Many far-left extremist ideologies not only fiercely contest this understanding of human conflict and societal problems but also argue for socioeconomic class struggle as the main reason behind all negative aspects of humanity. The question is much more than "race vs. class." Both ideologies have an ideological core "DNA" that negates each other's existence. However, Freeden maintains that ideologies are dynamic and flexible systems, which constantly change and adapt, especially regarding the more adjacent, cultural, and peripheral concepts attached to the core.

A second essential perspective on ideologies in addition to Freeden's concept of ideological morphology is the approach by Martin Seliger (1976). His work forms the foundation of what I call the ideological triangle, which explains the main psychological levels of effect on individuals and collective entities. All ideologies, according to Seliger, must have a problem definition with a viewpoint on existing order and power structures, a proposed solution to the problem, and a future vision in order to develop into fully functioning and self-enforcing systems of ideas. Each angle of the triangle, I argue, contains specifically arranged political concepts in the sense of Freeden's morphology that establish meaning and efficacy to each other. For example, a right-wing extremist ideology might stipulate the supremacy of the "Aryan" race and the threat of it becoming extinct due to a concerted evil conspiracy by hostile races (problem, viewpoint on power structures, and order).

In the fully de-pluralized (i.e., radicalized) system, only one solution can prevent that doomsday scenario: violent struggle against those "evil" races and their power structure. Finally, the future vision presented as the "glorious" end goal of all activism could be the white ethnostate, for example. Each part lends central meaning to the other. The desirability of the future vision (the white ethnostate in our example) would disappear without the supremacy of the "Aryan" race and the evil foe. Violent action (or any other form of behavior) would become needles without the ideological urgency of the problem and the herculean achievement the future vision would be. In this conceptualization of ideologies, I hope to avoid one of the most consequential mistakes usually accompanying the term: the focus on intellectual reflection and theoretical proficiency. Ideologies in fact "mix rational and emotive debate freely … After all, ideologies have to deliver conceptual social maps and political decisions, and they have to do so in language accessible to the masses as well as the intellectuals, to amateur as well as professional thinkers" (Freeden, 1996, p. 30). A person who does not know or understand the theoretical foundations of the ideology behind the milieu he or she is a part of is not necessarily less "ideologicalized" or committed to the cause. In other words, the milieu's ideology can impact the intellectual leader and the uneducated foot solder alike, but on different levels. Each part of the ideological triangle and the political concepts it contains can be transported intellectually and theoretically but also through emotional channels such as music, fashion, or games. This link between ideologies and social, as well as emotional, aspects of membership in extremist milieus was also pointed out by Donald Holbrook and John Horgan (2019), which I will pick up again in Section 6.4 when discussing lessons learned for preventing and countering extremism.

The ideological triangle approach fits well with Berger's (2018) concept of extremism. He also recognizes the indispensability of conflict and solution for these groups and milieus. In addition to the fundamental out-group hostility discussed, Berger sees a "crisis-solution construct" to legitimize action based on mutually exclusive identity definitions between in- and outsiders (Berger, 2018, p. 44). The ideologically defined problem is thereby inextricably linked to the enemy: "as extremist identities are constructed, the in-group begins to see the out-group as an unmitigated threat to its legitimacy. This threat creates a crisis, a pivotal event that requires an active response from the in-group. The extremist in-group offers a solution, consisting of hostile actions against an out-group in an effort to resolve the crisis" (Berger, 2018, p. 76). In the focus of this book, I consider those ideological milieus to be hostile when their identity is inseparably built upon hostility toward each other due to the previously discussed inconsistency of central political concepts at their cores.

Even though clearly many forms of extremist ideologies exist, in this book I will be concentrating my attention on three manifestations: far-right (or right-wing), far-left, and Islamic extremism. I am fully aware of the many controversies surrounding every one of these sweeping terms as they are all heterogeneous and non-monolithic phenomena even with partially overlapping currents (e.g., "National Bolshevism, "National Syndicalism," or "National Anarchism"). Therefore, no commonly accepted definitions exist for these three ideologies and their integral concepts are contested. Sometimes, side-switchers present their storyline in elaborate and extensive ideological-philosophical arguments attempting to signal an intellectual development process instead of a simple defection to the other side. Of course, it would go well beyond the scope of this book to retrace in detail the philosophical change in positions across decades for some of the side-switchers presented here. I also do not want to stray away from the individual storyline approach that puts the personal accounts at the center of the analysis by moving too deep into a philosophical assessment of ideological thought edifices. Unfortunately, an ideological "DNA mapping" as provided by Freeden (1996) for mainstream worldview systems (e.g., liberalism, conservatism, socialism) does not exist for extremist milieus so far. Therefore, I will revert to a minimalist working definition for each of the three ideologies my side-switcher cases left and joined, while briefly introducing special strands when necessary to explain an individual's storyline.

Far-right (or right-wing) extremism consists of an overlapping web of movements including but not limited to neo-Nazis, Christian Identity, white supremacists, ultra-nationalists, white power skinheads, and parts of the anti-government or militia movement. The key unifying component of the far-right extremist ideological family is the notion of being part of an innately superior race or nation that is under threat by lesser valued races or nations, for example, through race mixing or immigration (see also Simi, Windisch & Sporer, 2016, p. 6). Hence, their main enemies (next to the "races" and ethnic minorities deemed most dangerous or inferior to their own) are typically those political movements advocating equality and liberalism, in particular left-wing schools of thought.

Far-left (or left-wing) extremism consists of an overlapping web of movements and ideologies including but not limited to varieties of communism, anarchism, and socialism. Among the communists are, for example, Marxist-Leninists, Maoists, or Stalinists. The core unifying ideological components are either the forceful erasure of struggles between socioeconomic classes (e.g., through armed revolution and the forced redistribution of wealth and property); the removal of any governmental structures; or the violent destruction of right-wing extremism (i.e. fascism). Ideological far-left extremism must be differentiated from specific left-wing forms of activism and mobilization, such as anti-fascism as a philosophy or political culture on the one hand, or the black block tactic (for example), on the other. Of course, being opposed to fascism or racism as a matter of moral principles and democratic culture has nothing to do with the specific form of anti-fascist extremism that I am looking at here in this book. Far-left anti-fascism is typically a mobilization platform for different ideological movements in the wider left-wing spectrum. Historically, anti-fascist activism has been associated with anarchists most often, but there are also other ideological currents heavily involved in anti-fascism (Kenney & Clarke, 2020; Moore, 2020). It has been noted that far-left ideology and movements are rather malleable and therefore it is even harder to form a somewhat uniform conceptualization (Carson, 2016). Whether, for example, anti-globalist or environmentalist groups should be included, is contested, even though they might share many ideological components with the classical far-left. In terms of the typical enemy of the far left, these are usually capitalist forms of societies and their political or economic elites pushing for imperialism (e.g., the military-industrial complex), the police and law enforcement, as well as the "fascists" (which are often seen as composed of the elites and police), or the extreme right in general.

Finally, Islamic extremism (a term that has a pejorative tone for some audiences and is therefore not without controversy) is comprised of an overlapping web of movements including but not limited to Salafi-jihadists, legalist Islamists, or Shiite militants. The unifying ideological goal in this category is the protection of Muslims from a perceived war on Islam and the establishment of a society based on religious creed and authority. Many different terms are in use to describe this form of extremist milieu, ranging from "Islamist" to "radical Islam" or "violent Islamism." Since "Islamist" or "Islamism" first and foremost denotes a politicized form of Islam in general, I have opted to use the term "Islamic extremism" to make it perfectly clear that I do not consider the religion of Islam in any way to be directly linked to terrorism, violence, and extremist radicalization. I rather want to focus on a form of extremist milieus that use Islamic rationales, terminology, or theology to advance their own goals. Typically, the main enemies of Islamic extremists are all countries and societies not based on their interpretation of Islamic law, in particular those with man-made (i.e., democratic) legislation, as well as all nonbelievers (i.e., infidels). Furthermore, in the most extreme form (i.e., the Salafi-jihadists), even other Muslims not adhering to their strict understanding of the religion are declared infidels.

Of course, I am fully aware that those working definitions provide ample opportunity for criticism and that they might leave out or unjustifiably include important actors or ideological components.

A word or two are in order regarding the moral and ethical connotations of using the term "extremism" in a comparative way. As a researcher, my work aims to be as neutral and objective as possible, but as a human being with my own moral code, I of course do see an ethical difference between fundamentally opposing racism or an alleged global Jewish conspiracy as a matter of political conviction, for example. As I hope to show through the side-switching accounts presented here, indeed very different ethical and moral considerations played a role for defectors in specific pathways. To give one example: Those who switch from right-wing extremism to Islamic extremism often cite their continued anti-Semitism as a motive, while those defecting to far-left extremism predominantly want to hurt their former movement and repair some of the damage they feel they have caused. My own personal sympathy and understanding for one switching pathway over another should not lead, however, to looking away from the fact that all the side-switchers presented here drew social identity and status out of a conviction based on hostility toward another group of human beings, however morally unjustified this may be.

1.4   Milieu vs. Group

Throughout this book I will often use the terms "milieu" and "group," sometimes as a pair, or standing alone. According to the Cambridge Advanced Learner's Dictionary, a milieu is "the people, the physical and the social conditions and events in which someone acts or lives" (CALDT, n.d.). This places the emphasis on persons of significance, individual relationships, and incidents of relevance for a specific outcome. Another term to describe "milieu" is the "environment" around a person and his or her development in a certain direction. A milieu of radicalization could therefore be understood as a physical and mental space in which radical or extreme messages and individuals are encountered (online or offline), for example, in the form of recruiters, propaganda, rallies, concerts, or chat rooms. Milieus are much more dynamic and inclusive than "groups," which are typically understood as a fixed number of individuals forming an entity for a specific purpose and duration with clearly defined boundaries between insider and outsider. Even more formal would be the term "organization," which, for example, usually includes elements such as the subordination of the members' individual will to that of the collective.

Milieus also have physical, chronological, and relational dimensions at once. The founder of modern social psychology, Kurt Lewin (1936), posited in the 1930s that what he called "life spaces" include the physical environment from micro and meso to macro levels (e.g., the house, the neighborhood, the city, the country). But there is much more to it than merely the places of interaction:

one will have to represent his social environment, his relationship to other persons, their positions and personalities, and his own place in society, for instance his vocation. At the same time, his longings and ambitions will play a role, his fears, thoughts, ideals, and daydreams, in short everything that from the standpoint of the psychologist – read: social scientist - exists for this person. (Lewin, 1936, p. 18)

Along these lines, a milieu can be understood as the social and physical environment of various degrees of significance that surrounds the person in respect to shaping a his or her identity.

As milieus include significant relationships, emotions, events, experiences, subcultures, or places, the concept directly corresponds with that of "story-lines," which I will introduce in the following methodology section. Using milieus in addition to the more rigid "group" or "organization" allows for much more flexibility and appreciation of key factors and processes that the side-switching cases I will discuss here go through. It allows us to explore grey zones between official membership in a terrorist organization and associating oneself with it in the periphery or only online, without any physical contact, for example. Milieus provide the basis for the tracing of multidirectional individual trajectories as they unfold in everyday engagements with other people or ideologies. The "lived experiences" aspect of the milieu concept also includes elements that can go beyond an extremist ideology, such as feelings of grievances and anger, peer relationships, family, trauma, and crises. Many individuals who become involved with extremism and terrorism experience both: membership in a formal organization or group as well as more flexible association in fluid extremist milieus, for example, participation in chat groups, concerts, rallies etc. without becoming a full-time member of a certain entity. Lastly, it is important to point out that human beings can be part of many milieus, even within the same extremist "family." Each holds its own unique truth and reality, with specific norms and rules. In the perspective of Joel Busher and John Morrison, each milieu forms a "micro-moral world" (Busher & Morrison, 2018). Hence, we should be careful not to equate one specific milieu with the complete "truth" that constitutes the far right (for example) but rather as one possible little cosmos of values and interactions.

1.5   Methodology

It is of course tempting to profile all the cases of side-switchers I could identify and look for commonalities in their biographies or personalities. One could argue that those persons who shift between extremist milieus instead of leaving them altogether must have some kind of pathological or hardened desire for violence, hatred, adventure, and action, for example. This is, however, precisely not what I want to do here. Profiling terrorists and extremists has "failed resoundingly" (Horgan, 2008, p. 80) to use the famous expert verdict by John Horgan. This is because

neither psychological nor other research has revealed qualities unique to those who become involved in terrorism, or the existence of singular pathways into (and out of) terrorism. Though terrorist profiles exist in a broad sense, no meaningful (i.e., having predictive validity) psychological profile has been found either within or across groups. If anything, the composition of terrorist groups is remarkable for its diversity. (Horgan, 2017, p. 200)

I completely agree with him, that such a profiling endeavor has no future in serious analyses of either the terrorist or the pathways to radicalization. Following Horgan's lead, it is rather the meaning of engagement with the radicalization process, of which side-switching clearly is a part in the belonging phase of terrorist and extremist involvement (between entry and disengagement).

The methodology I will use to analyze the case studies presented in this book is based on the criminological storyline approach introduced by Robert Agnew (2006). He argued in 2006 that the typical way criminologists explain why individuals engage in crime was by referring to background (e.g., low self-control, delinquent peers) and situational factors (e.g., presence of tempting targets). This, however, ignores the individual perspective narrative behind the criminal engagement. Focusing on such personal storylines, according to Agnew, "can help us better understand the effect of background and situational factors on crime, better explain the variation in background and especially situational variables, and better control crime" (Agnew, 2006, p. 120). It is of course not my intention to liken a switch between groups, even violent extremist and terrorist ones, as criminal acts per se. As long as the instance of side-switching is not part of a criminal behavior (e.g., killing a person to gain entry by proving commitment and determination) and understanding that not all extremist groups are legally prohibited (thereby joining them would constitute a criminal act of material support for terrorism), I regard this phenomenon first and foremost as a significant personal development in a person's (radical) career. Linking the storyline approach with the criminological event perspective (Sacco & Kennedy, 2002), I conceptualize such incidents as multidimensional and situated within particular environmental and behavioral contexts. Criminological theory maintains that (criminal) events unfold over the course of three successive steps, including precursor, transaction, and aftermath stages.

Seeing side-switching as a personal event with such a high significance such as a criminal act in the eyes of criminologists, I argue, will make the storyline approach a fruitful methodology to explore what this form of defection actually meant for the persons going through it and how they explain it. Agnew has conceptualized a (criminal) storyline as, "a temporally limited, interrelated set of events and conditions that increases the likelihood that individuals will engage in a crime or a series of related crimes" (Agnew, 2006, p. 21). Each storyline has a beginning, a middle period, and an end. The beginning is typically started with a particular event that sets in motion a chain of interrelated situations, emotions, or other factors. This event is, according to Agnew, portrayed as something extraordinary and represents a deviation from day-to-day life. A key consequence of this starting event is, that it temporarily alters the individual's characteristics, for example, by increasing strain, reducing self-control, causing certain negative or positive emotions, and so on. The middle period is then comprised as the effects of this initial event, leading to the storyline's end through a resolution that restores the person's original psychological or physical state (Agnew, 2006, p. 121).

Translating Agnew's concept to side-switching, the storylines I will attempt to reconstruct throughout this book ideally include objective events and conditions that increase the likelihood of the defection for each affected person, but also his or her perceptions and reactions to the initial events and conditions (i.e., emotions such as anger, disillusionment, grievances). Furthermore, they should also inform us about relevant interactions with others (e.g., outsiders), the settings for these interactions, and all significant individual characteristics that might explain the side-switching incident. As suggested in Agnew's storyline methodology, I will attempt to include relevant individual characteristics, key events, and conditions of relevance to the defection. A key feature of that approach is that background factors such as, for example self-control, are not seen as linear and stable over time but rather dynamic and sometimes even erratic. Some persons could perceive significant shifts in their emotional state over days or even hours, depending on situational influences. One might be immediately more inclined to leave a group after a fight or discovering a very disillusioning incident of betrayal and hypocrisy. This state could then change in the following days when other group members intervene to mitigate frustration and solve the conflict. The person could also rationally begin to self-persuade that continued involvement in the group is still the best option.

However valuable the storyline approach is for my research questions, there are also some significant limitations to it. In criminological storyline research, multiple sources of information are usually available, including the narrative of the offender. Court files, interviews with peers and family members, or other documents are used to set the individual storyline in context and gain insight into how the person explains his or her involvement in crime vis-à-vis the surrounding environment's account. Where and how both storylines differ is an important indication of where to explore further for potential key factors. Extremist side-switching on the other hand is something rare (from what we know so far) and a phenomenon that occurs in a notoriously difficult to access environment. Even more so, it is very challenging to find detailed accounts of these storylines leading up to the defection and including all the elements that are necessary to fully understand why and how a person has decided and managed to switch between groups.

In this book, I will rely on mainly two sources for reconstructing these storylines: first, autobiographical content of the defectors themselves, usually in the form of books, interviews, or articles in which they at least describe what motivated them to change milieus across hostile ideologies. It must be acknowledged that in many cases, albeit not all of them, the side-switching accounts date from a time when the defectors had successfully entered the new extremist group and used their story to facilitate their integration. Clearly, there is a significant source of bias here, as it must be expected that the accounts are mainly designed to fulfill the goal of establishing some form of credibility in the new group, for example, by portraying the former in-group in an overly negative light. The story will also likely include praise for the new in-group and display elements that act as proof for the defector's ideological commitment to the new environment. There is almost no way to verify the accounts and storylines for most of the cases I will explore.

Furthermore, for some individual cases countless books have been written to discuss their actual ideological and psychological development with still open controversies. This is the reason why the focus does not lie on presenting factually accurate side-switching pathways as such, but rather narratives and storylines presented by the defectors, used by them to justify and facilitate the switch. In that way, I hope to understand how they explain the group migration to the new environment or to the public. Second, I will use additional sources such as press reports, court documents, or group discussions (e.g., in social media) about individual defectors or regarding the act of side-switching itself to shed further light on these storylines. Such sources are of course also affected by bias and oftentimes suffer from incomplete data and the obvious agenda to make the defector appear in a certain image. Luckily, it worked in my favor that those observers who stumbled upon the issue found side-switching across hostile extremist groups to be a curious and noteworthy phenomenon, so they pointed it out in their reports and attempted to explain it with their available evidence.

Identifying well-documented side-switching cases in the first place was even more challenging. As so little attention has been paid to this phenomenon so far, it is not possible to systematically search for it in terrorism or press databases. There is no commonly used vocabulary to describe extremist side-switchers and depending on the milieus defected from or to, much different emphasis is placed on each side. In my search for side-switching cases with enough information to attempt a storyline analysis, I leaned on many experts' and my own knowledge of individual cases via past research on extremism and terrorism. I also found snowball sampling (Noy, 2008) helpful as researching one particular side-switching case often led to identifying additional similar cases. In all likelihood, however, there are many more cases that I have missed and am not aware of. Even though I tried to collect as many storylines as possible and used all the sources at my disposal, the accounts explored here are nothing more than a first attempt at gathering more evidence about extremist side-switching and gaining a first in-depth look at it. Whenever necessary, I will provide the English translation of the original quotes.

1.6   Switching Sides in Context: What Do We Know So Far?

Why and how political attitudes are formed and developed have been major questions of political science, philosophy, and anthropology for centuries. Since knowing how humans come to believe certain fundamental political values and concepts to be true also means understanding how societies form, how they can be structured, and what makes them fail or succeed, this puzzle touches upon the very fabric of what it means to be a human, or in the words of Aristotle: "a political animal" (Aristotle, 1999, p. 5). Consequently, exploring where politics and political convictions come from, as well as the roots of the directly related nature of moral values, forms the basis of most religious and philosophical thought. This is not surprising, as the ever-lasting question of what is right and what is wrong feeds into how humans should conduct their lives, how they should interact with each other in a community and society, and how authority is perceived or administered.

Countless studies and treaties have been written about the development of political attitudes and their connection with moral values. Many factors have been thoroughly looked at by various academic disciplines, weighing the influence, among many others, of biology, neurology and genetics, cultural conditioning, socialization and familial upbringing, personal motivation and personality traits, socioeconomic status, ethnicity, regional context, gender, or religion (for a small selection of examples see Peter K. Hatemi et al., 2009; Peter K. Hatemi & Verhulst, 2015; Hess & Torney-Purta, 2005; Niemi & Klingler, 2012; Sears & Funk, 1991). To complicate matters even further, beyond the individual level development of political attitudes and moral values, the societal mechanisms involved in establishing collective norms that influence political behavior (e.g., voting) have also traditionally been a major focus of social sciences. To cite but one of the many foundational studies in this context, Seymour Martin Lipset's *Political Man* (Lipset, 1960) established, among other factors, the basis for understanding the direct relationship between economic development and democracy, as well the political manifest-ations of socioeconomic class differences, which since then have been the subject of extensive empirical validation.

Of course, it goes far beyond the scope of this book to dive into the question of why and how political attitudes develop in the first place. It is sufficient to accept the fact that the individuals and their biographical trajectories we will encounter in this book are clearly political animals in the strictest sense. All of them have chosen to devote large parts of their lives to a certain political cause, an ideology, or belief system. Instead of quitting extremist or radical activism at the point where they started to become uncomfortable with the situation, they switched sides and sometimes even clearly increased their activism. Some of them later quit extremism and politics altogether, but here we are mostly concerned with persons fundamentally changing the form and outlook of their political attitudes and convictions. Until quite recently, research on the change of political convictions and worldviews had little to say about this actually happening.

Despite evidence that people can spontaneously construct attitudes out of a moment's impression and might flexibly alter them due to contextual circum-stances (Converse, 1964, 1975; Haidt, 2001; Zaller, 1992), a remarkable stubbornness resisting change of views and opinions exists among humans, even when presented directly with factual evidence proving to them that they have been wrong. More so, when consistently challenged directly, many persons even increase conviction of their (faulty) beliefs (Nyhan & Reifler, 2010). It has been firmly established that a person's ideology can effectively prevent change in attitudes when facing evidence calling these opinions into question (Lewandowsky, Ecker, Seifert, Schwarz & Cook, 2012). This is due to the phenomenon called psychological reactance: a negative response to threats to volitional freedom. Reactance theory posits that when individuals perceive a threat to their basic need to choose their own opinions and actions, this can cause a negative form of emotional protection motivating these persons to reassert their power. This, in theory, aims to restore lost freedoms and independence (J. Brehm, 1966; S. Brehm & Brehm, 2013). In short, reactance serves to protect fundamental psychological needs, such as auton-omy, appreciation, and importance for others.

Reactance to attitudinal change, however, is not just a result of protecting one's own autonomy but also of avoiding an experience so thoroughly unpleasant for most humans that they are willing to continue with their erroneous views than to go through it: cognitive dissonance. This aspect of human psychology was first explored in Leon Festinger's (1957) seminal study of a cult that believed that the earth was going to be destroyed by natural disasters and the reaction of its members when the apocalypse repeatedly failed to happen at the prophesized dates. Especially those committed members who had invested heavily in the cult (e.g., who had given up their jobs and homes) were likely to continue activism for the cult and reinterpret the evidence in a self-assuring way (e.g., the earth was not destroyed because of the cult members' adherence to the beliefs).

Cognitive dissonance, a concept that has been extensively studied and supported by ample empirical evidence since Festinger described it, refers to a situation of conflicting attitudes, emotions, opinions, and behavior. The resulting sensation of psychological discomfort essentially leads the affected person to alter their attitude or behavior to reduce that unpleasant sensation and achieve what Festinger has termed cognitive consistency. According to cognitive dissonance theory, human beings are especially unlikely to change their attitudes or behavior if they either have already invested heavily into each or if changing the other is seen as the easier choice. A person who has, for example, been a member of an extremist group for a long time, spent time in prison for crimes committed in the name of the group's cause, and has broken up links to friends and family in the outside world, is highly unlikely to change the attitudinal framework underpinning and legitimizing those actions and investment. Changing the attitudes would mean to abandon the psychological justification for giving up so much for the group and its ideology. Changing the behavior (e.g., confirming to the collective norms in the extremist milieu) would in turn jeopardize the group membership and produce additional conflicts on its own. In sum, reactance and cognitive dissonance are two significantly powerful psychological barriers against attitudinal or behavioral change.

There is more, still. A third powerful individual-level psychological mechanism exists to shield humans from changing opinions and worldviews. Cognitive bias is a case in which "human cognition reliably produces representations that are systematically distorted compared to some aspect of objective reality" (Haselton, Nettle & Murray, 2015, p. 968) and there are many of them. One of the best known bias manifestations for example, is the so-called confirmation bias (Klayman, 1995), which in itself has several distinct variations and evolves around the human ability to ignore evidence contradicting one's own cognitive position and seek out such information supporting it. Far from being a natural design flaw, evolutionary psychology has argued that the numerous different biases help humans to protect the brain form essentially shutting down due to an overwhelming amount of new, contradictory, and difficult-to-solve problems in everyday life. While the evolutionary advantages of "keep calm and carry on" might have been significantly positive, the effects of that aspect of human psychology further decreases the chances of anyone making an easy transition between opposing political standpoints. Especially when those beliefs are deeply intertwined with membership in a social group, a second widely studied form of bias comes into effect, namely the in-group-out-group bias. Once a person considers him or herself to be part of a distinct social group (the in-group), which is a situation with much more extensive ramifications discussed later on in the context of social identity, that individual likely becomes a victim of systematic overestimation of the group's status and power, its moral values, as well as superiority toward outsiders (Mullen, Brown & Smith, 1992). Such intergroup discrimination based on individual bias happens in unison with increased closed mindedness and pressure toward uniformity with the group. Here, however, the particular nature of the out-group has a direct influence on the extent of that bias. Intergroup competition, similarity, and status differentials, for example, have an indirect impact on it (Brewer, 1979, 2010).

Furthermore, group belonging and collective identities shape individual political attitudes through the transmission of moral values embedded, for example, in emotional language intended to foster a member's commitment. Identity-based models of political partisanship and beliefs stress that cognitive processes like memory, implicit evaluation, and perceptual judgments can be altered by the individual bond to a social collective (Van Bavel & Pereira, 2018). Emotions, moral values, and cognitions interpreting and contextualizing contentious political topics, spread within a group much faster than between them, making it more likely that a highly committed member aligns his or her political attitudes with that of the group and protects it from change away from the collective norms (Brady, Wills, Jost, Tucker & Van Bavel, 2017). This mechanism seems to apply equally, if not more intensely, within virtual social networks and communities. Extremist milieus and narratives are oftentimes centrally developed around the evocation of emotions directed at moral judgments, such as grievances and anger about a certain injustice (Meier, 2019; van Stekelenburg, 2017), and so are social movements in general (Schrock, Holden & Reid, 2004; Van Stekelenburg, 2014). Social movements are "carriers of meaning and organizers and leaders do their utmost to create moral outrage and to provide a target against which this can be vented ... They use discourse and identity as resources to emotionally prime members for social movement recruitment" (van Stekelenburg, 2017, p. 936). When such highly emotional and moralized narratives targeting political attitudes about societal issues meet a technologically supercharged social network online, the proverbial "echo chamber" can lead to virtual cascades of extremist messaging akin to viral pandemics further increasing the individual alignment with the perceived or imagined community (Ferrara, 2017).

All of these mechanisms make the change of political attitudes exceptionally difficult it seems. Even more so from the perspective of a violent extremist, who would see his or her ideology challenged continuously and directly either by the surrounding mainstream society or the ideologically hostile group. So, when and how do such attitudes change? What are the circumstances capable of circumventing or dissolving these powerful barriers and protective mechanisms? In 2005, a team of Swedish researchers discovered a peculiar and, for the focus of this book highly relevant, type of human behavior they called "choice blindness." In the experimental study setting, the researchers presented participants with two photos of faces and asked participants to choose the photo they thought was more attractive. The photo was then handed to the participants after it had been skillfully replaced with a different picture of a person judged as less attractive without their noticing. Most participants accepted this version as their own choice and then even continued to argue for why they had chosen that picture (Johansson, Hall, Sikström & Olsson, 2005). This surprising mismatch between a person's choice and the ability to change the underlying rationale has since then been examined in numerous studies, including those looking at the phenomenon's applicability to the change of political attitudes.

It appears that choice blindness could be the psychological "backdoor" or "safety switch" for the mental one-way street created by cognitive dissonance avoidance, intergroup discrimination, cognitive biases, and reactance. Strikingly, as difficult as these mechanisms make individual attitudinal and behavioral change, choice blindness seems to easily sweep them away and induce partially fundamental and lasting individual shifts in political positions. In a 2012 experimental study applying choice blindness to participants' replies on a moral-political questionnaire (e.g., containing attitudes on the justifiability of violence and the Israeli-Palestinian conflict), over half of the manipulated responses were accepted and even defended by the test subjects (L. Hall, Johansson & Strandberg, 2012). In another experiment using the same principle, it was even possible to shift the political profiles and voting intentions across ideological opposites of nearly half the participants (L. Hall et al., 2013). The duration of this phenomenon's effects on individual change was demonstrated in 2018 (Strandberg, Sivén, Hall, Johansson & Pärnamets, 2018), when the unenviable experiment subjects were again brought to accept political opinions directly opposed to the ones they held at the beginning of the test. By using the same basic principle demonstrated in the 2005 study, false feedback regarding political issues was given to the subjects after a first round of questions about their attitudes. They were then asked to state their views directly after the altered feedback and again one week later. A significant change of attitudes in the direction of the manipulation lasted up to that week and the overall extent of the shift increased when the subjects were asked to explain their new position, thereby confronting them directly with the apparent contradiction.

What then might explain the effects of choice blindness and how does this relate to the initially described protective barriers against attitudinal change? One solution to the puzzle could be, that those who changed their attitudes wanted to avoid cognitive dissonance: the shame of admitting having accepted and defended a choice that was actually not theirs. Shifting one's position to appear consistent in the form of reclaiming the presumed error of judgment during the test as a conscious decision might be a psychological strategy to avoid a deeply embarrassing situation. It must be pointed out, however, that in the experiments cited, around half of the participants remained consistent in their political attitudes. Choice blindness clearly does not affect every person equally. Two key differences (among potentially many others) between the seemingly easy change of attitudes through choice blindness and the stubborn resistance against such change through the reactance, bias, and cognitive dissonance described, are the impact of motivated reasoning and individual choice.

In the choice blindness experiments introduced here, those participants who were asked to explain their apparent contradictory shift in attitudes were more likely to cement that change instead of acknowledging they had been misled and simply overlooked it. What Strandberg et al. have called "confabulatory reasoning" is shown to have a powerful impact on the change of a person's views through self-perception and self-persuasion (Strandberg et al., 2018, p. 13). Indeed, many different forms of self-persuasion and the following change in attitudes are known and have been empirically established. Among them is, for example, perspective taking, which can reduce ideological barriers across hostility (Noor & Halabi, 2018). Whether or not a person is aware that the attitude currently taken over is at odds with his or her own's can naturally influence the effect. As has been shown, defending one's own attitudes against an outside attempt to threaten them through reactance is deeply engrained in human psychology. It appears the key to breaking up cemented political views and changing them without suffering from any psychological damage or discomfort is to either convince oneself (and every-one around for that matter) that there is in fact no change at all. Claiming to stay truthful even while obviously changing core political positions to the exact opposite can be done, for example, through arguing that the original group itself may have lost its ways or that one particular core element of the ideology is so important that the rest was shed off in order to fully focus on that aspect in the new group. Throughout this book we will see the importance of such "ideological bridges" for extremist side-switching and defectors claiming to not have changed at all beyond the superficial group affiliation.

Clearly, a significant difference between accepting change and resisting it, lies in the option to choose one's preference. If the change is perceived to be a pressure against a person's will, reactance and resistance is the likely result. If, however, the situation provides an opportunity to correct a standpoint that a person might have outgrown or never fully agreed with in the first place, the attitudinal change could be seen as form of correction and alignment. This might even fit with cognitive dissonance in the form of reestablishing cognitive continuity. A person might have adopted a group's political ideology because of membership and not by individual choice. Alternatively, experiences in the group might have led to disillusionment and a mismatch between individual and collective identities. We will see that this happens regularly in dysfunctional collectives and high-strain groups, such as extremist and terrorist milieus.

Defectors' narratives oftentimes account for a personal grievance and frustration with the original extremist group, sometimes caused by their own actions and standpoints conflicting with the collective's and sometimes as a result of changes or decisions on the group level. In sum, reclaiming individual choice of preference regarding political attitudes in a situation of alleged contradiction between opinion and behavior appears to be a natural psychological antidote to the protective mechanisms against change. Constructivist perspectives on preferential choice and attitude formation have strongly supported this (Ariely & Norton, 2008; Slovic, 1995; Warren, McGraw & Van Boven, 2011). Regarding extremist side-switching across opposite ideological spectrums, the act of change itself could mean a reassertion of individual autonomy. This could be the case either because the defector truly has felt out of place and subjugated in his or her old group, or as a narrative strategy for persuading oneself and the new group. One important difference to the attitudinal change observed in choice blindness is, that extremist side-switchers clearly know that they must convincingly argue for a new political position directly opposed to their original one. However, as we will see, certain narrative constructs allow reconciliation of the two positions and create a "change without change" story arch.

1.6.1 Social Identity Theory

I have touched briefly upon the importance of the group membership and collective identities for the development and alignment of individual political attitudes and moral values. Moving beyond the individual level mechanisms behind formulating political views, holding on to or changing them, another key to understanding a person's move between social groups lies in in the dynamic relationship between the social collective and its members. That relationship has been described in the famous "Social Identity Theory" (SIT), formulated by social psychologists Henri Tajfel and John C. Turner in a series of publications in the 1970s and early 1980s (Tajfel, 1974, 1981; Tajfel, Billig, Bundy & Flament, 1971; Tajfel & Turner, 1979). In short, SIT postulates that people strive to achieve a positively valued social identity through categorizing themselves and others as members of competing social groups. I have previously mentioned in-group-out-group bias or discrimination as a key facet of human psychology. This type of bias typically forms the basis for a positive social identity. By evaluating the in-group more favorably than a relevant out-group, a person's own social status is elevated automatically through group membership. If, for some reason, a member might perceive a negative or decreasing social status resulting from the association with the group in relation to the competing one, SIT proposes three different reactions to the threatened social identity; one individual and two collective strategies. First, such negatively distinctive in-group members might attempt to achieve positive social identity through the so-called *individual mobility strategy*. This strategy means to leave (or attempt to leave) the negatively distinctive in-group and to join a higher-status group. Obviously, this strategy directly relates to this book's focus of extremist side-switchers, and I will discuss it in detail shortly.

The second possible strategy is called the *social creativity strategy* (Tajfel & Turner, 2004, p. 287). This reaction to negative social identity involves the attempt to redefine or alter the elements of comparison between the competing in- and out-groups to achieve a more positive outcome. One might change the dimensions of in-group vs. out-group comparison, for example. An extremist group member could also move away from judging his or her own group being the total number of members and new recruits in a contested social area like a town, state, or district. Instead, a redefintion could place other factors at the center of the comparison, such as political activism measured by the amount of distributed propaganda. In this example, the change in comparative dimensions could be described as a typical quality over quantity argument. Another form of social creativity strategy is changing the values assigned to each attribute of the group so that a negative comparison outcome is altered to be positive. In this manifestation of social creativity, the underlying value system of a certain comparative factor is reversed or rejected. Using again the previous example of a competition between extremist groups, a member might come to the conclusion that more members and recruits are in fact not a sign of positive status; instead, one might claim that the smaller a group is, since the more competitive its recruitment techniques are, the more elitist and high quality personnel would result. Finally, social creativity can also lead to shifting the comparable out-group altogether. A given extremist group's member might, for example, not look for other groups in the same ideological spectrum (e.g., extreme right) but for completely different or hostile ones, as we will see later in this book.

A third strategy described by Tajfel and Turner is the *social change strategy*, which involves an attempted change of the in-group's status as such. In essence, this means increasing the in-group status in the key comparative elements. An extremist group's member could, for example, try to raise its social status through increased activism in recruitment, by introducing new recruitment techniques or by directly challenging key features of the group that are perceived to be negative or weak. As this strategy for handling negative social status involves various forms of improving a person's in-group, the success of this coping mechanism depends on many factors and could easily lead to conflicts with the rest of the group, frustration, or disillusionment. If the individual using the social change strategy does not possess the necessary standing and authority in the group, failure with the possible result of ostracism could be the outcome. Furthermore, as extremist and terrorist milieus can be described as "normative enforcing" environments (Bates, 2011), attempting social change could also be interpreted by the group as a challenge to its core ideology and collective identity. It is obvious that once a person has failed to positively improve the in-group's social standing on key comparative elements and maybe even received punishment for this by the rest of the group, the outcome is likely to be a mismatch between individual and collective identities. However, this does not automatically mean that defection will happen. A group member must perceive the opportunity to leave the group and join a new one with higher social status, for example. In consequence, the questions when and why, as well as which social identity improvement strategy is selected and how it is influenced by external factors, have been major issues of debate among SIT-focused researchers.

The theory itself posits that individual mobility is generally preferred to the collective strategies (i.e., social creativity and social change). In what has been called the "macro-social emphasis" (Hogg & Abrams, 1988, p. 54), SIT identifies three factors impacting the individual choice whether to pursue a given status enhancement strategy or not: permeability of group boundaries (i.e., the perceived possibility to move from one group to another); stability of the intergroup hierarchy (i.e., the perceived likelihood of the status difference between the two groups being reversed in the near future); and the legitimacy of that status difference (i.e., the perceived justice of the hierarchy). In addition, individual ability (e.g., specific skills) might impact the perceived chance of successfully entering the new, higher-status group, thus influencing the decision to attempt the individual mobility strategy. Translating this to the realm of extremist side-switchers, SIT predicts that members of extremist milieus opt for defection when another group with higher status becomes available and joining it is perceived as a realistic option. Individuals with particular skills (e.g., bomb making, weapons handling, charismatic leadership, and recruitment) and knowledge (e.g., regarding the operations of the hostile group they are willing to give up) will find it easier to defect, if they are aware of their higher "market value." A theoretical concept adjacent to SIT, the Five-Stage Model (FSM), has also discussed the individual responses to membership in a disadvantaged or low-status group, focusing on minorities and their interaction with the mainstream culture and society (D. M. Taylor & McKirnan, 1984). Even more so than SIT, the FSM accentuates the preponderance of individual mobility as the preferred strategy, even when only symbolic permeability between groups (i.e., tokenism) exists. FSM also strongly suggests that social upward mobility is always chosen by those group members with the highest abilities and skills.

The individual mobility strategy of status enhancement and its macro-social emphasis, together with other potentially relevant factors (e.g., individual ability), have been widely discussed and tested in various social-psychological experiments. Empirical findings, however, indicate that the relationship between these factors and the likelihood of individual mobility is much more complex than initially stated by SIT. Regarding the impact of group permeability on individual mobility, Jackson, Sullivan, Harnish and Hodge (1996, p. 252) observed that experimental explorations have produced partially conflicting results. Ellemers, van Knippenberg, De Vries and Wilke (1988) first showed that group permeability impacts in-group identification in low-status groups, but only for high-ability individuals. In another experimental setting though, the contrary was found (Ellemers, van Knippenberg & Wilke, 1990). In this study, the impact of permeability was not moderated by group status. A third example of the complex individual mobility strategy from 1993 (Ellemers, Wilke & Van Knippenberg, 1993) identified the legitimacy and stability of group status as a potential influence on perceived group permeability, in addition to the previously known in-group identification. However, Ellemers, Spears and Doosje (1997) found that permeability had no effect whatsoever on in-group identification, meaning that just because another high-status group becomes available and can be joined seemingly easily, a member's bond to the group does not automatically dwindle.

Unfortunately, the list of studies producing apparently confusing results regarding influences on individual mobility and the role of group permeability or other factors continues. Wright, Taylor and Moghaddam (1990), for example, confirmed the positive impact of permeability on individual mobility but Jackson et al. (1996) reported the opposite from their experiments, namely that permeability influences the likelihood of collective strategies but has no effect on mobility. In short, the seemingly contradictory studies regarding individual mobility and group permeability have demonstrated one essential aspect of social identity: We are looking at a very complex interplay of various influential background factors that can significantly alter the individual strategy to remain with or leave the group but depend on the individual mixture of context, the group member's personality and status, as well as the world outside the group. One important point regarding that outside world should be added to the equation here, namely if the group member deliberating what to do about a perceived negative social status has actually had any contact with the potential candidate collective for becoming the new in-group. Indeed, direct contact with the relevant out-group might increase the chance for mobility through a sense of permeability (Tausch, Saguy & Bryson, 2015). In short, if I personally know a member of the competing out-group who can convey a credible possibility of being accepted there, my strategic outlook regarding the current in-group can drastically change. However, Tausch et al. (2015) also found that such direct contact does not automatically impact group commitment (i.e., the inclination to attempt collective strategies to improve the in-group's standing).

Interestingly, the influence of contact to those outside one's own group is something that has been observed many times in research on intergroup hostility, such as prejudice, xenophobia, or terrorism (here especially, in studies looking at external factors causing deradicalization and disengagement). I will treat this in detail in Chapter 6 but, for example, Allport's famous contact hypothesis stipulates that under optimal circumstances (e.g., hostile groups have the same status, cooperative collaboration toward a shared goal, repeated and regular personal interactions between members in a positive context, and the social desirability of exchange through collective norms) can significantly reduce the tension and in-group-out-group discrimination (Allport, 1958; Amir, 1969; Pettigrew & Tropp, 2000). Of course, this in itself does not mean defection to the out-group, but it certainly can reduce the perceived barriers and thereby produce a sense of potential permeability, if the group characteristics are not exclusive (e.g., based on ethnicity or gender). Still, contact with an out-group member or "significant other," be it a family member or someone previously seen as an ideological enemy, has been repeatedly identified as a critical factor in desisting from crime in general (e.g., Bovenkerk, 2011; John H. Laub, Nagin & Sampson, 1998; John H. Laub & Sampson, 2001; Maruna, Lebel, Mitchell & Naples, 2006; K. Walker, Bowen & Brown, 2013) and disengaging from terrorism in particular (e.g., Altier, Thoroughgood & Horgan, 2014; Dalgaard-Nielsen, 2013; Harris, Gringart & Drake, 2017; Koehler, 2016b; Williams, 2017).

Whether the individual strategy (i.e. mobility) is generally preferred to collective strategies (i.e. creativity and change) has also been debated, as stated previously. While SIT posits that this is always the case, experimental studies have again found conflicting evidence. In their experimental study involving 90 college students being randomly assigned to one of three conditions of group permeability (open, token, closed) and two different forms of social identity salience (none or existing), Lalonde and Silverman's (1994) results show that the individual strategy is usually preferred when group permeability exists. In groups closed off from each other, members' preference for collective strategies of status improvement increased but did not diminish their desire for individual mobility. Impermeable group boundaries, according to that study, simply led to equally strong preference for all strategies. When given a range of options, however, they will opt for mobility. Another perspective was provided by Boen and Vanbeselaere (2000), who made 187 male teenage study participants believe they were members of a disadvantaged group. They were then presented with a range of response options to choose from, symbolizing acceptance and combinations of individual and collective factors, as well as different permeability levels and individual ability (among other factors). In their test of the paradigm that individual mobility is always preferred when possible, Boen and Vanbeselaere did not find support for that claim. It appears that persons choose their preferred strategy for social status improvement based on a variety of mutually influencing factors, sometimes defying the rational choice approach embedded in SIT.

Individual ability is the third contested aspect regarding the mobility strategy introduced here (besides the impact of group permeability and priority over collective strategies). Ellemers et al. (1990, p. 234) observed that individuals with "highly esteemed characteristics" are less dependent on the group for positive identity. This notion, which has received some support in experimental studies (e.g., Boen & Vanbeselaere, 2000), indicates that such high-ability individuals might therefore be more likely to attempt to shift to a higher-status group. Afterall, it only seems logical that those who have much to offer are more easily accepted into the higher-status group and knowing this, are also more likely to choose such a social identity improvement. However, other studies have again found contradicting evidence (e.g., L. A. Jackson et al., 1996; Moghaddam & Perreault, 1992). Moghaddam and Perreault (1992) even came to the somewhat puzzling and counterintuitive conclusion that high individual ability reduced the chance of mobility, whereas a lack of ability increased it. They contended that the roles of group loyalties (i.e., in-group identification and commitment) and culture have not been adequately incorporated into SIT and FSM. In this intriguing study, it is argued that especially those low-status groups based on collectivist identities instead of the individualist perspective favored by SIT and FSM, may cause a highly esteemed member not to have strong desires to leave the group and potentially be exposed to discrimination and hostility. Furthermore, a stronger sense of belonging and commitment based on the shared collective identity could lead to an individual sense of duty and responsibility to use those skills and knowledge for advancing the low-status group's position in society, drawing the circle back to the collective strategies of status enhancement.

The aspect of the collective identity's importance for the individual members is very relevant for studying extremist side-switchers, since the milieus we are looking at are typically defined by strong collective identities and ideologies rooted in collectivist understandings of humanity. Simply speaking, we are looking at a field of competing groups defining themselves and each other in collectivist terms, such as race, religious creed, or socio-economic class. This ideological microcosmos is starkly detached (albeit not isolated from) the surrounding societies predominantly (as by the focus of this book and the case studies assessed herein) defined by an individualistic approach (i.e., Western democracies). Returning this argument to SIT, it has indeed been found that social identity salience (taking stronger importance for the group member than the individual identity), is important for the choice between collective and individual strategies (Lalonde & Silverman, 1994) and experiments by Ellemers at al. (1997) found little in-group identification to be a key determinant for social mobility.

Empirical evidence seems to support this plain and fairly logical argument: If I identify more strongly with the group in a way that my sense of individual identity depends on it or is defined by it, I will naturally choose to improve the social status of the group or change categories of comparison with a competing out-group before considering to leave it. Even when having psychologically distanced oneself from the in-group, it is still possible to seek out various social identity enhancement strategies at the same time. "Playing it safe" in regard to achieving a higher social status could mean that a group member can try to improve the group he or she no longer identifies with, including (and somewhat surprisingly) in-group favoritism (L. A. Jackson et al., 1996). Preferring the in-group and valuing it more than a competing group can but does not have to be linked to a higher self-identification with it. This is also well known from terrorism studies, where it is widely accepted based on empirical evidence that members of violent extremist groups can remain active and even committed while at the same time having forgone the ideological conviction (e.g., Horgan, 2005, 2009b; Koehler, 2016b; Marsden, 2017). Nevertheless, it is clear to understand the nature of the bond between an individual member and the extremist milieu he or she is part of in order to fully grasp the phenomenon of side-switching in this particular environment.

1.6.2   The Devoted Actor Theory, Sacred Values, Terrorism, and Social Identity

While SIT-based studies seldom use commitment research exploring the nature of in-group identification or social identity salience, a basic conceptualization for types of relationships between a group and its members is warranted at this point. Starting from Hirschi's (1969) control theory of delinquency, a strong bond between an individual and a social environment is influenced by the level of "attachment" (i.e., emotional connection to that environment); "commitment" (i.e., normal activities associated with that environment); "involvement" (i.e., perception of losing too much by quitting the environment); and "beliefs" (i.e., that shared moral values are essential). It can be assumed that an individual's in-group identification and social identity salience are higher when all four of these are distinct and perceived as such. In order to understand how a person's commitment to a group might change over time and what factors can increase or decrease it, Rusbult's (1983) social investment model provides a very useful concept.

Credit for introducing this concept to the field of terrorism research clearly belongs to Mary Beth Altier, Christian Thoroughgood, and John Horgan, who used it in their 2014 study to develop our understanding of when and why individuals disengage from terrorism (Altier et al., 2014). Key variables here for predicting if a person stays in or leaves extremist groups are the level of satisfaction one derives from involvement, the personal investments made into membership (e.g., prison time served, money spent for milieus–specific life-style items, employment given up in favor of activism for the group) and the attractiveness of available alternatives to the group. Satisfaction derived from group membership, according to Rusbult, is increased when a person invests more in being an accepted part of the milieu and is decreased when better alternatives deliver equal or better personal outcomes (e.g., status) for less cost. In short, the model suggests that commitment increases when people perceive poor alternatives to current involvement and have invested heavily therein. This is a logical expansion of the cognitive dissonance phenomenon intro-duced at the beginning of this chapter. When human beings have already invested valued resources such as time or money into a certain behavior, giving this activity up without an alternative that promises to somehow compensate or at least result in the same or higher satisfaction is psychologic-ally very difficult. It is more likely that a person keeps rationalizing why continuation of the activity or even increased investment appears consistent and feels cognitively balanced.

Turning the model on its head, if we want to have better chances at making someone seize involvement in extremist groups by disengaging completely or switching to another group, this should theoretically be supported by at least two things. On the one hand, offering cheap (in terms of social costs) and attractive alternatives provides what SIT sees as permeability to a higher-status group. On the other hand, it seems advisable to make the already spent investments look less important (or expensive). This can be done by using SIT's creativity strategy against the group's bond with its member by redefin-ing the underlying value system of those resources spent, for example, by removing the social stigma from being an extremist through participation in a deradicalization program or showing that it is possible to repair broken relationships and earn forgiveness. As to increase the attractiveness of that mechanism further, one could also make a convincing argument that those investments in membership in an extremist group are not lost but can still be harnessed for personal status gain. Former terrorists and extremists have written autobiographies, appeared on talk shows, participated in prevention programs, or created charities and foundations by using their biographies and knowledge about the insides of these milieus as an advantage (for a critical assessment of this practice, see Koehler, 2019a).

Still, we need to better understand the specific nature of collective identity and its impact on extremist group members. Social identity salience effects on individuals who are active in violent extremist or terrorist groups has been explored through the Devoted Actor Theory (DAT). Based on the concepts of "fused identities" and "sacred values" (Atran, 2017; Swann Jr, Jetten, Gómez, Whitehouse & Bastian, 2012), this theory explains why some members of such groups are willing to give up even their lives for relatively abstract collective norms, as well as ideological goals. Within violent extremism and terrorism, devoted actors are "deontic (i.e., duty-based) agents who mobilize for collective action to protect cherished values in ways that are dissociated from likely risks or rewards. Devoted actors represent a dimension of thought and behavior distinct from instrumental rationality in resisting material compromises over such values" (Atran, 2017, p. 69).

Within DAT, such deontic behavior is seen as the result of sacred values – "nonnegotiable preferences whose defense compels actions beyond evident reason; that is, regardless of calculable costs and consequences" – and so-called fused identity, which "occurs when personal and group identities collapse into a unique identity to generate a collective sense of invincibility and special destiny" (Atran, 2017, p. 70). While not equally important to every member, extremist and terrorist milieus are typically built around an ideology encompassing core values that are presented as "holy," "sacred," "divine," or otherwise sacrosanct. When those sacred values are attached to specific personal and collective goals, for example, to attain entry into paradise through martyrdom or save one's race from being exterminated by a perceived conspiracy, it becomes possible for some group members to develop a personal identity that is inseparable from the group. Success or failure as a person completely relies on success and failure of the group.

This effect is not only visible through behavior, such as killing or dying for the group's cause, but also in the neurobiology of a person who is so deeply convinced of those sacred values. In a fascinating brain scanning experiment, Pretus et al. (2018) performed functional magnetic resonance imaging (fMRI) measures on 38 volunteers out of a sample of 267 participants deemed vulnerable to recruitment into violent extremism. This vulnerability was based on expressed attitudes toward ideological violence in a previously posed questionnaire. Items, for example, included statements like expressed willingness to defend values by engaging in violent protest, financially supporting a nonstate militant group, joining a nonstate militant group, or fighting and dying on their own. As the study looked specifically at jihadist values, those were defined by elements dictating that "strict sharia should be applied to all Muslim lands," "all current Muslim countries should be replaced by a single borderless Caliphate," or "armed jihad should be waged against the enemies of Muslims" (Pretus et al., 2018, p. 3).

In the scanner, participants were assessed for their willingness to fight and die for in-group sacred values before and after an experimental manipulation involving a virtual ball-toss game that can be used for research on ostracism, social exclusion, or rejection called "Cyberball." Results of the experiment show that neural activity associated with sacred value processing among those predisposed to potential attraction to violent extremism as indicated by their pretest attitudes was significantly higher in the left inferior frontal gyrus. That particular brain region is known to be responsible for the retrieval of semantic knowledge and more specifically for the selection of information containing competing alternatives from semantic memory (Thompson-Schill, D'Esposito, Aguirre & Farah, 1997). This means that stimulation of this brain region through activation of sacred values can potentially impact a person's meaning-making mechanism, rule retrieval, and interpretation of certain symbols, codes, or other signs. Participants also expressed greater willingness to fight and die for sacred versus non-sacred values. It was also shown in this experiment, that it is possible to manipulate trivial values and "sacralise" them (here through social exclusion) to achieve the same neurobiological effects. In short, the study lends empirical support to the argument that sacralization of values interacts with willingness to engage in extreme behavior for those people vulnerable to radicalization or attracted to extremism.

Pointing toward a somewhat nebulous predisposition or attraction to violent extremist radicalization and its ideologically defined sacred values, it is obviously necessary to further interrogate where general morality fits in and how it relates to political attitudes. Which comes first and how do they influence each other? One widely cited explanation is provided through the Moral Foundations Theory (MFT) established by social psychologist Jonathan Haidt (2012). In it, Haidt posits that humans generate implicit evaluations and judgments of situations they encounter using psychological modules evolved to help them in solving social dilemmas, or in short, answering the question of what would be the right or wrong course of action. MFT suggests six foundations of moral reasoning: care/harm, fairness/cheating, loyalty/betrayal, authority/subversion, sanctity/degradation, and liberty/oppression (Haidt, 2012, pp. 9–11). Applied in research on political ideologies and attitudes, some scholars have found that persons who are sensitive to one or more of these foundational modules also correspond in alignment with certain political value systems, such as conservatism or libertarianism (Nilsson & Erlandsson, 2015).

However, a correlation should not automatically be interpreted as causality and the question remains whether moral values shape political attitudes (ideology) or the other way around. The latter was claimed by researchers arguing that human beings are more likely to adapt their moral code to the political group or community they see themselves as a part of (Peter K. Hatemi, Crabtree & Smith, 2019). This view is indeed supported by studies showing that a change in moral values does not significantly alter political attitudes as well and that moral foundations are not likely to be heritable, which is a condition for them being the outcome of an evolutionary development (K. B. Smith, Alford, Hibbing, Martin & Hatemi, 2017). That political attitudes and ideology have a much stronger influence on moral values than vice versa would fit well into the SIT, devoted actor, and cognitive dissonance frameworks. Assuming that radical or extremist milieus are based on particularly strong political ideologies and collective norms, members who identify with them based on their need for positive social identity likely adapt their morality to fit with the group's standard in order to achieve cognitive–behavioral balance. It does not matter if ideological beliefs or group membership came first. Members of far-right, far-left extremist, or jihadist groups will likely align the core moral foundations described in MFT to fit with the group if they want or need to stay involved (or do not have any alternative). Only giving one example here, extremist ideologies are focused on defining friend and enemy or in-group and out-group in strict binary terms, which we have already seen through the extremism concept by Berger (2018). Behavior toward friends and enemies (i.e., harm or care) is ideologically determined and expected of group members. Challenging this basic fabric of extremist milieus will very likely result in punishment or expulsion.

Bringing all these theoretical considerations and findings from experimental studies together, SIT and FSM predict (with some empirical support) that members of groups with perceived low social status will in some likelihood attempt to improve their social identity by defecting to a higher social status group under certain circumstances. Of particular importance for an attempted defection is the feasibility of joining the new group (permeability of group boundaries); if the person in question has any skills or knowledge making a transfer easier (individual ability); and if the psychological bond to the current in-group has been weakened (low social identity salience, little conviction in sacred values, defused identities). However, these are ideal conditions and as we have seen from many experiments' conflicting findings, making a decision to leave a group behind is complex and involves many factors influencing each other or yet unknown. All of these considerations also assume that a person makes rational decisions based on adequate information available to him or her. One can imagine a situation, for example, in which someone would like to leave a group and has the opportunity to do so but remains involved because of emotional attachment to friends or feelings of responsibilities and loyalty detached from social identity. Finally, we are not looking at ordinary social groups here, which can be left or joined with relative ease. In our present exploration, we are concerned with radical, (violent) extremist or terrorist milieus, which have multiple features making defection significantly more problematic. In the following section we therefore need to dive into terrorism and violent conflict research to better understand the peculiarities of these groups and membership in them.

1.6.3   Terrorism and Violent Extremism

Intergroup migration within the same ideological "family" during a radical career is a well-known phenomenon in terrorism research. Group splitting and infighting often lead to fracturing and shifting alliances, as well as the formation of new competing groups striving for the same ideological goal, tapping into the same recruitment pool, and trying to outbid each other by attacking similar enemies. Arguably, one of the best known terrorist group splittings that led to direct competition and violent conflict between entities sharing large parts of the same ideology is the al-Qaeda (AQ) and Islamic State in Iraq and Syria (ISIS, also known as ISIL, Daesh, or IS) divide. ISIS' roots as a coherent group go back to 1999, when its earliest predecessor was founded by Jordanian Salafi-jihadist Abu Musab al-Zarqawi under the name "The Organization of Monotheism and Jihad," lasting till 2004. Zarqawi, who was killed in 2006, then swore allegiance to Osama bin Laden and al-Qaeda and renamed the organization "The Organization of Jihad's Base in Mesopotamia," commonly known as al-Qaeda in Iraq (AQI).

On October 13, 2006, the group had begun to unite smaller insurgent factions under its leadership and rebranded again, using the title "Islamic State of Iraq" (ISI). On May 16, 2010, Abu Bakr al-Baghdadi was appointed the new leader of ISI. When the civil war in Syria broke out in March 2011, al-Qaeda affiliates also established a foothold there, with the largest group being "Jabhat al-Nusra li Ahl as-Sham," more commonly known as the "al-Nusra Front." Intergroup conflict began to arise in April 2013, when Baghdadi released an audio statement in which he claimed that the al-Nusra Front had been established, financed, and supported by ISI and would thereby join it to form a new group under the name of "Islamic State of Iraq and al-Sham" (ISIS). This was a direct challenge to the al-Qaeda central leadership and essentially an attempt by ISI/ISIS to transgress into a territory where it had no assigned authority. Not surprisingly, the leaders of al-Nusra and al-Qaeda rejected this claimed merger. Ayman al-Zawahiri, the head of al-Qaeda at the time, ruled against uniting the Iraqi and Syrian affiliates in June 2013, which in turn was rejected by al-Baghdadi. Ignoring the growing tensions with al-Zawahiri, who even ordered ISIS to be disbanded, operations in Syria continued. This resulted in a direct violent conflict between al-Qaeda and ISIS that lasted around eight months. In February 2014, al-Qaeda publicly disavowed any relations with ISIS (for a detailed account of the split see Zelin, 2014). In late June 2014, the group renamed itself yet again to "Islamic State" (ad-Dawlah al-Islāmiyah), declaring itself a worldwide caliphate.

Much has been written, for example, about the ideological differences between the groups, the multiple reasons for the split, and the consequences for the global jihadist movement (e.g., Arosoaie, 2015; Bacon & Arsenault, 2019; Turner, 2015). Even though both groups belong to the jihadist spectrum, the ideological differences are significant in some key questions. As Mohammed Hafez put it: "the Islamic State represents an exclusive, uncompromising, and puritanical vision of jihadism, while al-Qa`ida has rebranded jihadism as an inclusive, pragmatic, and populist pan-Islamist movement" (Hafez, 2020, p. 40). Important for the question of side-switching, however, is that the split caused an immediate pressure on fighters on the ground, potential recruits, and support networks around the world to choose a side and deal with defectors from the other camp. In addition to killing each other in open and direct conflict, both groups waged a propaganda war to win the "battle for the hearts and minds" of the jihadist movement. Statements of defectors from the other group were collected and used to portray the respective rival in a negative light (Zelin, 2014, p. 5). While naturally the stronger party at the time of the split (al-Qaeda) found itself in a position to stop defections to ISIS and therefore acted more negatively to those former members it could apprehend, ISIS needed experienced fighters and wanted to portray itself as the true future for the jihadist movement.

Still, even al-Qaeda has at times accepted and reintegrated former ISIS members in its ranks, when they had significant skills or knowledge, as well as presented a good opportunity to deal a propaganda blow to ISIS (Kajjo, 2016). Equally, ISIS changed its stand toward reintegrating defectors and apostates depending on its need for manpower. In an audio message by then–ISIS leader Abu Bakr al-Baghdadi released September 16, 2019, for example, the organization's head made an unusually strong argument for accepting the repentance of apostates who wished to return to the organization (Almohammad & Ingram, 2019). At the time of this message, ISIS had lost almost all its former territory and was in dire need of more fighters. Previously, ISIS had a much stricter policy toward former members it deemed to be apostates or defectors. Some were allowed to return after they had successfully gone through specific repentance procedures that included, for example, a renewed oath of loyalty, filling out repentance forms and signing related documents, as well as attending training courses reeducating themselves about ISIS' ideology. At the high time of ISIS, reintegrated former apostates even received a repentance ID and had to pay significant fees for its regular renewal (Al-Tamimi, 2015).

Group splits and fragmentation is a regular occurrence among terrorist organizations. Countless cases of splits leading to ideological and physical conflicts have persisted throughout the history of political violence. To name only two additional examples, the Irish Republican Army (IRA) and the Palestinian Liberation Organization (PLO) have both experienced dozens of internal splits and factions breaking off to form new groups in direct competition with them (Katzman, 2002; Morrison, 2013). In a theoretical model designed to help understand organizational splits in terrorist groups, Morrison (2015) suggests perceiving such schisms through a lens of the struggle for survival. Factions splitting off can be the result of a desire from at least one side to maintain a version of the original organization they both respect and recognize. This points to the previously mentioned importance of sacred values in extremist and terrorist milieus. Such groups are not ordinary organizations, even though they might at times pursue economic or political goals akin to other nonviolent actors. Especially their need to maintain stable sources of funding and an adequate human resource management have been likened to profit-oriented economic entities (e.g., Ligon, Simi, Harms & Harris, 2013; Logan, Ligon & Derrick, 2017; Mironova, 2019). Of course, there are many different types of terrorist groups with various goals, methods, and organizational structures (Marsden & Schmid, 2011). Still, they usually possess some forms of ideologically sacralized values setting them apart from one another and from nonviolent organizations. As Morrison (2015) points out, an internal conflict around the interpretation and obedience of these values usually precedes group schisms. A supgroup might move away if it no longer feels that the core values are respected or recognized by the parent organization, including the "correct" strategy, tactics, and personnel management. As soon as terrorist groups split into factions, the question arises of how to handle members shifting between them. Morrison (2015) also notes that the answer to this question lies in the strategy and power position of each side in the split. The parent organization, for example, could be in the process of strategic reorientation or attempting an ideological rebranding. Then it might make sense to tolerate "hardliners" to leave the group for the sake of its successful development.

Next to splits on the group level leading to competing and partially hostile extremist or terrorist entities, individual members of one specific ideological milieu might also move through many different organizations and roles during their militant careers. This is neither rare nor extraordinary, since staying true to the cause usually provides the legitimacy to choose a group more fitting to one's personal profile. A certain group might have become too violent or not violent enough. A member might have grown too old for a certain type of activism or simply changed his or her preferences for the lifestyle attached to a specific group. Individual circumstances might have changed (e.g., becoming a parent, finding a new job) leading to a growing incongruity between life's reality and group demands. While this could also result in disengagement and deradicalization, which I will discuss separately in Chapter 6, it is also one option to move to another group within the available extremist spectrum. Life stories of infamous terrorists regularly feature a history of shifting between groups, oftentimes accompanied by personal rivalries, ideological disputes, and disagreements over strategy and tactics.

To name but one example here, the biography of the Salafi-jihadi strategist and ideologue Abu Mus'ab al-Suri by Brynjar Lia (2007) details how he first joined the Syrian "Combat Vanguard Organization of the Muslim Brotherhood" in 1980, associated with the original "Muslim Brotherhood" (MB) in name, mostly, and differing from it substantially regarding ideology and tactics. The group chose this name as they, according to Lia (2007, p. 38), considered themselves to be the followers of the "true path" shown by Hasan al-Banna and Sayyid Qutb, the MB's founder and one of its most prominent thinkers. When al-Suri moved to Jordan, he joined the "real" MB, out of ignorance regarding the ideological differences and tensions inside the Syrian Brotherhood (Lia, 2007, p. 40). He rose to prominence and a leadership role with the MB but grew fiercely discontent with the organization after the Syrian regime had violently put down an attempted MB uprising in Hama in February 1982. As the MB leadership decided to seek political compromises with secular and communist regime parties as a result of the botched coup d'état, al-Suri resigned his position and condemned the group for "corruption" and "malfeasance" (Lia, 2007, p. 48). He left via Baghdad and Saudi Arabia for France in 1982, where he continued his journey through various jihadist factions till he ended up with al-Qaeda. Al-Suri is a perfect example of how terrorist groups change and evolve, as well as their members.

As one of the leading experts on the psychology of terrorism, John Horgan points out that "involvement in terrorism is a complex process of accommodation and assimilation across incrementally experienced stages. Potential and actual terrorists move between and within roles, although these migration and promotion processes remain poorly understood" (Horgan, 2008, p. 92). This role migration within terrorist and extremist milieus is essentially based on "a sense of positive expectation. As long as commitment and dedication to one's socialization further and further into the movement remains positive for the follower, the process eventually results in the formation of a new – or at least effectively consolidated – identity" (Horgan, 2008, p. 93). If this positive expectation is is not met for some reason, however, the person in question will experience exactly what we have learned initially in this chapter regarding cognitive dissonance; the effects of a decrease in social status and general frustration due to the mismatch of outcome vis-á-vis the resources spent (as in Rusbult's social investment model).

Instead of shifting to another group of the same ideological family, another option for a disgruntled member would be to leave behind the extremist milieu altogether. Disengagement (i.e., physical role and behavioral change) and deradicalization (i.e., ideological change) of violent extremists and terrorists have received growing attention among researchers in recent years (e.g., Bjørgo & Horgan, 2009; Clubb, 2017; El-Said, 2015; Horgan, 2009b; Koehler, 2016b; Marsden, 2017). This has led to a more nuanced understanding of the reasons and mechanism involved for someone to leave extremism and terrorism behind, including the development of increasingly detailed theoretical models and their empirical testing (Barrelle, 2015; Cherney & Belton, 2019a; Dalgaard-Nielsen, 2013; Khalil, Horgan & Zeuthen, 2019; Koehler, 2016b). I will revisit the countering violent extremism (CVE) debate, to which disengagement and deradicalization belongs, in Chapter 6 and discuss how it relates to extremist side-switching. Of interest now is that this line of research has identified many potential reasons for leaving extremist or terrorist groups, including disillusionment, internal conflicts, and ideological disagreements (e.g., Altier, Leonard Boyle, Shortland & Horgan, 2017; Altier et al., 2014; Harris et al., 2017). Interestingly and importantly, we will encounter these three motives to defect from an extremist milieu in the storylines of side-switchers very often.

All this research in the terrorism and deradicalization fields has looked at why individuals move between like-minded groups, split off from one another, or leave extremism and terrorism behind altogether. We know that extremist and terrorist milieus can be notoriously instable and put significant strains on individual members (e.g., Horgan, 2009b; Koehler, 2020; Simi & Futrell, 2010; Speckhard & Yayla, 2015; Weatherston & Moran, 2003). These groups are often riddled with internal conflicts, hypocrisy, errors in judgment, failure to succeed, and costly to be a member of (including the potential to lose one's life, freedom, or health). With all these characteristics of the life in extremist milieus pushing and pulling members out, the key question remains: why would someone choose to move to another group instead of leaving that lifestyle completely? It appears, at least to the outside observer, that joining a hostile extremist group across ideological boundaries is a much riskier strategy promising less benefits and unclear chances of success, compared to leaving behind extremism and terrorism and reintegrating into mainstream society.

So far, only two publications have considered extremist side-switchers. Next to my own article from 2019 (Koehler, 2019b), David Gartenstein-Ross and Laura Blackman (2019) have described this phenomenon as "fringe fluidity." Focusing on the specific subset of those individuals who have travelled from far-right to Islamic extremism, this study points out the potential ideological overlap, especially in shared out-groups, and the use of historical precedents allowing side-switchers to reconcile the apparently contradicting ideologies. In their eight individual case studies, Gartenstein-Ross and Blackman propose "fringe fluidity" as "an independent radicalization pathway," able to explain "how individuals who exemplify the phenomenon see the ideological synergy and historical connection between some aspects of neo-Nazism and militant Islamism as proof of their compatibility" (Gartenstein-Ross & Blackman, 2019, p. 11). They also point out that understanding the prior extremist involvement of side-switchers could be essential to "fully appreciating their ultimate beliefs and actions" (Gartenstein-Ross & Blackman, 2019, p. 1) and they suspect that "Islamist militancy" might be the "end point" of such shifts as they could not identify cases where it happened vice versa (Gartenstein-Ross & Blackman, 2019, p. 2). Speculations regarding the cause of this phenomenon in their study include "extremist personality type, a lower threshold for radical-ization into a new ideology once one is immersed in one extremist milieu, or two ideologies sharing a key enemy" (Gartenstein-Ross & Blackman, 2019, p. 2). One key necessity for the success of "fringe fluidity" described here are ideological commonalities between the extremist milieus the side-switchers cross. While most of those commonalities named by Gartenstein-Ross and Blackman are of rather general nature and could be found in essentially all forms of extremist and terrorist milieus (e.g. black-and-white thinking, all-consuming worldviews, totalitarian movements, clearly defined in-groups and out-groups), one potential specific ideological bridge could be anti-Semitism and the Jewish community as the shared key out-group (Gartenstein-Ross & Blackman, 2019, pp. 6–7). Indeed, most of their eight cases feature strongly expressed hatred against Jews as a predominant and coherent ideological motive. This is something that my own study of four side-switchers (of which one I shared with Gartenstein-Ross and Blackman's study) also strongly supports (Koehler, 2019b).

Another question we can only speculate about at this point is, whether we should be concerned about side-switching from a counterterrorism or CVE perspective. One main argument I will make throughout this book is that this phenomenon holds the risk of significantly increasing radicalization processes on the one hand, and making extremist groups more dangerous on the other. This is not necessarily the case because defectors might have "greater impul-siveness, or a lower threshold for action" (Gartenstein-Ross & Blackman, 2019, p. 3). One factor could be, that switchers likely will have to prove themselves to be trustworthy and convinced of the new group's cause, maybe through violent actions or extraordinarily determined recruitment activities. We have also seen through choice blindness, cognitive dissonance, and SIT research, that once persons persuade themselves of a certain explanatory narrative, their attitudes are likely to solidify as a result. Theoretically speak-ing, if you manage to successfully make a transition like that, it could lead to a more convinced and radical mindset.

A second argument I will make here is that with each defector, that person's ability, knowledge, skills, and other personal characteristics transfer to the new group as well. Some scholars have, for example, likened the way organized crime syndicates such as drug cartels synchronize their violent tactics to bacterial conjugation. As Jones (2019) has argued, individual members switching between violent groups take knowledge about certain tactics and methods of violence with them, allowing the receiving end of the defection to profit from that transfer almost like an infusion of successful "DNA" from another organism. This could make a group that integrates defectors more effective and provide a quicker learning curve by offering tactics that have been already tried and tested. However, it is not just tactical information that transfers with each defector, but also knowledge about the group's enemies, their names and addresses, their operations, and internal structure. Even those switchers coming from relatively marginal positions might help the receiving group to achieve a more accurate picture of its adversaries and thereby provide unique opportunities for improved action against them. Finally, switchers will also act as proof of ideological legitimacy. Likely the defector will make an effort to support those negative views harnessed about the new group's enemies. This could lead to an overall increase in the group's conviction and steadfastness. An indication of this dynamic was given by Daymon, van Zuijdewijn, and Malet (2020), who looked at career foreign fighters traveling from group to group (mostly within similar ideologies, though) in different conflict zones. During their careers, these professional foreign fighters accumulated resources, developed skills, and transferred them to each new violent actor, which resulted in significant advancements in terms of the positions held in group hierarchies and thereby social status. Another example is the role of defectors between various factions related to the IRA. Some observers fear that former members of "Continuity IRA" who have joined the "New IRA" might increase the latter group's ability to conduct terrorist attacks in Northern Ireland (Mooney, 2020b).

Gartenstein-Ross and I (Gartenstein-Ross & Blackman, 2019; Koehler, 2019b) have pointed out the importance of basic ideological commonalities such as shared enemy out-groups or joint concepts of honor, justice, and masculinity as potential bridges between the different milieus (see Chapter 5 for a detailed discussion). Embodied in the proverbial "the enemy of my enemy is my friend," this mechanism can indeed be a powerful force not just for side-switching but also for collaboration between ideologically hostile groups. One of the case studies in Gartenstein-Ross and Blackman's sample, Spanish neo-Nazi Diego José Frías Álvarez, remained committed to his extreme right ideology while also having been implicated in a mid-2015 conspiracy of a jihadist cell through the provision of weapons and suggesting attack targets (Gartenstein-Ross & Blackman, 2019, p. 16).

Another example would be the terror attack on the Munich Olympic Games on September 5, 1972. Eight members of the Palestinian terror organization

"Black September" entered the living quarters of the Israeli Olympic team and took 11 athletes as hostages. A failed German rescue attempt resulted in the death of all hostages, five terrorists, and one police officer, making the incident one of the most devastating and impactful terror attacks in German post–Second World War history. German authorities confirmed in 2012 that the Palestinian terrorists were working with and aided by at least two German neo-Nazis, who bought cars and worked as drivers for the attackers. One neo-Nazi even provided fake documents for the Palestinians (Kellerhoff, 2012). Such historical cooperation between certain extremist movements might point toward shared worldviews even across assumed hostility. This could mean that beyond the organizational competition, rivalry, and mutual identification as enemy, common ideological threads provide another yet unrecognized type of ideological permeability in addition to the organizational counterpart.

Unfortunately, little research has looked at the ideological overlaps and key motifs shared between different extremist environments, with notable exceptions mostly focused on common subcultural elements such as clothing and music styles or specific ideological components such as anti-Semitism (e.g., Michael, 2006; T. Morris, 2014, 2016; Patterson, 2016; Pisoiu & Lang, 2015) or anti-Americanism (which was noted to be a striking similarity between far-left and far-right extremism by Walter Laqueur, 2003, p. 153). Of course, each milieu has highly specific ideological components that by definition cannot be shared by another one, for example, the belief in a deity or the nonexistence of one (i.e., atheistic ideologies such as far left vs. Islamic and Christian fundamentalist or paganist far right). Beyond those, however, perhaps commonly shared elements could be identified. Unfortunately, uncritical and polemic attempts to "discover" certain ideological components in other extremist milieus have also led to infamous and unscientific labels such as "Islamic Fascism" (Göpffarth & Özyürek, 2020, p. 10). A much more fruitful approach to move beyond the rigid left–right religious extremist ideologies model has been the study and comparison of certain key elements behind them, for example, through the lens of totalitarianism research (Bale, 2009; Geyer & Fitzpatrick, 2009; Gregor, 2008; Kershaw & Lewin, 1997; Linz, 2000). Even though totalitarianism studies generally look at forms of government and statehood that are described as "totalitarian" (e.g., Nazi Germany, the Soviet Union under Stalin), they nevertheless are based on certain extremist ideologies comparable through some shared key features, such as a total and all-encompassing ideology based on conviction instead of critical thought, aiming to create a new and superior human being, suppression of any dissent, central and strict categories of an enemy out-group, subordination of the individual under the collective will, or militaristic lifestyles (e.g., Arendt, 1973; Friedrich & Brzezinski, 1965).

Nevertheless, it seems that some extremist milieus are ideologically closer than others. In their seminal study on (jihadist) educational profiles over-representing the STEM fields (i.e., science, technology, engineering, mathematics), Gambetta and Hertog (2016) also attempted an ideological comparison of far-right, far-left, and Islamic extremist milieus following from their hypothesis that certain personality types could be more or less attracted to different types of extremist ideologies. A stronger link between the far-right and Islamic extremists especially was pointed out there, since "left-wing radicalism is rooted in the Enlightenment and in a belief in scientific progress (however oddly framed by dialectical materialism), right-wing and Islamist extremists share an antiscientific worldview" (Gambetta & Hertog, 2016, p. 93).

Based on that assumption, the two scholars compiled a list of 15 Islamic extremist ideological core elements by consulting academic literature and other experts. It is useful to recount them here, as we will see many of them in the cases discussed throughout this book: traditionalism (including women's subordination); corporatist/organic view of society; hierarchical view of social order; acceptance of social inequality; authoritarian vision of order; rejection of popular sovereignty; anti-Semitism; restoration of a lost order; nostalgia of a mythical past; view of society as polluted and corrupt, in need of purification; membership of militants in a rigidly defined in-group; rejection of pluralism and political competition; monocausal view of origin and solution of social problems; violence as legitimate means of political action; rejection of Western cultural "imperialism"; and a lifestyle highly regulated by routines (Gambetta & Hertog, 2016, p. 95). In the comparison with far-right and far-left milieus, 13 elements were shared with the extreme right and five with the extreme left.

As the comparison was neither based on a systematic review nor was it the main focus of Gambetta and Hertog's study, this finding should be seen more as an indication, albeit a more detailed one, than is usually available elsewhere. Some aspects could clearly be subjected to critical refinement. For example, some far-left extremist environments clearly also exhibit very strong anti-Semitism, marked as nonexistent here (e.g., Hirsh, 2017; Norwood, 2013). Still, we must take the result of Gambetta and Hertog's comparison into consideration for understanding extremist side-switching, as the implications are far-reaching: "if we abstract from the transcendental beliefs that by definition concern religiously inspired groups, such as the Islamists, there is a near complete coincidence between the ideological cocktail of Islamist extremism and that of right-wing extremism" (Gambetta & Hertog, 2016, p. 97). From this point of view, if true, two key hypotheses regarding side-switching must follow: (1) it is more likely to occur between some forms of extremism than others (especially likely between far-right and Islamic extremism) and (2) that different types of personalities are attracted to those ideological clusters sharing fewer elements. Both are seen as confirmed by Gambetta and Hertog, who suggest three pre-ideological personality traits and one plausible complement shared by those individuals more likely to be attracted to far-right and Islamic extremism: the proneness to experience disgust; a strong need for cognitive closure; the strict distinction between in-group and out-group; as well as simplism (Gambetta & Hertog, 2016, p. 130; 150).

While Gambetta and Hertog's study is not a psychological or psychiatric assessment of personality traits and mental health issues among extremists and terrorists, their hypothesis that some persons might be predisposed to feeling a stronger attraction to such milieus than others has found some support in previous or subsequent research. The seminal work on the psychology of politics by Hans Eysenck, for example, indicates similarities between fascists and communists regarding their tough-mindedness, albeit only based on a small and exclusively British sample (Eysenck, 1968). Decades later, this notion was somewhat supported in the systematic literature review investigating the relationship between mental health factors and radicalization by Misiak et al. (2019). They found that empirical research has pointed to personality traits associated with radicalization such as identity fusion; the need for group identification; low levels of empathy; morbid transcendence; feelings of being treated unjustly together with harboring high levels of grievance; rational decision-making; dependent decision style; cognitive complexity; uncertainty; and an analytical cognitive style. Furthermore, personality disorders below the threshold for diagnosable psychological illnesses could be paranoid personality disorder, self-defeating personality disorder, and schizotypal personality disorder (Misiak et al., 2019, p. 57).

The mindset of extremists and terrorists is often characterized by patterns such as militaristic thinking and terminology, the glorification of the past, and of dying for a cause, utopianizing, or the dehumanization of the enemy (Saucier, Akers, Shen-Miller, Knežević & Stankov, 2009). It is important to understand that I am not trying to argue for a link between mental health issues or psychopathology and radicalization here. This is a heated debate including positions seeing a link as thoroughly disproven (e.g., Horgan, 2017; Rasch, 1979; Ruby, 2002) and those arguing for certain types of extremists with a higher chance of mental health issues, as well as measurement and definition issues leading to a false negative (Bubolz & Simi, 2019; Corner & Gill, 2018; Corner, Gill, & Mason, 2015; Lankford, 2018; Rollwage, Dolan & Fleming, 2018). I am not taking a side in this debate. Instead, the important takeaway from this research field is that for some individuals involved in extremism and terrorism, side-switching could be easier than exiting because even across mutually exclusive ideologies they might still recognize familiar psychological elements and feel much more "at home" compared to leaving the environment altogether. This could be especially true for those members who had their individual identities thoroughly fused with the one of the milieu; by switching to another collectivist environment they avoid the pain and cost of defusing identities to an individualistic society (see Sections 1.6.1 and 1.6.2 in this chapter).

As we have seen through social-psychological and terrorism research literature, leaving a group usually is preceded by some form of conflict or grievance leading to discontent and disillusionment regarding membership. This begs the question of what we know about the meso-social layer of interaction and exchange between an extremist group or environment and its members. Putting it more provocatively, how are such groups managing their personnel and human resources to achieve some form of continued commitment through conflict mitigation or the provision of benefits? Naturally, this depends strongly on the type of organization and milieu we look at, most importantly on the resources available for a group to, for example, pay members a salary, provide food, clothing, ammunition, or other necessities. It is well known that ISIS in its heyday was considered to be one of the wealthiest terror organizations in history, being able to provide educational, healthcare, and many other services for its members, including welfare benefits for families of fighters killed in battle (Jonsson, 2015). Smaller and less well-funded groups might resort to other forms of reward mechanisms, such as protection, a sense of loyalty and camaraderie, or the conveyance of individual significance and status.

Unfortunately, the positive forms of interactions between extremist and terrorist milieus with their members is something highly under-researched so far, with one of the most notable exceptions being the seminal study of Mironova (2019). We do know of course through many detailed studies about the importance of specific subcultural elements for recruitment, the construction of collective identity and construction of emotional-ideological bonds, such as music (Timothy S. Brown, 2004; Cotter, 1999; Futrell, Simi & Simon, 2006; Gråtrud, 2016; Hamm, 1993; Said, 2012); fashion (Miller-Idriss, 2018); social media (Frischlich, 2020; Holt, Freilich & Chermak, 2020; Huey, Inch & Peladeau, 2017; Venkatesh, Podoshen, Wallin, Rabah & Glass, 2018; Wahlström & Törnberg, 2019); video games (Al-Rawi, 2018; Lakomy, 2017); a shared food culture and sports (Miller-Idriss, 2020); or other leisure activities (Hegghammer, 2017; Simi & Futrell, 2010). Through such features of membership in an extremist milieu, a sense of normalcy, fun, and positive social bonding is achieved, which could lead to a buffering of negative aspects that might otherwise push a member to feel dissatisfied and leave. However, we do not have much information about how exactly groups and members react toward each other when confronted with conflicts and problems, or more specifically how the sphere of negotiation for continued membership actually looks like from the side of the member on the one hand, and from the side of the group on the other.

How then do extremist and terrorist groups react when they face defection? This could be an important indicator for organizational permeability, as well as a significant influence on the potential costs the individual switcher might have to expect. Severe punishment through acts of revenge, for example, could severely raise the costs of leaving to a point where it is simply too dangerous for the defector. In the terrorism and especially the deradicalization literature, ample anecdotal evidence exists about this phenomenon. Group sanctions are some of the strongest reasons for some defectors to abstain from leaving, but for those exiting from relatively marginal positions and not joining a directly opposing group it might be less of a problem:

some extremist groups let their members leave if they want to. New recruits who have been only on the periphery of the scene and not been initiated in any of the group's secrets may normally leave without any consequences whatsoever – at least if they do not switch to the anti-racists or run to the media with what they might know. (Bjørgo, 2009, p. 40)

Bjørgo continues, however, that if former members of extreme right-wing milieus leave middle or high levels of the group's hierarchy and if they should provide information to extreme left-wing groups, police, or the media, group reactions may include disappointment, observation, death threats, physical attacks, harassment, verbal threats, expression of content, and (rarely) killings. This is supported by other quite severe accounts of brutal punishments and threats against defectors who decided to work actively against their former in-group (Aho, 1988, p. 165; Horgan, 2009b, p. 47). In other cases, special arrangements between defectors and the group have been made, such as the practice of "separation contracts" by al-Qaeda described by Horgan (2009b, p. 37). The IRA even offered something like a vacation system to potential defectors, provided that no information about the organization was passed on (Horgan, 2009b, p. 93). Others, such as the Ulster Defence Forces (UDA), reacted with severe death threats (Horgan, 2009b, p. 114). Some groups have relied on blackmailing the potential and successful defector, either with crimes committed by them in the past or by threatening to disclose signed vows of loyalty by these persons to the public (Bjørgo, 1997, p. 224). Slander and public harassment of "traitors" is also common among some extremist groups (Bjørgo, 1997, p. 224).

In a study from 2015 based on interviews with five former German neo-Nazis and an analysis of twelve case studies, I wanted to get more insight into how, why, and when extremist groups react to defectors (Koehler, 2015b). Indeed, my qualitative evidence points to different types of defectors who receive different forms of reactions from the group, if the group is capable of reacting in a planned and coherent fashion. This largely depends on the position the defectors leave, the (incriminating) knowledge they have about the group, and the way they behave toward it after they have left (positive "dropouts," neutral "renegades," or negative "traitors"). This fits well with social-psychological research on group reactions to disloyalty in non-extremist settings. Levine and Moreland's model (2002), for example, predicts that groups facing strong competition will react harshly and negatively toward those defectors whom they perceive to create a disadvantage or threat for the group. In short, a defector leaving from mid- to high-level hierarchy with intimate knowledge of the group and joining a direct ideological enemy can expect severe reactions, including violence, at least in the far-right extremist environment.

Of course, extremist milieus can also be hostile to each other within the same ideological current, especially when there is direct competition for recruits, territory, power, or status (e.g., between ISIS and al-Qaeda). However, from the individual defector's point of view, it might still be easier to switch groups within the same ideological family. While he or she might nevertheless have to endure severe negative reactions from the former in-group up to execution, on the individual level there should be less cognitive dissonance theoretically.

Summing up this part of the chapter, side-switching is a phenomenon rarely looked at in terrorism and extremism research. We know that these milieus are prone to putting significant strain on individual members, be it physically or mentally, prompting many to quit the lifestyle eventually. Shifting between like-minded groups is well known and can also include partially severe conflict and hostility. Extremist and terrorist groups typically react harshly toward defectors who they decide to use their inside knowledge and skills to act against their former in-group, raising the costs for the defector and reducing perceived organizational permeability. There is, however, also indication that some commonly shared core ideological elements exist among otherwise hostile and directly opposed extremist milieus. This could create a form of yet unexplored ideological permeability functioning as psychological transit routes between different milieus. For further insight into the phenomenon, it might be helpful to look at another field of violent group-based conflict that experiences defections across enemy lines: civil wars.

1.6.4   Civil War Studies

Beyond social psychology and terrorism research, scholars studying civil wars have noted that side-switching, or what they call "opportunistic alignment" and "fratricidal flipping" across groups interlocked in armed combat with each other, is indeed a quite common phenomenon (e.g. Kalyvas, 2008). Nevertheless, the individual motives and processes involved remain a debated "puzzle in the context of ethnic civil wars" (Oppenheim, Steele, Vargas & Weintraub, 2015, p. 3), since ethnicity is usually seen as a key determinant of group alignment in conflicts and a very distinct group boundary allowing little permeability (Seymour, 2014). With such a conflict background, it is especially striking that individuals would leave the group fighting in support of their own kinship and join a faction likely to engage in armed struggle with their family, tribe, or community members.

It was suggested in some studies that especially relevant factors impacting the likelihood of side-switching in civil wars are the individual group shifter's degree of ideological conviction; the territorial control and organizational demands of the in- and out-groups; rebel group infighting causing members to flee potential reprisals; and relative power considerations (Seymour, 2014). In this sense, side-switching is usually explained by rational choice considerations. Joining the most successful faction or the one offering the best economic benefits in addition to escaping potential reprisals within the in-group is a logical course of action. Both the impact of economic considerations (increasing chance of side-switching) and ideological conviction (decreasing chance of side-switching) found some support in empirical research (Oppenheim et al., 2015).

Material incentives (i.e., economic considerations) have also been found to interact with political patronage and rivalry to make such opportunistic alignments more likely: "the risk of defection increases anywhere from three to four times in the presence of an intense and visible political rivalry that outsiders are willing to exploit through offers of military support; incentives to instrumentalize collaboration in pursuit of patronage-based rewards increase the probability of defection anywhere from four to eight times" (Seymour, 2014, p. 115). However, not all reasons for side-switching in civil war contexts can be attributed to such profane cost–benefit calculations. A report by the United Nations Office of the Special Adviser on Africa (UNOSAA), for example, describes the case of a soldier in the Great Lakes region who had started his fighter career as a child soldier in the Ugandan National Resistance Movement (NRM) (UNOSAA, 2007, p. 19). Since the mid-1980s, this person had fought and trained with militant organizations in no less than seven countries, partially with groups fighting each other. Instead of material gain, the report based on an interview with him, stated that he fully adhered to the various groups' ideologies he was with each time.

Even though research on defections in civil wars offers some relevant perspectives for extremist side-switching, it also underlies significant caveats. In this book, I am looking at migration across hostile violent extremist groups outside a civil war situation within a politically stable country, effective rule of law, and clear monopoly of force on the side of state authorities. Hence, conflict between the opposing groups, even though sometimes involving violence, is usually sanctioned through criminal justice and law enforcement and does not involve the use of tactics and tools of warfare (e.g., heavy weapons, artillery, tanks, intensive, prolonged, and repeated firefights). Therefore, military skills gained in open combat or irregular warfare, for example, which make side-switching in civil wars more likely due to the need for experienced and trained combatants, play only a minor role in the scenarios discussed here. Furthermore, extremist and terrorist groups in Western countries typically do not possess enough resources to offer significant material incentives, especially compared to the alternative social environment of mainstream society. Outside third-party patronage and sponsorship, which might indeed exist in that context to a limited degree (for example, in the case of Russia and Western far-right groups, see Shekhovtsov, 2018), extremist groups in the countries I look at typically do not possess actual physical support in their violent confrontations with opposing groups by a third–party state actor. Still, research about side-switching in civil wars supports some basic notions from social psychology: Individuals with a higher degree of in-group identification and commitment (i.e., stronger ideological conviction) are less likely to migrate to opposing groups and material incentives of some kind, and power considerations and in-group infighting increase the chance of defection for all others.

1.7   A Mystery, Still

Even when considering all the theoretical concepts and empirical research I introduced in this chapter, there are still many open questions and conundrums when it comes to extremist side-switching. First, extremist or terrorist groups based on hostile and mutually exclusive ideologies are unlikely to have open and pervious boundaries between each other. On the contrary, by definition hostile environments see each other with suspicion and enmity in the best of circumstances. Open hatred and violence are also likely forms of mutual reaction in this field. Speaking with SIT, hostile extremist groups are likely to have impermeable boundaries. It is not an easy task, for example, to simply walk over to a militant anti-fascist group as a well-known neo-Nazi and ask to join. Furthermore, many extremist groups react harshly toward potential defectors due to the risk of incriminating or otherwise sensitive information being passed on to opponents. Also, individual defections threaten a group's meaning-making system and therefore require adequate sanctions, up to the threat of violence and actually killing defectors. The severity of a group's reaction might also be impacted by the notion of "treason," since the switching we explore here involves a shift to an ideological enemy.

The receiving end of the side-switching might also be reluctant to welcome the defector, despite the valuable information and skills they might bring them. Having defected once, the risk of repeating this strategy of personal status enhancement should concern every group, especially if they need to rely on trustworthy and committed members. Not even a high level of individual ability and the possession of valuable skills will make this move more attract-ive necessarily. From the new group's perspective, high individual ability also makes another defection more likely, especially when this strategy has been successfully deployed once before.

We know from social psychology that intergroup situations filled with conflict, competition, and negative stereotypes impede rational thinking and collaboration, while also increasing in-group favoritism (Hausken, 2000). General mistrust and mutual devaluation are likely to be salient features within intergroup conflict, which may strongly impact the feasibility of the individual mobility strategy. Furthermore, group members may be motivated to hold on to intergroup conflict as a source of meaning (Rovenpor et al., 2019). In violent extremist milieus, at least some degree of collective identity is derived from that conflict, as such groups define themselves by ideologically based enemies and struggles. One should also not ignore the fact that activism in an extremist environment brings with it a high likelihood of having engaged in violent conflict with the very same milieu one is trying to enter. Confrontations between left-wing and right-wing extremists are, for example, quite regular, which has led to ample evidence and research on so-called cumulative or reciprocal radicalization, including other forms of extremism as well (Busher & Macklin, 2015; Eatwell, 2006; Ebner, 2017). Hence, there is some possibility for the side-switcher that he or she will enter a group or milieu that includes someone who has been a victim either of the switcher personally or the former in-group. All of this makes the attempt of switching sides to an enemy extremist group a psychologically and physically risky, daring, and unattractive business.

Another point that should give us pause when considering SIT's explanation for individual mobility, is the fact that it exclusively regards shifting as a way of entering a higher-status group. In a Western rule of law context, a shift from one extremist group to another does not credibly hold the promise of any status increase. Both groups are likely to be somewhat socially stigmatized, albeit granted with differences mostly on the side of left-wing activism. However, confrontations with law enforcement, high demands on individual commit-ment, and extensive personal risks will remain important strains on the switcher's life. Making a move like that is pure nonsense according to SIT. This is because the alternative of leaving extremism and terrorism altogether would provide higher personal status on nearly every conceivable level. Put simply, how could someone enhance their social status by shifting from one highly stigmatized group to another?

Most importantly, as DAT suggests, social identity is of major importance to members of extremist and terrorist groups. Their identities often become fused so that their sense of individuality completely depends on the group. Such groups typically demand high commitment and personal investment in support of specific "sacred values." To successfully execute the mobility strategy, individuals who have fully entered one violent extremist environment (i.e., not "bystanders" or "drifters") would need to overcome significant in-group identification and essentially "defuse" their individual identity from the collective on their own. Compounding this challenge, no help can be expected from either the in- or out-group.

In my attempt to solve this puzzle, I will use the biographical case studies presented in this book to argue that we need to understand three main mechanisms behind extremist side-switching. First, I posit that we must look carefully at the intersection between the extremist milieu and its members. At some point in this bond between collective and individual a conflict erupts and creates a temporal misalignment between the member and the group's identities on a fundamental level. The case studies deliver fascinating insights into the ecology of extremism and terrorism. How do groups react when being confronted with internal criticism; how do members try to negotiate a better social or ideological status before choosing the "exit" option? How do groups and members constantly reform their positions toward each other and how is it possible in the first place that side-switching is perceived to be a viable option? The way in which both sides react to this friction is of key importance in explaining why some extremists eventually decide to defect to the other side. Essentially, we must seek to explore how extremist groups manage internal conflicts and how their personnel management is perceived by those members who go on to leave. Even more specifically, side-switchers offer an opportunity to study when and how extremist human resource management fails, which could hold important lessons for counterterrorism and CVE.

Second, I build on Freeden's ideological morphology concept to show how extremist side-switching happens along ideological core "DNA" concepts, such as "anti-Semitism" or "violence," which alerts us to the existence of ideological permeability in parallel to organizational permeability. While on the group level, boundaries might be more or less closed off, the ideological dimension could allow for a much easier flow of thought and membership. This is possible because extremist milieus are by definition ideological spheres that operate and are held together on the premise of problem definitions, solutions, and future visions. Physical membership in the storylines of the side-switchers is often a side effect of ideological convictions. This perspective also helps to theoretically understand the possibility that some ideological directions of defections are easier to achieve then others. Third, I will argue that the option of leaving extremism altogether is indeed not the easiest one for side-switchers, both on organizational and ideological levels. Indeed, shifting to another extremist group oftentimes does require less identity restructuring and defusing on the side of the defector than compared with a complete disengagement or deradicalization. Some ideological core concepts must be reframed or repositioned, while most of them often remain intact in most of their storylines.

2   Nation, Race, and Anti-Semitism
Switching to Far-Right Extremism

On October 20, 1981, German police officers stopped a car with a group of neo-Nazis on their way to a bank robbery. Calling itself "Commando Omega," the clandestine terror cell hoped to finance their operation with the spoils from the heist. The group's main plan, however, was to assassinate judges and prosecutors targeting their far-right comrades, as well as defectors from their milieu. Once the car had stopped and one of its occupants exited the vehicle, a hand grenade was detonated resulting in a firefight with the police. Two of the right-wing extremists were killed and one from the group was wounded along with two police officers (Koehler, 2016a, p. 78).

Among the group was Peter Fabel (born 1961), who was later sentenced to four years of juvenile detention for attempting extortionate robbery, possession of illegal weapons, and explosives, as well as using a fully automatic firearm against police officers. According to the verdict, Fabel was the only child of his parents and achieved a medium-level education (certificate of secondary education). At age two, his parents got divorced and custody was given to the mother. Both parents developed a strong addiction to alcohol leading to Fabel spending most his time with his grandparents. He began vocational training to be a building fitter in 1977 but was dismissed after one year due to insufficient grades. Fabel struggled to find a job and only worked in short-term employment as a warehouseman between 1971 and 1981. In 1973, Peter Fabel attempted suicide via a medication overdose (BayObLG, 1983, pp. 26–27). About three years later, he began supporting the Communist Party of Germany/Marxists and Leninists (Kommunistische Partei Deutschlands/Marxisten-Leninisten, or KPD/ML). In 1977, however, Fabel switched to the extreme right-wing "National Revolutionary Workers Front" (Nationalrevolutionäre Arbeiterfront, or NRAF). In summer 1981, he shifted to sympathizing with the US neo-Nazi "NSDAP Aufbau und Auslandsorganisation" (NSDAP/AO) founded in 1972 by Gary Rex Lauck in Lincoln, Nebraska. In August 1981, Fabel was excluded from the NRAF. At the time of the sentencing for his involvement in the right-wing terrorist group, he already had numerous previous convictions for several acts of theft, damage of property, incitement of hatred, and criminal assault (BayObLG, 1983, pp. 28–30).

It is noteworthy that Fabel did not hide his extreme left-wing past but instead chose to write a personal portrait of himself in the monthly magazine of the largest German far-right prison support association named the "Aid Community for National Political Prisoners and Their Relatives" (Hilfsgemeinschaft für nationale politische Gefangene und deren Angehörige, HNG), which was founded in 1979 and banned by the German government in 2011. In its newsletter circulated among registered and paying members, political essays, addresses of incarcerated comrades, letters of prisoners, court documents, and other content was published. The August 1982 edition, about a year before the trial, opened with a short biographical piece written by Peter Fabel out of prison. In it, he explains:

Dear Comrades! . . . My name is Peter Fabel and I was born on May 28, 1961 in the old German Hanse town of Bremen. My job is as [a] worker. Because I come from a social-democrat family, the mindset of the so called "representatives of the working class" was not alien to me. But to recognize that the SPD [or Social Democrat Party of Germany] was neither a people's party nor a workers' party is not difficult for a teenager like I am. Those parties representing capitalism, like the CDU [or Christian Democrat Party] and the FDP [or liberal Free Democratic Party], did not come into consideration for me as well. Among everything, only the slogans of the KPD/ML appeared to be a better match for my ideas. So, in 1976 I did not become a member but a sympathizer of this group. The political realities of the KPD/ML, however, differentiated so much from the "preached" slogans and goals, that I quickly realized I will never be able to see the manifestation of my ideals within the framework of this party. After this bitter disappointment I joined the NRAF (National Revolutionary Workers Front) Bremen in 1977. It was there with the "fascist" enemy of yesterday that I found the path to what I envisioned in my deepest inner self. The social community of the deed. The National Socialism built upon the fundament of a folkish worldview revealed itself to be the realization of the goals of the working class and also the founder of a true nation [Volksgemeinschaft in German] without any class difference. Here no empty slogans and shallow phrases were used. The practice of National Socialism is the most convincing advertisement for itself. (original in German, translated by author; Fabel, 1982)

This letter is an extraordinary document for the simple reason that a person clearly involved in right-wing terrorism with some of the most extreme and violent parts of the far-right milieu "confesses" to have an extreme left background to his in-group shortly before standing trial. One potential motive for that might have been that Fabel feared his past would come to the attention of his fellow neo-Nazis through the court proceedings and that he therefore felt the need to preempt this inevitable disclosure of potentially embarrassing personal information. At the time, Fabel could not have chosen a more prominent place for his revelation, as the HNG was one of the largest extreme right-wing organizations in Germany and its magazine the central hub for exchanging information among the militant far-right long before the dawn of the Internet. Over three-quarters of the letter are dedicated to explaining his shift to the extreme-right milieu, indicating that the purpose of the publication was indeed to "own" and spin his narrative into a more favorable direction ahead of a potential forced coming out. In order to accomplish this, Fabel condensed three main elements into a concise side-switching storyline.

First, the overarching theme is his ideological goal to find a solution to the class struggle and in particular the manifestation of the working class interests rooted in his family background. Initially having been convinced by far-left propaganda, Fabel claims to have found only "bitter disappointment" over empty and shallow phrases, the second element in his narrative. Third, he highlights the action orientation within the far right and the more effective concept of racially based collective identities. In the extreme right, Fabel writes, deeds follow conviction making this milieu a superior answer to social problems compared to the far-left. There is no information about how the milieu reacted to his revelation but the fact that this key outlet decided to publish it as the first article of the issue clearly indicates support, at least from the HNG. It can also be expected that at this point knowledge about the group and actions Fabel was involved in had become widely spread in the extreme-right milieu. With a criminal background like this, he could hope for a reputation of ideological conviction beyond question among most of his fellow neo-Nazis. Ironically, two of his codefendants in the upcoming trial, the married couple and likewise militant neo-Nazis Christiane and Klaus Dieter Hewicker, would choose to go exactly the opposite way and publicly declare their defection from the extreme right to far-left anti-imperialist action (see Section 3.1 for their story).

Usually, the far left and far right are bitter enemies and regularly engage in violent and nonviolent conflict with each other. Typical and widespread hostile activities include doxing, that is, the publication of personal information such as names, addresses, workplace, etc. of members from the enemy group; verbal threats through music, rallies and, publications; and actual violent attacks. Especially within the militant anti-fascist current of far-left activism, the extreme right (in addition to the authorities), is by definition the main enemy and dominates the nature and target of most of its methods (e.g., Blank, 2013; Copsey, 2016).

Examples of violent actions targeting the far right include clashes in the United States between the two sides at the February 2017 Berkeley, CA protests against alt-right speaker Milo Yiannopoulos and during the August 2017 "Unite the Right" rally in Charlottesville, VA (LaFree, 2018). On the other side, far rightists widely see anti-fascists and the extreme left in general as one of their main political enemies and as the ideological embodiment of all those sociopolitical themes and characteristics they despise, such as immigration, tolerance for homosexuality, race-mixing, or pacifism. Far-right extremists have therefore also regularly targeted their left-wing opponents, for example, Anders Behring Breivik in his July 2011 terrorist attacks or James Alex Fields Jr. during the Charlottesville rally.

Beyond those modern-era hostilities, there is a long tradition of violent and nonviolent confrontations between these two ideological families, essentially dating back to the emergence of right-wing extremist political movements. Virulent street fights between Nazi stormtroopers (Sturmabteilung, or SA) and communists in Germany before the establishment of the Third Reich are but one example (Merkl, 1982; Rosenhaft, 1983), and the attempted extermination of left-wing political opposition by the Nazis in concentration camps after they had gained power, another. Long before that, these conflicts developed to a point at which members of the Nazi movement assassinated and terrorized left-wing politicians (Brenner, 2000; Southern, 1982; H. Stern, 1963), for example, German Foreign Minister Walther Rathenau (murdered in 1922) or leading German communists Rosa Luxemburg and Karl Liebknecht (both murdered in 1919). In Italy, the beginning of the reign of Fascism is often dated back to the assassination of socialist member of parliament and union leader Giacomo Matteotti by Fascists on June 10, 1924 (Killinger, 2016).

How then can side-switching between these two milieus be possible and successful? It appears that hating each other is very much engrained into the ideological and social "DNA" of these milieus. Despite this fact, however, we must not overlook that there were times even during the heated days of communist-Nazi street fights when both milieus either collaborated for political gain (e.g., the joint Nazi-communist strike targeting the Berlin public transport system in September 1932) or exchanged members either as part of a strategic infiltration or as a matter of side-switching because of an agenda and appearance that looked similar to the working-class audience. Especially the SA deliberately catered to socialist and anti-capitalist themes, while the Communist Party of Germany (Kommunistische Partei Deutschlands, or KPD) went through a phase of nationalization to win over some of the Nazis. Membership fluctuation between both camps appears to have been more heavily directed at the SA and other Nazi organizations, of which some divisions contained up to an estimated 70 percent of former communists (the motives of far-left defectors were diverse and included strategic infiltration or avoiding arrest but many came to abandon their previous ideology in the process; see Timothy Scott Brown, 2009, pp. 135–146). What specific storylines can be found among leftists who joined fascist, neo-Nazi, or other far-right milieus that can help us understand why individual members decide to defect along this ideological and physical barrier? The following chapter will try to reconstruct some of the pathways used to circumvent what appears to be a generally very impermeable intergroup standoff.

2.1   Horst Mahler

One of the best known German cases of side-switching is the notorious anti-Semite and Holocaust denier Horst Mahler, whose extremist career took him through such extraordinary and seemingly contradictory ideological milieus that his story was highlighted even in international research (e.g., Gartenstein-Ross & Blackman, 2019; Michael, 2009). Mahler was born in 1936 to devoted Nazi parents and raised strictly anti-communist. His father committed suicide in 1949, according to Mahler (Seitenbecher, 2013, p. 82), due to depression caused by Germany's loss of the Second World War. The death of his father and the ideology of his parents had a deep impact on him. Mahler repeatedly expressed continuous curiosity about the (for him) apparent contradiction between the loving and caring parents he remembered and their Nazi views (Seitenbecher, 2013, p. 84).

Mahler's mother remained a convinced National Socialist throughout her life and for a long time rejected the Holocaust or any other German atrocities during the war. Indeed, it appears that Mahler went through phases of rebellion against his parents by joining the far left to a certain degree and eventually circling back to them ideologically at the end of his extremist career (Seitenbecher, 2013, p. 85). Horst Mahler excelled academically from the beginning of his education. He received his high school diploma in 1955 in West Berlin and was the best in his class; he started law school right afterward with the support of the prestigious German Academic Scholarship Foundation (Deutsche Studienstiftung) reserved for highly gifted students.

By 1963, Mahler had already completed his first and second legal state examination. At that time, he began studying the writings of Marx and Lenin, at first out of a professed desire to disprove them in line with his anti-communist family background (Seitenbecher, 2013, p. 85). However, Mahler also felt impacted by collective German guilt over the Nazi era and the Holocaust, which provided another incentive to seek some form of redemption through communist teachings (Seitenbecher, 2013, p. 85). For a short period, Mahler was also a member of a right-wing student fraternity, at the time most likely as an act of rebellion against the university's authority (Seitenbecher, 2013, p. 85).

In 1956, he joined the Social Democrat Party (Sozialdemokratische Partei Deutschlands, or SPD), marking the beginning of his organized political activism. In 1959, Mahler moved on to the much more left-wing radical Socialist German Student Alliance (Sozialistischer Deutscher Studentenbund, or SDS), which became a core milieu for later far-left extremist and terrorist careers. He was expulsed from the SPD in consequence a few years later. Now the pace of his left-wing radicalization accelerated, leading to involvement in the "Association of Independent Socialists" (Vereinigung Unabhängiger

Sozialisten, or VUS). In 1963, Mahler was admitted to the bar, briefly slowing down his ideological and activist development. In 1970, however, he joined the Communist Party of Germany (Kommunistische Partei Deutschlands, or KPD) for a short time, after he had some significant successes as a lawyer focusing on commercial law. To illustrate his promising legal career in this period: Horst Mahler was the first German lawyer to be heard at the European Court of Human Rights in 1966.

Nevertheless, the political soon began to take over the legal commitments. In the same year, Rudi Dutschke (1940–1979), the iconic leading figure of the socialist student movement in West Berlin who was shot by a right-wing extremist in 1968 and later died of his injuries, asked Mahler to represent a foreign exchange student in court in order to prevent his extradition. Suddenly, everything began to change for him: "I now was the much in demand lawyer the students looked for. I defended their causes with all my heart and thus became a part of them" (original in German, translated by author, as cited in Seitenbecher, 2013, p. 93). Another motivation to become even more involved in the far left was a deep felt desire to become a member of those "other Germans" (Seitenbecher, 2013, p. 93) who fought fascism, and ignorance against those societal elements that had made the Holocaust possible.

Mahler continued to defend left-wing activists in court and cofounded the "Socialist Lawyers Collective" (Sozialistisches Anwaltskollektiv, or SAK). A key feature of Mahler's legal strategies began to appear: the use of the courtroom trial as a platform for political propaganda and weapon against the same legal order in charge of the process. Including repeated acts of defiance, for example, to obey with mandatory dress codes, Mahler also extensively used his pleas to promote ideological claims and statements. In the months of riots following the killing of the student Benno Ohnesorg on June 2, 1967, by a police officer, an event that significantly contributed to the collective radicalization of the left-wing protest movement, Mahler managed to take a public stance through his active involvement and partial leadership in some of the clashes (Seitenbecher, 2013, p. 239).

During one of the many court proceedings aiming to remove Mahler from the bar on November 4, 1968, about 1,000 students attacked the police outside the courtroom in his support and managed to cause the authorities' retreat. In the following months and years, Mahler increasingly and publicly defended the use of violence to advance political goals. Of course, he was not the only or even the most outspoken proponent of violent tactics, since large parts of the left-wing milieu saw the death of Ohnesorg as an act of war by the government against the movement. A series of three arson attacks against shopping centers in Frankfurt in April 1968 involved two of the later founders of the left-wing terrorist "Red Army Faction" (Rote Armee Fraktion, or RAF, also called the "Baader-Meinhof-Gang"): Gudrun Ensslin (1940–1977) and Andreas Baader

(1943–1977). This early coordinated act of politically motivated violence is widely seen as the beginning of the later RAF's formation.

In the following trial against the perpetrators, Horst Mahler defended Andreas Baader, which brought him in direct contact with an ideologically highly radicalized circle of extremists. During many conversations with Baader and his fellow defendants, Mahler increasingly internalized the propaganda of the deed, or in other words the priority of action over rhetoric. Throughout his life, Mahler claimed to have a strong desire to behave in accordance with his ideological beliefs. When on November 9, 1962, a failed bomb attack by the left-wing terrorist group "Tupamaros West Berlin" targeting the Jewish community center in Berlin (a deeply influential and controversial terrorist attack that led many defectors to the extreme right to point out the existing violent anti-Semitism in the far left) caused him to criticize the incident before his militant clients, Mahler failed to find an answer to the simple question posed in return: "if you know so well how to use violence, why don't you do it then?" (original in German, translated by author, as cited in Seitenbecher, 2013, p. 243).

The defendants of the arson trial received prison sentences of three years, appealed the verdicts, and later fled to avoid incarceration. Andreas Baader was arrested on April 4, 1970, and freed from captivity by a six-person team including Ulrike Meinhof (one of the first-generation RAF core members, 1934–1976) on May 14. Horst Mahler, as Baader's lawyer, had arranged the opportunity for the breakout and was involved in planning the event that would officially become the birth moment of the RAF. The group used firearms and severe violence against other humans for the first time, shooting two correctional officers and a civilian (Aust, 2009). As soon as the escape became public, Mahler went underground and went to Jordan together with Baader and eight more RAF members. A second group including Ensslin and Meinhof followed shortly after. There, the group attempted to acquire paramilitary training from the Palestinian Fatah. Some see Mahler as the leader of the RAF up until that point (Seitenbecher, 2013, p. 246), when ideological and personal conflicts broke out between him, Baader, and Ensslin. Mahler eventually lost the power struggle and further internal conflicts and a fallout with the Palestinians caused the group's return in August 1970. Mahler was arrested on October 8, 1970, after a series of bank robberies in which his involvement was strongly suspected but not definitively proven.

Even though Mahler did not participate in the murders and assassinations of the first RAF generation due to his early incarceration, he nevertheless had fully and openly supported terrorist acts with his speeches and writings. In the first RAF trial that followed, he was charged with facilitating the breakout of Andreas Baader, he was acquitted (the prosecution appealed). Mahler was again charged in February 1973 with forming a criminal association (among other points), found guilty, and sentenced to a total of 14 years in prison. He also was banned from practicing law.

As is the case with so many other side-switchers and defectors, his prison time together with increasing personal conflicts with his in-group eventually led Mahler to turn his back on the extremist milieu he was part of. In particular, the conflict with Baader and Meinhof (who had by now also been arrested and sentenced to prison) escalated quickly. The RAF leadership accused him of lacking determination and he in turn criticized their ideological and strategic concepts in his writings. It is of great importance that Mahler at this point completely rejected the RAF's national-revolutionary focus and argued for joining the armed resistance movements in developing countries. Mahler also refused to take part in the prison information system the other RAF members had created to secretly communicate with each other. The final break with the RAF happened during an appeal hearing regarding his Baader breakout trial in 1974. In a declaration, he publicly declared the RAF was following an "elitist and petit bourgeois concept of urban guerrilla," calling the group a newfound "nobility" (original in German, translated by author, as cited in Seitenbecher, 2013, p. 252). In the following bitterly personal RAF declaration officially expulsing Mahler from the group, he was called a "dirty, bourgeois chauvinist" and a "petty, mainly ridiculous figure" who had "never played a major role" for the terrorist organization (original in German, translated by author, as cited in Seitenbecher, 2013, p. 253). Despite the claims of the RAF leadership, it is clear that Mahler did indeed play a substantial role in the formation of the group (M. Fischer, 2014, pp. 211–263; Jander, 2006, p. 381).

For a short time, Mahler sought help from the communist party's prisoner support organization "Red Help" (Rote Hilfe, or RH). Even though he again left this group around 1976/77 citing the death of Mao in China and the following counterrevolutionary development there, his short involvement in orthodox Communism brought him ideologically much closer to a biologically based concept of fighting for the people's masses ("Volksmassen" in German). Horst Mahler was released from prison after serving 10 years and subsequently readmitted to the bar. In the decade after his release, he remained politically inactive for the most part.

However, he gained some public recognition as a terrorism expert after a conversation with the German minister of the interior at that time, Gerhard Baum, was published in 1979. In the conversation Mahler talked openly about his own motivation for joining the militant far left and attempted to explain the radicalization of the left-wing movement. As one of the RAF's cofounders and an open defector who had found, it seemed, his way back into the mainstream society, Mahler's perspectives and insights on left-wing terrorism gained a lot of interest. His shift to the extreme-right milieu became publicly visible in the late 1990s and continuously intensified. Together with two fellow right-wing extremist renegades from the 1968 far-left student milieu, Günther Maschke (see Section B1.3) and Reinhold Oberlecher (see Section B1.5), Mahler published a "canonical declaration about the 68 movement" in 1998, in which the trio claimed national-revolutionary motives and ideas as the core element of the extreme left during those days. Just a few months before, Mahler had given a laudation at the funeral of the right-wing conservative philosopher Günter Rohrmoser on December 1, 1997, whom he had met during his prison time. Rohrmoser was part of a governmental commission to research the mental roots of terrorism, which brought him to Mahler as an interview partner in the late 1970s. In the speech at his funeral, Mahler spoke about the alleged destruction of the German national consciousness as a consequence of the Holocaust (Seitenbecher, 2013, p. 333). In a later political leaflet from November 1998, he also started to warn against a "Muslim foreign invasion" (original in German, translated by author, as cited in Seitenbecher, 2013, p. 334) and the willing eradication of the (biologically framed) German people, both of which clearly are extreme right-wing tropes.

In the late 1990s, Mahler more and more drifted toward sovereign citizen ideology, arguing that the current German state lacked any legal legitimacy and publicly proclaimed the reestablishment of the Reich on November 9, 1999. He also began to speak at events hosted by the extreme-right "National Democratic Party" (Nationaldemokratische Partei Deutschlands, or NPD) and, given his legal expertise, took over its defense in the Constitutional Court trial deciding on the party's prohibition, which was requested by the German government. This (first) trial lasted from 2001 to 2003 and resulted in the NPD's and therefore also Mahler's legal victory, as the government's motion to ban the party was dismissed. Just as when he defended left-wing extremists over three decades earlier, Mahler began to identify himself ideologically with his clients.

In 2000, he had become a member of the NPD, which led to some resistance within the extreme right (Seitenbecher, 2013, p. 340). Some saw his left-wing terrorist past as the main reason to reject him, others saw his outspoken extremism to be a risk for making legal matters worse for the party. For decades, Mahler was one the personified ideological enemies of the extreme right and had therefore been the target of many campaigns against him. In 1977, for example, a local neo-Nazi group in Berlin placed a substantial reward for "killing the public vermin" (Volksschädling) (original in German, translated by author, as cited in Seitenbecher, 2013, p. 340). Nevertheless, Mahler also found strong supporters in the far right, mainly based on his undeniable legal expertise. After the verdict was delivered, he left the NPD and radicalized even further, calling for the complete abolishment of all parties. In his later activities, Mahler concentrated on the legal question of the German government's alleged illegitimacy and denying the Holocaust (a criminal act in Germany). For both positions, he excessively used any opportunity for publicity, especially interviews or the courtroom in the many subsequent trials against him. Mahler has been repeatedly convicted and sentenced for various politically motivated extreme right-wing crimes, such as Holocaust denial, threats of murder and violence, and the public use of (illegal) Nazi symbols (e.g., the "Sieg Heil" salute) or statements.

Horst Mahler's side-switching process and storyline developed over decades and was not driven by moments of epiphany or trauma, unlike many other cases presented here. Hence, Mahler had many different stages and opportunities to present an evolving narrative or rather a set of narratives explaining his ideological pathway. As a prolific writer and commentator seeking publicity, there are naturally extensive sources for probing his political mindset. Despite the plethora of statements and the undeniable chronological impact, it is possible to identify recurring and essential elements in Mahler's explanation for his extreme turnaround. First, he denied ever having broken ideologically with National Socialism. In a conversation with Franz Schönhuber (1923–2005), the extreme right-wing politician and former member of the Nazi SS (Schutzstaffel) as well as the original Nazi NSDAP party, that was published in 2000, Mahler stated:

What does that mean breaking with National Socialism? At the end, I was nine years old, I was not a National Socialist in the strict sense and therefore could not break with it. In particular, it was the engagement with time for me, which impacted me. I always had the problem with this history of my family, which finally had this relationship with the sadness and brokenness regarding the history of our people. My father perished because of that – and I loved my father beyond anything. I wanted to walk with my head up high as someone belonging to this nation [Volk] and not bow my head looking at Auschwitz. (original in German, translated by author, Schönhuber & Mahler, 2000, p. 163)

Another center element of Mahler's side-switching narrative is the outright claim that he never actually changed at all but rather developed a consistent and constantly progressing worldview. This rhetorical strategy, which also appears very often in other defector accounts, is arguably one of the strongest defensive mechanisms Mahler uses to shield himself from critique based on alleged opportunism or ideological betrayal. In a 2009 mainstream media documentary about him, Mahler, for example, said: "I do not have the feeling that I went from left to right or from right to left, but that this was a specific sequence which appears logical in itself, if one has taken a firm stand in that logic. This is a development which moves from within itself and leads to new insights without being a change" (original in German, translated by author, Mahler in Schulz, 2009, minute 15:30). What might seem as a somewhat cryptic but blunt denial of ideological change, Mahler elaborated elsewhere:

Some say that I drifted from left to right and then right away into the extreme corner. I don't have a lot to say about that. But I can assert: Back in the day we had an idea of what imperialism actually is. Today this is – a little bit romanticized – called "globalism." This is a world domination strategy of the money ... Back then, we recognized that this system is destroying the living fundamentals of the people based on the Marxist analysis of the political economy of the bourgeois society, which I still think is valid. Marx's suggestions regarding how to get over this system are obsolete and falsified today in my opinion ... And we started from that assumption. We said: this is it, this is what really determines the system and we need to overbear it. And today I see that the national forces – in particular the NPD – who back then attacked us viciously as traitors, have arrived exactly at this point. Today they see the economic connections of this system and say: This is the root of our woes. Because of that they are today anti-imperialist, anti-globalist and in that sense also anti-capitalist. We now meet in the opinion that this system – globally – can only be overcome if the national public economies [Volkswirtschaften] are reestablished within the framework of a strong national state ... This is the third way – beyond liberal capitalism and Communism. This is what we together strive for. Who then is "right" and who is "left"? (original in German, translated by author, Schönhuber & Mahler, 2000, pp. 184–185)

However, not only did the right-wing milieu change over time, so did the far left, according to Mahler:

We ascertain against all attempts to reframe in a lie the history of the 1968 revolt: The '68 movement was also a movement for national liberation of the Germans and in this sense a patriotic movement. This is simply seen differently today, because patriotism within what calls itself the "left" is by now called devil's work. Today many of the '68ers and their epigones only have antifa-reflexes left. Those who grew up in the '68 atmosphere don't even see anymore what it was all about and they don't even have the deed of the revolt as their own, which could instill pride in them. They drown in self-hate and hate against their people. They shout "never again Germany!" and "down with Germany!" and don't understand how they stabilize the very system that they hate too. Because they terrorize without a thought anyone who thinks differently on this point, they are basically a terror-formation against all attempts by our people to stand up as German nation and fight back against our enemies to take away the weapon of cultural relocation, which is tolerated or maybe even supported by the state. (original in German, translated by author, Schönhuber & Mahler, 2000, pp. 182–183)

In his storyline, the extreme-right milieu developed an ideological position that increasingly overlapped with Mahler while the far left moved away from their original position. Naturally, however, a narrative claiming that the opposite group moved toward the defector instead of vice versa still needs a component explaining why the former in-group had to be left behind. Not even Mahler claimed a total merger between the extreme left and right to a point where he simply belonged to both groups without having to make a certain group transition. Furthermore, the fact that his former milieu, as he claimed, ideologically degenerated, can also not in itself account for joining the opposing camp. Mahler does not prominently use his internal conflict with the other RAF members as the starting point of that part in the storyline. Instead, he over and over again in numerous different narratives recounts how an intellectual reflection process about the Marxist and Leninist works, as well as the philosophy of Georg Friedrich Wilhelm Hegel (1770–1831) during his prison time, eventually changed the fundamentals of his worldviews:

> The contact point [between left-wing and right-wing identity] is where I realized that this method of struggle has the opposite effect of what we wanted. And this understanding happened during imprisonment. I voiced it critically too. It has something to do with the possibility to separate yourself from the Marxist interpretation of history through Hegel. Marx didn't understand Hegel. Marx was a Jew. Jews have great problems in understanding Hegel. I have never seen one who really understood him. We were coined through a theory of revolution assuming the destruction of the unity of the people – class war. And then we saw all [the social issues] as class war. (as cited in Koehler, 2019b, p. 511)

And in more detail:

> I do not remember something like a "Damascus" moment. Of course: When experiences mount up and the circumstances change radically – the collapse of the Soviet bloc – you find yourself in a completely changed environment in which one lives and thinks. If I had something like a "Damascus" moment, then it was the lecture of Hegel in prison. With him I realized that the solutions Marx and in particular Lenin drew out of Marxist analysis of the bourgeois society were one-sided and abstractly negative and because of that don't fit the human nature and must lead into catastrophe . . . But is this recognition a "Damascus" experience? Did I change from supposed prosecutor of the "right" to the apostle of their faith? I do know the fatal tendency to want to remain correct. This is equally strongly developed in the "right" as in the "left." This impulse thoughtlessly changes any turn of a proven "leftist" to a notorious "rightist" into a confirmation for that one, that he is historically correct and that the "leftist" using the power of a "Damascus" experience finally has accepted this. Well, I do not want to take away this fun from anyone. In the sense of myself this process appears as the manifestation of the mutual and contradictory influence of both positions "right/left" on each other. It all gets crazy when the followers of the "left" camp now circumvent the painful recognition of this dialectic [the Hegelian philosophy] by expulsing their musing comrade and seeing in him an apostle of the "right" faith and consequently ostracizing him. Both lack the imagination that I might have placed myself right in between the two chairs and that this might be exactly the place at which the Germans who still want to be Germans will gather in the future. (original in German, translated by author, Schönhuber & Mahler, 2000, pp. 38–41)

Besides implicating that he never joined the opposing milieu by staying in between the far left and far right, Mahler also positions his study of Hegel at the center of his ideological change. In various other statements, he also connects Marx's alleged misunderstanding of Hegel to a Jewish conspiracy with the goal of fundamentally altering the collective German consciousness and suppressing the German nation. In consequence, Mahler even voices some form of surprise in his retrospective account: "contradiction is proof for the truth [according to Hegel]. But then it happens that one earns a position which one deemed to be completely impossible at first. This caused an anxiety which I sensed in prison that somehow a perspective or a completely new relationship with nationalism, with National Socialism could appear and then I ignored it. And then sometime in the 1990s there came a turning point where I said: 'I am ready. Now I engage with that'" (original in German, translated by author, Mahler in Schulz, 2009, minute 12:00).

However, the far left, according to Mahler, also failed to uphold basic human values of loyalty and compassion. Asked about any support he received from the left-wing milieu during prison, he replied:

Yes, but only to the point where I started to criticize them. This is an experience that we had to make over and over again in these turmoiled times: friendships, personal relationships always worked through ideological congruity within the circle of the '68ers. And if you left the track, you were removed from the human relationships as well. At first, this hurt, but it also led to some development of thought. Well, I somehow handled it. (original in German, translated by author, Schönhuber & Mahler, 2000, pp. 41–42)

It is obvious that Mahler is talking about the intensive conflict with the other RAF members during his imprisonment, which led to his expulsion from the group. Almost 26 years later, Horst Mahler still used language filled with emotions such as pain and disappointment about the treatment he received as a consequence of his criticism and the – in his view – betrayal of human relationships and friendship. Naturally, this position is somewhat forced, since Mahler himself repeatedly confirmed that the RAF milieu fully embraced the priority of the ideological cause and everything supporting the revolution was deemed morally justified. Hence, Mahler was fully aware of the fact that any human relationships in his former in-group only lasted so long as they were in line with the doctrine. The RAF's reaction, especially after the bitter ideological critique he delivered in public, could not really have surprised him. Coming back to his side-switching narrative: How does Horst Mahler explain the development of his passionate anti-Semitism and Holocaust denial, when in statements in the late 1990s he clearly acknowledged the industrial-style genocide and even voiced sympathy for the victims (Seitenbecher, 2013, p. 341)? Parallel to working as legal counsel for the NPD during its first prohibition trial in the early 2000s, Mahler also was asked to defend the German neo-Nazi musician Frank Rennecke, who was charged with Holocaust denial at the time. Mahler accepted the job and subsequently fully internalized the position of his client by working himself into the defense rationale:

First, this became visible in my laudation for the 70th birthday of Rohrmoser. At that time, I still believed in the so-called Holocaust and said to myself: "And if it didn't happen, as some think, you had to invent it in order to lift the intellectual history where it belongs". Then Frank Rennecke approached me, after I had agreed to defend the NPD, and asked if I could defend him too against the accusation of denying the Holocaust. Then I said: "Yes, I will do that". And then I defended him ... Yes. And then I didn't believe in it anymore, because I looked into the subject, what all the so-called revisionists had gathered. And it dawned on me that this is a huge propaganda lie. And then, of course, it left me. (as cited in Koehler, 2019b, p. 511)

Finally, Horst Mahler connected his newfound anti-Semitism with his anti-imperialist and anti-capitalist activism from the time in the far-left environment. In his narration, Mahler began to "understand," that an alleged Jewish conspiracy (i.e., Marx's misinterpretation of Hegel) had been used to cloud the Germans' recognition of the true forces behind capitalism and imperialism; a classic extreme right-wing trope:

But, for us, it was the term "US-Imperialism" at that time and now one sees clearer what US-Imperialism is, so the enemy is the same. The means to fight him have changed with the insights that grew out of this process ... No, no. You see, at that time I was not free from that consciousness, which had been planted within us through these lies: this feeling of guilt. That was a problem. This story governs my whole life and my life can only be understood through this story. (as cited in Koehler, 2019b, pp. 511–512)

The side-switching storyline of Horst Mahler, one of Germany's most prominent defectors form the far-left to the far-right extremist spectrum, exemplifies several key elements in defection narratives. Mahler openly acknowledges his left-wing terrorist past but denies any fundamental change. Instead, the milieus around him changed while he further developed his ideological understandings. In addition, interpersonal disappointment and a continued hatred for democracy, the United States, and the Jewish community act as a form of psychological glue between the opposing environments. Mahler quickly radicalized to a point at which he was too far gone even for most parts of the extreme right and his arguments were too immersed in legal and philosophical theories. Except for a small circle of fanatic sovereign citizens (called "Reichsbürger" in Germany) seeing a leading figure in him, Horst Mahler is now completely isolated. Mahler, however, was not the only renegade from the 1968 and militant far-left movement who ended up in the extreme right.

2.2   Iris Niemeyer

Iris Niemeyer belonged to a group of leading female neo-Nazi activists in Germany for some time in her life. Born in 1975, she graduated with a diploma in social work and pedagogy from the technical university in Münster after training as a nurse and working at a therapy clinic for drug addiction. By the age of 33 she had become the head of the children's section in a catholic child and youth center. Publicly she did not express her political views, even though she had been active in the extreme right-wing NPD party for years up until that point. In fall 2007, pictures of Niemeyer working at an information stand of the NPD women's association "Circle of Nationalist Women" (Ring Nationaler Frauen, or RNF) were sent to her employer. After being confronted with the irreconcilability of her political engagement with the ethical values of the employer, Niemeyer refused to distance herself from the far right. As a consequence, she was fired, against which she took legal action.

Niemeyer's appeal against the termination of her work contract found the support of the court. In order to avoid being forced to let her back on the job, her former employer agreed to a settlement and paid her off. Weeks after this incident, Niemeyer stepped up her political engagement and was elected chairwomen of the newly founded local NPD chapter (J. Lang, 2009). She also helped to set up a far-right online blog named "Jeanne D." (in reference to the French heroine Jeanne d'Arc) dedicated to providing legal and other assistance to fellow female extreme right-wing activists allegedly being "persecuted" by mainstream society (Dowling, 2008). In 2009, Niemeyer declared that she had left the NPD, but continued to promote extreme right-wing content on the "Jeanne D." blog. In August 2011, a local court ordered the website to be taken down and sent the police to search Niemeyer's home, accusing her of incitement of hatred, Holocaust denial, and the distribution of illegal far-right codes and symbols. She was sentenced to a monetary fine for these crimes in November 2014 and by then had disavowed the far right.

In the resulting public focus on herself and her engagement in the extreme right, Niemeyer gave a couple of interviews detailing the process that lead her into that milieu. An important part in her storyline is her grandfather, a doctor and "convinced anti-fascist" (original in German, translated by author, as cited in Mösken, 2012b), who was active in the resistance against the Nazis, lost his job, and was arrested because of this political activism. After the Second World War, Iris Niemeyer remembers him succumbing to a morphine addiction and dying when she was 11 years old. A key lesson Niemeyer's family drew from the experiences of her grandfather was that political attitudes should be kept to oneself. At age 17, desire for rebellion against the politically conservative environment she was growing up in drove her toward the left-wing oriented peace and environmentalist movement. Gradually stepping up her involvement with other like-minded students, Niemeyer also went to rallies and demonstrations, for example, to protest the construction of nuclear power plants.

At the time of her high school education, she was also an admirer and supporter of the left-wing terrorist RAF and read their statements with enthusiasm (Mösken, 2012b). The turning point for her political opinions came during her time at college while studying social work. It was then she sat in a lecture in which the professor spoke about the American–led reeducation policies in post–Second World War Germany with an attempt to "de-nazify" the German population. For Iris Niemeyer's narrative, this episode holds significant importance: "They have reeducated us. I am reeducated. And if I am reeducated, who am I really?" (original in German, translated by author, as cited in Mösken, 2012b). Even though the same professor also claimed that the reeducation campaign had ended, Niemeyer now in her late twenties began looking suspiciously at the Americans, thinking that they were still trying to supress the German people by controlling the media and through consumerism.

These specific thought edifices are not alien to the far-left protest movement, especially regarding the critical and sometimes conspiratorial interpretation of capitalist societies and the role of American influence on Germany. For Niemeyer, however, this was the start of what she calls the "search for the truth," as she began to understand that "what has been taken away from the Germans at that time was their patriotic spirit" (original in German, translated by author, as cited in Mösken, 2012b). This self-guided quest for answers was facilitated by personal impressions. During her college education, she was working as a cleaner and noticed that she was the only German-born worker on the team, resulting in ostracism: "I was always excluded . . . Everyone sat with their own kind . . . I mean which people you feel closer too, first one's own . . . It is just like that" (original in German, translated by author, as cited in Mösken, 2012b).

Around 2002, Niemeyer met her future husband at a techno party. At that time, he was a left-wing-oriented punk playing in a music band that actively supported anti-fascist actions and even engaged in violent attacks on NPD members (Mösken, 2012b). They discussed politics, literature, and philosophy, looking for answers together: "We were searching . . . It was not enough for us to be against the system somehow" (original in German, translated by author, as cited in Mösken, 2012b). Specific political questions came up, such as how the government is supposed to finance the social system if so many immigrants come to Germany. The couple mail-ordered the programs of all major parties but found them inadequate. A short-lived membership in the mainstream center-right Christian Democrat Party (Christlich Demokratische Union Deutschlands, or CDU) ended in frustration, since "no one took notice of us" (original in German, translated by author, as cited in Mösken, 2012b). Eventually, both contacted the NPD looking to join the party. The reaction of the extreme-right organization was to arrange a personal meeting and to find them worthy of inclusion. The local NPD chairman stated: "The party does not care where someone comes from . . . [What is] important is only what he wants to do for Germany now" (original in German, translated by author, as cited in Mösken, 2012b).

The couple was quickly integrated into the NPD and became active in street politics, distributing propaganda material and engaging in debates with potential voters. Even though Niemeyer points out that she did not agree with the openly neo-Nazi and anti-foreigner statements of some people she met in the far right, she nevertheless focused on the ethnocentric concepts of family and social policies. At the time she started her job at the catholic youth center, she had been an active NPD member for about three years. Her stance in the conflict with her employer about her extreme right involvement was that in a democracy everyone is free to believe what they want and that the party is not illegal. For her, political and professional life were two separate domains. Her firing came as a substantial radicalization boost and proof of her ideology to Niemeyer: "For me the dismissal was evidence ... A sign how strongly reeducated the people were" (original in German, translated by author, as cited in Mösken, 2012b). She described feelings of ostracism, shock, sadness, and anger as a result, recognizing that she somehow had arrived at a similar point as her grandfather, namely being excluded from society based on her political opinions.

Not surprisingly, the couple asked the NPD for help and the party saw a chance to use her case as a battleground against the system. With the support of a high-ranking far-right lawyer, Niemeyer quickly won her case in court but accepted the settlement offer instead of fighting it out to win a verdict in her favor. This decision later became the key reason for her conflict with the NPD, which accused Niemeyer of having been bought by the other side (Mösken, 2012b). At first, however, she founded a local NPD division with her husband, which led to direct confrontations with the anti-fascist movement. A key to Niemeyer's storyline is the victim perspective, in particular since she was attacked with pepper spray by left-wing activists. Through her personal contact with a leading NPD politician and convicted right-wing terrorist, Niemeyer got in touch with a fellow far-right woman who had lost her job due to political activism. Together, they created the initiative "Jeanne D." Since the extreme right was shocked that the two had chosen a French national heroine as their main reference, the webpage later claimed the name stands for "Jeanne Deutschland" (Röpke, 2012, p. 221). After a short time, the cofounder of the initiative left the administration team and Niemeyer remained in charge alone. Growing increasingly frustrated with the NPD, especially regarding the suspected heavy involvement of government spies and their pro-violent attitudes, both she and her husband eventually quit the party: "like that, the NPD will never get out of the [far-right] drawer" (original in German, translated by author, as cited in Mösken, 2012b).

As a consequence of her withdrawal from the NPD, Niemeyer began searching for other activists who, in her mind, were victims of public persecution for their political views. In the far-right environment, many of the most prominent "martyrs" for the cause are notorious Holocaust deniers. Iris Niemeyer began posting articles in support of those she considered equal to her own, including the former RAF cofounder and now adamant neo-Nazi Horst Mahler (see the previous section). She also began to take over their conspiracy theories as yet another focal point for her struggle with the mainstream culture: "Every murder, every war is inhuman but you can talk about it and you can question it, why then not with the Holocaust as well? This is the culture of guilt inflicted upon us Germans" (original in German, translated by author, as cited in Mösken, 2012b). Only once, Niemeyer called a civil society deradicalization program but when she was asked to leave her ideology behind, she backed off: "This would be treason for me" (original in German, translated by author, as cited in Mösken, 2012b). A key element in her side-switching and self-defense narrative is the continuity of nonconformity: "I will not be forced to wear a muzzle. I am a rebellious person and have never conformed to society and the world" (original in German, translated by author, as cited in Mösken, 2012a). Due to her increasingly extreme positions, she has not been able to find a job for years as the legal conflict around her website has escalated. During the trial in 2014, however, she claimed to have disengaged from the extreme right, deleted all the website content, and quit far-right groups.

Iris Niemeyer's side-switching storyline is built around two main components: victimization and ostracism on the one hand, as well as rebellion and resistance against a perceived moral authority on the other. In her youth, Niemeyer chose the far-left pacifist and environmentalist position as the most effective way to distance and revolt against her parents and the obdurate conservative surroundings she was growing up with. For many teenagers at that time, the RAF was the main alternative to the establishment; young, active, committed to nonconformism, and without compromise. Their goal to force alleged fascist structures and continuities of the new Germany from the Nazi Third Reich to reveal themselves publicly through provocative violent acts (aiming to create a counterreaction from the state showing its alleged true nature), also transported an all-encompassing attack against parental and governmental authority, hierarchies, and societal expectations. Very likely the rejection of and scepticism against the state and Western models of society that is so deeply engrained in far-left milieus provided a natural connection point with far-right conspiracy theories of US reeducation attempts aiming to erase German culture and patriotism. Her own personal perceptions of ostracism and victimization, for example, being the only German at her job and being eschewed because of that, fed into her confirmation bias already nurtured by growing suspicion from learning about the reeducation.

Additional important aspects in her narrative are the notion of "being taken seriously" and "freely stating one's opinion." Niemeyer and her husband distanced themselves from mainstream politics initially because they felt they were not being listened to. The far-right NPD on the other hand, was quick to offer their interest and attention. In the following conflict with her employer, Niemeyer was finally pushed away from non-extremist society, even though she does not seem to have had any particular interest in core extreme-right ideology. Rather, it was the only remaining option for continuing to voice her dissent and criticism. Finding like-minded individuals to push back against a perceived undeserved victimization was the driving factor for Iris Niemeyer's activism in the far right. Because of that, she began to take over some ideological positions that arguably helped her to integrate into that group of victims. For Niemeyer, these were Holocaust denialism and related conspiracy theories.

2.3   Julian Fritsch – "MaKss Damage"

Another modern era case study of switching from left-wing to right-wing extremism is the German neo-Nazi rap musician using the stage name "MaKss Damage." He was born in July 1988 in Gütersloh, Germany, under his real name, Julian Fritsch. He made his first public appearances as a musician in the extreme-left milieu when Fritsch described himself ideologic-ally as "Stalinist." For many left-wing peers, however, he appeared more like a "National Bolshevist" and was labeled as such, which indicated his political proximity to the extreme right even while he was active in the far-left scene. "National Bolshevism" as a somewhat incoherent ideology originated in the German Communist Party (KPD) in the aftermath of the First World War. At that time, this political current aimed to unite quarreling communist factions with dissident nationalist groups in the German army through joint opposition to the Treaty of Versailles (Ascher & Lewy, 1956; Von Klemperer, 1951). One of the prominent thinkers leading this movement was former Social Democrat politician and writer Ernst Niekisch (1889–1967), who during the 1920s argued that a synthesis between radical nationalism and Soviet Bolshevist Marxism would be the most promising future direction for Germany. Not unlike Mussolini's attempt to reconcile nationalism with socialism (see Section B2.1), in that time period various different political movements fought bitterly over which ideological component should be the dominant one and where the ideological roots of the concept should be placed (i.e., within nation and race or within socioeconomic class struggle). National Bolshevism can be seen as the excursion from the socialist side into nationalist ideological territory. In the Soviet Union, Josef Stalin (1878–1953) and his policies between 1927 and 1953 were greatly influenced by many core ideas from this particular school of thought (Brandenberger, 2002).

Hence, the differentiation between Fritsch's self-description and that of his peers is a subtle one. Nevertheless, he did make himself known as militant and convinced left-wing extremist with his music. In his early lyrics, he praised left-wing terrorist organizations but also idolized the September 11 attacks and anti-American violence. Other regular song themes from the beginning of his career were anti-Semitism, anti-Zionism, and fierce critiques against those parts of the extreme left opposing statehood in general and the German state in particular, which was a natural consequence of his ideological positions as a National Bolshevist. Fritsch's ideological transformation to a neo-Nazi was complete in the early 2010s, after about two years of transition period, when he publicly revealed his new worldview in a videotaped interview with extreme-right propagandists. Nowadays, Fritsch continues to produce rap music using the same stage name but with entirely neo-Nazi contents. His lyrics now primarily promote racism, xenophobia, and violence against both the Jewish community and the left-wing scene to which he used to belong (Büchner, 2017). Parallel to his musical career, Fritsch studied law at two German universities.

Julian Fritsch's side-switching storyline has been presented to the public in two interviews; on the one hand during the far-right propaganda piece I mentioned, and on the other for a live on-air interview he gave to a mainstream youth-oriented German radio program. In both of these interviews, Fritsch describes his defection process as "waking up" and the realization of numerous ideological and personal contradictions within the extreme-left environment.

Age 15 to 16 is normally a time at which most are completely drifting and just start to look for their identity, something which is not given to them today. It was just like this: I had a very left-wing group of friends, through them blundered into Antifa, you could say that. I never really belonged there; I was active in different communist groups, where I always had conflicts about opinions regarding moral values but also politics and other things . . . I simply wasn't a good communist. And then I started being honest with myself and taking the path I am walking now. (original in German, translated by author, as cited in Koehler, 2019b, p. 509)

The roots of this internal crisis of "being true to oneself" were elaborated by Fritsch as hypocrisy and the lack of converting ideological convictions into actions within the far-left milieu:

The left-wing scene reflects contradictions en masse: It includes contradictions within itself; it talks about one thing, brings words on the one hand and does not let any deeds follow, or only a deed with the complete opposite effect. I had to experience that a couple of times. This has greatly impacted my personal love for this cause, which is completely gone now, and it is not possible any longer for me to live that lie and to act as if I would still be standing behind this cause. (original in German, translated by author, as cited in Koehler, 2019b, p. 509)

His storyline evolves around the question of being "true and honest to oneself," as well as the moral value of having actions following out of an ideological conviction. That particular ideological core issue in his narrative is the role of the nation and race. Fritsch portrays himself as having always fought for Germany and the German people, which, given his Stalinist/ National Bolshevist ideology, certainly does hold some consistency. The way in which his nationalist ideas failed to respond with the larger far-left milieu, which in his view increasingly turned to anti-nationalism, became the main reason for his defection in the storyline:

There is no opposite pole in the left-wing scene against anti-Germans. Of course, I tried to root against these people with my music; that was extremely important for me, that these people don't find a place among leftists or anywhere, and yes, the left-wing scene has shown that it is not willing to oppose this self-destructive current and, with that, it more or less signed its own death sentence. (original in German, translated by author, as cited in Koehler, 2019b, p. 510)

This part of Fritsch's storyline also contains a classical example of Social Identity Theory's social change strategy. He too claims to have tried rescuing his in-group from ideological fallacy before turning toward defection. The reason for choosing the far-right side is presented as a logical consequence of this conviction: "If I want to do something for Germany, I have to work together with nationalists, of course, because they have defended positions that are much more social and socialist, that are much more understandable, than the leftists ever did in the last 20 years" (original in German, translated by author, as cited in Koehler, 2019b, p. 510). Furthermore, Fritsch describes being welcomed very "warmly" by his new comrades and highly praises the sense of unity, comradeship, and bonding in his new movement. However, he also recognizes that the far right entails greater personal dangers than the far left: "We expose ourselves to a much higher risk. This only shows our strength of will, for what we stand for and what we are ready to sacrifice, that we are fighters, that we stand behind what we say, that we realize that with full force: This is a thing that a leftist cannot possibly understand" (original in German, translated by author, as cited in Koehler, 2019b, p. 510). With this part of the side-switching storyline, Fritsch extends a rhetorical olive branch to the far right by praising their masculine and warrior-like qualities, which the far left lacks in his opinion.

Fritsch's narrative explaining his defection across the left-wing vs. right-wing extremist spectrum emphasizes ideological consistency, as well as a failed attempt to improve or save the old in-group and the superior social status and situation in his new environment. Fritsch had invested heavily in the far-left movement and was publicly known as a left-wing extremist. He also risked his musical career as nothing could have guaranteed that his background would not have stood in the way of acquiring a new fan base. However, his skills and knowledge about the far-left movement also made him an attractive convert for the extreme right. Portraying his new milieu as riskier and more dangerous than the old one is an interesting peculiarity. In Fritsch's narrative, this supports one of his key themes: the will to fight for one's own beliefs. Accordingly, higher risk increases his narrative's consistency.

2.4   Virtual Confessions and Digital Debates

Modern extreme-right milieus are dependent on various forms of online infrastructures for many different reasons. Even those groups, organizations, or subcultural networks that still heavily rely on offline activities such as concerts, rallies, sports, or parties need the Internet to communicate about these events, coordinate, recruit, or advertise. On the other end of the spectrum are those groups and milieus that were created in the virtual space, exist almost entirely online, and sometimes make the step into the offline reality. In short, the Internet and extremist milieus, in particular the far right that has recognized and utilized its potential from the first online days onward (Ray & Marsh, 2001), are inseparable today. The following section is not concerned primarily with the role of the Internet in far-right radicalization or extremist recruitment (for overviews and introduction into this topic, see Koehler, 2014; Meleagrou-Hitchens, 2017; Von Behr, Reding, Edwards & Gribbon, 2013) but focuses on the manifestations and visibility of side-switching in extreme-right online environments.

Especially with those far right milieus that are heavily digitalized, such as for example the so-called alt-right and its various connected and overlapping online subcultures on platforms like 4chan, 8chan, gab, or Discord (for a general introduction into these various milieus, see Daniels, 2018; Hawley, 2017; Main, 2018; Nagle, 2017; Zannettou et al., 2018), countless users who self-identify as far right in all its forms (including open neo-Nazism and Fascism) have transported the predominant portion of their social life inter-action into these digital spheres. The development of extreme right virtual communities and collective identities evolving around specific online platforms has become an increasing area of research interest and it was shown that these social media and interaction hubs can become the sole center of gravity in the lives of far-right activists (e.g., Bliuc, Betts, Vergani, Iqbal & Dunn, 2019; Bowman-Grieve, 2009; Caren, Jowers & Gaby, 2012; De Koster & Houtman, 2008; B. Kleinberg, van der Vegt & Gill, 2020; Thompson, 2001).

While understandably some research has focused on extremist, pro-violent, or particularly radical posting content (e.g., Scrivens, 2020), it should not be surprising that those virtual communities also include discussions of everyday life issues, as likewise the offline far right has been found to be much more multifaceted and diverse regarding everyday activities beyond violence and political radicalism (Simi & Futrell, 2010). Arguably, it is much easier to share interests, emotions, or intimate details of one's past with someone online behind a protective wall of perceived anonymity and at least some form of technically mandated distance. This should not mean that these online milieus are less meaningful to the users than offline interactions. On the contrary, through the partially intensive interactions and exchange of most detailed thoughts and feelings, extremely strong social bonds and fused identities with the virtual community can develop and take over every aspect of some users' lives.

All of this becomes relevant for our present endeavour to understand extremist side-switching, as sometimes members of far-right online milieus have either openly admitted their pasts in other hostile ideologies or discussed this matter in general with other users. As it is the nature of today's online content, most of these statements and discussions are brief and cannot be compared with the detailed storylines presented throughout this book, which are often based on autobiographies, extensive interviews, or self-authored articles about the defection process. Nevertheless, the posts and discussion threads that I was able to retrieve provide fascinating and important insights into the way some of these side-switchers in the modern virtual extreme right frame their defection from a hostile milieu; how they are perceived and received by other in-group members; and which ideological or rhetorical elements can play a significant role when confessing to side-switching online. In the following section I will concentrate on two online platforms that had great influence and importance for various militant far-right networks: the IronMarch (IM) forum and extreme–right discussion servers on Discord.

IM was a discussion-based forum with social media elements founded in 2011 by a Russian right-wing extremist using the alias name "Alexander Slavros" (Team-Ross, Bevenssee & ZC, 2019). The platform was designed as a transnational social networking site with a dedicated focus on neo-Nazism, neo-Fascism, and white supremacism. IM went offline in November 2017 and during its time of existence had become infamous for its open and virulent support of violence, anti-Semitism, racism, and terrorism through large portions of its content. IM also acted as a depository for extensive militant extreme-right literature collections and hence became the nucleus and birthplace of multiple neo-Nazi terror cells and organizations, most notably but not limited to the US "Atomwaffen Division" (AWD) (Ware, 2019), the British far-right terror group "National Action" (NA) (Allen, 2017; P. Jackson, 2014), and the Australian "Antipodean Resistance" (AR) (Poulter, 2018).

In the spring of 2018, a new website called "Fascist Forge" (FF) went online and many of the previous leading administrators, including Slavros, were also prominently involved. In November 2019, anti-fascist hackers made a large cache of IM data available to researchers and investigators, which provided the opportunity to explore the neo-Nazi site in pursuit of mentions and discussions of side-switching. Discord, on the other hand, is a proprietary freeware Voice over Internet Protocol (VoIP) application and distribution platform designed to facilitate the creation of communities evolving around gaming, education, and business themes but it predominantly caters for the needs of the online gaming scene. Discord specializes in text, image, video, and audio communication between users in chat channels. Due to its strong anonymity and privacy policies, Discord became an important platform for the alt-right movement and quickly gained notoriety for the excessive far-right discourses and hate speech on many of its themed discussion servers (Bernstein, 2017) until the company was forced to take action after the violent extreme right August 2017 "Unite the Right" rally in Charlottesville, Virginia (Roose, 2017). In a hacking operation not unlike the one targeting IM, far-right Discord servers were secured and made available for researchers, journalists, and investigators online.

The first thing one notices when exploring extremist side-switching through the various posts and discussions in these two forums is that often users are very open about their past in far-left milieus and appear to show little concern about this fact potentially damaging their reputation or causing any backlash in the form of ridicule and cyberbullying, called "shitposting." In one better known example, a young man named Kamden Musser from Columbus, Ohio, received national attention after having been identified as a neo-Nazi demonstrator in pictures from the October 2017 "White Lives Matter" rally in Tennessee that were circulated widely in the media to signal the angry fanaticism of many far-right activists who participated. Through interviews with him and his family, journalists tried to trace the extreme-right radicalization process (McCoy, 2018) that had taken him to membership in the "Traditionalist Worker Party" (TWP), a militant openly neo-Nazi organization active between 2013 and 2018 that was founded by Matthew Heimbach (a once leading white nationalist who now claims to be a reformed former extremist with a past in far-left politics, see Section 5.7). On Discord, Musser, who used the handle "K Martin," cheerfully recounted his experiences with a journalist from the *Washington Post* newspaper and hoped that at least the popularity would help him to make his milieu better known. Before the media attention had started, Musser mentioned some details about his past in various messages, for example in November 2017, that placed the start of his far-right radicalization process in the year 2010, when he got "redpilled," a widely used alt-right reference to the popular Hollywood movie series *Matrix*, meaning the awakening to the "true reality." He also credits Matthew Heimbach's speaking skills with bringing him into the movement.

Before joining Heimbach's TWP, Musser casually describes previous extreme-right activities, such as having been a member of Vanguard America (a neo-Nazi organization active since around 2015) or far-right militias. In January 2018, Musser, to the amusement of the other discussion thread participants, posted three pictures of himself holding a gun and wearing a Soviet style hat saying: "me c. 2008 when I was a commie" ("K-Martin," 2018). The overall topic of the thread at that point in the discussion was evolving around "awkward childhood" photos and Musser even bragged about his courage to share these photos. In a short string of messages, he explains: "I've come a long way. We all have . . . Now that I'm a fascist I became 1000% more chad . . . really makes you think. Well maybe not fascist but deff NatSoc. a lot changes in 10 years. ugh i was gross looking. AND a commie" ("K-Martin," 2018, spelling as in original). The term "chad" is also widely used in virtual alt-right and Incel ("Involuntary Celibate") milieus to denote a man who can attract female sexual attention based on his muscular, tall, or wealthy nature. It is also noteworthy that Musser, like many other cases we will encounter in this section, makes detailed ideological differentiations regarding his own positions, such as clarifying that he sees himself as National Socialist and not a fascist. Except a small note in passing that expressed agreement with Musser's statement that a lot has changed since childhood for many of the members in the forum, no one appeared to take particular notice of the pictures and the revelation of his past as a communist.

Other Discord users also did not seem to mind sharing this kind of information. In one discussion thread from July 2017, a couple of discussants began expressing their disdain for "antifa" and the left in general because of what they considered to be poor aesthetics. During the conversation, two users nicknamed "Ronny TX" and "Tedium," the latter a known former communist in the forum, began talking about their own personal side-switching accounts:

TEDIUM: Antifa is so boring. Leftists used to be a whole lot more interesting when they didn't have to pick between 69 different SJW [or Social Justice Warrior] causes. Just no war but class war, let's fuck some shit up.
RONNY TX: This is redundant. You don't need the rainbow to make an Antifa flag gay
TEDIUM: Now you have to have rainbow committees and all this dumb shit.
RONNY TX: @Tedium don't go Commie on us
TEDIUM: I left that shit behind in high school. lol you don't have to worry . . .

. . .

RONNY TX: I was a Commie in 9th grade because I didn't know the difference between one kind of authoritarianism and another. Plus they had nice aesthetics. Then I realized the economics were bad, and then

> I learned about the social policies of the whole thing and that
> modern leftism is all gay and everything I've ever hated. I learned
> that Fascism was closer suited to my style of Authoritarianism. That
> or National Socialism.

. . .

TEDIUM: Yeah, @Ronny TX it took me a while longer, but I got there. I was a
              senior or junior when I first read Hitler's speeches. That did it for
              me. The rest fell into place.

RONNY TX: @Tedium yeah, it seems like I was a junior or senior when I stopped
              being a Commie, and I was a generic Conservative for a while.
              Towards the end of my senior year I became a NatSoc
              ("Ronny-TX," 2017c, spelling as in original).

This short exchange of viewpoints regarding leftist aesthetics and the
mutually shared side-switching experience did not raise any comments from
other users, who even often posted completely unrelated messages in between
the conversation of "Tedium" and "Ronny TX," appearing indifferent. Both
users locate the leftist past in their high school time and while "Ronny TX"
was initially impressed with left-wing aesthetics, he later found his "style of
authoritarianism." For him, lack of understanding serves as the explanation for
"not knowing better" at the time, in addition to realizing that the ideological
system of Communism, in his view, espoused moral values he claimed to have
always rejected (in particular queer sexuality).

He also appears to make a differentiation between Fascism and National
Socialism, hinting an advanced level of ideological knowledge on both
systems of thought. "Tedium" on the other hand admits having spent more
time as communist. His defection to the far-right was facilitated by reading
Adolf Hitler's speeches, or so he claims. Following the trail of "Ronny TX" in
the same thread, additional remarks are provided about 17 days later. Now, the
discussion is centered around the leading alt-right person Richard Spencer and
the upcoming August 2017 "Unite the Right" rally in Charlottesville. A lively
debate about whether to participate in the rally under Spencer's auspices
involved many users rejecting the core idea of bringing the extreme right
together under the leadership of a man openly rejecting fascism. This sparked
some intense back and forth about Spencer's ideological positions and the
arguments in favor or against joining his efforts. In this exchange, "Ronny TX"
circles back to his own past and interestingly recognizes the value of less
radical milieus (like Spencer's group) for converting new recruits to their own
cause. In this user's mind, side-switching is a gradual process of getting used
to more and more extreme ideas by slowly advancing into the extreme right
camp, even though individual trajectories are acknowledged:

THE INQUISITOR: @Thomas Ryan Why as Fascists should we tolerate a man who
                    tries his best to suppress Fascism in favor of his own
                    lukewarm mysterymeat "nationalist" liberalism?

THOMAS RYAN: If you wish, you may attend the rally and attack him yourself.

THE INQUISITOR: Attack as in politely discourse on white nationalist philosophy?

SOME GUY: I don't think Spencer suppresses us. He doesn't even countersignal us. He's a SWPL [or Stuff White People Like] nationalist and a stepping stone to the more hardcore groups like VanAm [or Vanguard America].

...

THE INQUISITOR: @Some Guy Behind the scenes Spencer and co try everything they can to keep National Socialists from upstaging them ...

RONNY TX: The entire point – and the weakness – of the Unite the Right event is to unite Right Wing groups. Not all groups there will be Fascists. Not all groups will even like Fascists. Identity Evropa is no fan of Fascists, for instance. But we're there to unite right-wing groups, regardless of whether we're all the same ideologies. We may not particularly like Spencer, but he's among the groups we're uniting with. Remember, one of the core tenants of Fascism is Strength through Unity.

...

THE INQUISITOR: @Ronny TX If we're uniting under Richard Spencer, then the event is WORSE than nothing

RONNY TX: @Nathan TX Remember when Lee was in IE [or Identity Evropa]? He left partially because they didn't like Fascism, partially because they charge for membership

...

RONNY TX: @The Inquisitor not under, alongside. He's the face of the Alt Right whether we like it or not. Everyone between normies and us redpills people a little more until they become more like us. People like Spencer, so they put him first on the poster. We're not there primarily for him.

SOME GUY: @The Inquisitor I am going [to] need more context, not just a 9 second snippet. I agree he doesn't go far enough, but he's still a decent ally. He brings people to our side and that's great.

RONNY TX: I was a moderate republican once. It was people like Steven Crowder, Paul Joseph Watson, Milo Yiannopolos, Black Pidgeon Speaks, etc. that got me to where I am now. They redpilled me a little bit, then I moved further and further right until I could no longer stand them. That's why I like those groups even still, because if we just had the Fascists, we'd never convert anyone.

...

THE INQUISITOR: @Ronny TX Funny you mention that. I didn't make the transition right away but the first redpills I ever took were from an IronMarch-tier fascist

RONNY TX: And everyone makes their journey differently. I definitely
                   received some redpills from more extreme sources at the
                   beginning, but the little ones along the way really helped. In
                   any case, we have plenty of enemies, we need more allies.
                   We're going to UTR for building alliances, not for Spencer.
                   If he wasn't there, it would be better, but we can't let him
                   ruin our opportunity ("Ronny-TX," 2017b, spelling as in
                   original).

Regarding the ideological overlap with the far left, two short but very
insightful comments by "Ronny TX" and "The Inquisitor" allude to anti-
capitalism as the key link. Shortly before, a message from a person clearly
opposed to the far right with hints of far-left ideology was posted to the forum.
One particular part in that outsider critique against the extreme-right milieu
sparked the comments:

RONNY TX: "The true fight is with Big Money!" [a partial quote from the
                   outside message, author's note] Well, kinda. It happens that
                   our enemies overlap with theirs in that regard – big money
                   happens to also usually be Jewish.
THE INQUISITOR: Take the Strasserite Pill: we need to kill the Jews because the Jews
                   are the bourgeoise.

. . .

RONNY TX: Nah, the NatSoc pill: we need to kill the bourgeoisie because the
                   bourgeoisie are Jewish ("Ronny-TX," 2017a).

In this short exchange about which "pill" (i.e., which argument) is best for
converting potentially left-wing anti-capitalists to the far right, detailed knowledge about the early Nazi movement's internal ideological conflict between
the "left" wing led by the brothers Otto and Gregor Strasser and the "right"
wing led by Hitler, shines through (for some further details on this conflict, see
Section B2.2. on Richard Scheringer and Section 3.1). It should be added that
these far-right online milieus oftentimes are very interested in discussing the
most effective "pills" to "wake" others and convert them to their own positions. Therefore, whether to use the Strasserite or National Socialist position
could also be a matter of tactic instead of personal conviction for "Ronny TX"
and "The Inquisitor." The following example thread shows how the far-right
online milieu partially frames and understands facilitated side-switching, or
more precisely converting new followers from the ideological outside world.
While far from being an uncontroversial topic in the discussion, the main issue
of debate is whether someone from the outside with hardened liberal and left-
wing views can actually change. Here, too, one user opts in by providing their
own left-wing background as a proof of concept:

BANKS=GAY:	All my friends are either sjws [Social Justice Warriors, slang for people holding liberal or left-wing views, author's note] are politically uninformed/apathetic. I think friendship and politics should never mix unless they mix it first
FITZYDOG:	I consider their politics a good indicator of their ability to critically think, and if there is none, I make a wide berth around them
BANKS=GAY:	Just a good way of making yourself a[n] ideologue asshat and ruining friendships
ANGUS:	the first step of trying to become friends is so that they don't see you immediately as a Russian nazi when you start trying to help them out of their programming
BANKS=GAY:	Smart people can have dumb politics. Saying they cant is like saying smart people cant be bad at math
ANGUS:	the npcs [Non Playable Character, an alt-right phrase with roots in the online gaming community denoting supporting characters who offer a quest or recite dialogue to further the plot without any mind or control of their own, author's note] are mostly just misguided and fed the wrong information by people who know how to use their impairment . . .
FITZYDOG:	This far into the programming? You can't convince these people now . . .
BANKS=GAY:	Fuck. Then im still a communist . . .
GOBLIN_SLAYER_FLOKI:	Depends on the level of npcism

. . .

ANGUS:	I didn't say it would work, but when you see a dying animal, you want to help it, your *gut* reaction is to help it not immediately give up on it, and sometimes you can actually fix it
GOBLIN_SLAYER_FLOKI:	Immideate reaction is a bullet
BANKS=GAY:	Wtf is that even supposed to mean. Yesterday or 2 years ago, if theyre "too far into the programing,its too late" it shouldnt matter

. . .

GOBLIN_SLAYER_FLOKI:	Anyone can be reprogrammed tbh. Its just how much work it takes
FITZYDOG:	If they haven't realized what the hell is going on in October of 2018, then theres no reason to even try
GOBLIN_SLAYER_FLOKI:	Wrong some are just ill informed
BANKS=GAY:	I was a commie who unironically wanted to kill Trump and his supporters not long ago.
FITZYDOG:	And you no longer are

BANKS=GAY: Exactly
ANGUS: everyone can be salvaged, it's something I like about religion
                        despite the glaring flaws, they know that someone can
                        be given as many chances as they need to see the light
GOBLIN_SLAYER_FLOKI: My wife was sjw leaning when i met her. Like deeply.
                        Over the years of retraining she is now libertarian
FITZYDOG: I'm not saying it's impossible to change peoples opinions,
                        only that the people who's opinions CAN be changed
                        would have already done so by now, and the others who
                        are going to keep on being retarded will probably
                        consider Trump to be evil incarnate 30 years from now
ANGUS: it's entirely possible that they've been kept through
                        circumstance in a bubble that doesn't allow any other
                        viewpoints in

. . .

ANGUS: considering that universities and cities are basically like
                        giant secluded far left ideology zones

. . .

ANGUS: you need to be raised to have an open mind, what if you
                        were instead raised to have one idea because your
                        parents were brainwashed by their surroundings.
                        there's still a person in there, they just need to be
                        shown the light in a way that is meaningful
FITZYDOG: @Angus So unless you physically remove them from
                        these places, I still see no hope for them
ANGUS: that might actually have something to do with it

. . .

ANGUS: that's the thing though, there is a way
FITZYDOG: @Angus If you were not raised to have an open mind,
                        I have even LESS hope for them ("Banks=Gay,"
                        2018, spelling as in original).

Other discussions on Discord about winning over left-wing activists to the far
right, for example, focused on the appeal of the ideological milieu as such. To
achieve a higher success in converting leftists, the users in the following thread
debate training each other in rhetoric and "larping" (from "live action role
playing," or acting) as communists to learn how to think and talk like them
(in essence a red-teaming exercise):

ARNAR: We need to get a more "revolutionary" spirit, follow the footsteps of
                        Anarchists from the 80's up until now. If we can steal
                        communism's thunder of being known as "The fun" ideology,
                        then we'll be golden

P14#4031:	we are the fun ideology. We need to show that …
RAM3N:	people aren't interested in having children or families though however. a lot of people don't anyway, as it seems
ARNAR:	Because, from my experience, I know plenty of older guys who lean on the Marxist side now but used to be full-blown communists "back in the day". That basically shows that just being exposed to an ideology during your early years can have a lasting impact on what you believe in
P14#4031:	I think we need to train ourselfs in rethoric
DELETED USER:	Larp as leftists and challenge each other. I've seen other groups do it. It's rather effective.

. . .

| P14#4031: | Well, there is stuff out there on YouTube about rethoric. We could practice holding a speech planned and spontaneously |

. . .

ARNAR:	We need to replace Marxism with Ethno-Centrism.
P14#4031:	We dont need to discuss a lot, its more about getting to know each other.
RAM3N:	natsoc
ARNAR:	Natsoc would actually be preferred, yeah. We're trying to appeal to whites after all. I doubt anuddah shoah is ever gonna happen, at worst we'll just end up with what we have now but whites benefit from it ("Arnar," 2017, spelling as in original).

There are numerous other isolated comments by users on far-right Discord servers simply stating that they are "former commies," usually saying this was in their high school years. In most cases, this received no or only minor interest from other users, typically expressing understanding for why someone might find this ideology attractive in that age (e.g., for thinking everyone gets free stuff). Few instances include exchanges with forum members claiming to have always been far right, displaying any real interest in why the side-switching took place. Usually, discussion threads evolve around a certain key topic such as gender issues, environmentalism, or aesthetics and then involve users sharing their opinion on the collectively despised mainstream or left-wing positions based on their own background with the other side. In most of these cases, being left wing is presented as a not uncommon developmental phase during teenage years, among many others. In one example of such brief exchanges, a couple of users confess to having had such phases in their past:

ZALFIR: i was a tree hugging hippy and digital rights activist

MIRI: Egalitarian

ASTROTORCH: I never went that far I dont think, like I knew the communist manifesto back to front but never went much in for the gender politics stuff. made me cringe a bit

. . .

HAM SANDWICH: poofta [slang for homosexual, author's note] communism is cringe

. . .

COW: Gender politics are cringe.

V3XXED_GIRAFF3: at one point after i went out the socialist phase i started veering to stuff like the edl [or English Defence League] and shit

. . .

HAM SANDWICH: two types of commies. Chad [Incel slang for strong, masculine, and attractive, author's note] commies. and poofta commies

QUESTGIVER: i was a commie, then i went to china for a year and stopped being a commie

V3XXED_GIRAFF3: just the commie and alt-right phase

. . .

ASTROTORCH: I never had the Ayn Rand [(1905–1982, Russian-American writer)] / naïve libertarian phase a lot of the Americans seem to have

TURTLE: Ayn Rand is interesting.

WERTHOM: I was a communist in like 7th grade

HAM SANDWICH: my 14 year old brother is currently going through his raging anti-feminist stage and it makes me cringe so hard

. . .

ZALFIR: seems like a lot of people go through the angry phase, Ham ("Questgiver," 2019, spelling as in original).

A similar rhetoric of previous communist phases also appears in the following example discussion thread, which originated in arguments about how to "red-pill" or convert left-wing activists to the far right as well. In this case, some users include the utopian nature of far-left ideologies as a major aspect in the "awakening" of some participants. One user interestingly points out that defectors can make for the most committed anti-communists and thereby raises their status in the discussion significantly:

FAUSTUS#3547:   Infographics don't convert the enemy. They convert normies.
                Or they at least get them thonking a bit.

...

NO.#3054.   People completely convinced by an ideology cannot be
                   swayed by mere infographics. People that are
                   undecided can be, but that largely depends on the
                   person. I loath to paraphrase Inception, but a fully
                   formed idea is *impossible to force away*. You
                   simply cannot. Consider your own conversion to
                   whatever ideology you belong to now. Unless you
                   grew up with it / have always been swaying that way,
                   it was likely a long, long process you can't really put a
                   finger on. I used to be a honest-to-god atheist commie,
                   but I think 4chan + seeing my nation self-destruct was
                   enough to sway me in the right direction.
FAUSTUS#3547:   Same, IMO the most ardent anti communista are
                   former commies.
DELETED USER: it's simple nature versus unnatural accepting and embracing
                   reality, vs rejecting reality outright and pretending the
                   world is somehow a magical pixyland for your special
                   little self
FAUSTUS#3547:   To be completely honest though, when i was in my commie
                   phase I knew the world was an unfair, rought place but
                   thought these things could be overcome with collective
                   action. Then I realized my motivations for these
                   changes were flawed and there was no reason to make
                   the world fair.
REDFROSTGAMES.COM: I wonder why you used to be a commie
KNEON#7841:   I was an ardent center libertarian as a kid and I'm slowly going
                   right and up ("Faustus," 2018, spelling as in original).

Rarely do far–right Discord users – with or without a side-switching background –
discuss far-left ideology in as much detail as the various forms of extreme-right
systems. One example, however, provides insight into such a discourse in part
influenced by defectors from the extreme left. In it, a distinct differentiation is
made between Anarcho-Communism (anncom or ancom, also called stateless
communism, a particular form of communist ideology advocating for the aboli-
tion of all state-like institutions while retaining personal property, along with
collectively owned items, goods, and services), Trotskyism (the school of communist thought led by Leon Trotsky, 1879–1940, a main rival of Josef Stalin),
and Stalinist Communism. Not surprisingly, Anarcho-Communism is seen as the
worst through the perspective of an ultra-nationalist far-right milieu:

SPORUS: ancom is degenerate

. . .

SPORUS:	back when i was a commie i was baste & redpill'd to trotskyism
JORDAN PHILIPS COCKRAM:	Communists cant solve economic calculation problem and the knowledgepovlem
SPORUS:	anything but trotskyism is degen

. . .

SPORUS:	"b-b-b-b-but stalin told me not to like it!" shut up boomer ("sporus," 2019, spelling as in original).

These example discussion threads from Discord partially display a surprising openness toward side-switchers from the far left and the idea of engaging with the opposing milieu's core ideas, rhetoric, and aesthetics to facilitate that process. There is little to no rejection of defectors, even when they engage critically with elements of the far-right ideologies typically supported in the forum. It appears, that those defectors weighing in with their own side-switching accounts do not fear being ridiculed or mocked for this fact and indeed, I could find very little evidence of this in the threads I looked at more closely.

However, one might argue that the nature of Discord supports this specific climate, as even within far-right dominated servers and threads, the nature of the platform does include a baseline chance of encountering individuals from other ideological camps. IronMarch (IM) on the other side was a social networking site entirely dedicated to fascists and neo-Nazis. The moderators and administrators made no secret of the website's goal, namely to spread and support extreme right ideology worldwide. Active adherents to other ideologies were very unlikely to be tolerated, with the possible exception of Islamic extremists to a certain point and until a defector to that form of extremism murdered two neo-Nazis (see Section 4.4.2 for the Devon Arthurs case and Section 4.5 for a discussion of conversion to Islam in far-right online milieus). At least in respect to the seemingly unconcerned admission of former far-left commitments, IM does not fall behind Discord much. Numerous IM users began their involvement in the platform by openly stating this fact, thereby introducing themselves to the community. Others included this information in their profile page's short biographical sections. I could not find clear examples of this leading to any kind of negative reaction at all. On the contrary, in many cases more senior IM users greeted the new members back with admitting to be "former commies" as well.

Nevertheless, in some marginally more detailed conversations and reply posts, little hints about potential reservations from other factions within the IM far–right online milieu indicate that the far-left defectors considered themselves some form of special breed as opposed to the rightists without such a biographical shift. For example, on May 16, 2014, a user nicknamed "Clive Bissel" wrote in a reply to a new IM member: "just warning you, most of us are

Hitlerists here. That said I don't know why you think you'd be doomed for saying you were a former commie; most fascists were" ("Clive-Bissel," 2016, spelling as in original). Even the founder of IM, "Alexander Slavros," professed being a former communist and clearly stated that he considers this to be a significant advantage on the far-right side:

... can be argued that we actually know the left better than it knows itself. There's dumbasses on our side or at least who pretend to be on our side who don't know shit about fascism OR communism so eh. I'm a former commie so I know communism and I know exactly how little communists know of themselves from our worldview. See we got a broader scope. ("Aleksandr-Slavros," 2014, spelling as in original)

However, this view is not shared by all side-switchers. "Raycis," for example, wrote in March 2014:

I was a communist for a brief edgy stint during my early teens, and then I gradually shifted from liberal progressive, to libertarian, to conservative, to tradical, to fascism. People keep saying that Communists and far-leftists make the best converts, but I'm not seeing it. I think it's easier to take a racist conservative / libertarian who is fed up with the modern world and convince him to adjust economic views and nudge his philosophy a little more in the right direction than it is to change a leftist with good economic views but with a stubbornly or even aggressively delusional world view to a fascist world view. ("Raycis," 2014, spelling as in original)

On the other side, those right-wing extremists without an ideological shift in their biography are sometimes seen as being a kind of separate community within the far-right online milieu that was IM. In a more revealing conversation, two former extreme left-wing activists discussed the risk of negative reactions in the forum. This conversation also fascinatingly includes open admission of incomplete ideological transition, that is, still holding many dedicatedly communist views out of tradition or even conviction. The following lengthy thread impressively shows how some side-switchers actively work on their ideological development and trajectories, clearly showing a strong sense of agency even to the degree of painful individual personality work. The two users involved go through extensive and detailed discussions about issues of race, anti-Semitism, economics, development aid, white nationalism, and religion, among other topics. The level of depth in that conversation can certainly be regarded as unusual even for IM. The following excerpts aim to focus on the relevant exchange on side-switching, even though the economic or religious debate is equally revealing regarding the ideological state of mind of both users:

THE YANK: Right on. So what exactly is Peronism?
DELETED USER: Peronism is the socially liberal economically fascist ideology of Juan Péron, former President of Argentina. It advocates social justice and corporate nationalism and overall is not that disagreeable with from my POV.

THE YANK: Interesting. Iv'e had an interest in Strasserism for a while, maybe
                   i'll have to look into Peronism. Any recommended reading?

. . .

DELETED USER: Yw. I take it you're a white nationalist?
THE YANK: Not at all. I do not feel white nationalism has anything to do with
                   genuine National Socialism. Do you?
DELETED USER: Yea. I don't feel I could ever be a white nationalist. I don't feel
                   more superior to my nephew or the majority of my friends at
                   school, reading Strasser makes me consider nationalism more
                   seriously from when I was a communist not too long ago.
                   I don't think I'll ever publicly call myself a national socialist
                   because of the negative sentiment with the term.
THE YANK: Right. I personally don't mind being associated with the term
                   despite it's negative reputation. It's what i believe in, and
                   that's that. And yes, Strasser had some interesting works. I'm
                   assuming you've read "Germany tomorrow"? If not, i can send
                   you a link to where you can read it in full text online. By the
                   way: What made you switch from communism? Do you still
                   hold any sympathies for communist ideology?
DELETED USER: I do hold any deep communist feelings and tendencies. It's hard
                   toget over something you were for 3 years >.>. I also am
                   something hated by many here, which definitely is a big factor
                   on me hesitating to identifying as a communist. *as a fascist.
THE YANK: There's a small, but still alive, left-wing presence on the forum of
                   the more socialistic fascists. Many of them don't get on as
                   regularly as the right-wingers, but they're still here and you
                   can see them post and message them from time to time. And i
                   personally had a hard time getting over anarchism at first, but
                   after a while i just saw it for what it was. Over time, you'll
                   realize that communism is just utter filth, don't worry.
DELETED USER: I haven't fully left communism. I came here to meet people like
                   yourselves. Most of my social community are communists or
                   something similar to that.
THE YANK: Like i said, either you will leave communism, or you'll go back to
                   it. You'll find in the future, that there is no other way, really.
DELETED USER: Yea. I don't think I'll be staying a communist–too many
                   ideological conflicts.
THE YANK: Glad to hear it, comrade.

. . . [lengthy debate about currency policies and economics, author's note]

THE YANK: That's about the same as what i had in mind, actually. Good to hear
                   i'm not the only one who came to this conclusion.
DELETED USER: Then again, I have a feeling a large percentage of the people here
                   are not social-nationalists at all, just republicans who are more
                   racist than most people.

THE YANK: Yeah, I think you may be right about some of them.

...

THE YANK: Let me get your opinion on some people and topics: – George
                  Bernard Shaw – Mao -Stalin - Both Mussolini and Hitler (just
                  wondering your opinion on Hitler since you seem to identify
                  more with Strasser, and i wanted to get your opinion on the
                  man who created fascism as well). Also: – Agrarianism ...
DELETED USER: ... Mao Even when I was a communist I was opposed to Mao
                  (I was a hoxhaist). Mao did nothing except overthrow a corrupt
                  leader–and that's all he should be accredited like that, he was
                  not a saviour of China or even a good theorist. –Stalin A good
                  leader during the hitlerite invasion of the Soviet Union, and
                  industrialized the SU rapidly, that's what he is responsible, and
                  that's what I credit him with. – Both Mussolini and Hitler (just
                  wondering your opinion on Hitler since you seem to identify
                  more with Strasser, and i wanted to get your opinion on the
                  man who created fascism as well). Benito Mussolini was a
                  decent leader until the later years of his rule when he started
                  behaving more irradically and allied himself with Hitlerite
                  Germany in its advocation of European Civil War which is a
                  negative thing both for the European Peoples and for the
                  world–it led to many negative things. Instead of doing this he
                  should have allied Italy with the rest of Europe against the Red
                  Horde. The Hitlerite war led to the accession of the Soviet
                  Union to the status of a world power. Hitler I view in a
                  negative light obviously, he started and advocated civil war
                  between Europeans, supported the reactionaries, and overall
                  abandoned the entire reasoning behind National Socialism ...
THE YANK: What exactly made you decide to leave communism and become a
                  fascist?
DELETED USER: ... Study, simple study ("The-Yank," 2014, spelling as in original).

Compared to Discord, IM seems to have been comprised of a somewhat
more intellectual membership interested in extensive and detailed ideological
debates, but also with higher interest in learning about new users' stories,
motives, and reasonings. The previously mentioned user "Clive Bissel," for
example, approached another IM member in October 2013 out of curiosity
regarding the side-switching from communism but also was careful to avoid
any misunderstanding and therefore included very direct compliments and
positive words of welcome. In the ensuing conversation familiar topics such
as disillusionment with utopianism or nationalism vs. internationalism appear,
but so does the question of cooperation between the left and right embodied by
dictators such as Yugoslav Communist leader Josip Broz, commonly known as
Tito (1892–1980). For the approached defector, a simple online search for

opponents of communism out of disillusionment allegedly led him to the neo-Nazi forum Stormfront and from there on deeper into the far-right milieu:

CLIVE BISSEL: Hey man, I was just wondering what it was which convinced you and made you take up fascism over communism. IIRC [short for If I Remember Correctly, author's note] you were a communist and a supporter of Tito. It got me thinking recently since I re listened to Rockwell' Nazism the only answer to communism speech, re read some more NatSoc literature and remember some of my own research and the stuff written in Mussolini's Intellectuals about the goofed predictions and the very real historical reality that "communists" had to make concessions to right wing principles on a more extreme level than even fascist groups. I remember a south slav on another forum I used to post on and got on well with who spoke with positivity of Tito's "fascism". I did some research on this myself and found that he transitioned to a co-operative based economy and it worked much better than "communism" did in other economic areas. I'm not that fond of the co-operative model, not on a large nationwide scale anyway because there are better models but after my recent revision it seems to confirm my convictions more than ever about communists having to make concessions to the "right". Excuse the rambling. You're a valuable member to have and an asset to fascism, as I've always said on here I value a former communist over a flavour of the month libertarian queer. I'm going o be making a thread probably in the next few days solely for communism; it'd be great if you could offer input either in that thread or over PM, especially since you came here as a communist and ended up being a fascist. Have a good weekend brother.

ZHICA: Good day! Well, I was communist-ish. I was still exploring my views but Communism seemed reasonable. At the same time, I had a soft spot for nationalism. Watching various vids on youtube about demographic decline in Europe and other white nations, and being a European myself, this just didn't sit with me. There were aspects of communism that I didn't mind, but the main thing was the internationalism that I didn't like. They want all of the means of prod. to be owned collectively, but I don't think that could work on an international scale. Also at the same time, I had an intense dislike for Revleft-style leftism (a la 1960). So I searched up on google: "revleft sucks", to see who shared my views on the revtards. It was mainly stromfront threads but then I came upon Ironmarch. After I joined I read a little more about what Fascism was really about (though I still have a lot to read) and it just appealed to me more. It was anti-global capitalism and at the same time anti-internationalism and pro-nationalism. I felt it was perfect for me. Thank you! Looking forward to the thread as well.

CLIVE BISSEL: That's very reasonable; I think the fact that communism is utopian is the thing that can turn people off from it, I've found communism mainly appeals to intellectuals (who always end up dead under real communism, or atleast the closest thing to it – like Cambodia). Communism degenerates further 2 ways, it goes to either the extreme lengths of totalitarianism and death or to the left and becomes a hodge podge of contradictions or soemthing else entirely, anarcho-communism, "stop liking what I don't like" anarchism. The internationalism vs nationalism debate is of upmost importance. There's a huge ideological and principled difference between something like WU(FE)NS and international Jewry (Marxism) . . . Nothing has changed concerning the tactics of real leftists. I don't know when I'll put the thread up it gets a bit busy, espc. during the weekend with the kid other stuff.

ZHICA: Very true, the utopianism is definitely another big one. It's hard to sell something if it seems too based on hope rather than actual practical possibility. Though, this wasn't a problem for the Obama campaign, but then again American liberals tend to be pretty dumb. Communism and Anarchism today certainly do attract a lot of morons and weirdos (ex. Anarcho-queer). From university profs all the way to 14 year olds on reddit/revleft. I used to not mind Jews that much, but seeing how big of an influence they've had in the West I just can't ignore them. All the social justice movements, banks, and even in the media, vastly owned by Jews. Why would such a small minority need so much power? Something is definitely a little off. The one thing I've noticed about the left is that they don't live in reality. They never think realistically about anything – history, race, etc. – none of it. They constantly look through the lens of their ideology of equality and all that jazz, instead of just examining things logically. In my opinion, modern leftism is simply just an undiagnosed mental illness . . . ("Clive-Bissel," 2013, spelling as in original).

Interestingly, IM, like Discord, saw debates among former left-wing extremists regarding the various different types of far-left ideologies and which ones are arguably more prone to leading into the far right. In contrast to the Discord thread presented, Trotskyism was seen as one rather rarely relevant far-left current for side-switching:

DELETED USER: . . . I am also an atheist and former Trotskyist. It's quite amusing how we're very similar . . .

HADIT: Yeah, i noticed our similar views. I like how you're a former trot like me. Seems like most of the former commies on this forum were either marxist-leninists or anarchists.

DELETED USER: . . . Yeah, a lot of the former communists here were anarchists and non-Trotskyite Marxist-Leninists. The owner of this website when I used to talk to him loved the shit out of Stalin. Dig through his posting history, because he goes over Russian history pretty thoroughly even if it's ideologically biased. I'm close friends with some of the people on here, so I can introduce you to some cool people on Skype. They're nice people for the most part, but some are on the crazy side (at least for my own sake) . . .

HADIT: . . . His Stalin obsession kinda bothers me though. He's a russian nationalist, and Stalin obviously had a huge influence on Russia. But still, kinda weird seeing a fascist idolizing one of the biggest anti-fascists to ever live ("Hadit," 2014, spelling as in original).

Another difference between Discord and IM regarding the visibility of side-switching is the fact that the latter platform contains numerous detailed testimonials from defectors who attempt to explain their transition, albeit unfortunately not in as much detail as seen in other storylines in this book. In the following, I present but two exemplary posts of this nature from IM, out of roughly a dozen. The first testimonial was written by a user from New Zealand nicknamed "John Q. Public" who joined the forum late in May 2017. Just five days into his IM membership, he posted the following statement about his ideological development, placing utmost importance on US neo-Nazi George Lincoln Rockwell (1918–1967) for his conversion, but also speaking about disillusionment with utopian ideological goals:

I was a teenage communist and became a racist. Rockwell made me do it. Hello Ironmarch, I'm a 25-year-old man from Wellington, New Zealand. I was raised in an apathetic, liberal and atheist household. My political awakening began when I was about 13 years old. I found it hard to believe that anarchists were simply some sort of chaos worshipers, and decided to investigate it online. As it turned out, there was a whole canon of political and philosophical literature surrounding it. Of course, I swallowed it all. Aside from sparking a far more vigourous interest in politics, this experience taught me at a young age to distrust simple narratives that we are expected to uncritically accept. So, starting from the very bottom – Anarcho-Communism – I climbed up through the New Left and Stalinism. Thankfully I snuck through before all the 96 genders trans-unicorn business really blossomed. In any case, it didn't take long to figure out that class consciousness and proletarian revolution were the fever dreams of a baseless ideology, a presupposed conclusion eternally in search of a reality which affirms it. Worth noting is that at some point during this period I found my way to Stormfront, where the case for nationalism was made to me. It was, of course, common sense, but being young, I didn't understand why white civilisation was more deserving of preservation than multicultural universalism. The seed of moral relativism, planted back in the anarchist days, finally bore its ugly fruit, and set my search for truth back by a decade. So from about the age of 17 I languished in an individualistic civic nationalism, and felt pretty clever about it, too. I thought that I had finally come to the common sense, adult, time-tested view of things. The old cliche of the "Talented Tenth" and case-by-case judgment of individuals kept any racial questions at bay. I still had a very materialistic, "Guns, Germs and Steel" view of inequality on the civilisational scale. The other races were simply blank slates born in unlucky circumstances, and that alone covered for any failing they might manifest. Even then, I didn't like being around blacks, but I wouldn't ever have admitted that. I maintained a casual curiosity about "extremist" politics, but felt comfortably superior to such ideas. Though I didn't know it, I had the Cathedral affirming my views, after all. My ideological view of the world was comfortable, as long as I remained willfully ignorant of certain issues which would cause cognitive dissonance. Cognitive dissonance is extremely uncomfortable anyway, so it was easy to justify avoidance. Here I remained, until about a year ago. It was listening to George Lincoln Rockwell's (maybe you've heard of him) university speeches that finally did me in. There was a man who knew how to present an idea, and make any contradiction sound to your own ears like defiance of common sense. His case for Human Biodiversity using the manifestly obvious differences between breeds of animals, and the sudden suspension of this logic "when it comes to this magical animal that walks on two legs and calls himself Man" was devastating. This was quickly followed up by Stefan Molyneux's presentation on HBD, supplying the data confirming what one can tell just by looking at the face of an African. This one-two punch was a killer. The floodgates opened. A whole new dimension of understanding stretched out before me. The world finally, genuinely, started making sense, without any uncomfortable doubts niggling away at the back of my mind. I was no longer trapped having my outlook on the world decided one person at a time. The tiny prison cell of individualism (and not noticing demographic patterns) looks spacious, but only because the walls are mirrors. Seeing things through an ethnic lens simplified what I saw, now that I had no need of the involved mental gymnastics to preserve my old view. I realised that what I had been searching for through my political sojourn was identity and purpose. Finally I had found it, written in my genes, the very fundamental stuff of which I am made, all along. I discovered pride and tradition and community. I was a White man, and for the first time, I knew it. Naturally, anti-Semitism followed. I don't imagine that it takes anyone long. One sees it everywhere, once he starts looking. After listening to the first several episodes of Mysterium Fasces when they came out, I went to Church. This made the reality of objective Truth and morality obvious, and made me twice the anti-Semite that I had been. Suddenly it wasn't merely ethnic self-defense; it was opposition to rebels against Truth and Nature itself. Finally, I understood that Evil is real, and that it has a face, and a long, hooked nose. I found Ironmarch through Mysterium Fasces being featured on the Daily Stormer, with Anglin himself on episode 1 ... established your bona fides, but to my shame I fell for the meme that the Ironmarch forum was an internecine internet drama factory which sacrificed pragmatism for ideological vanity. As it turns out, it seems that everyone else alienated themselves from you, instead ... Finally, a chance contact on Facebook encouraged me to join you guys here. I'm keen to get a more detailed understanding of National Socialism and racialism. First on the reading list is White Power. Thanks for reading. ("John-Q.-Public," 2017, spelling as in original)

A second example for such a defection testimonial comes from a user nick-named "Samus Aryan" who joined IM in October 2017 and was based in North Carolina. His biographical post came shortly afterward as well, just five days after becoming an IM member. In it, he describes his ideological development from communism via anarchism to National Socialism but also goes on to formulate what partially reads like an application letter, detailing his personal skills and interests in order to find a useful task for the far-right community he just joined. This can be seen as a textbook example of Social Identity Theory's (SIT) intergroup migration explanations in part, as the offering of valuable skills and knowledge is very clearly presented in the direct context of professing to a long-term ideological development process that originated in the far-left milieu.

Age: 28 Profession: construction assistant/secretary (measure jobs/bid/estimate/e-mail) Country: North Carolina, United States Political history: I was a communist briefly in my teens and an anarchist for 7 years afterwards, being national socialist for a good two years now. I now believe anarchy is always a temporary transitional stage as there will eventually be some form of government to take its place. Being national socialist truly is the most rebellious ideology of our times, as they say national socialists are the new punks Reasons for joining: Before national socialism I was an ancap then an individual-ist anarchist when I realized communism and capitalism are both spooks. I now realize we all have a duty to our people and trying to be an ethical egoist isn't all its cracked up to be. Egoists really are full of themselves, I do however, now believe that national socialism rewards individuals doing what they do best all while serving the greater good. I ditched pretty much all my friends cause they hate "nazis" so much, they still don't know I'm national socialist I still want their trust as I'm trying to dig up intel about Antifa from them. That and becoming straightedge had me realize a lot of the reason I was friends with other people was drug and alcohol related. Misery loves company, although I'm a hell of a lot lonelier I am living a more rewarding, healthier life. Im trying to reciprocate ideas instead of listening to the same ol' one-sided pessimistic crap I'm used to. I'm here for friends but I mostly want to commit to real world action where ever I'm needed. I wouldn't mind starting or joining a local NS chapter, I've already convinced an old friend to be national socialist and want to meet others in the area. Skills: I'm always restoring an old electronic and modifying technology in general. I'm never ever happy with the way anything looks or functions normally and make it a point to modify every little possession to make it my own aesthetically or functionally. I'm huge into quality over quantity and am quick to get rid of any unnecessary clutter. I am very organized and love arranging things. I think aesthetics are important especially with first impressions, dressing well is a form of politeness. I've worked at sign shop, I understand people are lazy and like information simple and to the point. I'm very observant at noticing flaws, has good eye for detail and eyeballing things. I can do most things in Photoshop, can hand draw, can make/apply vinyl decals, prints, wheatpaste and stencils. I also make glitch .gifs and can glitch out analogue video I'm an amateur tailor. Most my clothes now were either waxed, patched, dyed, painted, shrunk, stretched, had new buttons put on, or repaired in some way by myself. Can do simple embroidary, Im very tedious when hand sewing. I can resize t-shirts and turn them into tank tops. I can also sew pillows, armbands, and basic things like that. I do a lot of kettlebell, mace, and Indian club exercises. I'm not the strongest I could be but have really good stamina from biking often. I'm a naturally good swimmer and am taking freediving classes soon to be able to dive 60 feet without a tank. Interests: Things I've found interesting in the past at least: extensions of the body, tools, artificial intelligence, dimensions, mandela effect, simulations, reincarnation, conspiracies, dharma, natural order, religions, and anything esoteric. I was a transhumanist like 2 years ago but I've grown out of it, prosthetic limbs and stuff are fine but life was meant to be experienced in the natural form we are in. I like tinkering with things and am ashamed to admit I'm a "hobbyist", I'd like to put my creativity into something less selfish and more practical. ("Samus-Aryan," 2017, spelling as in original)

Fascinatingly, IM also contained a couple of user statements about multidirectional side-switching, meaning, for example, repeated transitions between communism and neo-Nazism back and forth or interruptions of far-right extremist trajectories with intermittent phases of activity in the far left. Such pathways are quite counterintuitive and contradict some parts of the literature on intergroup transitions and the development or change of political attitudes (see Section 1.6). Such regular switchers must appear highly unreliable and untrustworthy to each milieu they are active in. Hence, one should normally assume little interest in publicizing such behavior, especially since concealing it would be easy online by simply using different nicknames, throw-away email addresses, or IP scramblers, etc. In one such case, a user calling himself "Peter" explains this back-and-forth switching with the emotional effects of each milieu's ideology. His narrative is strengthened for the far-right audience by implying that all in all, he has always been a committed rightist, but diverted to communism now and then:

Hello, my name is Peter and I am an eighteen year old male and reside in Ontario. My family is Anglo-Saxon, blood is a mix of Bulgarian, Irish, and English. After reading the works of Julius Evola, I have started to consider myself a Traditionalist. I was first a communist in middle school, I read the communist Manifesto and Das Kapital(a hard time understanding it at the time). Eventually I converted to Socialism, then oddly enough I became infatuated with Ayn Rand and Objectivism. Ever since I was little I knew I was a white Canadian Christian who wanted to live in such a way and live in a society that lived in such a way. Thus Communism never exactly held complete control over me, I read the works of various Fascistic Intellectuals and have always leaned towards the far-right(or what is known as the far right). I will also admit I tried to force myself to be a communist more than once, being a part of the right wing brings pessimism and a sense of hopelessness into one's thoughts(for me at least), and the thought of ultimate victory seems low. However, when I was a communist, I thought ultimate victory was but inevitable and I was a much happier individual to know my beliefs would triumph in the end. Though I could never ever buy into the cultural marxism and generally the communist mind set. I have always returned to the right wing eventually, and for over a year and a half I have studied Traditionalism and have found myself firm in my beliefs. I recently got accepted into university for philosophy and well that is it really. I hope the stay here will be enlightening and fun, my deepest apologies if my introduction was difficult to understand, I am quite tired while typing this. ("Peter," 2015, spelling as in original)

Another user nicknamed "New Canadian Empire" can serve as an additional example of intermittent far-left "excursions" during extreme-right radicalization processes. It surely is highly extraordinary to see a narrative involving a move from neo-Nazi skinhead to Stalinist Communist and finally to Italian style fascist:

As a child I took in the whole rainbow nonsense. But then again I think we all did at one point. However I remember being dissatisfied with many policies that were brought up by the ruling liberal party that were so bad even a child could see the foolishness. But then I had a streek with national socialism. But I was more or less a skinhead screaming Gas the Kikes! Race war now! But more of less oblivious to the greater theory. Then I was a communist. Lordy be was I ever. I admired Stalin for battling the enemy with unremittent force. Or how Ho Chi Mihn fought the Americans from Beyond the grave. But then I found out all that other stuff. Dat cultural revolution ... Trotsky Dat buriccratic blunder fuckery Several years ago I started to read up on Mussolini's policies and it was like the light had been lit. I joined the Army Reserve Went to the sandbox ... Came back Went back to school Joined Iron March Its just a never ending hate filled story. ("New-Canadian-Empire," 2013, spelling as in original)

In sum, I looked at those two extreme-right online platforms to explore how extremist side-switchers to the far right communicate their trajectories in the virtual space and how their communities received them. Through their debates and discussions, I gained unique insights into the framing process of defection. Through those online milieus, it becomes possible to partially trace the evolution of side-switching storylines and gather narrative fragments by those switchers in different stages of the process. Of course, many defectors who outed themselves on IronMarch or Discord did so long after they had completed the transition. Few examples, however, show the personal agency in this individual identity management and the reconstruction work a side-switcher automatically has to go through in order to adapt to the new social environment, its collective norms and values, and the details of "correct" participation. This can even mean learning a new language in part, as the new milieu might react negatively to certain trigger words, codes, or symbols that were considered unproblematic in the old in-group. As an unknown IM user wrote in June 2013:

I was a communist until recently, but I realized that nationalism is better than internationalism, and that communism is unrealistic. I've been lurking around this forum, and I still hold a lot more far left views that the average Iron Marcher. Also, I'm probably going to sound like a communist some of the time. I'll try to avoid using communist expressions." ("Deleted-User," 2013, spelling as in original)

It is somewhat surprising to find no significant negative or even cautionary reactions to side-switchers. At least on IM this might be due to the fact that the forum's founder himself is a defector from the far left. Such side-switchers are generally welcomed openly and very positively. Users discuss a lot how to facilitate and increase defection from the far left by using the most effective "redpilling" arguments and strategies. Especially the IM forum saw itself as a place of extreme-right ideological learning and development, which is why partially detailed and highly differentiated theoretical discussions between various ideological currents took place. Multiple discussion threads indicate that many users recognized and acknowledged at least some basic ideological relationship between the far-right and far-left thought system families. Underlying core themes such as "race," "nation," or "religion" in addition to more complex political issues such "economics" are used to debate individual right or left extremist dictators and thinkers' positions within and across the milieus. This allows for the recognition and creation of ideological subclusters on the platforms, for example, more left-leaning Strasserites or National Bolshevists. Interestingly, this ideological plurality on a "sub-atomic" level (they still remained committed to the extreme right in general) includes many arguments and philosophical "lineage tracing" that some scholars of fascism and National Socialism have identified as well (e.g., Gregor, 2008; Sternhell, Sznajder & Ashéri, 1994), thereby lending empirical support to the ongoing efficacy of this ideological kinship in parts. As the Discord user "Ronny TX" put it most pointedly, side-switching might essentially be about finding one's favorite style of authoritarianism.

2.5   Conclusion

The case studies we have seen so far display a wide variety of potential motives and pathways for members of far-left milieus who joined the extreme right. Generally speaking, many "discovered" the role of the nation or were looking for a group that was more committed to anti-Semitism than their previous groups. Despite partially severe criminal activities or outspoken support for violence, ideological arguments are more prevalent in explaining the decision to defect to the other side. Nevertheless, we see story elements evolving around masculinity, a warrior ethos, or courage (for example, in the cases of Julian Fritsch in Section 2.3 or Benito Mussolini in Section B2.1). The far left is presented as weak, cowardly, and hypocritical. Horst Mahler combines his militancy with the claimed intellectual breakthrough after having studied Hegel in prison and realizing that Marx fundamentally misinterpreted his philosophy.

We can also see a strong component of resistance or rebellion against what is portrayed to be societal or milieu-specific injustice, for example, in the storyline of Iris Niemeyer. Beyond the individual and detailed storylines, discussions and side-switching confessions in the digital realm have given us an inside perspective of a milieu that can be remarkably integrative and flexible in terms of including outsiders coming from traditionally hostile ideological backgrounds. It would be far too easy and misleading to simply dismiss this fact as a lack of interest in doctrines or the history and contents of the ideology.

Online discussions in those far-right virtual milieus can quickly escalate into highly detailed exchanges of arguments and facts regarding even seemingly remote and specialized theoretical or policy related topics. One cannot find outspoken hostility or rejection against those who profess to have switched sides or are still in the process of learning about the far right. Of course, the far-left milieu as such is despised and very much vilified but there is also a significant amount of debate about how to better convert leftists to their side, and defectors are warmly welcomed. It appears that there is little shame or fear of disclosing such a past, at least in those far-right online milieus I looked at for the purpose of this book. Given the strong historical and ideological links between the far right and the far left, causing some scholars to go as far as calling fascism, for example, a variant (Gregor, 2008) or a revision (Sternhell et al., 1994) of Marxism-Leninism, this might be understandable. However, the strong awareness of the need for social integration of defectors and the mechanisms put in place to avoid scaring them away are rarely observed characteristics of far-right milieus.

3 Joining the Far Left

For seven years, "Jan," who did not want to use his real name in the article about him, was active as a neo-Nazi skinhead in Germany. He does not easily fit into the stereotype of a violent and uneducated teenager with a broken family background who enters hypermasculine extreme–right subcultures, such as the skinheads, while looking for a new family. At the time of his interview with a German newspaper in 2012 (Kolodziejczyk, 2012), Jan was in his late twenties and still used the skinhead outlook, the fashion, tattoos, and haircut.

However, at that point he was active in the militant far-left scene and had replaced his neo-Nazi tattoos with portraits of communist thinkers and anti-fascist symbols. As the skinhead subculture roughly splits into far-right, far-left, and unpolitical currents, the need to change his appearance was, with the exception of the tattoos, mostly marginal for Jan. On the inside, however, Jan's mindset had changed drastically. He does have a high school diploma (the German "Abitur," which is slightly more advanced than the Anglo-American counterpart) and is described as sophisticated, eloquent, and well-read by the journalist who spoke to him. Jan described his parents as neither left-wing nor right-wing but unpolitical instead. During his teenage years, he started to develop a "bourgeois, right-wing conservative mindset" (original in German, translated by author, Kolodziejczyk, 2012) and developed an interest in extreme right-wing literature on race and conspiracy theories, anti-Semitism, and Nazi propaganda. He then started to go to concerts with his friends, where he met more organized and radicalized extreme right-wing peers. With those insider contacts, it was easy for Jan to get access to more hardcore neo-Nazi literature and he especially liked a more elitist magazine called "Funkenflug" (translating to "flying sparks," the main outlet for an elite neo-Nazi organization outlawed in 2009). From that point on, his extreme right-wing career progressed rapidly.

More conflicts at school went hand in hand with increased activism for his extreme right-wing group, a far-right skinhead gang. For this group, Jan ran an anti-Semitic webpage, authored numerous articles, and sang in a neo-Nazi rock band (Kolodziejczyk, 2012). When offered a position within one of Germany's largest extreme-right parties, he declined with an already burning hatred against the political establishment and any parliamentary solution to societal problems. However, soon after Jan had finished his high school degree, he fell in love with a young woman who embodied everything his ideology had taught him to despise. Jan started to read up on racist literature to find any piece of information proving to him that this relationship was permissible. Even though he did eventually convince himself of the relationship's ideological legitimacy, other members of his extreme right-wing milieu did not share this viewpoint. Accusing him of treason and "racial defilement," other neo-Nazi skinheads threatened Jan, telling him to choose between being on their side or against them. Jan continued his relationship and left the group, but without changing his ideological views. Nevertheless, the former in-group interpreted this move as an act of betrayal and started harassing Jan's family and girlfriend. In search for protection he turned toward the "political enemy" (original in German, translated by author, Kolodziejczyk, 2012), meaning the local organized extreme-left anti-fascist milieu. At first, the reaction from the far left was cautious at best, as it seemed simply too incredible that a well-known and committed neo-Nazi such as Jan would indeed be involved in an intimate relationship like that. After some fact-checking and interviews with Jan and his girlfriend, they started to engage more openly and set conditions for helping him to leave the far-right environment.

For Jan leaving the extreme right-wing ideology behind did not come as a natural consequence at this stage yet: "I was still extreme right-wing. I simply wanted nothing to do with the fascists, the bully skins, who have been my friends before" (original in German, translated by author, Kolodziejczyk, 2012). For the anti-fascist far left, the only way to leave the far-right milieu was to quit the thinking behind it as well and therefore they provided Jan with left-wing literature and counter-narratives to extreme-right arguments. In Jan's perspective, this was the real turning point: "As I had read myself into right-wing extremism, I now read myself into the left-wing scene" (original in German, translated by author, Kolodziejczyk, 2012). Even though his relationship causing the defection broke up for nonpolitical reasons, Jan found a new social environment and activities, reflecting about his time in the far right: music concerts, parties, and intellectual discussion circles. At no point in his side-switching storyline did Jan actually consider cooperating with the authorities or one of the many German governmental deradicalization programs. Calling himself a "convinced left-wing extremist" (original in German, translated by author, Kolodziejczyk, 2012), Jan still hates the political system, which in his narrative appears to be the ideological bridge between the two milieus.

The case of Jan provides us with an example of emotional and intellectual defection drivers. Once his milieu forced him to choose between the far right and his girlfriend, they created an emotional conflict of interest eventually resulting in disengagement. The ideological part of the side-switching process came through reading and critical reflection nurtured by a new social environment. As we will see in the next chapter, which looks at defectors from the extreme right who joined far-left milieus, many in this category use moral and ethical arguments to explain their personal responsibility to contain some of the damage they helped to create. We can also read much about anger and revenge against a milieu that left those side-switchers' lives in thorough disarray.

3.1 Christine and Klaus Dieter Hewicker, Odfried Hepp, and Left-Wing Anti-Imperialist Currents in 1980s German Right-Wing Terrorism

Klaus Dieter Hewicker was born in 1956 as the only child of his parents. In 1972 he finished his schooling with the certificate of secondary education ("mittlere Reife" in German). Afterward, he began his training to be a legal assistant, which he completed in 1975. As he failed to find employment in this profession, Klaus took over a job as production worker in a car manufacturing factory. Between 1976 and 1977 he served in the German army as part of the mandatory conscription at that time. Once he had returned from the military, he moved between various short-term and unskilled employments before serving a prison sentence between July 1980 and March 1981 resulting from a 1979 sentencing for incitement of hatred, distribution of illegal extremist propaganda, and damage of property. The court verdict states that he met his future wife Christine in 1977 and became engaged one year later in 1978. An attempt to live together in their own apartment failed due to financial problems and the couple had to move in with Klaus' parents. After getting married in 1980, they left Germany in August 1981 for France and later Belgium, where they joined other militant German neo-Nazis and plotted terrorist attacks and robbed a bank (BMI, 1982, pp. 26–27).

After the heist, both Hewickers were arrested in November 1981 together with a third extremist and extradited to Germany in January 1982 (BayObLG, 1983, pp. 18–19). In the eyes of the court, Klaus Dieter Hewicker began his extreme right-wing career early and was already an enthusiastic reader of far-right literature at the age of 16. In 1974, he became a member of the extreme–right NPD party and became a leading figure in its youth organization. Three years later, in 1977, Klaus declared his exit from the party as his ideological positions had developed to a point at which the NPD appeared too bourgeois and conformist. In the ensuing years, both Hewickers joined much more openly neo-Nazi organizations and participated in illegal activities such as distributing propaganda or smearing extreme-right graffities. As the verdict reads, Klaus Dieter Hewicker renounced his right-wing extremist ideology in prison and began to promote his "own version of anti-imperialism" (original in German, translated by author, BayObLG, 1983, p. 20). He was sentenced to seven years in prison for serious extortionate robbery (BayObLG, 1983, p. 6). His involvement in a terrorist organization was not part of the charges, as German law at the time excluded terrorist activities outside the country.

Christine Hewicker was born in 1959 as the youngest child of six siblings. She finished her schooling with a certificate of secondary education and a vocational training as a bakery saleswomen in 1978 (BayObLG, 1983, p. 23). Her radicalization process is explained by the court as being due to an early brotherly influence, which brought her into contact with the neo-Nazi movement. In 1977 Christine became a member of the NPD youth organization, where she met Klaus Dieter. Together with him, she declared her exit from the party in 1978 and participated with him in the same activities and neo-Nazi groups, resulting in various criminal convictions for distributing illegal propaganda and damage to property. The verdict also states that Christine Hewicker, like her husband, renounced extreme right-wing ideology in prison and started to "more or less" (original in German, translated by author, BayObLG, 1983, pp. 23–24) hold the same views as him.

She was sentenced to six years in prison for serious extortionate robbery (BayObLG, 1983, p. 6). Her 2001 autobiography gives a detailed account of her childhood, radicalization into right-wing terrorism, and ideological change. In it, Christine remembers a loving and caring family environment until when she was 14 years old and a former school friend of her oldest brother returned from Berlin as a convinced NPD member. In her small village, the extreme-right political ideology met little resistance among the teenagers who were generally bored due to a lack of alternative distractions. Gradually, all her brothers became involved in the far right. Furthermore, the village was close to barracks of British troops, which regularly passed through on training exercises and created a perception of foreign occupation (Hewicker, 2001, p. 13). While xenophobia was something Christine first learned from the NPD, a certain frustration about the country's separation in East and West Germany was already present:

Even before I got to know the NPD, I felt stressed [about] the relationship between the FRG [or Federal Republic of Germany, West Germany] and the GDR [or German Democratic Republic, East Germany]. Oftentimes, it made me deeply sad that a country was separated and whole families were destroyed by that. I always wanted that these families were allowed to reunite and I found support for my opinion in the NPD … I felt really good among the NPF comrades. (original in German, translated by author, Hewicker, 2001, p. 15)

Increasingly, Christine was included in the social activities of the extreme-right movement, for example, camping and singing events. Her parents never protested this, likely because they had no clue about the political motivation behind her involvement. In contrast to other radicalization pathways, however, she was able to maintain a nonpolitical circle of friends for a while and finish her school education. This changed only after she met her first boyfriend in the far-right milieu, who was regularly engaged in violent confrontations with the far-left scene and nurtured additional ideological beliefs in Christine, such as anti-Semitism and anti-capitalism (Hewicker, 2001, pp. 16–17). The fact that her boyfriend later died in a car accident involving a British soldier also played a role in her growing hatred against the troops "occupying" Germany. For Christine, the main facilitator for her extreme-right radicalization was the social interaction with like-minded teenagers. Violence and romantic relationships resulted in further ideological commitment expressed through aggression against all political opponents (Hewicker, 2001, pp. 18–19). Her milieu also provided status and confidence: "How important I felt, when I had something 'intelligent' to add! Yes, I was somebody!" (original in German, translated by author, Hewicker, 2001, p. 20).

Christine describes an early aversion against the hard-core neo-Nazi paroles glorifying violence. For her, violent acts only made sense as a part of conflicts with the far left. After she had met her future husband Klaus in 1977, her life started to change more significantly. Most importantly, the couple began moving from legal to illegal political activities and left the NPD for more extremist organizations. Ideologically the reason for quitting the party was radicalism: "We accused the party of having a tendency towards the bourgeoisie, conforming with the system and lack of initiative" (original in German, translated by author, Hewicker, 2001, p. 28). Around 1977, the Hewickers met other militant neo-Nazis, among them some who would later become involved in terrorist groups as well. Based on personal friendships, the couple gravitated toward clandestine and highly violent sub-milieus. They gradually left the few remaining halfway legal extreme right-wing groups they had found more or less acceptable until that point (Hewicker, 2001, pp. 28–29). International far-right networks form another key element in her storyline. From very early on in her involvement in the extreme-right milieu, Christine traveled to gatherings, concerts, and rallies in neighboring countries such as France and Belgium. There she made further connections to other militants and later found support for her own terrorist plots. Regarding the side-switching, those international contacts provided essential ideological input through personal relationships. In 1979, discussions in Christine's militant milieu indicated a growing admiration for the left-wing terrorist RAF:

One day in March 1979 we sat together with a couple of comrades in a restaurant and talked about how the future could look like and what we could do against the state in the upcoming time. It was dropped that the work of the RAF should not be rejected actually. I cannot remember who said that, but everyone there supported that notion. Hence, we started thinking about how we could work similarly and we imagined kidnappings of a high ranking politician or something like that. (original in German, translated by author, Hewicker, 2001, p. 42)

Not surprisingly, such discussions quickly raised the suspicion of the German authorities and soon some members of that specific circle were arrested and charged with forming a terrorist organization called "Otte," named after its alleged leader and a close friend of Klaus: Paul Otte (Koehler, 2016a, p. 200). It was just a matter of time before the police would focus attention on the remaining neo-Nazis, including the Hewicker couple. Indeed, they were already seen as key witnesses in the trial against Otte, so they began plotting an escape to France. As her husband sat in prison for various other crimes at that time, Christine Hewicker started to explore her ideology: "Since I was on my own, I somehow began to make my own thoughts about the political situation in Germany and the world. For the first time completely without the influence of some comrades but infected by the virus of hate, my interests moved far beyond the borders of the FRG. I developed a tremendous empathy for the fate of the Palestinian people" (original in German, translated by author, Hewicker, 2001, p. 47).

Further conflict with the law also increased her hatred against the authorities, resulting in an amalgamation of her personal ideological struggle for "justice and humanity" (original in German, translated by author, Hewicker, 2001, p. 53) with the fight against the German justice and police system. On August 6, 1981, the couple fled to France and met with other militant right-wing extremists. There, they also connected with Arab militants: "I liked it a lot to finally be in touch with representatives of those people I so much pitied. And I knew that the men of the Palestinian fighter group 'Al Fatah' were happy about any European support. The idea to maybe fight against the FRG and later against the Israeli state together no longer was a utopia" (original in German, translated by author, Hewicker, 2001, p. 55). Out of France, the group plotted a bank robbery in Germany to finance their terrorist plans and during the preparations met with Walther Kexel, another militant neo-Nazi who would later form the right-wing terrorist "Hepp-Kexel" group together with his coconspirator Odfried Hepp (Hewicker, 2001, p. 58). The group conducted at least five armed robberies and 11 explosive attacks against US military personnel (Koehler, 2016a, p. 206). The link to Kexel and Hepp is significant for Christine's side-switching narrative. In the early 1980s, at the height of right-wing terrorism in Germany and Europe (Hoffman, 1982, 1984, 1986; Koehler, 2016a), a very small number of militants and their groups within the extreme right milieu attempted to ideologically and practically link up with far-left and international ethno-separatist terrorism (e.g., the Palestinians, Basque separatists, the Irish Republican Army, or with the German RAF). The reason for this might have been the desire for international recognition of their actions (particularly as some framed the violence as a liberation struggle against a foreign occupation), but also internal ideological debates influenced by the vibrant global terrorist landscape.

In fact, heated internal debates over specific tactical and ideological directions regarding the militant far right's future led to numerous bitter disputes and fragmentation of the milieu at that time. In 1983, Odfried Hepp and Walther Kexel became the most public representatives of the self-declared left-leaning anti-imperialist wing among right-wing terrorists. They published a political manifesto, which very few right-wing terrorists did in Germany, arguing for a joint right–left front against the "imperialist" and "Zionist" West (see more shortly). Christine Hewicker's retrospective narrative includes a detailed memory of the ideological debates within the militant far right in that period, which circled around specific leading figures of National Socialism and their respective currents in the Nazi movement (e.g., Ernst Röhm, the Strasser brothers, and the SA). As with many other side-switchers from the far right to the far left (and vice versa), the strategic and ideological tension between a focus on the national (e.g., racism) or international (e.g., anti-imperialism, anti-Zionism) level became a key issue for Christine and her close environment:

Slowly, our group began to split into two political directions. The clique from Hesse that had formed around our friend Walther Kexel had explicitly distanced itself from Hitlerism and oriented toward anti-imperialism, while the opinions about the political future of our group were very much divided. Klaus and I discussed and argued with the others. Wie agreed and then fell out with each other again. Kurt was a uniform fetishist and a great admirer of the revolutionists around Ernst Röhm [1887–1934, a leading Nazi and head of the SA]. So he never opposed our view that Adolf Hitler never would have gotten into power without those men, even though the NSDAP followers murdered them later. And with those fighters Adolf Hitler and his henchmen could never have thrown Germany into such misery as they later did. Because the revolutionary forces of the SA, like Gregor Strasser, Otto Strasser, Walther Stennes, etc. would have understood that and this is why many of them left the movement. What remained was a bunch of little bourgeois Hitlerists that soon started to flirt with Western-bourgeois capitalism . . . It was clear that that the wheel of time could not be reversed and that neither the core idea of the NSDAP nor the later path of Hitlerism with its fatal consequences was to be revived. We were neither "right" nor "left" and the Federal Republic should never bow to American imperialism or be turned into a Soviet republic and we agreed that Germany should become a free country in every situation. However, Kurt was a fierce hater of Jews and even though he had influenced me and the others a lot with his opinions, anti-Zionism had only a minor role in the ideas about the future struggle against the Federal German government. Opinions differed slightly about that among us though. And Wehrdorf too had problems accepting the newly oriented thoughts away from Hitlerism towards anti-imperialism, even though he was not totally against it. Personally, I – like Kexel, Klaus and some other comrades – had totally submitted to the thought that American-Zionist imperialism, which was extending its tentacles to all directions in the world, must be fought. The final stage of capitalism interlocking with industrial and banking monopolies must be stopped from gaining influence in our country to prevent it from letting our people die spiritually, mentally, and morally ... Huge gaps opened op within the right milieu in Germany. On the one side, there were the bourgeois nationalists, the posh faithful Germans, the NPD. and similar parties and groups. Then there were the uniform fetishists who really did not have any political understanding and wanted to raise their low self-esteem with provocative appearance ... And then this new group called the "Anti-Imperialist Liberation Army" emerged, to which I felt associated. Now we suddenly were traitors to the cause and enemies of our former comrades, even though we never actually wanted that. (original in German, translated by author, Hewicker, 2001, pp. 61–62)

Internal ideological differences aligned with power struggles, which resulted in partially open hostilities in the Hewickers' group. However, many members also made strong efforts to resolve conflicts: "Almost every time Klaus and I were able to reconcile the brawlers. Sometimes, Kurt laughed at us and threatened us. But always the calmness and camaraderie we had known returned to us" (original in German, translated by author, Hewicker, 2001, pp. 62–63). Hewickers' group relived the early Nazi movement split between the Hitler and Strasser/Röhm factions to a certain degree and both camps in the small terrorist cell included strong personalities claiming physical and ideological leadership. For a short while, the group was successful in navigating these internal tensions and maintaining some form of unity. Everyone received an agreed upon share of the money stolen during the bank robbery, which happened on September 23, 1981. Christine and the others proceeded to use most of the money to buy more weapons and explosives from French and Arab extremists, while resurfacing conflicts with those members standing for the "Hitlerist" interpretation of National Socialism finally led to their expulsion and mutual threats.

Ideological differences coupled with claims of leadership therefore resulted in the eventual splintering of the group (Hewicker, 2001, p. 64). The cell, now using different names such as "Commando Frank Schubert," "Black Front," or "Antiimperialist Liberation Army," planned its relocation to Belgium when some of Christine's close friends and fellow right-wing terrorists were stopped by the police on their way to a bank robbery in Munich, Germany. In the ensuing shoo-tout with the authorities, two neo-Nazis were killed. Among those arrested was Peter Fabel, a right-wing extremist who would later divulge his communist past in a neo-Nazi magazine (see the introduction in Chapter 2). This incident, according to Christine, caused some of their international supporters to distance themselves from the group and eventually information regarding their whereabouts was leaked to the Belgian police and led to their arrest and subsequent deportation to Germany.

By going through various stages of prison and investigative custody (in Belgium and Germany), Christine Hewicker credits this phase in her extremist career with fueling a fundamental hatred against governmental authorities and the judiciary. Nevertheless, she and her husband also used the time for an attempt to convert fellow right-wing extremist comrades to their new ideological positions via mail exchange. This, however, was not met with a lot of success, foreshadowing a potential negative backlash to their deviation from orthodox neo-Nazism:

Because my husband and I had changed out political opinions by now (to anti-imperialism), it was imperative to convince the comrades of this new position in the following time or, if necessary, cut off those contacts. Even before our arrest, we had found like-minded souls with Walther Kexel and Ottfried Hepp [his first name is correctly spelled Odfried, author's note], while almost all other comrades could not understand our position. Gradually, all those contacts stopped ... The fact that Ernst Balke [one of those who left the group in conflict due to ideological differences] continued to send threat letters to me in prison did not bother me much. I never took him really seriously anyway. (original in German, translated by author, Hewicker, 2001, pp. 78–79)

As Christine was held in a separate prison, she had no chance to meet her husband in person for more than half a year after their arrest. When they first had the opportunity to see each other again, Christine remembers surprise about the lack of any positive emotions for her husband, indicating a growing psychological detachment from him and the relationship. In September 1982, she began a hunger strike and wrote a letter addressed to the German parliament and government. This document, together with a later public declaration during the trial, is highly revealing regarding the ideological mindset of this former right-wing terrorist and the development of her side-switching storyline:

I hereby declare to commit to an unlimited hunger strike since Monday, October 11, 1982. Reasons: As a representative of the "Anti-Imperialist Liberation Army," I protest: 1. The massacre of Palestinian civilians in the refugee camps of Shatila and Sabra (West Beirut), which bestially killed hundreds, maybe even thousands, old people, women and children (February 15–18, 1982). 2. The anew invasion of Zionist troops in Beirut. 3. The response of the German government to these incidents stated above as well as the general behavior of the government towards the Palestinian people, to the PLO and to the actions of the Zionists in the Middle East. I therefore demand: 1. Withdrawal of all foreign troops from Lebanon ... 8. Complete abjuration of the German government from American-Zionist rule. 9. Cessation of all money transfers from the FRG to Israel, which make it possible for the Zionists to field powerful armies and make the German people complicit in their policy of extermination ... (original in German, translated by author, Hewicker, 2001, pp. 86–87)

Other demands included the release of all political prisoners in Germany or the full recognition of the PLO and the Palestinian state. With that declaration, which not surprisingly had no discernible impact whatsoever, Christine aimed to step up her public ideological rebranding as international ethno-separatist. Her new focus was the liberation struggle of the Palestinians and the fight against "American-Zionist" global rule, an expression that indicates partially anti-Semitic conspiracy theories and left-wing anti-imperialist sentiments. Indeed, sympathy for the Palestinians has been and still is a major ideological inroad for right-wing extremists, who can use the issue of illegally occupied territory to link racial anti-Semitism with anti-Zionism.

As I pointed out previously (see Section 1.6.3), collaboration between neo-Nazis and Arab (particularly Palestinian) extremists and terrorists was not rare, at least from the European perspective. As for many other terrorists before and after her, prison also provided an opportunity for Christine to reflect on her positions and positively engage with members of the ideological out-group. This further increased the defection process from the far right: "I had problems dealing with myself around mid-82, when I began to critically review my previous opinions and my lifestyle. Somehow, I longed for calm-ness, my family and for love" (original in German, translated by author, Hewicker, 2001, p. 89). She recounts meeting a Jewish woman in prison and getting along well with her, for example. Not unlike the case of Richard Scheringer (see Section B2.2), Christine also puts some significance on per-sonal interactions with left-wing terrorists in her narrative:

While I was still sitting in isolation detention, two members of the Red Army Faction (RAF) were admitted to my prison. Sieglinde Hoffmann [born 1945, was a leading figure in the RAF's second generation; sentenced to 15 years in prison in 1982 and to life in prison in 1995; she was released on probation in 1999, author's note] right away got two cells next to me and Verena Becker [born 1952, sentenced to life in prison for attempted murder of two police officers in 1977, was a member of different left-wing terrorist organizations, including the RAF; she turned informant for the intelligence and was pardoned in 1989, only to be sentenced again to four years in prison in 2012 for accessory to murder, which had only become known then, author's note], with whom I later could establish contact in regular detention, got those two cells across Sieglinde Hoffmann. Once I was released into regular detention, it became possible for me to instruct fellow inmates to shield me off from the eyes of the prison staff during my free time in the yard so that I could have brief conversations with Verena Becker from time to time ... Even though it never got to a point of intensive contacts with the RAF members, we had to admit that we shared similar views regarding the state and its servants. While I did not really get "warm" with Sieglinde Hoffmann, I had to recognize that I found Verena Becker extremely likeable and if my transfer had not been interrupted, an intensification of our contacts would have been possible since I had not at all distanced from my opinions to fight the German state. And in Verena Becker I found a person who could contribute a lot of valuable ideas to my anti-imperialist thoughts. (original in German, translated by author, Hewicker, 2001, p. 91)

Until the start of her trial in June 1983, Christine Hewicker spent most of her prison time engaging in bitter personal letter exchanges with judges and prosecutors, as well as following the news about arrests of those former fellow neo-Nazi terrorists who were still on the run. Together with her husband, she did anticipate the trial to be an important public platform for promotion of their new ideology. During the court proceedings' first days, both Hewickers read out individual trial declarations explaining their disavowal of neo-Nazi ideology and turn to anti-imperialism, marking the peak of their side-switching storylines. In Christine's statement, the process is framed through a mixture of autobiographical and anti-capitalist elements:

During the last years, I have thought a lot about the problems facing the global population. Generally, I think and act following my feelings only, but I must say it makes me sick to my stomach when I think about what I have found out during my observations and reflections. I simply cannot understand why humans who have reasons and emotions are able to ignore the atrocities and inhumanities that happen in the world ... The so-called civilized humanity fights a war of consumption to a degree never seen before, "all against all" and "everyone against everyone" creating suffering for children, the sick, the unemployed, the poor and the minorities ... Why? Because the world of capitalism and quest for power alienates humans and isolates them ... It is the omnipresent principle of profit which slowly but certainly extends it tentacles into every sphere of life and engulfs us and those spheres. And what about the human being? Think about the South and Central American people and countries, who are exploited by US imperialism like always. Or think about the Palestinians, who are exiled from their homes, tortured and killed by power hungry money-Zionists. The Zionists have the Americans and the Europeans, led by the FRG, behind them ... Minorities are belittled because of their religions or worldviews, they are despised or discriminated. There is no sign of freedom of religion or opinion. Foreigners are not only seen as pieces of dirt by anyone on the street but the Federal German government even supports racism. For example, when they support, even indirectly, racist and Nazi groups. Why? Because the foreigners who have been brought here to work for us are now useless. Because the corporations have transferred their factories into Third World countries for cheaper labor and unemployment is rising in our country. And because those foreigners now cost too much for our state ... I was fourteen when I was confronted with politics for the first time. Back then, the NPD was a temporary fashion and I regarded the NPD as a tool to express and live out my childish ideas and wishes. Maybe now, as you have heard my thoughts, you can understand that with my adolescent optimism and naiveté I became easily impressed by such a group. Back then, the NPD was the main contact point with people who actually tried to change something of this catastrophic situation. However, in the course of our relationship, I had to find out that here, too, nothing but empty slogans were propagated. Looking for consequence, I moved to more extreme right-wing groups. But I quickly realized that here as well mostly teenagers with criminal tendencies or seeking to polish their lacking self-esteem through showing off their fetishes were active, presenting their brown or black uniforms, assault foreigners or shout[ing] "Heil Hitler." Because the fascists know, that nothing much will happen to them from the side of the state, other criminal acts are perpetrated and disguised with a political coat. Of course, there are also some convinced National Socialist[s]. But they have standpoints which I cannot support with a clean conscience. This is why I have separated myself from the fascists. I want equality and humanity for all human beings and all people in the world. This requires anti-imperialist resistance! It is a resistance against anything that facilitates inhumanity and makes human beings mental and spiritual cripples. Because of that, I distance myself from all anti-human groups and among others from the fascists. Because of that, I sympathize with all supressed people and groups, like the ETA, IRA, the PLO and the South and Central American guerrillas. As an anti-imperialist, my goal is to change the FRG into a free and independent Western Germany, which does not obey blindly the quest for power of imperialist states ... I wanted to show you, how coming from an extremist point of departure only an extremist solution was an option. I will not testify to the charges brought against me in the trial, because I am not willing to accept this fascist trial through my presence. I strongly distance myself from the Nazis charged here and I have nothing to do with them ... (original in German, translated by author, Hewicker, 2001, pp. 107–113)

The extensive declaration that was reprinted in Christine's autobiography aims to deliver a sweeping blow against capitalism and imperialism, including an attempt to link them to the alleged overall moral numbness of the population, destruction of the environment, international conflicts, suffering of women and children, suppression of minorities and whole ethnicities, politicians' corruption, or the malfunctioning social policies. She explains the existence of neo-Nazi groups with the lack of perspectives and meaningful responses to societal challenges by the German government, which would drive teenagers into the arms of right-wing extremist groups who made promises to deliver solutions. It is also noteworthy, that Christine seems to have included many positions of left-wing terrorist groups such as the RAF in her statements, for example, the claim that capitalism automatically produces fascism (a central social-philosophical concept used far beyond left-wing terrorist groups to explain the emergence of totalitarianism, fascism and Nazism, see: Adorno, 1950; Arendt, 1973; Horkheimer, 1939; Scheuch & Klingermann, 1967) and more specifically that the German government actively uses and supports far-right groups to control minorities out of open sympathy for them.

She also attempted to explain her own attraction to the extreme right and her fundamental disassociation from it. Ideologically, her side-switching pathway was made possible through neo-Nazi nationalism, which created the first mutually shared basis for collaboration with Palestinian ethno-separatist groups. Of course, the PLO at that time was nationalist in the sense of fighting for national liberation from Israeli occupation, but their overall ideology was based on left-wing anti-imperialism (Chamberlin, 2011). Additional links with the internationalist and anti-imperialist struggle of postcolonial liberation movements were anti-Zionism and anti-Americanism, both of which also formed the core of many neo-Nazi groups. Naturally, the extreme right-wing derivation of these positions was rooted in biological racism and anti-Semitism in particular, while on the left-wing ideological aisle macro-social and global political determinism based in the Marxist analysis of society formed the guiding rationale. Indeed, these ideological links, how remote they might appear, have effectively made the transition between the two milieus possible for many of the cases discussed in this chapter and the next one.

The Hewickers, however, did not only use the trial to present their new positions. Since the goal of those extreme-right ideological renegades was to win the support of the far left, they also directly engaged with the opposite milieu and campaigned for an alliance. On April 11, 1983, the German left-wing oriented newspaper *taz – Die Tageszeitung* published large excerpts of a declaration by both Hewickers, which the paper claimed to have received directly via mail at the end of March:

We take the arrest of Walther Kexel in England on February 18, 1983 as an opportunity to insistently point out again the necessity for a coordinated approach of all undogmatic, anti-imperialist and non-pacifist forces ... We believe that puny group interests are surmountable especially among those who call themselves undogmatic, because it requires remembering the highest principles of anti-imperialism, anti-racism and anti-fascism in order to arrive at the broadest front of resistance possible. We, repeatedly previously convicted former Nazi activists Klaus Dieter and Christine Hewicker, have drawn the conclusion of a mental learning process ... US imperialism is the militant arm of the USA and US capitalism respectively and is responsible for unmeasurable suffering for decades. (original in German, translated by author, *taz*, 1983a)

The Hewecker document, according to the *taz* newspaper, also claims that an "analysis of Western bourgeois capitalist exploitation order" leads to the necessity of "anti-imperialist liberation struggle" and "socialist revolution" (original in German, translated by author, *taz*, 1983a), aiming for a unified Germany as a solution. Regarding their own far-right past, the *taz* quotes the document with the following: "The only thing we regret is that we do not understand the motivation that has pushed us back then anymore" (original in German, translated by author, *taz*, 1983a). In the discussion of the declaration, the newspaper appears to be unimpressed, if not highly suspicious. It writes about the "fascist socialized Hewickers" who speak in "oracles" and "national-revolutionary tones" (original in German, translated by author, *taz*, 1983a). Another point the paper highlights is, that the Hewickers somewhat curiously focus on their terrorism charges, which had already been dropped by the prosecution at the time the document was written. In the eyes of the *taz*, this only serves the purpose of claiming a reputation as politically persecuted activists equal to far-left groups (*taz*, 1983a). Maybe it was this rather skeptical and critical reception of their declaration that made Klaus Dieter Hewicker follow up with a letter claiming foul play. First, correcting some factual inaccuracies in the previous report (such as age and state of the trial), Klaus directly denied ever having sent the declaration to the *taz* and authorizing its use. In his view, the newspaper somehow got its hands on a draft he was working on and produced a completely contradictory picture by "tearing it apart" (original in German, translated by author, *taz*, 1983b) with arbitrary quotes and wrong interpretations. Klaus continues:

We are not the "long term fascist socialized Hewickers" but living examples for the opposite! ... Yes, I was with the rightists and I stand up for that and now I am not there anymore! Who wants to come now and judge me and take away my personal development? ... And now crystal clear: I am neither a "right-wing activist" with group interests "currying a favor" with the left to offer an alliance, nor a "left-wing" fascist or expression of "ideological confusion and real crisis"! ... Nothing with so-called national-revolutionary tones the *taz* insinuates! ... Nationalism is nothing more than the stupidity and resentment of petty bourgeois, caused by and always increased by the bourgeoisie for their revanchist plans and profits – and therefore there can never be a "national-revolutionary" movement between "right" and "left"! ... I have nothing in common with the right anti-Americanism ... If a part of Germany was liberated, than to the honor of our people by the Red Army! Furthermore, there is no "solidarity" between right and left in the FRG in 1983 and there must not be one! Anti-imperialism is not a diffuse thing but happens on the left and nowhere else! ... The anti-imperialist liberation fight is not a nationalist matter, which must be strengthened, but it necessitates a national liberation, which can only be international at its fundamental core ... With the best wishes, Klaus Dieter Hewicker. PS: I am not at all sorry about destroying the worldview of the *taz*, which obviously, like so many "others," holds the opinion that "once being a neo-Nazi" equals remaining one for the rest of one's life. (original in German, translated by author, *taz*, 1983b)

Through this extraordinary exchange of opinions between a former neo-Nazi terrorist and a public far-left news outlet, one can discern various contentious elements between the two sides. Among them is the *taz* critique that the Heweckers would now portray themselves as national revolutionaries, meant as a derogatory and repellent category for those who consider themselves to be true leftists. Again, the specific question of the nation's role in fighting imperialism becomes a key issue between left and right. Another argument evolves around the nature of anti-Americanism and its roots in the Hewickers' argumentation. Obviously, the *taz* suspects some form of disguised German biological or cultural supremacism. While the left-wing paper interprets the declaration as an extreme-right attempt to join forces with the left and profit off their strategic and tactical skills, the Hewickers insist that they have truly defected and not just extended olive branches from the far right. Klaus-Dieter's defense shows frustration and disappointment over the left's refusal to take their change of heart seriously. It is noteworthy, however, that the use of anti-Zionism so present in the trial declaration was missing in both statements directed toward the *taz*.

Considering the historical context in Germany at the time of this exchange, the newspaper's position becomes understandable. Indeed, many high ranking and fully committed neo-Nazis had begun to strategically court the far left for various reasons, including US right-wing extremist Gerhard "Rex" Lauck, who called for joint political activism with all leftist groups (Rosen, 1989, p. 72) and leading German neo-Nazi Michael Kühnen, who wanted to reach a form of "keeping still agreement" (original in German, translated by author, Hagen, 1983) with the far left. Over a decade later, militant neo-Nazis and National Bolshevists would even create their own organization devoted entirely to creating a joint front between the far right and far left: the "Combat Federation of German Socialists" (Kampfbund Deutscher Sozialisten, or KDS), active between 1999 and 2008. The leadership of the KDS included active neo-Nazis and communists but never managed to gather more than a few dozen members (BMI, 2000, p. 38). Nevertheless, some contemporary analysts and observers feared a vanishing distance between right and left militancy (e.g., Horchem, 1988).

Interestingly, such ideological hybrids that might act as intermediaries between otherwise mutually hostile positions (e.g., "National Communism," "National Bolshevism" – see also the case of Herbert Crüger in the Preface of this book) also exist today and in countries other than Germany. In Sweden, a political party called "Framåt Sverige" (Forward Sweden) brings together former neo-Nazis and communists in a position dubbed "left nationalism" and features classical left-wing political goals (e.g., anti-capitalism or a stop to privatization) next to typical far-right topics (e.g., ending immigration and anti-multiculturalism). One of the group's leading members is former neo-Nazi and convicted bank robber Christopher Karlsson (formerly John Christopher Rangne, who was active in the right-wing terrorist group White Aryan Resistance). Within a short report about the group by the Swedish anti-fascist magazine *Expo*, Karlsson is quoted with stating his motives to shift toward the left: "I left the political direction you are referring to 25 years ago, a quarter of a century. I left this because I had found a different political orientation. A direction that made it impossible to continue in the circles then, i.e. a distancing ... When I saw that there was an alternative that sprang from the left, I chose to get involved again" (original in Swedish, translated by author, Vergara, 2020).

Moving back to the storyline of Christine and Klaus Dieter Hewicker, as well as the far left's lack of welcoming support for their ideological shift, one must differentiate between those attempts by active neo-Nazis to collaborate with far-left groups and actual side-switching from the extreme right. It is clear that the *taz*, for example, saw the Hewickers' declaration as part of a far-right strategy and not as true defection. In consequence, the hoped for positive echo from the far left remained absent (Rosen, 1989, p. 72). On their own side, however, Christine Hewicker and her husband received quite enthusiastic but negative responses: "over this and my husband's declaration ... our former comrades were furious. Michael Kühnen talked about 'mean treason' and others simply found it 'sickening'" (original in German, translated by author, Hewicker, 2001, p. 113). The Hewickers remained isolated from their old group and found no acceptance in the new one. In her continuing storyline, Christine Hewicker describes that she increasingly felt hopeless as well as betrayed by the judiciary, resulting in an unsuccessful suicide attempt in 1984. In the same year, she also decided to move away from extremist lifestyle and activism, which set her on a collision course with her husband. In November 1984, Klaus Dieter Hewicker wrote to his wife in a letter that he wanted a divorce, which was legally completed in December 1985 (Hewicker, 2001, pp. 130–132). Surprisingly, her exchange of letters with a judge and prosecutor, which was quite combative at times, evolved into friendships over time, which significantly helped her deradicalization process. After release from prison, she found a new partner, vocational training, and job. Still using the name Hewicker, Christine wrote in her autobiography in 2001:

Still I stand by the complete content of my trial declaration from June 23, 1983, although today I do not have any radical thoughts against German judges, prosecutors and politicians anymore and do not want to fight with my life for it. I have realized by now, that violence is not the right way to remove injustices. With every piece of my heart I still stand behind the Palestinian people and suffer with every injustice that is being done to them. I felt and still feel somehow aligned with the Palestinians and campaign for these humiliated people robbed of their homes whenever possible. After all, I think I can achieve through defensive argumentation that the ignorant and disinterested Germans start thinking critically about the situation in the Middle East and that they do not see the Arab people as primitive. (original in German, translated by author, Hewicker, 2001, p. 194)

As has been mentioned in Christine Hewicker's autobiography, she and her husband were not the only right-wing terrorists moving toward left-wing international anti-imperialism at the time. Particularly important additional cases are those of Odfried Hepp and Walther Kexel, already briefly mentioned. During the early 1980s, the "Hepp-Kexel" cell became one of the most active and militant right-wing terrorist groups in Germany (Koehler, 2016a, p. 206). Odfried Hepp was born in 1958 and experienced the divorce of his parents in 1971 at the age of 13. One year before, in 1970, Hepp had already become a member of a neo-Nazi youth organization where he radicalized to the point of full-scale commitment and devotion to National Socialism. After completing his high school degree (Abitur) in 1977, he served in the German military. At the same time, he transferred to the more extreme right-wing "Wiking Youth" organization (founded in 1952 and banned in 1994), where he advanced to leadership positions.

A short-lived attempt to achieve a university degree in construction engineering was ended by a pretrial detention spanning from late 1979 to early 1980, as well as a looming prison sentence earned for various extreme right-wing crimes Hepp had perpetrated together with his own military sports group (Wehrsportgruppe, a type of far-right paramilitary organization). After his release and waiting for the upcoming trial, Hepp contacted the leader of one of the largest extreme-right military sports groups: Karl Heinz Hoffmann (leader of the Wehrsportgruppe Hoffmann, or WSG). The WSG, which was founded in 1973 and banned in 1980, produced numerous right-wing terrorists responsible for some of the most devastating and deadly attacks in post–Second World War Germany (Koehler, 2016a, p. 235).

To name only one example, on September 26, 1980, former WSG member Gundolf Köhler detonated a bomb at the entrance of the Munich Octoberfest, killing himself and 12 others, with over 200 wounded (Koehler, 2016a, p. 210). Shortly after the WSG had been made illegal, some members left Germany for Lebanon to build a camp there and receive training in insurgency tactics by the PLO (Koehler, 2016a, p. 236). In order to avoid the trial, Hepp and three of his fellow neo-Nazis fled to join the WSG's foreign division in July 1980, where they remained until June 1981. In Lebanon, Hepp and some of his close friends experienced a desperately overwhelmed neo-Nazi group struggling with infighting and mutual violence, lack of morale, and discipline. A first escape attempt was intercepted by Palestinian militants. Hepp and other escapees were repeatedly tortured in the following interrogations.

When he finally made it back to Germany, he was immediately arrested and sentenced to 16 months in prison. He was released early in December 1981, after which he met his later coconspirator, Walther Kexel (born in 1961, committed suicide in prison after being found guilty of creating a terrorist organization in 1985). Both formed a clandestine militant extreme right-wing cell, which took shape in late 1982 and included a total of six members. The group used bank robberies (five in total) to raise funds for weapons, cars, and hideouts. Their main target was the US military presence in Germany, which the group targeted with at least 11 explosive attacks between October and December 1982.

During the peak of the "Hepp-Kexel" group's terrorist activities, the two leaders had already begun to develop a new ideological reasoning and strategic concept (Hewicker, 2001, p. 58), which they put down in a short pamphlet entitled "Farewell to Hitlerism." The text was published by the left-wing *taz* newspaper together with the alleged declaration of Christine and Klaus Dieter Hewicker on the same page in April 1984. It read:

Farewell to Hitlerism. This declaration became necessary because in "national" circles people were talking nonsense about us on an ever-increasing scale. With this explanation, we now bid farewell not only to Hitlerism, but also to all bourgeois manifestations of nationalism, as well as to the fascists of the so-called Nazi movement. Hitlerism of 1933–1945 consistently led the German people into the ruin of 1945, in which we are still stuck today ... While in the beginning the NSDAP had very good revolutionary forces, in the course of time they left the "movement" (Otto Strasser, Walther Stennes, Gregor Strasser, etc.), because it more and more exposed itself as a bourgeois Hitler party. While Ernst Niekisch, for example, clearly recognized that the enemy was Western bourgeois capitalism and not Russian Bolshevism, the NSDAP began to flirt with the West even then. This then led to Hitlerism attempting to court England's friendship in a degrading manner, after it had gained power and the last revolutionaries around Ernst Röhm – without whom Adolf Hitler would never have come to power – were murdered ... After an alliance was reached very quickly with Russia in 1939, they attacked the same on June 22, 1941, probably the most unfortunate day in our history. This "Eastern Campaign" brought unspeakable suffering to the German and Russian people ... Perhaps a few words about historical National Socialism, which we do not equate with Hitlerism. The NS had correct and good starting points, for example in social, family, youth and cultural policy. Thanks to the existing abilities of its leader, Hitlerism succeeded in putting these good points into practice in fragments, and so the people who were enthusiastic about it did not oppose Hitler's subsequent rampage ... We were shocked to discover that the extreme right has slipped more and more into a Hitler cult, which differs from other sects or religions only in that it does not yet slaughter sacrificial animals and fogs itself with incense. Anyone who still thinks Adolf Hitler is our leader and Chancellor of the Reich today can only be advised not to call such unrealistic nonsense politics, but to create some kind of church community in which one can then exchange and worship the relics – Jesus Christ, the cross, the Bible, etc. – for Adolf Hitler, the swastika, "Mein Kampf." This is above all an appeal to young comrades who are still searching to not submit to the dogma of Hitlerism, but to question it critically, as we, who were once caught up in this narrow-mindedness, have done too. Just like Hitlerism, we strongly condemn bourgeois nationalism, which is once again flirting with the bourgeois West or even openly calling for an alliance with it. In the meantime, we can be glad that there is a wall through Germany, because it guarantees that there are still 17 million healthy Germans in the eastern part of our country, while here the people are dying mentally and emotionally. These two anomalies of nationalism are joined by the third, that of Nazi and uniform fetishism. We don't want to talk about this one, because whoever builds up a fetish because of his personal desire for satisfaction and lack of consciousness for his personality is not to be taken seriously politically. Therefore, it must be said that these three bad habits of nationalism do more harm than good for the real cause of our people, the anti-imperialist liberation struggle. We do not doubt that there are still good, revolutionary forces in this scene, but this does not change our fundamental rejection. Our aim is not to turn back the wheel of history and reestablish a Hitler-style state, but to conduct an undogmatic liberation struggle that will ensure the survival of our people. In this struggle against Americanism, we are in favor of everyone who, like us, has realised that only when the activist youth, who exist in left and right circles, overcome their dogmas and join together in the struggle for liberation, do we stand a chance. Of course, we also welcome foreign anti-imperialists living in Germany who want to take part in our struggle. Finally, we would like to emphasize once again that we are neither "right" nor "left" and we do not want to turn Germany into either an American federal state or another Soviet republic. We do not consider a system that suits Russia to be transferable to our country. But we do not underestimate the anti-bourgeois-capitalist thrust of Bolshevism and it is our wish and will to live as a neutral Germany in peace and friendship with Soviet Russia. We have tried to remain as objective and unemotional as possible in this declaration, although this was not always easy given our boundless contempt for a large part of the Right. In this sense – forward in the anti-imperialist liberation struggle! (original in German, translated by author, Hepp & Kexel, 1983)

The publication of this short manifesto authored by some of the most wanted right-wing terrorists caused a small sensation in the German public. The left-wing milieu, however, remained unimpressed and no significant positive or negative reactions to this call for a united struggle are known. On the contrary, just a couple of months before the publication of the Hepp-Kexel manifesto, far-left leaflets had furiously called out against the fascist "Guerilla Diffusa," fearing that their goals might be blurred with those of the neo-Nazis and that attacks could be perpetrated in the name of anti-imperialism that the extreme left could not justify through their own propaganda (Fromm, 1998, p. 377).

But was the public statement by Hepp and Kexel a genuine ideological move toward the far left or rather a strategic attempt to gain support from other militants without giving up their core values? It is impossible to tell for Walther Kexel, but at least Odfried Hepp left some information in that regard. In a 2004 authorized biography written by psychologist Yuri Winterberg and journalist Jan Peter (Winterberg & Peter, 2004) based on extensive interviews with Hepp and his family, the experience in Lebanon is presented as the key in a seemingly true ideological defection. While sitting in a Palestinian prison after his first escape attempt and being tortured for information, Hepp started to reflect upon his glorification of the Holocaust and suddenly imagined himself in the position of those forced into the concentration camps (Winterberg & Peter, 2004, p. 112). However, Hepp does not develop a hatred against his captors, something his racist and neo-Nazi ideology could have easily led to, especially directed against foreigners and Arabs. Instead, something of a respect for the discipline and commitment of the Palestinians grew within him. Hepp began to realize that the German neo-Nazis in Lebanon are merely playing tough:

even though Odfried has not yet abdicated his neo-Nazi ideals, Lebanon has changed him. For example, the military sports group, led by Leroy Paul [a fellow neo-Nazi], drives with jeeps through a close Palestinian refugee camp ... A year ago, Odfried would have shrugged this off. Now he is ashamed. None of them have really experienced war, while the Palestinians have suffered civil war, bombardments, displacement, and camp life for decades. (original in German, translated by author, Winterberg & Peter, 2004, pp. 134–135)

Back in Germany, the vanishing respect for the wannabe right-wing guerrillas continues to drive an ideological wedge between Hepp and the far-right milieu:

Indeed, he [Hepp] makes the experience that the insights he gained in Lebanon meet deaf ears among the Müllers [a neo-Nazi couple hiding Hepp after his return] and their various guests. Racist blindness and glowing hatred against anything even sounding left wing unites them even though they also have differences. Hepp on the other side diagnoses that with such stubborn fantasts it is not surprising that in Germany there is no effective "patriotic liberation organization" like he still envisions; however now incorporating his knowledge about the Palestinian liberation struggle and enriched through his discussions with left-wing PLO activists – his acquaintance with another worldview. On the one hand still a convinced nationalist, Odfried increasingly recognizes the paltriness and insignificance of the German right-wing scene. His whole circle of friends are right-wing extremists and he does not want to lose them at once, even though they are useless for an organization he has on his mind. (original in German, translated by author, Winterberg & Peter, 2004, pp. 150–151)

Hepp found a like-minded soul searching for new ideological answers in Walther Kexel. Their defection process accelerated in the first half of 1982 and came as a complete surprise for most of their fellow neo-Nazis. In January, Hepp had distributed a leaflet in the far-right milieu glorifying Hitler as a great statesmen (Winterberg & Peter, 2004, p. 165), before executing an astonishing turnaround in public. The biography, however, points out, that the ideological break might indeed not be as fundamental as it appears, since Hepp and Kexel were still operating in an ideological framework between patriotism, socialism, and anti-imperialism, connecting their thoughts to National Bolshevik currents in the extreme right-wing organization they had been members in. In the public declaration "Farewell to Hitlerism," Hepp and Kexel extensively reference Ernst Niekisch and the Strasser brothers, who advocated a joint right–left front against democracy in the Weimar Republic in the early years of the Nazi movement.

Hepp, according to the biography, was dreaming of a "German variant of the PLO" (original in German, translated by author, Winterberg & Peter, 2004, p. 67) as a revival of the "Black Front" of the 1930s. Note here that Christine and Klaus Dieter Hewicker also switched to using this label in the late phase of their terrorist activities, which is of great importance as it is a direct historical reference to a specific ideological movement in Germany before the Second World War. The "Black Front" was a National Socialist micro party created by Otto Strasser after he had left the NSDAP in July 1930. Together with his brother Gregor Strasser, the two had stood for a strong socialist element within the Nazi movement, which increasingly clashed with Hitler's racist faction (see also Section B2.2 on Richard Scheringer's case for a more detailed discussion). First named "Combat Federation of Revolutionary National Socialists" (Kampfbund revolutionärer Nationalsozialisten, or KGRNS), the new organization held a congress in October 1930 and called for anti-imperialism and collaboration with the Soviet Union. However, the group remained marginal and mainly integrated disillusioned SA members (Schüddekopf, 1960).

By referencing those early Nazis, Hepp and Kexel clearly signaled that they intended to remain ideologically connected to the extreme right. Personally, Odfried Hepp continued to develop a fascination and admiration for the professionalism of left-wing terrorist organization such as the RAF and the "Revolutionary Cells" (Revolutionäre Zellen, or RZ). To advance his goal to "play in the big league," Hepp met with PLO representatives in East Berlin and Garry Adams, the head of the IRA's political arm Sinn Féin, in Ireland to discuss collaborations (Winterberg & Peter, 2004, p. 175). While the first intent of their declaration might have been to maintain some link with the far right, the reactions following its publication showed no sign that this might have been possible. On the contrary, Hepp and Kexel were immediately attacked as traitors in extreme-right leaflets and magazines.

The two reacted in kind and quickly the distance between them and their former milieu became insurmountable (Winterberg & Peter, 2004). The question of treason and constant infighting in the far right was a key issue that drove Hepp and Kexel further toward the left, which in their eyes was free of such quarrels, and such an environment impressed them because the authorities failed to penetrate militant groups such as the RAF for years due to the lack of members willing to defect. A bitter and personal response to "Farewell to Hitlerism" from leading neo-Nazi and Hepp's former idol Michael Kühnen resulted in a public feud with the two, in which they sarcastically wrote (addressing Kühnen): "Your position in charge of the waste heap has the purpose of keeping away unwanted elements from the revolutionary liberation struggle and diverting them toward the historic trash dump to which they belong. We wish you much of success in this important task!" (original in German, translated by author, as cited in Winterberg & Peter, 2004, p. 182).

It is fair to say that a failed side-switching attempt by Hepp and Kexel, as well as the Hewickers, resulted in their ostracism from both sides, leaving not much room to find a new milieu. Walther Kexel is even reported to have begun using the label "anarchist" in the time before his arrest (Winterberg & Peter, 2004, p. 194). At least Odfried Hepp was able to find a new ideological home by first linking up with the East German Stasi and working for them as an informant and operative, beginning in February 1982. It was with their help that he was able to flee looming arrest in February 1983. After hiding for a couple of months in the GDR, the Stasi sent Hepp to Damascus in Syria, aiming to use him for international tasks. However, Hepp decided to liberate himself from Stasi control and moved on to Tunisia, where he joined the Palestinian Liberation Front (PLF) and managed to gain a leadership position in it.

His new task for the PLF was to establish a network of weapons depots in France for potential terrorist attacks, so he moved to Marseilles in May 1984. Astonishingly, Hepp remained in touch with the Stasi, which seemed to not have taken an issue with his independent actions. In fact, now the Stasi could gather information from the inside of Palestinian terror groups through Hepp (on the quite extraordinary collaboration between Hepp and the Stasi, see Blumenau, 2020). Finally, Hepp was arrested on April 8, 1985, in Paris. He served two years in a French prison before being extradited to Germany, where he was again tried and convicted in October 1987. He was sentenced to another ten and a half years in prison, which he left in December 1993.

The side-switching storylines from Christine and Klaus Dieter Hewicker, as well as Odfried Hepp, are part of a short-lived attempt by right-wing terrorists in the 1980s to benefit from the much superior organizational skills of left-wing terrorist groups such as the RAF. In addition, a global uptick in post-colonial ethno-separatist insurgencies and terrorist groups also impacted the militant far right in Germany and Europe. The most prominent international terrorist groups at that time were both decidedly nationalist and anti-imperialist out of historical necessity. During the height of the Cold War, national liberation struggles almost automatically aligned with the East–West clash of political systems and left-wing anti-imperialist Marxism provided a very effective way to ensure political support against the old colonial powers from their opponents on the communist side.

Ideologically, this anti-imperialism also formed a natural basis to justify violence against those perceived as illegitimate oppressors. For some German and European neo-Nazi terrorists, the combination of nationalism and anti-imperialism came as a natural advancement for their own cause, especially since they saw Germany as a territory occupied by the Allied Forces. Anti-Americanism and anti-Zionism almost automatically resulted from the virulent anti-Semitism in the extreme right-wing milieu. Framing their cause as part of the global liberation struggle against Western capitalist imperialism and quasi-colonialism in Germany opened a completely new strategic and tactical angle for the far right. For some neo-Nazis, the perspective of ethno-separatist liberation became an even more convincing ideological concept than their previous positions based on now obsolete and antiquated revisions of classical Nazism.

Interestingly, anti-Zionism as a potential bridge to extreme right-wing anti-Semitism featured only marginally in the Hewickers' and Hepp's storylines. While still present in Christine Hewicker's trial declaration, it was completely absent in the material send to the *taz* newspaper, as well as Hepp and Kexel's "Farewell to Hitlerism." Those storylines are rare examples of comparatively well-documented failed side-switching attempts. Naturally, if an extremist is unsuccessful in joining the opposite milieu, publicizing this has little value, especially if the outcome is to remain in or rejoin the former in-group. The German far right mostly rejected the strategic attempts to form an alliance with the extreme left by Hewicker and Hepp and responded with open hostility. The far left on the other side interpreted these approaches as a simple strategic disguise that even created a risk of alienating its own support base. It seems that the Hewickers and Hepp chose a pathway of public declarations and discourse with the left-wing milieu to present their new positions, without securing any backup in the new environment they targeted. Overall, their side-switching attempts were ill-conceived. They had little to offer to the far left, which was in a clearly superior and much more powerful position regarding the generally recognized quality of organization, militancy, and commitment. In addition, the timing of approaching the extreme left from their position was unfavorable, since a couple of other dedicated neo-Nazis had already begun to strategically court the left without showing any signs of significantly moving away from their core beliefs.

3.2   Ray Hill

Ray Hill is one of the cases of far-right extremist activists who got involved with anti-fascist work. Hill, who detailed his life in an autobiography in 1988 (Hill & Bell, 1988), was born in 1939 in in Mossley, Lancashire, Great Britain. Before entering the extreme right in the late-1960s by joining Colin Jordan's neo-Nazi "British Movement" (BM), he served in the armed forces for three years and worked in various unskilled labor jobs. Hill describes this time in his life as "miserable" with an increasing conviction that "people like myself were suffering as a direct result of immigration into this country" (Hill & Bell, 1988, p. 26). Via newspaper advertisement, Hill learned about the "Anti-Immigration Society" (AIMS) and joined it first, before moving on to the closely connected but more radical "Racial Preservation Society" (RPS). In his words "The RPS, if nothing else, appeared radical, and addressed itself directly to what I felt was the big issue . . . the RPS came across as an organization of people with conviction – clear sighted, committed and courageous" (Hill & Bell, 1988, p. 31).

Hill got into direct contact with the "National Socialist Movement" (NSM), which was later rebranded into the BM, through a booklet written by Colin Jordan about a global Jewish conspiracy. Immensely impressed by Jordan's personality, he made a third move toward more extremist positions and joined his group, quickly becoming the organizer of the local Leicester chapter in 1968 and Jordan's election campaign agent in 1969. This marked the first peak of his ideological conviction: "I threw myself totally and enthusiastically into the heart of things. I was an organizer, a leader, an orator, totally committed to the national socialist ideology I had embraced" (Hill & Bell, 1988, p. 21).

After a violent altercation at the end of that year, Hill was charged with assault and actual bodily harm. Together with his wife and two-year-old daughter the young family decided to emigrate to South Africa before Hill was due to appear in court.

Living and working in apartheid South Africa became a first opportunity for disengagement for Hill, albeit a rather involuntary one. Simply by being away from the British far-right scene and getting a new job to provide for his family, a somewhat natural distancing process took place. Around 1974, Hill realized that "I had been out of active politics for a few years. I had not really missed it, I must admit, and I suppose in some respects, by South African standards, I had mellowed just a little. Not exactly a liberal, I was nevertheless not the hard-line Nazi who had packed his bags and quit Leicester for years earlier" (Hill & Bell, 1988, p. 48). However, after an accident left him struggling to find work without any form of social welfare support, Hill again entered a period of frustration and grievances. "I did resent bitterly the position in which I and my family now found ourselves. For all the calamities which had been visited upon us ... we had received no help at all ... hearts seemed to be bleeding profusely for the 'poor, oppressed black' in the townships" (Hill & Bell, 1988, p. 48).

Not surprisingly, this state of mind and emotion led to reengagement with far-right extremism. In 1978, Hill writes, "I dipped my toe, a little hesitantly at first, back into the waters of racist politics" (Hill & Bell, 1988, p. 48). His group of choice became the South African branch of the "British National Front" (BNF) – the "Herstigte National Party" (HNP) – which was running mainly on a platform of fiercely opposing any attempt to reform apartheid and return to a more just and equal society. At first writing articles for the main HNP propaganda outlet, Hill again ventured on to a more extreme organization: the "South African National Front" (SANF). Within that group, he even reached the level of chairman and used his experiences from his time with the BM to orchestrate various publicity stunts and rallies. However, this is also the point in Ray Hill's storyline where his commitment to the extreme right-wing cause began to collapse once and for all.

The first blow to his devotion and social identity as a member of the SANF was dealt to Hill's ego by the simple perception of lack of trust and power. Even though he was chairman of the organization, Hill describes as frustrating that "I had not actually been involved in the decision to begin this particular campaign. That's not to say that I disagreed with it, but I did feel just a little put out at having been excluded from the discussions in the party leadership which preceded it" (Hill & Bell, 1988, p. 58). A significant mismatch between a member's claimed status and influence on the one hand and the actual power attached to the position on the other is an often-cited reason to become disillusioned with a group. Frustration about this lack of actual status within the group continued to gnaw on Hill when other factors began to reinforce his distancing process too.

> Increasingly, certain matters were being discussed in a tightly-knit little caucus which seemed to be operating like some secretive cell . . . I became increasingly persuaded that I was regarded as something of a useful idiot: making the speeches, and fronting for the party, but being kept deliberately in the dark by a group of very sinister individuals who were now firmly in control. (Hill & Bell, 1988, p. 61)

As described by terrorism researcher Julie Hwang (2015) through the concept of "reinforcement loops," Hill's experience of not being awarded with the influence and recognition he felt the position of chairman deserved, created a form of cognitive opening in which other external factors were consciously and subconsciously taken in to support that initial disillusionment; a process we have come to know as information bias (see Chapter 1). We can clearly see how Hill was impacted by cognitive dissonance through his chairman position in which he represented the group with conviction on the outside (behavioral level), while at the same time feeling left out and disrespected from the group itself, which eroded commitment (attitudinal level). This tension eventually had to be remedied but at first, Hill continued playing something of a role. Albeit feeling devalued within the group's leadership, he continued to "staunchly" (Hill & Bell, 1988, p. 58) defend what the SANF was doing to the press and public. The second and definitive impact on Hill's conviction came in the form of specific incident with significant emotional repercussions. Together with his daughter, he drove to the Hillbrow district of Johannesburg for a social visit with some family friends. After an enjoyable and relaxed time, he decided to stop for ice cream at a small café on the way home. It is enlightening to consider Hill's description of the following event in full:

> Directly opposite our pavement table was a truly pathetic-looking Indian family, squatting at the roadside with what few possessions they owned tied up in bundles of blankets. Wandering across the road I asked the husband what the problem was. When he replied that they had been evicted by police from the house they had been living in for the last year, and that the police had blamed the NF, I felt a knot tighten in my guts. How on earth could I begin to tell him that I was responsible for what had happened to him? On one level I wanted to show my sympathy for this poor family, stuck out here in the streets with nowhere in the world to go, but this simple human response was ruled out by the knowledge that I was to blame for their predicament. I muttered something unintelligible, dragged my daughter away from her ice-cream and, almost literally, fled from Hillbrow feeling thoroughly ashamed. Of one thing I was suddenly sure: never again could I be party to visiting such misery on human beings. It would be difficult enough now living with the consequences of what I had already done, and I could not ever contemplate adding to it. My days as a racist were over. (Hill & Bell, 1988, pp. 58–59)

This direct confrontation with the consequences of Hill's actions spreading the SANF agenda was intensified once he arrived back home and remembered a very similar story of a family's eviction reported in the local press. In this news piece, Hill was quoted as a representative of the extreme right-wing party he chaired in defense of that action. His immediate highly emotional reaction was: "Utterly disgusted with myself, I threw the paper into a corner and went to bed" (Hill & Bell, 1988, p. 60). A third development next to the frustration of lacking influence and the emotional shock from the confrontation with the consequences of his involvement had also taken its toll on Hill's ideological convictions and commitment to the far right. In the months prior to the Hillbrow encounter, Hill describes how he had "strange as it may seem, already established friendships with a couple of Jewish chaps who had been extremely kind to my family and myself when times had been hard" (Hill & Bell, 1988, p. 60).

Even though these newfound friends new about Hill's political positions, they did not seem to hold any negative feelings against him. Ray Hill reflects quite clearly upon the dynamic interaction between all three factors. The friendship with members of the Jewish community had "softened" Hill's beliefs that "other races – especially Jews – were the enemy of whites" but in itself it did not lead to any "blinding light revelations" (Hill & Bell, 1988, p. 60). What was needed for the slowly decreasing commitment to the group to manifest was a traumatizing event: "The catalyst was that Sunday afternoon in Hillbrow, which left me shaken, confused and ashamed. At home I was broody and preoccupied that fateful Sunday evening, and eventually I knew that I could not live with myself if I carried on as before. 'No, it's over,' I decided" (Hill & Bell, 1988, p. 60). Around the same time, Hill's wife was pressing for a return to England as the economic situation of the family was not improving. With all that had happened, the decision was made to leave South Africa.

Ray Hill's storyline up to this point explains why he decided to disengage from the extreme right, but it does not shed light on why he eventually came to work with the far left against his former peers. He could have easily walked away and began a new life after his arrival in Great Britain. At this critical juncture in his life, pondering whether to leave this environment for good, Hill reflects on his options:

I could, of course, have simply walked quietly away, telling the party I wanted no more to do with it. Or I could have gone in for some public recantation which would, no doubt, have had some damaging effect on the Front, even if only in the short term. But preying on my mind was the conviction that just getting out would do little to repair the damage that I now knew I had inflicted on innocent victims, almost certainly from the day that I had first been baptized into the world of the extreme right. Most of this would never be known to me – perhaps that is what makes such extremism so easy to settle into.

For all the time you spend propagandizing, issuing inflammatory leaflets, or organizing provocative demonstrations, you are rarely around to appreciate the consequences. The seed of hate which you plant in someone's mind may only come to fruition years later, when its lineage to your own contribution has been well obscured by time and intervening events. And, while you are located firmly on the fringes, you rarely see any direct consequences of your campaigns for policies rooted in racism and national socialism. In that respect, Hillbrow was out of the ordinary: I was directly confronted with the dreadful playing out of events which I had had a hand in shaping. I had met a family which I had thrown into the streets, and I knew there were probably many, many more. Hillbrow was only the result of my most recent efforts: what of the possible consequences of the previous ten years of political activism? It was not enough, now, simply to walk away, shamed or otherwise. Something in the way of reparation was called for. Weighing up the risks to myself and to my family, I decided to stay on, acting out the role of dedicated racist demagogue, but using any information to which this gave me access against the Front. (Hill & Bell, 1988, pp. 61–62)

In Ray Hill's storyline, a moral obligation to damage his former in-group directly followed his emotional state of shame, guilt, and frustration that had been caused by a combination of internal mistrust, positive contacts with out-group members deemed as enemies, and a confrontation with the suffering his actions had brought to others. In short, Hill wanted to make good on his past mistakes. In the six months before the Hill family departed back to England, he passed on internal information to leading members of the Jewish community that helped them to arrange opposition and counter-measures against SANF activities. It is of great importance in Hill's storyline that he describes how this double life activity actually provided a sense of purpose and feelings of relief: "I must admit, although I had to keep up an appearance of being angry and outraged, that inside I was crowing with delight" (Hill & Bell, 1988, p. 65).

Ray Hill returned to Leicester in 1980 where he renewed his membership in the British Movement. After his first taste of working as a spy to damage the extreme right, he continued to look for ways to do so in the United Kingdom, even though more emotionally draining experiences increased his desire to disengage completely. One of such incidents involved other members of the extreme right whom Hill associated with ranting about how they would "rape little Jewish girls" (Hill & Bell, 1988, p. 88) once they had taken over political power. In particular, Hill decided that it was his moral obligation to thwart specific plans for establishing a foothold by the neo-Nazi "British Democratic Party" (BDP) led by lawyer and former National Front chief legal adviser Anthony Reed Herbert. Hill knew well about the anti-fascist magazine *Searchlight*, which regularly exposed extreme-right activities and activists. Interestingly, Hill's storyline connects his explanation of why he decided to pass on inside information to *Searchlight* to his emotional disgust of Anthony Herbert, who was furiously angry about the magazine's reporting, because he knew that "these were the people who could make best use of the information which came my way" (Hill & Bell, 1988, pp. 92–93).

Marking the beginning of Hill's activity for *Searchlight* as a mole in the extreme right, an information cache he passed on to the magazine via telephone was initially intended to be a one-time activity. He wanted this to be the "last modest fling before I slipped away from politics and resumed a normal family life" (Hill & Bell, 1988, pp. 92–93). However, Hill was asked by his *Searchlight* contact to meet up in person and get to know each other. At first, the question about his identity became a matter of debate, but eventually Hill decided to reveal who he was. He informed the *Searchlight* person introduced as "Derek" that no more information was to come from him. At a second meeting a couple of weeks later, Derek "very gently approached the subject" of Hill's future intentions with "consummate skill" (Hill & Bell, 1988, p. 94). During the unfolding conversation, he was probed intensively about his moral obligations and viewpoints on Searchlight's methods with a very clear direction:

By the time I realized where his line of questioning was leading, the outcome was really a foregone conclusion. If my assessment of Reed Herbert and the BDP was accurate, and if I was truly opposed to what he was trying to do, then perhaps, given the unique opportunities open to me, I had something of a duty (although Derek avoided using such a strong word) to stay with him and exploit my connection. (Hill & Bell, 1988, p. 94)

In short, Ray Hill was recruited into *Searchlight*'s activities by a charismatic and skilled member who used Hill's state of mind – his feelings of guilt and shame – to strengthen the perception of a moral obligation. Again, the personal positive contact with an out-group member ideologically defined as the enemy became the key in Hill's storyline of side-switching. Later in the process, social-identity rewards became an essential motive to continue with leading this risky and exhausting double life:

Many times, I am convinced, I would have been on the verge of cracking up had I not had the support and encouragement of my friends and colleagues at Searchlight. Often, when things were bearing down particularly hard, I travelled to London to meet one or two of them just for a few sociable hours away from the madhouse world I had involved myself in. Over a few drinks, we would chat about cricket, or our families, or any of the million or so ordinary things that other people can chat about whenever they fell so inclined, without having, as I did in my usual company, to make sure every conversation was peppered with pejorative references to blacks or Jews. The batteries recharged, I would return to Leicester refreshed and throw myself once again into the fray. (Hill & Bell, 1988, p. 94)

Guided by *Searchlight*, Hill would provoke internal conflicts within the extreme-right movement and pass on information leading to several police investigations for planned acts of violence. Ray Hill revealed himself to be a mole in 1984 in a media documentary that focused on the links between the British far right and international terrorism. His revelations about various terrorist plots and national as well as international connections caused widespread confusion and shock in the far-right scene. After his public outing, Hill became a regular columnist for *Searchlight*.

3.3   Tim Hepple

As the second informant of the anti-fascist magazine *Searchlight* in the United Kingdom who detailed his story of involvement in the extreme right and side-switching, Tim Hepple followed in the footsteps of Ray Hill. It should be pointed out upfront, that Hepple's case is somewhat controversial as to his true motives and actions in the far right and during his involvement in other milieus afterward. Some argue that Hepple was nothing but an agent provocateur creating backlash against the left-wing environment (O'Hara, 1996, pp. 18–19). For the topic and focus of this book, his true intentions are less important than the storyline presented to justify the side-switching. While *Searchlight* magazine might have received strong criticism from other parts of the far left, the publication still remains one of the most important anti-fascist sources of information on the extreme right. Working with *Searchlight* would be considered an act of treason within the far right in any case, even though other more militant left-wing groups might have existed or still exist.

During his far-right career, Hepple helped infiltrate the headquarters of the extreme-right British National Party (BNP) the National Front, and witnessed the creation of the right-wing terrorist group Combat 18. His own involvement in that milieu resulted from soccer hooliganism. In the 1980s, he was a hooligan at the Reading football club at first. By 1983, he had developed an interest in politics that circled around opposition against the nuclear disarmament campaign, anti-communism, and the desire to be part of an elite (Hepple & Gable, 1993, p. 1). In August 1984, his parents, who were teachers, moved to Lancashire and while Hepple was studying in a library in Lancaster, he came across a copy of the paper *Nationalism Today*, one of the National Front's (NF) official publications. The magazine "greatly impressed" (Hepple & Gable, 1993, p. 1) him and after writing to the NF leadership he increasingly immersed himself in far-right propaganda. Hepple joined the National Front (NF) the same year.

However, in 1986 he won a scholarship to the Royal College of Music in Glasgow and moved to Scotland. This indicates that Hepple was certainly not the stereotypical extreme right-wing activist, as he managed at least for some time to follow interests and professional networks outside of his extremist milieu. After his arrival in Glasgow, Hepple not only changed his soccer club affiliation (to Glasgow Rangers) but also his far-right group association with the BNP. This came about by pure coincidence when after a Loyalist rally Hepple "bumped into" (Hepple & Gable, 1993, p. 2) two leading BNP members who were selling their own extreme-right magazine. He was invited to socialize with them and quickly integrated into the very active Glasgow BNP division, which at the time received little far-left opposition (Hepple & Gable, 1993, p. 2).

During violent clashes around BNP rallies elsewhere, Hepple experienced the difference between the BNP and the NF and found the latter to be lacking discipline and organization. Much of his recollections reflect a time of rivalry and conflict between the NF and the BNP, which can also be found in the case studies of Ray Hill and Matthew Collins in this chapter. Led by John Tyndall (1934–2005, chairman of the BNP from 1982–1999), the BNP was arguing that open promotion of Nazism would be counterproductive to finding new recruits and achieving meaningful societal impact. Tyndall, who had also led the NF before and left in conflict, was a controversial figure in the British far right, as many extremists did not support the "soft" course of his BNP. However, the NF was more or less defunct at that time and this internal rivalry created much of a paralysis for the overall milieu.

Regarding his own motivations to join the far right in the first place, Hepple remembers:

I just wanted to smash the state, to show my anger, to hate somebody. Like many others I was scared about the future and had little respect for myself. I wanted to be part of a gang and I really enjoyed slagging people off and getting in fights. The BNP provided me with some sense of identity and belonging. To some extent I fell for the idea that Nazism was an extreme form of opposition to the government. The BNP was the vehicle for expressing hatred and violence. By late 1986 I thought myself to be a hard-line national socialist with little interest in plain old nationalism. Every time I heard a Hitler speech I virtually lost control. I don't know exactly what it was – the tone of voice, the power, the spectacle? He certainly held a tremendous fascination for me. (Hepple & Gable, 1993, p. 3)

In December 1986 Hepple left Glasgow and went back to England. He continued his studies of music at Sheffield University in 1987 while at the same time being a prominent BNP activist in Leeds, where he tried to recruit new followers to the cause with a focus on soccer club supporters. In Sheffield, Hepple encountered a much more organized and active anti-fascist resistance to the far right. Despite his attempt to complete a university degree, Hepple did not shy away from violence and organized an attack on a meeting of left-wing students at his school. He also experienced the effects of internal quarrels within the far right, for example, during a meeting involving John Tyndall, who anxiously defended himself against criticism of not being a real Nazi. Among other incidents, this left Hepple disillusioned with the BNP:

More than anything else, this incident showed me what a pile of backstabbing scum BNP "loyalists" really were ... Things were never the same after this ... These and other developments between late 1987 and mid 1988 served only to shatter my faith in the BNP and the whole movement in general. From September 1987 to June 1988, I travelled to rallies the length and breadth of the country, spending hundreds of pounds. The demands on activists were high. (Hepple & Gable, 1993, p. 8)

At first, the disillusionment did not stop his commitment to the milieu, even though this placed high financial costs upon him. In addition, Hepple also experienced violent attacks by anti-fascists, which also did not deter him in any way. On the contrary:

I was attacked by two masked anti-fascists with clubs and ended up in hospital with six stitches in the back of my head, a badly damaged left leg, a broken or bent nose and a neck brace. This attack in no way deterred me. It redoubled my will to fight and led me from then on to vary my route home, vary daily routine and go more "underground". I took to stickering at two and three in the morning, sometimes walking miles, and pushing leaflets under the windscreen wipers of stationery cars. In addition, I carried an acid-type spray in an old Windolene squirter bottle and a large iron bar. They weren't going to catch me again. They never did either. (Hepple & Gable, 1993, p. 8)

Starting at the end of 1988, Hepple began working with another infamous British neo-Nazi, Eddy Morrison, to revitalize support for the BNP in his region. Morrison, who suffered from manic depression, was shunned by many in the far right. Hepple, on the other hand, developed a close friendship with him and found their meaningful relationship gratifying:

I felt as if I was doing some good for somebody at last and positive emotions began to take a hold ... Experiences like this were enough to convince me that there was a lot more to Morrison than met the eye. I began to see things in terms of people being victims of capitalism or at least a system which ground people down and took away their respect. National socialism and "survival of the fittest" may have a certain credibility, but would it not be possible for people to cooperate and share their problems, find the answers? Eddy continued to drift in and out and I continued to play a cat and mouse game with him, trying to hide his alcohol ... although I was supposed to be a hardened national socialist, I found myself revolted at this spectacle [of Morrison telling new recruits made up horror stories about minorities]. It just stopped me in my tracks and made me realise that for years I had not thought about what I was doing or the effect my activities might be having on others. When you're in the movement you and your "comrades" poison each other's minds with hatred on a day to day basis and you are so active that you just get on with the job in hand without thinking. Because you close your mind off to all other options, you cannot envisage life without the movement; you just do not imagine the possibilities of any other way of life. (Hepple & Gable, 1993, p. 13)

Very much like the other defectors from the far right to the far left discussed in this chapter, Hepple experienced the impact of meaningful personal relationships in combination with a direct confrontation regarding his own close-mindedness. He witnessed how his comrade Eddy made up stories about minorities to radicalize new recruits. Hepple must have realized that many of the narratives he believed in might have originated in the same way. In his side-switching narrative, these two factors (feeling of gratification from helping his friend and realizing he had potentially been lied to) formed the first cracks in his conviction and commitment. In the following months, Hepple pursued his intellectual curiosity on the issues about which he had so far blindly believed the far-right narrative. He also openly began exploring other ideologies and reflecting on their value from his own standpoints. Nevertheless, a change of personal environment and additional experiences he had in real life substantially facilitated the process:

You can only stay a nazi [*sic!*] by blocking out all other options, beliefs and ideologies. Unfortunately for the BNP and fortunately for me I began to read books in the Independent bookshop in Sheffield as well as radical gree, socialist and anarchist publications. My interest in the green movement developed at this time – late 1988 to early 1989. I had already rejected all forms of Marxism as no better than fascism. There were equally high body counts in the USSR and Nazi Germany. Although many Marxist[s] condemned Stalin, a basic look at Trotsky showed me another bloodthirsty butcher who murdered millions of peasants, "white Russians" and opponents between 1918 and 1924 in his role as Red Army leader. Marxist[s] in general were just as dogmatic and unthinking as the BNP, it seemed to me, opposite sides of the same coin. Living at home in the countryside helped as well. I got a feeling of inner peace and contentment out in the sticks "in harmony with nature". I ready a number of books about green issues ... I also read a lot of Third Position stuff that I picked up from Glen Taylor in Leeds. At Christmas 1988 during the holiday a girl in my village was going out with a black guy. Despite everything, I couldn't think of one good reason why they shouldn't go out together. In this tranquil setting race theory just seemed plain stupid. Early in 1989 I set of for an organisers' conference at the new BNP HQ in Welling. On the way down I remember reading Mein Kampf and looking for answers to my objections. There weren't any, but during the conference I got carried right back into things. The ties were not yet ready to break. When you've given years of your life to a cause in such a fanatical way, it's remarkably difficult to believe or admit that you have been terribly wrong. Late 1988 to early 1989 was the beginning of certain doubts, which came around mainly because of the sick characters that inhabited the BNP and associated groups. (Hepple & Gable, 1993, p. 13)

Interestingly, one can recognize elements from Richard Scheringer's story-line (see Section B2.2) in the narrative of Time Hepple. Both began looking for specific ideological questions in the core fundamentals of their extreme-right milieus, only to find none. Furthermore, in what is a textbook example of describing cognitive dissonance (facing the prospect of acknowledging one's own error is harder than to continue and ignore the doubt), as well as the simple reason to stay involved because of the large amount of resources already invested (Rusbult's investment model, see Chapter 1), Hepple rationally reflects upon the barriers preventing his defection. Once back among his peers, doubts and feelings of uncertainty quickly vanished. This short but insightful part of Hepple's storyline shows us yet again how important the social environment and peer-group interaction are for extremist milieus in maintaining commitment and mitigating the potential risk of losing members. Failing personal relationships and internal conflicts, however, were impossible to brush away in this way and soon Hepple was reminded about the "sick characters" he had found to be the dominant kind of members in the BNP. One incident followed his participation in a London BNP leadership conference and stands out. Upon his return to Sheffield, Hepple informed his friend Eddy about personally slanderous remarks by Tyndall directed at his comrade. This naturally led to an angry confrontation between Morrison and Tyndall, which, however, caused them to put blame on Hepple:

I don't know what crooked deal the two worked out, but there was obviously a reason for their cooperation in this matter and they turned on the messenger. I was that messenger and the next day I received a vicious call from an enraged Morrison accusing me of working for the Special Branch [UK police] via Garry Gable [editor of the anti-fascist magazine *Searchlight*] ... I was so upset that I cried, not an easy admission to make. Tears of anger at betrayal. Morrison couldn't stand Tyndall one bit and just weeks earlier we'd been planning to overthrow Tyndall in the BNP equivalent of a palace coup. I had helped Morrison during his illness, listened to his deepest psychological problems and secrets. I'd lie for him to BNP comrades. Well, that was it, finished. Now that it came to it I felt really empty and totally alone. The only friends I had were in the BNP and now I'd been dumped. (Hepple & Gable, 1993, pp. 14–15)

Instead of quitting, Hepple still looked for any straws to cling to and wrote an emotional letter to Morrison as "one last chance" (Hepple & Gable, 1993, p. 15). His friend Morrison reacted in a conciliatory manner, but the BNP leadership accused Hepple of deliberate attempts to split the organization and set a tribunal session for a hearing. Afraid that this would only lead to his lynching, Hepple decided to boost his standing in the far-right milieu by invading a left-wing student union meeting. The following brawl received wide press coverage and armed with such indisputable proof of his commitment, Tyndall had no other option but to change course. The fact that he was able to manipulate the far left so easily only increased Hepple's negative attitudes toward them: "After this series of comic events, which reinforced my belief that the reds were pathetic weaklings and that fascism had a psychological effect on them, making them incapable of action, I decided to give the BNP one last go" (Hepple & Gable, 1993, pp. 15–16).

Hepple had missed a chance to break with his milieu, partially because he had experienced the far left to be weak and susceptible to manipulation. The consequence of this, however, was significant, as Hepple increased his involvement with a newly found sense of belonging. He took over a major role in organizing the 1989 far-right rally in Dewsbury, which led to fights with opponents and multiple arrests. For Hepple, the Dewsbury clashes pushed him much deeper into the extreme-right milieu: "I had a tremendous feeling of power and exhilaration leading hundreds of young thugs to the rally site next to the town hall past the police. That day we completely destroyed the opposition, who, like in Bermondsey two years earlier, found that their international Marxist ideologies could not help to explain or stop the tribal hatred of white youths on the rampage ... Whatever happened from now on, I had at least done something infamous" (Hepple & Gable, 1993, p. 17). In the aftermath of the rally, Hepple's friend Morrison suffered a fallback into psychological problems and alcoholism, resulting in "all the energy and good work [going] down the tubes" (Hepple & Gable, 1993, p. 17). The thrill of power and violence was not enough to keep Hepple involved for long. His storyline now reaches the most important turning point:

Tremendous disappointment at the leadership of Tyndall, the character of Eddy Morrison and my disillusionment with nazi [sic!] ideology combined to make me reconsider my whole system of beliefs for the next 12 months. This involved a lot of souls [sic] searching, re-education, reading, confusion and hassle, leading up to a decision to do the right thing and volunteer to help Searchlight ... What had started as a dislike for the assortment of cranks and lunatics inside the BNP had led to a complete hatred for the BNP and its [sic] disgusting nazi [sic!] ideology. It had to be stopped. (Hepple & Gable, 1993, p. 17)

In Hepple's side-switching storyline, internal conflicts in the far-right milieu take a dominant role in the immediate aftermath of developing these doubts in the ideology. This is yet again a classic example for dyadic reinforcement loops described by Hwang (2015), which mean that corresponding push and pull factors involved in deradicalization and disengagement processes strengthen each other. The result of disillusionment and internal conflicts was a substantial deterioration of commitment for Hepple. He left Sheffield after his second year without any perspective or direction for his life. As he was also unemployed, Hepple first joined the military but only found a "cold hard world where the narrow-minded ideas that I thought I supported were fully exposed for what they were" and an organization "that promoted the worst aspects of racist thought and intolerance" (Hepple & Gable, 1993, p. 17). In consequence, Hepple left the military in early 1990 and started working at a local motorway service station until January 1992. It was during that time of reorientation he found a new political interest as well, albeit none that would bring him away from the far-right:

During this period I involved myself in what I considered to be worthwhile causes, especially the local anti-poll tax group in Lancaster, my home area. The potential and possibilities of radical politics were brought home to me at the marvellous poll tax riot of March 1990. I have never seen anything like it. The atmosphere was amazing and I will never forget that day. I tried to open up tentative links with the Third Position, run by Paul Shepherd in Blackpool. I even managed to meet Roberto Fiore, errand boy for Italian terrorist bombers, and Colin "Saddam Hussein" Todd ... It was quite clear that although the Third Position had altered the emphasis in its propaganda and adopted a revolutionary tone, its arguments with the mainstream fascists of the NF and BNP were arguments *within* fascism. For them it was a question of style, content and window dressing. They were still after the Jews, blacks, minorities, etc. *ad nauseam*. (Hepple & Gable, 1993, p. 17, italics in original)

Through Hepple's storyline, one can easily spot the fascination with radical opposition, action, and rebellion. Rather than questioning the overall milieu based on the various negative experiences he had, Hepple was merely shifting to other forms of "radical politics." Hepple became a local spokesperson for the Anti-Tax Poll Union and met "some really decent people" (Hepple & Gable, 1993, p. 17) in the group as well, when the long-term effects of his earlier disillusionment caught up with him. He finally made the decision to contact *Searchlight* and to pass on information to the enemy. His motive for this was a mixture of seeking redemption to calm his own consciousness, clearing his name among anti-fascists, and last but not least revenge against those who had wronged him (in his view):

But something was nagging me. I was sick of both naked and institutionalised racism and intolerance but I felt that this was not enough. For a time I helped out at a night shelter for the homeless in Lancaster, but I felt that my previous activities could not be so easily pushed into the past and forgotten, either by me or by those anti-fascists I had come across during my recent nazi [*sic!*] days. I had heard all about *Searchlight* and as far as I was concerned this was the only organisation that bothered the fascists psychologically or mentally. Of course anti-fascists on the street had bothered me, but you could always evade them, fool them and lose them. *Searchlight* was different and it had an uncanny habit of getting its stories about the extreme right more than 90 per cent correct. I felt like a lost soul in need of a "religious conversion", so I rang *Searchlight* and told the chap on the other and of the phone who I was and said that I wanted to give them any useful information that I could. He had certainly heard of me but was friendly nevertheless ... I wrote *Searchlight* a long letter detailing the various lunatic activities I had been a part of (as if they didn't already know) and some days later I got a phone call form Gerry Gable. This was quite a traumatic experience for me. After all, this was the supposed human incarnation of all evil for the BNP and up to a year before, 1989, I had accepted this unthinking view to some extent. Having said that, I felt a lot better to have talked to somebody who knew, I suspect, just what I as going through and who also knew the sort of sadistic scum who had been part of my life for over seven years. I now felt that I had made up in some small way for my previous activity. (Hepple & Gable, 1993, pp. 17–18, italics in original)

Hepple volunteered to work for *Searchlight* without any monetary compensation (so he says in his narrative). It is not unimportant that he found himself in a perfect position to become a key informant, which provided him with a highly effective bridge of transition to an equal or higher social status. Very tellingly, in his storyline Hepple differentiates between anti-fascist activities such as *Searchlight* and other parts of the far left, such as Marxism. This is a significant aspect for studying side-switchers, as they sometimes continue to make quite detailed separations among the milieu they defect to according to their own goals and motives. Hepple, for example, expresses strong contempt for the Marxist left while at the same time fully supports the anti-fascist left:

> I soon learned that vast sections of the left were "pissing in the wind", but my main disgust was reserved for the specimens of the not so radical Marxist left, who seemed to jump on every bandwagon and talk more dogmatic nonsense than the entire nazi [*sic!*] movement put together. I eventually found a home of sorts in the animal rights and direct action movement as well as in the radical green movement, attending various Green party conferences, seminars and meetings. My main interest was in radical green politics and I continued to read as much information about this as possible. (Hepple & Gable, 1993, p. 18)

Unfortunately for Hepple, his involvement in green anarchist groups created bigger problems a couple of years later. *Searchlight* states that in the group he was a member of, without the knowledge of his handlers, extreme right-wing infiltrators came across Hepple and used his inside information on the far right to expose him as a traitor (Hepple & Gable, 1993, p. 18). It is not by coincidence that Hepple's storyline shows remarkable similarities to that of Ray Hill, discussed previously. In fact, Hipple recounts meeting Hill and being impressed by him: "like me, he had initially been disgusted by the personalities within the extreme right, which had then led him to realise that the whole nazi [*sic!*] ideology was historically unsustainable and morally unacceptable" (Hepple & Gable, 1993, p. 18). It is likely that the two also conversed about their mutually shared quest for redemption and vengeance against their former comrades in detail.

In 1991 Hepple ended a relationship, which left him "like a fish out of water" (Hepple & Gable, 1993, p. 18). However, this also provided him with more free time to work for *Searchlight* and after a meeting with Garry Gable, Hepple was convinced to reenter the BNP with the goal of strategic infiltration. This provided significant status and gratification for him, as one of the main goals was still to hurt those he had come to despise: "I somehow knew that this moment would come, but now the time was right. I felt as if I had matured a lot since leaving the BNP in June 1989 and that I was now ready to inflict some serious damage on the BNP" (Hepple & Gable, 1993, p. 18). Hepple's contempt for Marxist forms of the far left blurred somewhat in the following years since he considered himself to be working for the left in general. During a situation in which it appeared that a violent clash between the right and the left was inevitable, Hepple remembers: "Marvellous we had thought, just a rabble of wimpy reds. The next moment the smiles turned to looks of horror as a quite different group of around 20 large characters turned up ... I remembered that none of these guys would know that I was really on their side" (Hepple & Gable, 1993, p. 30). Like other *Searchlight* informants discussed, Hepple eventually experienced psychological distress from his role as a spy who not only hurts those far rightists he despised but also his former friends. In April 1992, he writes, "the long term psychological strain of working inside the BNP finally took its toll and I decided to gracefully retire" (Hepple & Gable, 1993, p. 24). *Searchlight* contrasts this brief statement with an account of its own:

In fact Hepple had undergone a personal crisis. Although he had volunteered to work for Searchlight and the anti-fascist cause, he was still subject to periods of doubt about whether it was right to "grass'" on people like Edmonds who had from time to time shared his last slice of bread with him ... He wrote us a letter saying he was not sure who was right and who was wrong and how, whilst Edmonds was a dedicated nazi [*sic!*], he had a good side to him as a husband and had provided Tim with food when he was broke. Maybe, he thought, some of the stories he had heard among some his green anarchist contacts were right and that the nazi [*sic!*] claim that Searchlight was run by Zionists was true ... We knew full well that when Hepple came to us he still thought violence was an acceptable part of life. (It was only after O'Hara revealed in his booklet in spring 1993 that he had seen Hepple's letter to the green anarchists that we understood how Hepple had exposed himself by contacting a group that had became a hunting ground for the fascists and nazis [*sic!*]. (Hepple & Gable, 1993, p. 34)

Searchlight's perspective on Hepple's withdrawal from work as a mole is significant, as it shows how side-switching, if incomplete, can throw the defectors into constant limbo and psychological turmoil. All the psychological barriers involved, such as cognitive dissonance avoidance, reactance, social identity enhancement strategies, and so on (see Chapter 1) are not resolved. There is no closure for the person and if somehow the old milieu is successful in getting "back into the head" of the person undergoing such a process, it can easily lead to a draining process of moral self-destruction. In 1993, Tim Hepple was revealed to the public as a mole in a TV documentary, effectively ending his involvement in the far right. To sum up is motivations to switch sides, Hepple writes at the end of his storyline:

but I hope that what I have written here and what I say in the future can [be] said to have damaged the nazi [*sic!*] movement in some way. I was able to get right to the heart of the BNP's headquarters operation for three months in 1992 ... Having said that, I feel I have been able in some way to make up for my past activities and I believe very strongly now that the idea "once a nazi always a nazi [*sic!*]" has been proved to be wrong. I had to step back and look at what I was doing – to myself, my family and to innocent people in the long dark years from my early teens until I found the courage to ask for help and the chance to give something back to a society with which I had been at war. (Hepple & Gable, 1993, p. 35)

3.4   Matthew Collins

Matthew F. Collins was born in London in 1972 and was active for the "British National Party" (BNP) and the "National Front" (NF) for about six years in his youth. For almost three of those years he worked as an informant for the anti-fascist magazine *Searchlight*. In his autobiography, Matthew Collins describes this double life and the process leading to switching sides much differently than Ray Hill. For Collins, there was no relatively short moment or period of revelation that led him to a position of hatred for and complete rejection of his former in-group. Even though he did develop those feelings, switching sides did not come as easily to him. Collins writes:

I was also torn about what I was doing. I knew so little of life, so very little of the reasons for the hatreds that had driven a younger me and I understood even less why I had kept on going and kept on doing it when all the time I had longed for and dreamed of an opportunity to get away from it all and live a life less confronting and emotionally draining. (Collins, 2012, p. xxiii)

Collins was born into a working-class environment and grew up without a father, who had left the family with his babysitter. Incidentally, she and her family were the only "black people I had known" (Collins, 2012, p. 2). There was some level of contact with his father later on though, which also brought him in touch with everyday racism transmitted in the form of paternal stereotypes and racist slurs used to explain away poverty and grievances: "Was all this the fault of the [slur] and [slur]? Once they had been pointed out to me they suddenly and miraculously seemed to be everywhere, even at school and on the estate. I'd never even noticed them before" (Collins, 2012, p. 5). In his retrospective storyline explaining his pathway into the far right, Matthew Collins continuously points out broad feelings of anger and frustration about many things (e.g., economic deprivation) and pressing desires to find answers to questions he carried around. In school, Collins quickly ended up in conflicts and describes himself as violent and aggressive: "No one challenged me and I felt no one was listening. I was certainly becoming the worst sort of bully" (Collins, 2012, p. 9). He already had read about the NF, which made him curious but at the time Collins could not find a way to contact anyone from that organization.

At the age of 14 he started to work at a fruit market and yet again found his racist stereotypes affirmed by his coworkers. His curiosity and search for meaning or purpose increased to a point where he could barely understand what was happening to him:

Who was going to listen to my complaints? What actually were my complaints? I couldn't articulate what I was feeling because I didn't understand it. Something had to happen, anything. The absolute and endless periods of boredom, either locked in school or locked in my bedroom, seemed to drag by while I sat plotting all the things I was going to do when I had the chance. Never once did I list what these things were, never once did I convince myself of anything. (Collins, 2012, p. 11)

In short, Matthew Collins was an angry and aggressive young drifter desperately searching for his place in life.

At this moment in his storyline, two critical things happened. First, Collins watched on TV German neo-Nazis performing a funeral march for Rudolf Hess, the former deputy of Adolf Hitler, and idolizing a "martyr" in the extreme right. To young Collins' mind, those extremists in their uniform clothing appeared "impressive" and "brave": "People my age, with courage and conviction, trying to commemorate one of their own, betrayed by liars in foreign governments. I was leaderless and I was bored. Where was my Rudolf Hess?" (Collins, 2012, p. 12). Second, the far-right BNP outlet "British Nationalist" was put under the Collins family's door one Saturday afternoon. With enormous excitement, Matthew Collins took and hid the paper, devouring it in his room: "My body trembled as I held it in my hands and read every inch of its pages. This spoke to me, this said so much without actually making any real sense to me. It made me feel small and, at the same time, the more I looked at it, the more obvious it was that this was my calling" (Collins, 2012, p. 13).

Collins wrote a letter to the BNP and received a call inviting him to attend one of their rallies, which kickstarted a fast-paced career in the British extreme right ultimately leading him to become the South London NF organizer and a volunteer working in the BNP's head office. Through meetings and personal conversations, Collins slowly started to integrate more and more of the ideology into his life, which increased his violent confrontations in school, for example. However, the social identity aspect clearly was the main motivation for him in this phase, calling his far-right environment the "most magnificent drinking club in the world" (Collins, 2012, p. 20). By chance, Collins came across the NF and started to become involved in their activities as well (mostly distributing leaflets), leading to even more excitement and social status: "Here I was, finally doing something useful. We were like a secret army" (Collins, 2012, p. 23). Not surprisingly, this newfound status, excitement, and identity in combination with the preexisting anger and frustration led to a thirst for (violent) action and adventure (2012, p. 32). In his storyline, the far right elevated his status and provided him with power: "you would strike fear into people ... You could feel how you physically intimidated someone" (Wynne-Jones, 2011) and "I thought I was morally right. I felt untouchable ... In the group we felt empowered with a family spirit" (Boycott, 2002). With further ideological indoctrination, his originally crude racism developed into anti-Semitism with a particular focus on anti-communism and anti-capitalism.

The initial turning point in Matthew Collins' storyline came during a violent brawl in Welling, southeast London. In 1989, the BNP was opening its new head office together with a far-right bookshop in the area. A group of mostly elderly women protested this by calling a community meeting in the local Welling library, which was attacked by about 40 far-right extremists, including Collins. Instead of what he had expected to be an honorable fight between men, he and his comrades were brutally dashing at mostly defenseless women. In Collins' perspective, this event and the following mystification of the "battle of Welling" within the far right, started a critical reflection process:

I couldn't see what freedom of speech and fighting for British democracy had to do with stamping on little old ladies' heads . . . It was real hatred. I began to see it was all about destroying people's lives. Violence was the only way they could affect change. I was standing in the library watching people getting their heads kicked in for attending a debate and discussion. I thought: I'm on the wrong side." (Wynne-Jones, 2011)

Furthermore, the way in which his far-right peers began to talk about the attack and glorified it directly confronted him with a mismatch between real events Collins had witnessed and his in-group's recount: "I thought, this is unbelievable, and it set me thinking. These were the same people who'd told me the Holocaust didn't happen and now they're telling me what a wonderful thing it is that 40 grown men attack a meeting of women" (Boycott, 2002). These reflections were accompanied with intense feelings of shame and guilt: "I was a fucking coward to have done such a thing. I began to realise that this was what race wars were about, the innocent attacked and their dignity destroyed. If my mother had known, she would have disowned me on the spot" (Collins, 2012, p. 55). After this turning point event, Collins began to sporadically call *Searchlight* magazine to pass on information. *Searchlight* as such was the most popular anti-fascist outlet and many far-right extremists would regularly read it just to check if they had been included in the latest issue, or in other words: if they had been seen as significant and dangerous enough by their enemies to justify writing about them.

Interestingly, Matthew Collins did not consider switching sides at this point: "but I was concerned about the psychotic nature of some of the people around me. I just wanted to redress the balance. I decided to ring Searchlight anonymously. Everyone in the BNP knew the staff at that magazine were evil baby-eating communists. I began to give Searchlight information: about correspondence, what the campaigns were going to be, who'd been arrested for what" (R. Taylor, 2008). The power of social identity and commitment to a group was too strong for him, yet: "I couldn't just quit. It was my life. I'd forgone everything for the far Right [*sic!*] by this time. They were my only friends, my social life, everything. They were psychopaths, but they were my friends" (Boycott, 2002).

However strong and important these friendships were, Collins gradually started to recognize the toxicity of these relationships: "I had friends now, as I always had done, but the nature of these new friendships meant that I would probably have to fight and die with or for them ... All of these friendships were built solely on our hatred and distrust of others" (Collins, 2012, pp. 110–111). As a slow process, more and more pieces of Collins' emotional bond and rational fascination with the extreme right broke away. "The more I delved into the NF, the more I felt like it was a big lie. The whole charade of political persuasion and principles based on class equality and freedom were little more than my own dreams and rhetoric. The NF was ideologically and ethically empty and my illusions were being steadily shattered" (Collins, 2012, pp. 123–124). Very much in line with existing research on disengagement processes from extremist milieus, Collins also started to realize the material costs of his membership once the emotional commitment had started to erode: "they were rapidly making me as financially bankrupt as they were themselves morally bankrupt" (Collins, 2012, p. 125).

One of the key features of Matthew Collins' side-switching storyline is, that the distancing process did not manifest in a steady and unidirectional way. Instead, for him the question of continuous involvement and passing on information to the enemy very much depended on what Helen Ebaugh (1988) has called "role residuals" (p. 182) in her seminal study of role and identity transition processes. In Collins' own words: "though I was falling out of love with being involved in the NF, I quite enjoyed being the full-time Nazi about town" (Collins, 2012, p. 134). These still existing fragments of conviction also included ideological elements, which interacted with his increasing doubt:

I still believed in my race, still believed I was the victim of being born my colour and my class ... And yet in three years moving between the NF, the BNP and all the small satellites where I was allowed to relay my fears and even, at times, encouraged to attempt to critique them, could I honestly say that the far right really spoke for me at all? (Collins, 2012, p. 144)

At some point, his far-right extremist milieu even managed to restore some of the lost faith and renew positive excitement about the moral value of the social relationships within it. One example of this dynamic relationship between Collins and his far-right milieu is visible through his peers' reactions after a violent altercation with an opponent. Organizing a headhunt for left-wing extremists for revenge, Collins was positively surprised to experience such degrees of loyalty: "I was touched. My faith in the brotherhood of man was renewed" (Collins, 2012, p. 150). Nevertheless, the shame and guilt after the Welling library attack still weighted heavily on his conscious and eventually overpowered any remaining positive experiences with the far right. Until this point was reached, Collins tried to convince himself of being able to improve his in-group and of still being a committed insider:

> I realised that I did not want any of this, I didn't want to save the NF. It felt as if my stomach had been ripped out, I was empty. I really couldn't give a toss about saving the NF or the BNP. What was going on? I put the phone down as it suddenly felt as if my world had turned in on itself. Violence fucking hurt, I could see my battered face in the mirror but that was not bothering me too much . . . There and then nothing about the NF or even the BNP seemed to matter. I had been ringing Searchlight occasionally, every time I had these pangs of guilt, which had started immediately after the Welling incident, but I had also been struggling with how blasé I was at times about how easy and enjoyable it would be for me to put certain people onto lorries or trains heading off "east" . . . I steadied myself in the front of the mirror: "I am still a National Socialist, I am still a white Aryan, part of the master race," I assured myself. (Collins, 2012, pp. 154–155)

In Collins' storyline, the initial turning point of the Welling attack led to feelings of guilt and shame, which gradually deteriorated his emotional bond to the extremist milieu. A second event was necessary for him to finally make a fundamental change. During one of the very few leisure events Collins attended that did not involve his extremist peers or ideology, he was confronted with unpolitical and from his point of view, "normal" people. In a similar fashion to Ray Hill, those outsider contacts made him reconsider his position: "I decided that night that I should change my life . . . My heart was empty as my life, my pockets were full of lint and my jeans ironed with creases down the middle" (Collins, 2012, p. 181). However, instead of switching sides for good, it was more the hate toward his current milieu that drove this change: "I hadn't suddenly become an anti-fascist, not even an anti-racist . . . But it was the fascists I hated, not myself. My own mates and comrades. My only friends were all fucking mad. Mad, bad and very, very dangerous" (Collins, 2012, p. 184).

After a couple of anonymous phone calls to *Searchlight*, Collins was asked if he would be interested in a personal meeting. Similar to Ray Hill's experience, it was the charismatic and friendly human contact with members of the other side who made a difference. Nevertheless, there was no conversion moment for Collins: "After the meeting I felt a bit numb. I also had to ask myself honestly what my motivation had been for doing it" (Collins, 2012, p. 188). The choice to intensify the cooperation with *Searchlight* magazine came as a natural consequence of its status within the far right: "This magazine was totally dedicated to fighting everything I had for so long thought I stood for . . . The truth was, I was changing. Why take two steps forward, followed by three steps back? I didn't enjoy the company of fascists, perverts, thugs and incompetents" (Collins, 2012, p. 189). The meetings with *Searchlight* staff continued and Collins was driving toward these with a mixture of "curiosity, and fear as [to] what trouble" would result from them. It was more temptation by excitement than a higher moral duty to damage those he deemed to be dangerous at that point in his storyline. During the meetings with *Searchlight*, Collins was asked to describe various contacts and events with the far right, which made him realize the actual threat he was continuously facing by simply being around his right-wing extremist peers:

> If meeting Searchlight had been an attempt to unburden myself, it was not having the desired effect. It was a dreadful, intimidating meeting. To them I was obviously still a, very confused, Nazi fanatic with an irritable bowel. I was obsessed about what I had said to them and what they would do with the information. No arrangements had been made to meet again and neither of them had ventured a hanky for my tears. Why were they trying to break an already broken man further? (Collins, 2012, p. 193)

Far from receiving any kind of absolution and positive status enhancement at that point, Collins' situation even worsened as *Searchlight* reported on a person based on his information, which led to a legal confrontation between the magazine and the person in question. This conflict could have easily led to Collins being forced to give witness testimony in court with the automatic consequence of his outing as a traitor to the extreme right. For a short period of time, Collins' love for *Searchlight* faded, even though he continued to distance himself from his old life, for example, by removing all the neo-Nazi paraphernalia from his room (Collins, 2012, pp. 203–204).

But then *Searchlight* changed its approach toward Collins to a more amicable style, likely because they had now decided that the young neo-Nazi was sincere and trustworthy to a certain degree. An essential change for his relationship with *Searchlight* came in the form of Gerry Gable, a legendary figure both within the extreme right and left, as he was involved in the founding of the magazine as its editor. In stark contrast to the image Collins had derived from extreme-right propaganda about Gable, he did find a father-like figure in him: "This man was supposed to be a monster, if not the monster behind all of the great conspiracies, and here he was with me, chatting away like he was my Dad about holidays in the sun" (Collins, 2012, p. 207). Just like in Ray Hill's storyline, the unique position Collins was in helped to persuade him to stay involved as a mole instead of quitting altogether. This, however, was a very straining process that led to Collins feeling torn apart:

> Leaving behind those thoughts of race-hate and very slowly approaching light was like leaving a prison. It was only ever a day release though, because I now had to live a lie. I could tell no one about my new choice of direction. The level of excitement in my life had grown, but it was now fraught with danger. Even now I shudder when I think about the close shaves I was having barely able to do anything a normal person would do in my situation. I felt like a cheating husband while my poor colleagues were like my wife at the kitchen sink. Meanwhile my new lover, Searchlight, wanted me to keep fucking my wife, keep bending her over the dishwasher. And that was all

fine, all fun and rewarding, but if I meet the girl of my dreams, what should I tell her? (Collins, 2012, p. 222)

To a large degree, Collins' attraction to *Searchlight* consisted of adult and serious conversations on the one hand, and his by now raging hatred for his far-right peers on the other. He even recalls telling *Searchlight* goodbye many times, only to find himself calling again due to yet another threatening development in the extreme right he wanted to report (Collins, 2012, p. 234). There was no specific pro-social morality driving his side-switching yet: "I was involved only because I hated the mad fuckers. I was also scared of them though" (Collins, 2012). Eventually, Collins' double life led him to a point at which he was passing on such critical information about highly militant groups and activities in the far right that it became widely known in the milieu he was a mole, resulting in significant risk to his life. In consequence, Collins went into hiding in Australia from 1993 to 2003 until he returned to the United Kingdom and into the public as the subject of a BBC documentary in 2004. Finally, his side-switching storyline found its end through the closing narrative:

My mission had begun back in that library in Welling, where I had finally seen with my eyes wide open what fascism really meant. I can remember that split second when everything a young boy ever needed to know about [the] dangers of the life I had chosen played out in front of me ... But Welling library was the moment everything changed for me. There followed a loss of faith and a further, deeper confusion about where I would go to now, where I would fit in comfortably: if not fascism, what did I want out life? And here I am, over twenty years on, desperately trying to ensure that somehow there will be no more young kids like me, walking blindly into the dark and soul-destroying path of racism. (Collins, 2012, pp. 305–306)

Collins' narrative did not spin around his guilt and shame the way it did for Ray Hill. The need to repent for one's past by destroying what one has helped to build does not feature prominently in his storyline. More important in this side-switching account is the desire to prevent repetition of one's own past in the life of another young malleable mind. Collins continues his work with his own anti-fascist organization called Hope not Hate, for which he runs his own informant network within the extreme right.

3.5   Conclusion

Defection to the far left in the eyes of the side-switchers we have gotten to know here through their storylines is a highly moral and ethical imperative. Their narratives are deeply infused with expressions of guilt, shame, and the desire to correct past errors. Sometimes, as in the cases of Richard Scheringer (see Section B2.2) or Christine Hewicker, this explanation for transitioning to the opposing far left is extended beyond personal-level morality to global issues of injustice and grievances. Anti-imperialist or anti-capitalist liberation struggles of the oppressed and exploited can become an immensely powerful element in side-switching. Of course, ethical and moral arguments are not absent from defectors to the far right, but overall, their storylines much more often present the process as the outcome of a rational development or maturation in contrast to the emotional social justice–oriented commitment they claim is fueling the left.

Interestingly, the defection narratives presented in this chapter seem to somewhat validate this claim. Persons leaving the far right grapple with a recognition of injustice and social toxicity originating from their own milieus. Whether or not this is originally derived from ideological reflections, the consequence is usually the devastation of the meaning-making framework in the mindset of those defectors. We hear little about nuanced ideological or theoretical arguments from these side-switchers. Rather, they provide us with narratives created around at least one of two main components: fundamental opposition against the Western political and economic system (including but not limited to capitalism and parliamentary democracy) or the deep rooted moral responsibility to destroy the far right. None of the defectors we learned about here considered the state or Western society to be capable or willing to fight social injustice or the extreme right to a degree that would meet their own grievances and conceptions of what is necessary to do.

The substantial lack of trust in the mainstream society can be the result of continued direct confrontation with the government (for example, in the cases of Richard Scheringer in Section B2.2 or Christine Hewicker, who both never seized their struggle against the state during their side-switching). Not choosing to disengage altogether can, however, as well be the outcome of a "moral slingshot" that catapults defectors from one side of the political–moral spectrum to the other. The stronger they feel that the guilt has perpetrated serious ethical wrongdoings not just to induvial victims but to the society at large (e.g., by creating and leading violent far-right organizations), the lesser the chance of perceiving the mainstream society as an adequate place to live in. Moderation is not an option for them, at least not for some time after the transition, because their ideological and ethical reconfigurations are much more far-reaching and fundamental than in the cases we studied in Chapter 2 and the Bonus Chapter. What is left intact, however, is the desire for activism against an evil enemy, be it capitalist imperialism or the fascists.

4   Fighting on the Path of Allah
Joining Islamic Extremism from the Far Right and Far Left

The Norwegian police were surprised and concerned, to put it mildly. In September 2010, a special tactics and weapons police team had searched a tattoo studio in Oslo as part of an investigation against organized crime syndicates. They found weapons, Norwegian army uniforms, and fake identification cards that allowed the owner to enter military installations. Furthermore, the tattoo studio also seemed to have been a central meeting hub for militant neo-Nazis of Russian origin, as the 33-year-old owner Viacheslav Datsik himself was a notoriously criminal and violent right-wing extremist with a martial arts fighter background. He had escaped from a Russian psychiatric prison and illegally entered Norway just months before the raid. Once in Oslo, Datsik began to recruit other Russians living in the city and established what seems to have been a militant clandestine cell preparing for serious criminal acts. Russian authorities demanded his extradition, which led to a court hearing on the matter in early 2011.

On the day his deportation back to Russia was decided, 22-year-old Oleg Neganov was sitting in the court room among the many followers of Datsik. Neganov had come to Norway with his family at the age of 17 and clearly expressed his extreme-right ideology in public, for example, posting pictures of himself giving the Hitler salute on social media (Svendsen, Alayoubi & Jentoft, 2017). Five years later, in April 2016, the British newspaper *The Telegraph* reported about various spectacular application forms filled out by foreign recruits wishing to join the jihadist terror organization ISIS. Among them was a 27-year-old calling himself Abu Amir al-Russi who claimed to have been a competent helicopter pilot, sniper, and tank driver from Norway. Abu Amir indicated his Russian roots by his kunya, an Arabic name construction used by many jihadist foreign fighters as nom de guerre (Ensor, 2016).

Through access to the ISIS files, Norwegian newspapers were able to identify Al-Russi in 2017, who was in fact none other than Oleg Neganov. Oleg had never received any helicopter piloting or advanced military training, but he was still considered to be dangerous. Interpol placed a wanted notice on him in the same year, citing charges such as recruitment for and participation in a terrorist organization (Svendsen et al., 2017). Oleg's life had obviously changed drastically after Datsik's deportation and it is possible to piece together some parts of this change. It is known that he participated in far-right rallies and was involved with various extreme-right violent groups or persons between 2010 and 2011. At that time, Oleg took part in a violent attack and was charged with a weapons crime in 2010, as well as with serious theft in 2012.

However, Norwegian media reports indicate that he also announced his conversion to Islam in fall 2011, posting a picture of himself reading the Quran and raising his index finger in a gesture showing his faith. In that post, Oleg also took over a new name, Amir Aminov, showing an intermediate step before further developing his new identity as Abu Amir al-Russi (Johnsen, 2019). The young man wrote about his conversion in a blog post and explained that he went to a mosque in 2011 out of curiosity about Islam. There he received a Quran in Russian as a gift and began studying it: "the more I read, the more I began to understand that Allah's religion is the truth … I got answers to all my questions and was ready to become a Muslim" (original in Norwegian, translated by author, as cited in Svendsen, 2019). Oleg renewed his Norwegian visa in March 2013 but must have left for Syria shortly afterward. At that time, he intensified social media postings with Islamic extremist content and by June 2014 he was one of 368 trainees in an ISIS training camp near Raqqa. In May 2019, Abu Amir al-Russi aka Oleg Neganov was arrested close to the Syrian-Jordanian border (Johnsen, 2019). On July 26, 2020, he was convicted of membership in a terrorist organization and sentenced to eight years in prison in Iraq (Svendsen & Alayoubi, 2020). Not much is known about the immediate reaction among Oleg's neo-Nazi friends to his conversion to Islam, but there is some reporting that displays great surprise and turmoil. One person who new Oleg at the time was quoted in a press article saying that "if the goal is to use violence, the way from Hitler to the IS is short" (original in Norwegian, translated by author, as cited in Svendsen et al., 2017), through which he wanted to show what he regarded as Oleg's main motive and ideological bridge between the two extremist milieus.

Chapter 5 will focus on defectors like Oleg, who converted to Islam and joined Islamic extremist groups coming from a previously far-left or far-right background. It is of the utmost importance not to conflate conversion to Islam with extremist side-switching. Many former extremists and terrorists converted to various religions, including Islam, and shed their radical worldviews in the process. A religious conversion must by no means be associated with extremist radicalization in any direction. In fact, it most often leads to a moderation of beliefs and a personal stabilization within a pro-social network, especially when happening in prison (Hamm, 2013).

For those who do venture on to join extremist milieus within Islam or use an Islamic collective identity, a conversion (even if only for a superficial appearance) is a necessary requirement to be accepted into the environment. In the storylines in the next sections, we will learn about personal journeys into different forms of extremism and personal crises or curiosity leading to the adaption of Islamic extremist views and ideological concepts. Most of them came from the far right and interestingly attempted to combine their previously held convictions with the newfound Islamic extremist ones. We did not see this as a phenomenon at all in the earlier chapters dedicated to switching between the far left and the far right. In those categories, defectors almost always went to significant lengths to disassociate themselves from their old milieus and to point out a clear ideological break. Not so with the persons we will get to know in this chapter. The first case, Sascha Lemanski, for example, wrote about the ideological unity of Islam and neo-Nazism against an alleged Jewish conspiracy against the German people in order to retain his links on both sides of the extremist aisle.

4.1   Sascha Lemanski

The case of Sascha Lemanski, a German convicted and sentenced to prison for a jihadist motivated terror plot, is one example of side-switching between extreme right-wing and Salafi-jihadist milieus that arguably led to a significant escalation of the radicalization process. He was born 1991 in Germany. From what is known about his upbringing, he had to endure hardships and neglect, which brought him to drug addictions and mental health issues. Lemanski never completed formal education and lived in homeless shelters for some time. He also accumulated significant financial debt. His father physically abused his mother and one of Sascha Lemanski's first criminal convictions was for beating his own pregnant girlfriend. Living in a supervised community for "high problem adolescents," he became a father at the age of 19. This relationship failed, as did another in which he fathered a second child (Munderloh, 2018).

Lemanski lived off social welfare and lost the custody rights for his children when he became active in the extreme right-wing environment in the early 2010s. He published multiple video statements on various social media sites, mainly targeting Muslims, immigrants, and the Jewish community. Sascha converted to Islam in the mid-2010s, shortly after changing his place of residence to a smaller town for a new intimate relationship. Unfortunately for him, his new environment was dominated by a strong anti-fascist movement that still considered him to be a neo-Nazi and eventually posted his personal information together with the label far-rightist online. During the following two to three years, his radicalization reached the point of plotting a jihadist terrorist attack with explosives, together with three other coconspirators. He was convicted of preparing a "severe act of anti-governmental violence" (original in German, translated by author, Niemann, 2017) and sentenced to more than three years of imprisonment in 2017. His violent extremist behavior and attitudes did not decrease in prison. On the contrary, in 2019 he lured a guard into his cell and attempted to kill him through a stabbing attack using forks and shouting "Allahu Akbar." For this, he was convicted of attempted murder and sentenced to another 14 years in prison in 2020 (dpa, 2020).

According to one of his former girlfriends, who also belonged to the extreme right-wing milieu, Sascha Lemanski repeatedly and stubbornly tried to convince his neo-Nazi peers of his opinion that Islam and National Socialism are closely related ideologies. She also described how Lemanski, at that time identifying as a neo-Nazi, gradually withdrew from his extreme right-wing group after he met resistance to his ideological positions (Munderloh, 2018, p. 56). At the same time, he ran a modestly successful extreme right-wing online video blog. During his 2017 trial, Sascha Lemanki described how he quickly integrated into Muslim online communities and received positive feedback, for example, as a site administrator and self-professed authority on the Quran. A year after his conversion, the authorities first noticed his potential jihadist radicalization when Sascha Lemanski started to share extremist codes and symbols online. When they searched his computer, the police found jihadist and neo-Nazi material (Munderloh, 2018, p. 57).

Around that time, Lemanski also published an article on an extreme right-wing online blog and argued that Islamophobia was essentially a tool of the global Jewish conspiracy to turn Germans against Islam. He explained that "[t]he German Empire and National Socialist Germany were true friends and brothers of Islam. Today, strangely, those patriots and nationalists are the ones acting against Islam – led by Jews and Zionists, who are not clearly visible at first sight" (original in German, translated by author, as cited in Koehler, 2019b, p. 507). Even though his attempts to convert fellow neo-Nazis to his interpretation of ideological unity between right-wing and Islamic extremism were met with outright rejection and ridicule, Lemanski still actively maintained a friendship with at least one of his former peers. This person, who openly identified himself as a convinced neo-Nazi in court, was tried for aiding Lemanski in his terror plot and lived with him for some time after he had become a radicalized jihadist (Munderloh, 2018, p. 60).

Sascha Lemanski's defection storyline is clearly dominated by anti-Semitism. During his trial, he explained that the targets of his bombing plot – police officers and military personnel – were "servants of Jews" (original in German, translated by author, Munderloh, 2018, p. 62). Anti-Semitism was also a key motive in the videos he released during his time as a neo-Nazi and he repeatedly used this theme to explain the ideological bond between National

Socialism and Islam/jihadism. In addition, the Salafi-jihadi victim narrative of Islam being globally suppressed by a Jewish-led West, for example, by pushing Germany into war with Islam to provoke a new "Holocaust" against Muslims, seems to have strongly resonated with him. This motif is also closely aligned with one of his arguments as a neo-Nazi: that Jews are allegedly working to bring about the death of the German people.

Sascha Lemanski's defection storyline pictures the milieu transition as a natural consequence of his core ideological beliefs, which he felt received more positive feedback in his new group than in the old one. He described Islam as the last line of defense against an alleged global rule of Judaism and hence combined this belief with a narrative of heroism against those evil forces trying to destroy Germany and Islam. Although he faced reservations and partial resistance over his attempts to proselytize former in-group members, Sascha Lemanski continued at least one friendship, which was stable enough to turn into a source of support for his terrorist plot. This indicates that there did not seem to be any issue with a lack of group permeability for either side. He also clearly received status and identity improvement within his new group, after two failed relationships (with at least one extreme right-wing partner) and substantial threats from another enemy (the extreme left). Ultimately, group membership in the extreme right seemingly became more costly than rewarding for Sascha Lemanski, especially since he had not invested heavily in the neo-Nazi milieu at that point (e.g., through criminal convictions, violence, or prison sentences), which might show that he perceived himself to be in the "wrong" group early on.

4.2   Bernhard Falk, aka "Muntasir bi-Ilah"

Bernhard Falk was born in Germany in the year 1967; he was the son of a teacher. He studied physics at the German technical university RWTH Aachen after he achieved the best high school degree score in his state the year he graduated (Intelmann, 2014). Falk was first arrested for left-wing motivated crimes in the early 1990s, after which his criminal activities escalated in severity until he was convicted of carrying out attacks using explosives and four cases of attempted murder in 1999. He was sentenced to 13 years of imprisonment for his terrorist activities in connection with the left-wing extremist "Anti-imperialist Cells" (Antiimperialistische Zellen, or AIZ).

The AIZ saw itself as the successor of the left-wing terrorist "Red Army Faction" (Rote Armee Fraktion, or RAF), which shortly before the first AIZ communiqué on May 22, 1992, declared that they were renouncing violent attacks in April 1992 (the so-called RAF de-escalation declarations). This distancing from violent methods caused a rift within the militant far left and groups such as the AIZ sought to continue the armed resistance. Between

1992 and 1996, the AIZ conducted at least nine attacks using arson and explosives against politicians, police officers, leading members of the employers association, and diplomatic buildings. Bernhard Falk and one codefendant were the only two members of the AIZ the German authorities were able to apprehend and it is now unclear if the cell ever had more than those two members. The AIZ, however, appeared as a somewhat unusual left-wing terrorist cell, as it also received strong criticism from within the far-left milieu. During the end of its violent campaign, the AIZ increasingly incorporated positions in favor of Islamic extremist ideologies and groups, as well as a glorification of religiously based martyrdom concepts. Furthermore, the AIZ used its declarations to criticize the wider left-wing environment. Naturally, this resulted in an almost complete isolation of the group in its own ideological spectrum. This ideological distancing process on the group level somewhat mirrored the personal developments of its members. In one letter claiming an explosive attack against the residence of a politician from the Christian Democratic Party from September 1995, the AIZ for example stated:

In the international anti-imperialist struggle, revolutionary Islamic and communist groups are leading at the moment. The struggle has escalated in the way that these groups have also carried out actions in the metropolises of imperialism; in the FRG [Federal Republic of Germany], these are the actions of the Kurdish comrades. Unfortunately, it is now the case that the FRG left and those who are fighting worldwide are strangers to each other. And of course, in many ways it was quite euphemistic when we saw ourselves as "part of the resistance in the FRG" in our first declaration (22.4.92). Many in the FRG left refuse the exact confrontation with those who fight in the FRG, because they cannot comprehend certain forms of action. Still others from the FRG left are only looking for opportunities to distance themselves – this is not a good precondition for mutual communication ... Even in situations in which it would be absolutely necessary for the FRG left to act positively, the mutual lack of understanding prevents any further development. This is particularly clear with regard to political prisoners: just as the French left had to deal with the fact that the majority of political prisoners in France are of Maghreb origin and come from the Islamic resistance, it is also about time for the FRG left to realize that the majority of political prisoners in the FRG are of Kurdish origin and come from the communist resistance. Despite the situation of mutual misunderstanding that we are aware of, we think it is important to express what we consider objectively necessary and right (original in German, translated by author, AIZ, 1995).

A bitter ideological critique like that, published as part of a letter claiming a left-wing terrorist attack, necessarily had to result in strong rejection from the remaining left-wing milieu and is indicative of an already smoldering ideological emancipation process within the AIZ. Bernhard Falk converted to Islam shortly before starting his prison term. Released early in 2008, after serving nine years in prison, he subsequently became an outspoken and well-known activist within the German Salafi-Jihadi milieu. His main activities focus on online media productions as well as prison support for incarcerated fellow "brothers" and "sisters."

While he is mostly nonviolent now, his ideological positions do include the promotion and legitimization of violent acts, specifically against the USA, as well as the defense of jihadist terror organizations, such as al-Qaeda (von Hein & Felden, 2018). Due to his very public and outspoken position, he regularly presents his own storyline in autobiographical videos or interviews in an attempt to explain his ideological development and side-switching process. Bernhard Falk sees his defection from the extreme left as a natural and consistent development. In the period shortly before his arrest and prison sentence, Falk witnessed a general trend among his left-wing extremist peers to discontinue their violent struggle against the German state. At the same time, he encountered Muslim students at his university and engaged with them on philosophical and theological questions. He also learned about Muslim activism against Western (especially US) "imperialism" around the world.

Naturally, the process of his conversion to Islam holds the center of his side-switching narrative and is deeply connected to a search for meaning and perspective in his life at a time when the militant far left lost momentum:

At the same time, I noticed of course that as I already have indicated the RAF at the beginning of the 1990s was in the process of disbanding and the spirit was also gone. I was of course then confronted with, yes, with fundamental questions fundamental questions. I had devoted my best years during my university studies to these things and was now faced with a completely new situation as were the others ultimately. For me it was discussing the question of meaning which everyone then answers for himself; what sense the commitment makes; what perspective this commitment has in the long run; and I have then, and I think this is a natural reflex, looked at everything I had available from my previous life. I have revisited what I have and what I had learned from Christianity, what I had from Marxism, what I had also learned from other influences and so then I just realized at the beginning of the 1990s how more and more Muslims became active worldwide and that Islamic groups which have shown resistance against imperialism in many different forms emerged. And because I was someone who was internationally active early on, I was interested in it. By the way, this was not unusual in the RAF environment, the RAF was always an internationalist group that has always perceived the worldwide change. So, my interest in the international situation was actually only a natural consequence. I simply saw that in Palestine or in Chechnya or in North Africa, everywhere the Muslims were on the move as a force that the New World Order ... was opposed [to]. So, I was thus confronted with a double development. On the one hand the dissolution of the RAF here in the Federal Republic of Germany, the decline of the autonomous movement and the whole environment, the whole radical left environment, on the other hand with the emergence of Islamic groups. And this got me curious of course and I immediately looked at the basis of Islam. Specifically, I went into bookstores in Aachen where I studied at that time and tried to get Islamic books. I started with a Quran translation as far as they were printed in German language at the time. I also had a number of students with whom I was able to discuss such questions ... so I started to deal with Islam and of course I took a completely different turn in my thinking, whereas before I had only thought ahead for a very short time just to fulfill my student duties and I have been involved in the environment of the RAF, I have, so to speak, always thought only until the next week. Now I started to think longer and more about the long-term perspective, the meaning of life as a whole, which is a valuable commitment, a commitment that extends beyond the next few years and the meaning of that and so I gradually more and more identified with Islam. (original in German, translated by author, Falk, 2012, starting minute 15:28)

Falk's first reaction to this newfound interest and fascination with Islam was to argue in favor of joining Islamic terrorist organizations in a united front against Western imperialism within his left-wing milieu. This, however, was not greeted with a positive response:

I was one of the few, well at that time I belonged to the left-wing scene, I tried to call upon others to solidarize with Islamic groups ... and this was strongly rejected. So, while I was finding more and more answers for the questions I had, I realized the strong reservation towards Islam among the leftists I had contact with ... Most leftists are atheists and they are such strong atheists that they reject working with someone who is religiously convinced ... So, it was my sympathy for Islam which led to my own isolation. (original in German, translated by author, as cited in Koehler, 2019b, p. 508)

Hence, Bernhard Falk was and still is well aware of the atheistic positions in the far left. The categorial rejection of his arguments also led to emotional pain and disappointment, which still features strongly in his storyline: "I am still shocked today and sad at the same time because in the end they were my ideological comrades who then just wanted to have nothing more to do with someone like me" (original in German, translated by author, Falk, 2012, starting minute 20:36). From Falk's viewpoint, his left-wing extremist environment changed to a point where he felt unable to adequately continue his struggle and be part of an active movement:

I was facing the problem that many in the Left were ceasing their activities. And then you ask yourself the question of the meaning of life, how one wants to continue to act. I don't think that the end of the Soviet Union should lead to an end of anti-imperialist activities, because the problems in the world have not been solved and, therefore, the engagement must continue. I realized then that many Muslims are active, and this motivated me to look into it more and everyone more or less constructs the meaning of life for himself and, for me, that became Islam. (original in German, translated by author, as cited in Koehler, 2019b, p. 508)

As a consequence, Falk felt pushed away from an increasingly inactive and, in his viewpoint, ignorant far-left milieu, while he developed a strong feeling of belonging within Islamist circles at the same time:

Personally, Islam answered the question of meaning for me, that life here on earth is only a part of the way ... and the real perspective is what happens afterward. We have the task here on earth to strive as far as we can in this effort, we can be arrested, we might suffer injuries, we might die even for this cause, but the real perspective comes after that. That means we are obliged to do as much as we can for the just cause and then we get a reward that exceeds a dimension we cannot even imagine. That means Islam has practically answered my personal search for meaning. That is one point and the other point is if you look at it in a narrower political context, of course I not only felt but actually became part of a complete effort of all Muslims worldwide who are working for this goal to be active against imperialism, that is to say I noticed this while I was losing more and more comrades on the one hand but gained more and more brothers on the other. And as sad as the one thing was, as hope-giving was the other and that gave me a lot of strength ... and in the end you are alone in the cell with yourself and Allah and think[ing] about the meaning of life and if you have no reasonable basis then you can't hold out. (original in German, translated by author, Falk, 2012, starting minute 20:45)

It is noteworthy that Falk still uses left-wing terminology (e.g., "imperialist"), which underscores his claim to have continued the same ideological struggle, albeit from a different position: "also this whole conflict with US imperialism, with the Zionist state structure, with the Federal Republic of Germany as such, all these are of course things that run through my activities of the last 20 or 25 years like a red thread" (original in German, translated by author, as cited in Koehler, 2019b, p. 508). Regarding his past and the conversion narrative, Falk sees both as a source of added value for his role and status in the Islamic extremist milieu:

I think that I can convey a certain authenticity to the brothers because I went through these stages ... I am thankful that I could experience all this because I believe that I have found a deeper access to Islam than many others, possibly even those who grew up in a quote-on-quote Islamic culture and never had to really engage with the contents. I had to gather, piece by piece, every aspect of that knowledge. (original in German, translated by author, as cited in Koehler, 2019b, p. 508)

Bernhard Falk's side-switching narrative describes a critical juncture phase dominated by a deep personal crisis. For Falk, this crisis entailed the softening of his extremist peers combined with self-induced isolation through attempts to advocate support for Islamic groups. He also pointed out that only some of his Muslim friends, and none of his left-wing peers, visited him in prison. This social aspect, combined with his renewed determination to be part of a global, active, and successful anti-imperialist movement, is decisive in his narrative: "so the Islamic movement has grown really strong globally, and it became a factor that the imperialists cannot get around, and this gives enormous hope to perceive and feel oneself as part of a community that stands for a just cause, and this is a very nice thing" (original in German, translated by author, as cited in Koehler, 2019b, p. 509).

Falk does not seem to have encountered any resistance within the Islamic extremist environment due to his former atheist past. However, his high personal investment in the anti-imperialist struggle might explain the strong focus on continuing in his main ideological positions. Interestingly, his codefendant from the AIZ trial, Michael Steinau, also converted to Islam. He, however, took a completely different route than Falk. Separated from Falk in investigative custody, Steinau started to write letters out of prison praising Iranian militias and befriended the neo-Nazi terrorist Kay Diesner, who awaited his trial for killing a police officer and the attempted murder of a left-wing book seller in the same prison (Carini, 1997). This immediately led to a break with his lawyer, with Falk, and with the left-wing solidarity movement that initially attempted to support him in custody. In the same letter, Steinau called for Islamic resistance against the "infidel" German state and the release of Diesner. Claiming that Diesner had in fact become his best friend in prison with many mutually shared ideological positions, Steinau announced that he wanted to "fight together" (original in German, translated by author, Carini, 1997) with him.

Summing up the side-switching storyline of Bernhard Falk, the combination of a personal search for meaning in life with the loss of momentum and activism in the far-left environment pushed him toward "Islamic resistance movements." Falk looked for those ideological milieus that continued the aniimperialist struggle on the one hand and that provided a more holistic ideological basis on the other. This dual process was facilitated by the left-wing milieu's failure to respond to his newfound interest in Islam with anything but rejection, something that is still presented as a source of pain in his narrative.

4.3   David Myatt

David Wulstan Myatt was born in Tanganyika (today mainland Tanzania) in 1950. During his life Myatt was involved in different forms of violent extremism, such as neo-Nazism and Islamic extremism. Since 2010, however, he claims to have rejected all extremist ideologies and turned the attention of his prolific writing toward general philosophy, esotericism, ancient Greek literature, and poetry. Undoubtedly, a main driving factor behind Myatt's various political-extremist engagements was an ideological and philosophical quest that led him to and through various worldviews or schools of thought. Some scholars have seen Myatt's case as a proof of a growing overlap between neo-Nazi and jihadist milieus (e.g., Michael, 2006).

With his extensive and highly militant writings that defended his violent neo-Nazi or Islamic extremist viewpoints, Myatt naturally caught the attention of the public and academia (e.g., Gartenstein-Ross & Blackman, 2019; Kaplan, 2000; Perdue & Johnson, 2012). He grew up in Tanganyika (Tanzania), where his father worked as a civil servant for the British government. In his later childhood, the family moved to the Far East and in 1967 he relocated to England together with his two sisters in order to complete his schooling (Myatt, 2013, p. 6). Back in England, Myatt intensified his interest in oriental philosophy, especially through a fascination with martial arts (Myatt, 2013, p. 7). For a short time, he also enrolled in college to study physics, which would later become increasingly burdensome for him and cause him to drop out. His first contact with the extreme right happened by chance at the age of 15. One day Myatt passed by a street brawl that involved some far-right extremists and due to his strong interest in martial arts and street fighting, he joined in. Myatt was aware of the political affiliation of some of the persons involved in the fight, as he had spent some months reading about National Socialism before this incident:

Without thinking, I waded in to help him. There was that exhilaration, again. That love of direct physical violence I had felt before. A few more young lads joined the melee, and then it was over, and so we went, quite naturally, to some nearby Public House to celebrate our victory. Their accepting camaraderie was wonderfully refreshing, and many hours were spent, drinking – and talking politics. Not that I was then ignorant of their type of politics. Indeed, I had spent many of the previous months eagerly reading about nationalism, about National-Socialist Germany, and especially about Adolf Hitler, inspired by an account of the actions of Otto Ernst Remer, on that day in July 1944 during the Second World War. Such loyalty; such a sense of duty; such honour; such forthright warrior action. (Myatt, 2013, p. 4)

A desire for violence and conflict mixed with his quest for living out a romantic warrior hero identity was the initial driving force. For him, the "honorable warrior" would be the precursor of a new society built upon the ideals Myatt found in national socialism. Through his intensified contacts with the extreme right, he thought that he found "a similar type of people. Or at least, those who could, given training, direction and guidance, purpose, be such people. Young; enthusiastic; who seemed to share something … and who … seemed to enjoy and welcome violence" (Myatt, 2013, p. 14). By following up on invitations to participate in events, Myatt met personal acquaintances of Colin Jordan (1923–2009, a leading British neo-Nazi), whom he later contacted directly.

Myatt immensely idolized Nazi Germany at that time in his life: "It also seemed to me then – and for a long while afterwards – that Hitler's National-Socialist Germany was, and should be, the archetype for such a new society: that NS Germany embodied most, though not all, the ideals I then saw as necessary to the creation of such a new, warrior, society imbued with a Galactic ethos" (Myatt, 2013, p. 14). Called a "true seeker" and "fixture on the British National Socialist scene since the early 1970s" (Kaplan, 2000, p. 216), David Myatt joined Colin Jordan's neo-Nazi British Movement (BM) in 1968, partially working as a bodyguard for Jordan during one of his many rallies. It is reported that his entry into the far right was facilitated by his strong spiritual quest and interest in Nazi-occultism, which he discovered, for example, through writings from Savitri Devi (nom de plume of Maximine Portaz, 1905–1985, a French writer portraying Adolf Hitler as a Hindu god) at the age of 16 (Kaplan, 2000, p. 216). Myatt himself writes of his excitement and enthusiasm about being involved in a movement alongside people he deemed "worthy" of building a new society: "These were exciting times, and there really was a feeling, among the rank-and-file, that the NF was growing in such a way that, in a decade or more, it might be able to win or seize power" (Myatt, 2013, p. 19). During this process of intensifying his political involvement, Myatt's still ongoing university education became a tiresome alternative life more and more, which he eventually dropped completely to fully focus on is extremist activism:

Compared to all this, my life at University seemed, and indeed was, boring; dull. Thus it seemed natural, inevitable – especially given my friendship with Morrison – that I move to Leeds, and become involved with street-politics full-time. Which I dutifully did . . . Thus, and yet again, there was a certain period of drifting, by me, until a particular course of life seemed obvious, even to me. My next year was a learning process. Learning about people; learning more about political propaganda; speaking in public; organizing and participating in street fights and demonstrations. That is, it was a learning of the Art of the revolutionary political agitator. I loved the life. (Myatt, 2013, p. 20)

Interestingly, Myatt also remembers positive interactions with members of the opposing left-wing extremist milieu during his university time, where he was well known as a fascist:

I did, however, find one political person – who belonged to some minor Marxist-Leninist group – who understood this, and who thus took the opportunity to get to know me and with whom I had many friendly discussions about politics, and life in general. And it was he who – along with a few cultured non-political individuals – somewhat helped restore my belief that humans were, or could be, rational, cultured, beings. Perhaps I should add these few cultured non-political individuals – three young men and a young lady – were all (as we now say) "gay". Indeed, with only one exception, all my friends at University were gay, in those intolerant days . . . when such a preference, such a nature, was often kept secret because [it was] still regarded by the majority of people as reprehensible and somehow "perverse". As for me, I simply enjoyed their company; their culture; their sensitivity; and which culture and sensitivity was, or seemed to me at the time, rather lacking in most if not all the other students I met, studied with, or had occasion to interact with. (Myatt, 2013, p. 21)

Through further integration into the extreme right, especially facilitated by the mentorship from Colin Jordan, Myatt intensified his Nazi beliefs and developed a quasi-religious fanaticism for that ideology in combination with the almost obligatory Holocaust denial: "To me, then, National-Socialism seemed to embody everything that I felt was noble and excellent: a new, modern, expression of the Hellenic ethos which I had greatly admired ... one of my most treasured possessions came to be a signed photograph given to me by Major-General Otto Ernst Remer" (Myatt, 2013, p. 22). Myatt's political goals were to establish a "warrior society" modeled after Nazi Germany. This, he figured, could only be done through violence:

I further came to understand that in order to create the new warrior society, it was necessary to disrupt, undermine, destroy, overthrow – or replace by any practical means – all existing societies, and all governments, and that while electoral politics might be one way for National-Socialists to take power, direct revolution or insurrection was a viable alternative. Therefore, with the dedication of a fanatic, I set about doing just that, ready, willing and prepared to use violence in order to aid and achieve political goals. For I then considered that sacrifices were necessary in order for these goals to be achieved, and that, once achieved, the violent struggle would have been worthwhile, even if it cost me my own life, or that of others. Thus, I placed some idealized vision of the future before my own personal happiness – indeed, my own happiness became the struggle for, and the practical realization of, that vision of the future. (Myatt, 2013, p. 23)

It is no surprise that Myatt let actions follow such beliefs and in the 1970s he was sentenced to prison for leading a skinhead gang into a brutal attack on immigrants. In his autobiography, Myatt describes prison as a "useful and interesting experience" (Myatt, 2013, p. 23), where he made further contacts with other extremists and learned new violent skills. More arrests and convictions followed. His career in the far-right scene took Myatt to the secretary position of the BM Leeds branch and to become a member of the organization's national council in 1973. He also was the founder and first leader of the National Socialist Movement (NSM), cofounder of the National Democratic Freedom Movement (NDFM), which was active in Leeds, England, in the early 1970s, and founder of the "Reichsfolk" group, all of them distinctive neo-Nazi organizations.

During his further radicalization, Myatt became involved in paramilitary clandestine violent neo-Nazi groups between the 1970s and 1990s, such as Column 88 and Combat 18, in which he took over leadership positions. In particular, the terrorist underground fit well with Myatt's sense of elitism and vanguard identity: "here, I felt, was the spirit, the comradeship, of The Third Reich, of the Waffen-SS, of genuine National-Socialism, come alive again, something which, I knew from direct personal experience, was often so sadly lacking in the other NS group I had previously encountered" (Myatt, 2013, p. 26). In this last quote, one can easily recognize that Myatt felt some kind of frustration about a lack of loyalty, comradery, and commitment within the larger extreme-right milieu. Indeed, this disillusionment led him to become a monk in a Buddhist monastery before he was sent to prison again. After his release, Myatt still pondered whether to go back to extreme right-wing violence and politics. In his autobiographical recollections, enthusiasm for the cause seems to have disappeared due to the lack of camaraderie and moral values in the movement:

As for me, for over five, often violent years, radical street politics had been an important part of my life – often, the most important part; and I had dedicated myself to the struggle, undeterred by prison. But my naivety, idealism, and optimism had all but faded away. For experience had revealed to me that the honour, loyalty and commitment to duty I expected from fellow political comrades was often absent, and that the leadership of all NS, all pro-NS groups and even all of our kind of nationalist organizations was woefully bad; un-charismatic and incapable of inspiring the loyalty required. Instead of idealism, loyalty and honour there were continual feuds, continued disloyalty, and little or no honour, manifest most often as this dishonour was in the spreading of malicious rumours behind people's backs. (Myatt, 2013, p. 30)

In combination with this disappointment regarding the reality of interpersonal relationships within the far right, Myatt, according to his storyline, also developed a new and much deeper desire for a more holistic philosophy:

The truth I felt, the truth which thus became so revealed, was that I did not know; that I did not have all the answers; that I had begun to doubt everything that for years I had so passionately, even fanatically, believed in. The truth that maybe, just maybe, I might not be able to find all the answers by myself, unaided; that maybe, just maybe, there was someone out-there, or something, who and from which I might learn, who and which might guide me toward a deeper, a better, understanding of myself and this world. That maybe, just maybe, in that particular allegory I might find some answers. (Myatt, 2013, p. 33)

Throughout his life, David Myatt writes, he has been on a quest for spirituality, sense, and purpose. After both the frustration about lack of commitment in his milieu and the desire for a more meaningful worldview had increased significantly, Myatt decided to try out yet another religion and became a Christian monk. For about a year and a half, he tried to integrate into the order of Saint Benedict. However, after several incidents mostly involving Myatt rebelling against the strict cloister rules and the theological teachings, he realized that he had an "un-monastic attitude" (Myatt, 2013, p. 39) and left this particular detour from his extremist pathway again. In the following years, David Myatt entered his first marriage and claims to have kept away from politics, even though he remained in contact with Colin Jordan and John Tyndall (1934–2005, another leading British fascist). He also wrote a couple of articles for the extreme-right magazine *Spearhead*. Myatt's storyline at this point described a wide-reaching disengagement form his previous extremist lifestyle, but after the death of his first wife, he reengaged with the far right:

Life was never simple again, after that. For I had returned to writing about National-Socialism . . . Why this return? To be honest, I cannot really remember. But I have more than a vague suspicion that Sue's death had affected me more than I, at the time, cared or even dared to admit. Something seemed to have departed from my life: a personal vision, a dream, perhaps, of us – of Sue and I – growing old together; of a life of contented sharing, where the world was only our life together . . . I was, quite simply, in love and content, as I knew she was. So, perhaps I replaced my personal vision with another one, retreating back into the world I had known before. The world of NS politics; of striving to create a better world, for others, based on the values of honour, loyalty and duty. (Myatt, 2013, p. 51)

Not surprisingly, Myatt's experience regarding the overall quality of inter-personal relationships and commitment did not significantly change with his involvement in clandestine groups like Combat 18 or Column 88. On the contrary, he quickly realized that the situation was even worse: "There seemed to be little honour; even less genuine loyalty; and the usual spreading of malicious rumours and of gossip. Furthermore, few people – if any – were prepared to risk their lives or their liberty for the Cause they claimed they believed in" (Myatt, 2013, p. 54). This very proof of devotion to a cause – the willingness to sacrifice one's life – was something Myatt found impressive in the actions of Islamic extremists around the world and this sparked his motivation to engage more with Islam, as well as study its main principles. In addition, his narrative includes a rather mundane rationale: "For a new strategy had occurred to me, and this was that a religion might be very useful, or at least some kind of religious approach . . . I began to seriously study Islam, initially more to see what I could learn from it and perhaps apply to that NS Cause I then still believed in" (Myatt, 2013, p. 54).

In short, Myatt openly states that he wanted to infiltrate Islam to learn about the cause of fanaticism of some of its followers in order to apply it to the extreme right. During his time with Combat 18, he traveled to Egypt for that goal and began to personally immerse himself in Muslim culture and religion, noting a fascination with Arab nationalism. Again, he found himself impressed by individual commitment and devotion through personal conversations and – upon his return – experienced a cultural shock: "I returned to England to find bad-manners, arrogance, materialism, decadence, and for the first time in my life I felt somewhat out of place among my own people" (Myatt, 2013, p. 55). All of this happened around 1998 and in his autobiography, Myatt explains that "there was no sudden decision to convert to Islam. Rather, it was the culmination of a process that began a decade earlier with travels in the Sahara Desert" (Myatt, 2013, p. 55). Many years before his conversion, Myatt also recounts that he had bought a copy of the Quran and occasionally read in it. However, he had "no desire, felt no need, to study Islam further" (Myatt, 2013, p. 56). As the side-switching storyline continues, David Myatt began to study Islam initially to use it for advancing his neo-Nazi cause but then he found it genuinely convincing. Again, intellectual fascination for a different manifest-ation of the "warrior ethos" paired up with personal impressions:

After some months of studying Islam, during that Summer of 1998 – my new strategy regarding some religion completely forgotten – it occurred to me that the Way of Al-Islam was indeed a good way to bring-into-being a new, a noble, society with a warrior ethos, and the more I read about the life of the Prophet, Muhammad, the more I came to admire him. There did, indeed, seem to be something remarkable, something numinous, something divine, here, in both the life of the Prophet, Muhammad, and in the Quran, and so – inspired and naively enthusiastic again – I trundled off to the nearest Mosque. For nearly half an hour I hesitated – for these were the people I had spent thirty years trying to get out of Britain. How would they react to the former leader of the neo-nazi NSM walking into "their" Mosque? ... They were so pleased and so friendly that I admit that, then, tears came to my eyes, and I really felt I had, finally, arrived at the right place. (Myatt, 2013, p. 57)

After this key event, Myatt enrolled in an Arabic class and claims to have rejected nationalism, national socialism, and racism. He also took over the new Muslim name of Abdul-Aziz ibn Myatt. A slightly different storyline was presented by Myatt immediately after his conversion in an essay entitled "My Conversion to Islam" dating back to 1998. Naturally, the likely target audience for this narrative was the Muslim community and hence does not include the strategic goal of using the Islamic faith for the advancement of national socialism. In this version, David Myatt develops his conversion around two main experiences: taking over a new job on a farm and his personal impressions during his travels to Egypt. As for the first element of his alternative storyline, the new job, Myatt writes:

My conversion really begin [*sic!*] when I started a new job, working long hours on a farm, often by myself. The close contact with Nature, the toil of manual labour, really did restore my soul, my humanity ... I felt the truth of the one and only Creator in my heart and in my mind. For the first time in my life, I felt truly humble. (Myatt, 1998)

Following this sensation of oneness with nature, Myatt describes how he (guided by Allah) began to read the Quran and found "logic, reason, truth, revelation, justice, humanity and beauty" (Myatt, 1998), which sparked his interest in learning more about Islam. Through this process, Islam "answered all the doubts, all the questions" (Myatt, 1998) of his past 30 years. Especially the "dignity, honour, trust, justice, community and truth" (Myatt, 1998) of the prophet Muhammad and the first generation of his followers impressed him deeply. In consequence, "conversion became not a question, but a duty" (Myatt, 1998). Practically, Myatt's transition to Islam was facilitated through personal interactions with Muslims and travels to Egypt:

In terms of the "Western" explanation that most Westerners will seek in order to try and understand my conversion, I suppose my journey toward Islam began when I first went to Egypt and, as a tourist, visited a Mosque. The Adhan – the call to prayer – had begun and I was struck by its beauty. It is fair to say my heart responded to it in a way that, at the time, I did not understand. Then, I knew little about Islam, but each time I visited Egypt I learnt a little more. I talked to several Egyptians about their religion, and bought a copy of an English translation of the Quran. The little bits I read made a lot of sense to me, and the more I learnt about Islam, the more admirable it seemed to be. The more Muslims I met, the more I admired them. (Myatt, 1998)

Interestingly, Myatt also kept using his other side-switching narrative that focused on a strategic infiltration of Islam at least for some time after his conversion. This might have been due to the fact that he actually did remain engaged with extreme right-wing milieus, for example, through writings and interviews. Naturally, this would create the need to explain the "double life." In an interview published in 2001 by *Invictus* magazine (run by US neo-Nazi Harold Covington) and posted online on one of Myatt's various online blogs around August 2002, the narrative about the conversion still was:

But with Islam I had an ulterior motive, at least initially. In addition to seeking some aid or support for the overthrow of ZOG [Zionist Occupied Government], I wondered if it might be possible to create some kind of Aryan Islam – some kind of group to express Aryan culture and identity within the confines of Islam. In the end I concluded it was not possible, just as once again I found only National-Socialism to fully and rationally answer all the questions about life, existence, and our identity, as human beings. (Myatt, 2001)

Even articles he wrote under his Muslim identity were called a "ploy" or "deception, to confuse and if possible divert the attention of the enemy" (Myatt, 2001). This was not the only indication that Myatt might have tried to keep both ideological worldviews active in unison. After his conversion, he authored and published some extreme right-wing texts, such as *Why National-Socialism Is Not Racist* and the essay "The Holocaust: Truth and Reason verses Zionist Propaganda," in which he denied that the Holocaust ever happened. In a 2003 interview with George Michael, he stated: "As for myself, I am committed to Folk Culture, which I understand to be the esoteric aspect of National-Socialism: what National-Socialism is evolving to become" (as cited in Michael, 2006, p. 145).

Indeed, David Myatt put significant effort into arguing for a shared ideological core between National Socialism and Islam (or more specifically Islamic extremism). In his 2003 essay "National-Socialism and Islam – The Case for Cooperation," for example, he claims that the "real" Islam upheld by jihadist groups like al-Qaeda, the Taliban, and Hamas differs from the "tame, emasculated, 'moderate', 'democratic' Islam, which the Zionists and their lackeys in the governments and agencies of the West seek to create and which they wish to see practised by Muslim countries ... authentic Islam – like National-Socialism – is profoundly anti-democratic ... The honourable warriors of this authentic Islam are the natural brothers-in-arms – the natural allies – of true, authentic, National-Socialists, exemplified as this National-Socialism" (Myatt, 2009, p. 7). For Myatt, a shared code of honor and hatred against

Western democracies, as well as Judaism, would create the basis for an "Aryan Islam," meaning an Islamic theology infused with his understanding of national socialism, in order to create a natural ally for Western right-wing extremist groups in Muslim countries. Myatt also repeatedly stated that in his perspective, the only effective challenge against "imperialist Zionism," his main ideologically enemy, would come from Islamic extremist groups (e.g., Michael, 2006, pp. 143–144).

David Myatt not only kept an open dialogue with his former extreme right-wing milieu through writings and interviews long after his conversion, he also developed a particular Islamic extremist mindset and position. Among his articles written as Abdul-Aziz ibn Myatt are, for example, extensive praise for Osama bin Laden, the Taliban, and al-Qaeda, as well as some of the most elaborate and sophisticated justifications for suicide terrorism in the English language (Weitzman, 2010, p. 16). In his previously mentioned essay "National-Socialism and Islam," for example, suicide attacks including against civilians are described as righteous duty:

This sacrifice is not "suicide" – the Western Media using the incorrect term "suicide attacks" or "suicide bombings" in an attempt to discredit these martyrs, their organizations, and authentic Islam itself. Such martyrdom operations arise from the Islamic duty of Jihad – for Muslims believe they have a duty, given by Allah, to fight injustice, oppression, and tyranny, and to reclaim any Muslim lands which have been occupied or taken by non-Muslims. (Myatt, 2009, pp. 43–44)

Up until the late 1990s, David Myatt had not been a widely known or prominent figure of the extreme right in the British public perception. That abruptly changed in April 1999, after the London nail bomb attacks over three successive weekends (between April 17 and 30). The homemade bombs killed three people, including a pregnant woman, and injured 140 victims. On May 2, 1999, the authorities charged 22-year-old neo-Nazi David Copeland with murder. Copeland was a former member of the British National Party and Myatt's NSM. The attacks targeted minority communities and resulted in six concurrent life sentences for Copeland. In combination with the surfacing of the right-wing terrorist tactical manual *A Practical Guide to the Strategy and Tactics of Revolution* authored by Myatt around 1996, connections between him and Copeland were quickly drawn in the public. The strong media interest in Myatt, according to his narrative, also put additional strain on his second marriage. However, ideological and theological interests had taken priority over the relationship for him before and so Myatt continues to express deep regret about not having been able to recognize or prevent his wife's suicide. With yet another traumatic incident in his life, David Myatt was thrown out of his ideological stability again, which led him to discard his newfound religion:

In the weeks, the months, following Fran's death, Islam became personally irrelevant to me, for as I wrote at the time, I felt it would have been just too easy for me to depend upon, to turn to, to rely on, Allah, on God – to have one's remorse removed by some belief in some possible redemption, to have one's mistakes, errors – "sins" – voided by some supra-personal means. To escape into prayer, Namaz. Can there be, I began to wonder, hope, redemption – some meaning in personal tragedy – without a Saviour's grace? Without God, Allah, prayer, Namaz, submission, sin, and faith? Gradually, painfully slowly, I seemed to move toward some answers, often as a result of personal letters written to friends. For the act of so writing – of trying to so express my feelings, my thoughts – seemed to aid the process of interior reflection. However, for a while at least, I maintained a public Muslim persona, stubbornly clinging as I did to some notion of duty; to the pledge of loyalty I had given on my conversion to Islam, a pledge I still then, and for some time afterwards, felt I was honour-bound to honour, and it would take me some eighteen months of an intense interior struggle, and further development of the ethics of my Numinous Way, before I resolved this very personal dilemma. (Myatt, 2013, p. 65)

This solution to his internal dilemma became a complete cessation of his involvement in Islam with a public declaration to have left the religion in 2010, followed by promotion of his own religious philosophy, which Myatt calls the "Numinous Way" and renouncement of extremism. Since then, he has focused his writings mostly on poetry, translations and commentaries on classic Greek mythology, and philosophy. In this short discussion of David Myatt's side-switching narratives and partially conflicting storylines, it becomes clear that he is a complex persona who defies simple answers to the question of why he changed groups and milieus so often and so fundamentally. It is also obvious, that during large parts of his life, Myatt was driven by a search for meaning and purpose, as well as intellectual desire to find or create the all-encompassing and perfect political philosophy. At least based on his own writings regarding the transition from the far right to Islamic extremism, a strong recurring element is the fight against an alleged "New World Order," meaning Western and Zionist imperialism in his opinion.

Islam, for Myatt, provided a welcomed basis to further explore and spread his own version of national socialist ideology, wrapped into sacred values like "honor" and "nobility." Anti-Semitism therefore can be seen as a key element in his side-switching storyline. It is quite extraordinary that Myatt kept open and amicable relations with the extreme-right milieu, even years after his conversion. The fact that most of his neo-Nazi writings are still essential reading in many militant far-right groups and circles further shows that his double narrative strategy that aimed to avoid being seen as traitor seems to have worked at least to some degree. A possible explanation could be that Myatt managed to find an ideologically "correct" language using certain triggers (e.g., honor, duty, discipline, warrior ethos) to build sympathy between the different milieus and for his own position. In fact, he could rightfully refer back to historical precedents of alliances between Nazi Germany and Muslim countries or leaders (Michael, 2006, pp. 112–119). His outspoken extreme positions during his neo-Nazi and Islamic extremist involvement might have also shielded him from the accusation of opportunism. Still, David Myatt's defection processes are unusual when compared with the others presented here. In his storyline, it is all a constant intellectual strive toward metaphysical enlightenment.

4.4   Extremist Converts in Court

In 2008, the British newspaper *The Independent* reported on the case of former neo-Nazi and member of the British National Party (BNP) Stephen Jones (N. Morris, 2008). At the time of the coverage, Jones was being held in isolation within a segregation unit in Whitemoor prison, Cambridgeshire, for three weeks on suspicion of trying to recruit fellow prisoners to the jihadist terror group al-Qaeda. Notably, the paper reports, this was the first time an inmate had been put into isolation to prevent attempts to radicalize other prisoners. While the story about Jones' background remains somewhat vague, it is hinted that he converted to Islam in prison and became extreme in his religious views. Jones was serving a life sentence when, it is suggested, other extremist Muslim inmates converted and radicalized him. His previous extreme right-wing background was seen as a major additional risk factor for Jones, in terms of his own ability to recruit others. A Prison Officers Association member is quoted by the BBC on the case saying "if you can get someone that's so right wing converted then a normal prisoner is going to have absolutely no chance" (Chidzoy, 2008).

Twelve years later, in 2020, a remarkably similar case was reported, again through British newspapers. This time, the public discussion developed around the question of what to do with high-risk prisoners who had come close to the end of their prison terms and were about to be released. In the context of the February 2020 Streatham (London) stabbing attack, leaving two victims injured and the attacker Sudesh Mamoor Faraz Amman shot and killed by the police, this issue had become immanent. Amman had been sentenced in 2018 to three years and four months in prison for disseminating terrorist material and collecting information that could be useful to a terrorist. While he was a college student at the time, he shared an al-Qaeda magazine and voiced support for the terror organization ISIS. Shortly before the Streatham incident, Amman was released from prison (January 2020) and remained under active surveillance by the authorities due to the significant risk to the public he posed in the eyes of the police (Dodd, Sabbagh & Syal, 2020). During his time in prison, Amman had befriended another inmate, identified only as "X" in the news reports. This person was also getting close to his release and considered to be a "high risk and highly vulnerable prisoner" (Hymas, 2020). "X" had been sentenced to prison for far-right terrorist activities as well and converted to Islam in prison. Regarding his personality and motives, the press quoted Chief Magistrate Emma Arbuthnot with: "X's views have veered from one extreme to another, he has a deep seated psychological need to feel part of a group" (Mellor, 2020). Again, this case was special as it was one of the first to be discussed after a legal change by the British government to keep high-risk inmates detained even after their sentence had ended.

Little is known about the backgrounds, radicalization trajectories, and conversion stories of these two far-right defectors to Islamic extremism besides the fact that both completed the journey to a point at which were considered to pose significant security risks. Of course, Stephen Jones and "X" are just two cases that made it into public reporting. Religious conversion by inmates with all kinds of different backgrounds leading to the onset of violent extremist radicalization or the spin of existing extremist views into a different direction in prison can be regarded as a simple statistical probability. Once extremist ideologies are present in a closed environment, either through inmates who have been sentenced because of their actions for such extremist milieus or imported through external sources (e.g., literature, mail exchange, visitors), there is at least a chance that some prisoners might find those views attractive.

The prison environment as such can cause existential crises, boredom leading to the search for new experiences and perspective, or the simple need to socialize with other inmates and receive their protection. In most cases, however, a religious conversion in prison has been found to be a source of behavioral improvement and emotional stability (Hamm, 2013). Whatever the effects of the conversion to extremist interpretations of Islam in prison for far-right inmates might be, the specific nature of the high-security environment they are located in makes it difficult to get an impression about their motives and side-switching process, as well as stories. Other than interviewing these persons, little information can be expected to be publicly available.

It is at least slightly different for a handful of comparatively well-documented cases of people who shifted their allegiances and worldviews before entering the judicial system. In these cases, court documents and press reports have provided some insight into their driving factors, the way those persons combined opposing extremist ideologies, and their reception in the milieus they were active in before the conversion. One example would be the case of German convert Thomas Usztics, who was sentenced to a prison term of four years and three months for his membership in the jihadist terror organization "German Taliban Mujahideen" (Deutsche Taliban Mujahideen, or DTM) in December 2012 (Gartenstein-Ross & Blackman, 2019, p. 16; Steinberg, 2013, p. 173).

Even though his activities after converting to Islam in 2008 and subsequent involvement in jihadist terrorism, including his travels to and combat experiences in Afghanistan, are far better known, there is some information about his past as a neo-Nazi. As Usztics had returned disillusioned from the fight in Afghanistan and regretted joining the Taliban, he cooperated in court and provided testimony. He was born in Hungary but grew up in Berlin and was introduced to right-wing extremism by his uncle. In the reported pieces of Usztics' storyline, however, his far-right past is presented as a marginal and insignificant period in his life, preceding a drift into drug abuse and addiction. In court, Usztics explained that he experienced some form of "inspiration" (original in German, translated by author, Mielke, 2012) and bought a Quran. Whenever reading the holy text, he stated, the use of drugs did not appeal to him. Islam fascinated him, because the religion seemed peaceful and calm during a time he felt lost and in psychological turmoil. After his conversion, he convinced his wife to follow him and was introduced to more radical groups via a friend (Mielke, 2012).

Another example would be the case of American teenager Corey Johnson, who stabbed to death a 13-year-old victim during a sleepover on March 12, 2018. Johnson, who was 17 at the time of the incident, had been a long-term friend of the kids he attacked that night, including the boy he killed (Wang, 2018). As for the motive, he stated that the other kids had admired celebrities like gods and mocked his faith (Wang, 2018). Johnson was not unknown to the authorities, as he had raised concerns many times already for violent and threatening behavior and excessive interest in other forms of extremism, namely neo-Nazism, as early as middle school. At least since 2016, the FBI was watching his online activities as they began involving communication with ISIS and expressions of jihadist views. Local police knew about his outspoken support for the Ku Klux Klan and anti-Semitic, as well as anti-LGBT, comments since his seventh and eighth grade. This interest seems to have intensified throughout grade 10, when around December 2016 Johnson's sister reported his fascination with Adolf Hitler, anger management issues, and bullying of other kids. At that time, the teenager also used a swastika as avatar on his Facebook page and crossed the tipping point for local authorities to reach out to the FBI's Joint Terrorism Task Force.

A meeting of different agencies about Johnson in January 2017 linked him to an online jihadist–framed threat made against a British high school in October 2016 (E. Kleinberg & Peters, 2018), which had to be evacuated and searched in consequence. By then, Johnson's mother reported to the authorities that her son's interest had expanded to include other dictators such as Josef Stalin or Kim Jong Un and that he had begun to study Islam, as well as that he changed his dress to Muslim attire. In March 2017, Johnson was interviewed by the FBI and denied any affiliation with ISIS but admitted his admiration for senior al-Qaeda recruiter and strategist Anwar al-Awlaki (1971–2011). He was warned and told to cease his extremist online activities, but in February 2018 federal agencies had determined that Johnson's actions now created enough concern to justify an arrest, which, which would have happened just a couple of weeks after the stabbing occurred (for this timeline of the case see Wang, 2018).

Court records provide some, albeit limited, insight into Johnson's development, who after being arrested claimed the name "Mustafa" (E. Kleinberg & Peters, 2018). At least in his statements to the authorities regarding the killing, Johnson filled his rhetoric and explanations with partially detailed jihadist ideology. He claimed to be a prisoner of war against the unbelievers, quoted Jordanian jihadist and emir of al-Qaeda in Iraq Abu Musab al-Zarqawi (1966–2006), and praised British, French, as well US jihadist motivated terrorist acts as "successful attacks against the crusader coalition" (as cited in E. Kleinberg & Peters, 2018). Johnson experienced many potentially traumatizing childhood events, including numerous long-distance moves, the divorce of his parents, and the his father's death due to a drug overdose. It is known that he was supposed to take antidepressant medication, which he stopped a week before the killing. Johnson also began to try excessively to convert his closest friends and to show them ISIS videos on his cell phone, even the night of the sleepover and stabbing attack (E. Kleinberg & Peters, 2018).

The main difference in the cases of Sascha Lemanski or David Myatt, who have also had conflicts with the legal system, is that no elaborate storylines exist among the individuals discussed in the following section. Nevertheless, they are too significant for the focus of this book to forgo, especially since highly relevant information for the overall analysis was given by family members, friends, other associates, or digital evidence. For example, assessing the way those former US neo-Nazis (all of them came from the American far right) acted online after their conversion in their original milieus and how they were perceived by their peers holds important insights for our exploration in this book. The cases in question are Emerson Begolly and Devon Arthurs. Two additional case studies (Nicholas Young and Joseph Jeffrey Brice) can be found in the online Bonus Chapter to this book.

4.4.1   Emerson Begolly

On January 4, 2011, Emerson Begolly, a 21-year-old man from Pennsylvania, was arrested in connection with al-Qaeda–inspired terrorist acts. His online activities that led to prominence in jihadist chat rooms began in 2008. As an indication of his committed involvement in the virtual jihadist milieu, Begolly was a manager of the al-Qaeda–affiliated Ansar al-Mujahideen English Forum (AMEF). At the time, the occasional college student lived at home and used various aliases, such as "Abu Nancy," "Goatly" (referring to his rural farming family background), and "Asadullah al-Shishani." Online, Begolly made the acquaintance of other extremists, many of them arrested, charged, and sentenced later on, for example, Colleen LaRose (dubbed "Jihad Jane" in the press), who was sentenced to ten years in prison in January 2014 for a jihadist assassination plot, or Khalid Aldawsari, who was sentenced to life in prison in 2012 on charges of attempting to build a weapon of mass destruction.

Another part of his online activities was to argue for terrorist attacks against the Jewish community, financial institutions, civilian planes, trains, and military installations. To support his calls for action, Begolly also uploaded a 101-page manual providing instructions for how to manufacture a bomb, among other terrorist instructional material. In the subsequent police search of his parents' home, authorities found multiple weapons. During his arrest, he attempted to reach his gun and bit the FBI agents apprehending him (Gartenstein-Ross & Blackman, 2019, pp. 12–14; Klausen, 2016, p. 38). The jihadist trajectory that led to his indictment in July 2011 and sentence of more than eight years in prison in June 2011 for using the Internet to solicit others to commit terrorist attacks and weapons charges, followed his extreme right-wing involvement. Begolly's extensive online posting behavior, which included a picture of him as a child dressed in a Nazi uniform, caught the media's attention and fed into analysts' comments on his radicalization processes.

From what is known, his father, who was a white supremacist at least for some time into his jihadist radicalization as well, introduced him to the extreme right at age 11 and facilitated his development of far-right attitudes, for example, by dressing him up in that Nazi uniform. By the age of 14, Begolly contacted the neo-Nazi organization National Socialist Movement (NSM) and was appointed head of the Pennsylvania division of the NSM's youth division, the Viking Youth Corps, in 2003 (Nelson, 2011). A crucial investigation into his beliefs and mindset at that time resulted in online messages between Begolly and other NSM members being obtained and analyzed by the Southern Poverty Law Center (SPLC). They reveal a deep commitment to extreme-right ideology. Most importantly, Begolly wrote a lengthy autobiographical post on November 2011 entitled "My Story, My Life," which was quoted in parts by the SPLC. As a key element of the explanation for the way into the neo-Nazi milieu, Begolly recounts incidents of harassment by Latino and mixed-race students starting in the fifth grade without any intervention by adults. Conflicts such as these became worse in junior high school, where he was suspended and labeled a threat and required to undergo mandatory counseling after a violent altercation (Nelson, 2011). Neo-Nazism provided him with a sense of emotional stability and an explanation for the injustice and grievances he perceived:

I am not quite sure where to begin my story, and I am wondering if it has a beginning at all … I have always agreed with the National Socialist philosophy, even before I knew there was one! … I discovered my Fuehrer, Adolf Hitler. I read about National Socialism in a book and it seemed so great! It was the answer to all my problems. At school I said that Hitler was a great leader, but the students branded me a fool. But, I stuck to my beliefs, the Truth. (as cited in Nelson, 2011)

Begolly continues to recount conflicts in school, while at the same time he also claims to have been regarded as extraordinarily intelligent with high-grade achievements. A few weeks into high school, he "put down the school system for being 'too jewish [sic] and pro-mixing'" (Nelson, 2011) and made comments that voiced understanding for school shooters. Eventually, he was given the option to either leave the school or go to court: "So I quit school at age 13 and began home-schooling. [I] discovered the NSM. I e-mailed [C]ommander Schoep … He said I would be a good member. So I joined" (as cited in Nelson, 2011). It appears to be clear that the continuous conflicts in his school were somewhat premeditated by the racist and anti-Semitic stereotypes planted in him by his father.

The far-right milieu naturally seemed the only logical and stable social environment for Begolly and his storyline makes a clear point about being driven into the arms of the NSM by the alleged failures of a multicultural educational system. However, the fact that he is diagnosed with Asperger syndrome, an autism spectrum disorder whose symptoms include extreme difficulty with social interactions, likely also played a significant role for the problems he encountered during his school education. It is not clear exactly when, how, and why Begolly converted to Islam before becoming active on jihadist online forums around 2008, but the content was explicitly anti-Semitic in nature, even with an Islamic extremist wrapping. It is reported that in 2009, after he registered as an online student of Pennsylvania State University, he attended a pro-Palestinian rally on campus in early 2009 and presented himself as a Chechen (Siegel, 2011). In those early posts as a jihadist, Begolly encouraged attacking synagogues, Jewish schools, and day-care centers (Siegel, 2011). What eventually would alarm the authorities, however, was increasingly militant anti-Americanism by the end of 2010 and early 2011. Begolly began to call for attacks against US "police stations, post offices, synagogues, military facilities, train lines, bridges, cell phone towers and water plants … civilian planes, financial institutions" (Siegel, 2011). Conversations between him and other jihadists online that were retrieved by the authorities mention America's alleged "war on Islam" as the main reasons for this development.

It is fair to say, that Emerson Begolly's relationship with extreme-right ideology remained complex, even after his conversion to Islam and radicalization into jihadist milieus. While he included white supremacists (next to black supremacists) as targets in his calls for terrorists attacks at least by August 2020 (Indictment: United States of America vs. Emerson Winfield Begolly, 2011, p. 4), residual far-right ideology and even sympathy shines through in many of his statements and conversations. As part of the exhibits presented to the court during Begolly's detention hearing in January 2011, extensive chat conversations between him and a fellow jihadist were made public. In one exchange from November 2010, he states that his father was aware of him being an administrator on the AMEF forum and allegedly would not care about this. Begolly's father, according to this conversation, displayed hatred against then-President Obama for allegedly wanting to "kill white people" and did not mind his son's involvement in jihadism because of "presumably" being part of his "own militia" (Exhibits from the Detention Hearing: United States of America vs. Emerson Begolly, 2011, p. 16). In the same conversation, Begolly, who used the the nickname "Abu Nancy," also expressed his admiration for Adolf Hitler but denied being a racist: "i like Hitler. so what? Im not racist against black ppl. or asian. or whoever" (Exhibits from the Detention Hearing: United States of America vs. Emerson Begolly, 2011, p. 28, spelling as in original). This somewhat surprising statement is contradicted about six minutes later in the same chat:

i think biggest threat to america is damn mexicans but yet they spend billions giving to israel and dont secure the boarder. why??? they come in illegally and hurt innocent ppl like rob old ladies and rape little kids yet here is the fence??? ... where is the watch towers? ... persoanlly if america were not at war with islam i would not hate it but i am angry they dont do something abotu the aliens. killing kuffar is one thing but when ppl r getting raped and robbed who have nothing to do with anyway it is upsetting. ppl like my gram, sry, i just had personal experiences i told you my gram was robbed. (Exhibits from the Detention Hearing: United States of America vs. Emerson Begolly, 2011, pp. 30–31, spelling as in original)

Begolly appears to be mixing racist far-right stereotypes that arguably stem from his time in the neo-Nazi movement or his militia-oriented father with his jihadist narrative framework. He seemingly expressed a moral priority in combination with personal experiences of injustice against helpless victims, which would supersede "killing kuffars" (meaning killing infidels). In a separate conversation with the same chat partner, Begolly also recounts his father as abusive, that he had kicked his mother during the day of the exchange. According to Begolly, his father also used violence to make a "man" out of him when he was small (Exhibits from the Detention Hearing: United States of America vs. Emerson Begolly, 2011, p. 35). However, there is no indication that Begolly took these negative experiences as a reason to reject his father's white supremacist ideology. On the contrary, he even casually uses extreme right-wing language and slurs, for example talking about "typical liberal kikes" (Exhibits from the Detention Hearing: United States of

America vs. Emerson Begolly, 2011, p. 37) when expressing his anger about strict gun laws in many countries. The anti-Semitic slur is widely present in today's far right and adds to the extensive expressions of hatred against Jews and Israel in Begolly's posts and conversations. While other target groups and enemies appeared to vary over time, anti-Semitism clearly stands out as the ideological continuity between the two extremist milieus.

Additional links to his extreme-right past repeatedly shine through in his conversations. For example, Begolly envisions a "redneck ... southern style" (Exhibits from the Detention Hearing: United States of America vs. Emerson Begolly, 2011, p. 56) lynching as a form of execution he would enjoy for an enemy and describes the anti-government extremist and (at least) white supremacist–leaning Oklahoma bomber Timothy McVeigh (1968–2001) as "a hero" he wished to surpass in "going down like him" (Exhibits from the Detention Hearing: United States of America vs. Emerson Begolly, 2011, p. 63). On one occasion, Begolly explained his dislike for the US Democratic party and displayed his political-moral code of ethics: "i dont like republicans, i hate them, but i hate democrats worse cause they r for queers and abortions and anti firearms ... the republicans destory other countrys the dems destroy america" (Exhibits from the Detention Hearing: United States of America vs. Emerson Begolly, 2011, p. 72, spelling as in original). While the rejection of abortion and queer sexuality could be found in Islamic extremist milieus as well of course, the specific notion of democratic liberalism "destroying America" is a sentiment most widely seen in ultra-conservative, radical, and far-right environments. It is fair to speculate that these far-right anti-government ideological talking points originated and resonated with Begolly's father militia involvement and his own time in the neo-Nazi NSM.

There is no indication that there was a break of some sort that might have led him to critically distance from far-right ideology or language. On the contrary, the fact that he so openly referenced anti-government terrorists like McVeigh and used clearly far-right terms and codes without fear of alienating his Muslim chat partner, means that he saw no contradiction or problem in combining the two ideologies. This speculation is supported by another episode in his chat. With some excitement, Begolly tells his fellow jihadist that he recently met a member of a far-right militia and goes on to build sympathy for that milieu: "they r trainin just like i am. at the present time i dont think they pose a threat to the mujahideen cause their only plan is to keep blacks out of their areas but maybe in the future they may pose a threat ... but not in the present" (Exhibits from the Detention Hearing: United States of America vs. Emerson Begolly, 2011, p. 73, spelling as in original). This was stated by Begolly in November 2010 and about four months before, he had posted a somewhat more elaborate version of the imagined common nature of far-right anti-government militias and jihadist groups:

The American Revolution. Dear brothers and sisters, this is just a brief overview of possible scenarios ... Revolution. Civil war. Mass chaos. Race riots. Whatever you call it, it boils down to the same. The toppling of America from within itself at the hands of its own people. What could cause such events to take place? The common answer is martial law declared upon the people by the state. Why is martial law declared? Well, that in [sic] actually unimportant as to why. Maybe the mujahadeen carry out attacks. Maybe the assassination of obama by skinheads leads to mass race riots. Maybe California tries to declare independence. Maybe even the government in all of its corruptness orchestrates events itself in an effort to gain ultimate control. Whatever the case may be, if it results in some sort of civil, then what would come to place next. Many groups operate within America, aside from what would be deployed, which would likely be the National Guard and police forces. Christian militias, white militias, black militias, crips, bloods, mexican gangs, nationalistic militias for Alaska, minutemen. These are just some of the groups. But what about Muslim militias? What about the MUJAHIDEEN? Where shall be the able bodies young man who will protect their brothers and sisters not only against a government crackdown, but also against rival gangs and militias? Preparation::: Education ➔ Training ➔ JIHAD. Ultimately the government will fail ... at the hands of these various groups. Why? First because in America people do have guns and will fight. Second, because a majority of the people will not support martial law. Third, because during the civil war, the government will go broke from no Texas. Fourth, many national guardsmen may become disillusioned and either fight the government or dessert because the lack of pay. Fifth, because as Abraham Lincoln said "a house divided cannot stand." A civil war between all factions, as it as it clearly would be in this case, as opposed to north vs. south or even just people vs. government would draw out all resources, especially from the government, who even though they pack the most firepower, like needed resources such as the farmland and support of many groups. How long would the war last? Allah knows ... The end result ... Insha Allah no more United States. The what? A new government that all people support? Various different countries for separate groups? Allah knows ... But ultimately and most importantly, what shall become of the Muslims living within America during this war? Insha Allah we shall fight under the banner of La Illaha Lila Allah. Insha Allah we shall emerge victorious. When next for us? An independent state for Muslims in north america? A mass migration back to Islamic countries? Or continued Jihad against all factions until Islam dominates north American, which it shall, Insha Allah. (Exhibits from the Detention Hearing: United States of America vs. Emerson Begolly, 2011, p. 104, spelling as in original)

In this fascinating combination of stereotypical far-right apocalyptic visions regarding a looming race war and the collapse of the US government after defeat by the various armed groups that oppose martial law (a key extreme-right narrative, as laid out in the *Turner Diaries*, see Berger, 2016) with a jihadist-framed call to form a mujahideen militia, Begolly appears to be right in the middle between the two milieus, while still leaning heavily to the far right. In this post, he does not advocate an all-out war against the infidels, for example, and does not seem to prefer emigration to a Muslim-majority country to build the caliphate. Instead, in his mind at that point, the mujahideen are a form of Muslim militia who will protect each other once the race war starts. The use of Muslim terminology and the optimistic statement that Islam will dominate North America after the downfall of the US government cannot mask the fact that the particular nature of his arguments, conspiracy theories, and solutions to the seemingly upcoming crisis are predominantly based in far-right anti-governmentalism and extremism.

The lack of arguments in favor of a spread of the Muslim faith through violence and thereby securing control over the territory (a classic jihadist narrative to solve conflict with Western infidel countries) shows that Begolly's mindset is focused on removing an allegedly corrupt government that does not have the support of the people. Considering his ideological past (mainly anti-government militias from the side of his father and the neo-Nazi NSM), this post apparently aims to reconcile the paternal influences with his newfound extremist interpretation of Islam. The statement does not contain any anti-Semitism, racism, or white supremacy, which is noteworthy, since in later conversations he rarely missed an opportunity to express hatred toward Jews. Other posts shortly before and after this one, however, do contain much clearer jihadist language and narratives, so this statement regarding militias and the looming racial war in the USA might be seen as a particularly relevant residual from his previous ideological milieu (especially since it still resonates in his conversations a couple of months later).

In addition to this ideological side of Emerson Begolly's storylines (as far as they are known through the documents and his posts), it must be pointed out that there seems to be also some form of therapeutic outreach. I have argued in a separate publication that extremist milieus not only pose risks of damage to the mental health of their members but also contain elements that could provide quasi-therapeutic effects, for example, a strong sense of belonging, community, explanation, understanding, and sympathy (Koehler, 2020). Begolly at one point in the chat conversations provided to the court explains his hatred against liberalism and queer sexuality with an incident of abuse and molestation by a Christian minister at the age of 13 or 14. This experience is given as the reasons he "really started to hate this society" (Exhibits from the Detention Hearing: United States of America vs. Emerson Begolly, 2011, p. 75). It is hardly possible to ignore the attempt to receive some form of help or consolation, especially since he openly states: "i am still traumatized" (Exhibits from the Detention Hearing: United States of America vs. Emerson Begolly, 2011, p. 76, spelling as in original).

In addition to confessing such intimate details of his past (regardless of whether they are true or not), Begolly also expressed concern very openly about his constant violent fantasies (including those with a sexual component) and his fear that his chat partner might think of him as a "psychopath" (Exhibits from the Detention Hearing: United States of America vs. Emerson

Begolly, 2011, p. 70). As has been initially pointed out, Emerson Begolly was diagnosed with Asperger syndrome and clearly suffered from severe mental health issues throughout is involvement in the two extremist milieus. Therefore, it is of course difficult to establish with certainty how much of his commitment to right-wing or Islamic extremism was influenced or driven by these mental health factors. Nevertheless, the case of Emerson Begolly's side-switching appears to be an almost natural development of his virulent anti-Semitism and anti-liberalism by growing out of the extreme-right milieu into the jihadist sphere, while he retained many of the thought patterns and concepts nurtured by his father and the neo-Nazi environment.

4.4.2 Devon Arthurs

Of the two cases presented in this section, Devon Arthurs (born in March 1999) is the most significant one. Not unlike Sascha Lemanski (see Section 4.1) he retained intact friendships and even a close personal involvement in the far-right milieu even after his conversion and subsequent jihadist radicalization. On May 19, 2017, Arthurs left the apartment in which he lived in Tampa Palms, Florida, together with fellow neo-Nazis and walked to a nearby smoke shop carrying a firearm and began to threaten customers. After the arrival of the police, Arthurs was arrested without resistance and directed the officers back to the apartment, where, he informed them, the bodies of two of his comrades could be found. At the same time, another neo-Nazi friend and alleged leader of the group, Brendon Russell, who served in the National Guard at that time and had just returned from an exercise in full military dress, suffered a nervous breakdown after finding his two dead roommates. Arthurs admitted to shooting 22-year-old Jeremy Himmelman and 18-year-old Andrew Oneschuk earlier that day (E. Hall, 2017).

Regarding the motive of the killing, he stated to have acted in anger over the neo-Nazis' mocking of his Muslim faith and their plot to conduct acts of domestic terrorism, which he sought to prevent in this way (Dearen, 2017). Other statements about the reason behind the killing included raising aware-ness about anti-Muslim sentiments and "to take some of the neo-Nazis with him" (as cited in Beckett & Burke, 2017). In the subsequent interrogations, significant mental health issues became evident and even Arthurs himself stated that he wanted help to get them under control, fearing to "be insane" (Sullivan, 2018). Facing two counts of first-degree murder in addition to kidnapping and firearms charges, Arthurs was psychologically and psychiatric-ally evaluated twice in 2018 and ruled incompetent to stand trial. He spent more than a year at the Florida State Hospital where he received treatment with the goal of restoring his mental health to a condition in which he would be fit to stand trial. In December 2019, mental health experts testified that Arthurs was diagnosed with schizoaffective disorder and underlying symptoms of schizo-phrenia, bipolar disorder, and autism. One expert detailed his condition by describing that the accused quickly gets distracted with unintelligible speech, as well as the experience of auditory hallucinations – voices that criticize and accuse him. According to the testimony, Arthurs also believed that he could communicate with his dead roommates (Sullivan, 2019). Restoring Arthurs to good mental health was deemed impossible by some experts in the hearing (Sullivan, 2019), which resulted in another court decision of incompetency to stand trial in May 2020 and his return to treatment (Sullivan, 2020).

Before his conversion to Islam about one year before the killing at the age of 17 (Mathias, 2017), Arthurs was a member of the militant neo-Nazi terror group "Atomwaffen Division" (AWD) since roughly 2013 according to police records (Tampa-PD, 2017, p. 118). AWD has been increasingly active since 2015 and originates in the USA. Its ideology is based on existential nihilism, accelerationism, and virulent neo-Nazism, as well as anti-Semitism. The group's doctrine was laid out by American far-right extremist James Mason in his 1980 book *Siege* (Ware, 2019) and led to numerous murders and terror plots across the United States. There is little information about his extreme-right radicalization process, but the court documents state that in September 2014 Arthurs' father received a copy of Adolf Hitler's *Mein Kampf* in the mail and got so upset with his son that an argument (including a physical altercation over the book) led to Devon's decision to move out and live with his mother. The records also state that the father had no idea about his son's conversion to Islam and described him as having "ever-changing" (Tampa-PD, 2017, p. 129) ideologies.

The notion of ideological fickleness is also supported by statements from an online acquaintance of Russell and Arthurs: "I know this seems like a crazy red flag, but he would jump from one ideology to the next ... He was an atheist. Then Catholic. Then Orthodox Christian. Then Nazi. Then Muslim. He latched onto ... anything that looked cool" (as cited in Altman & Marrero, 2017). As for the motives and process for Arthur's conversion to Islam and his jihadist radicalization, a detailed media investigation based on extensive interviews with many of his peers and an assessment of chat conversations, revealed some important details. According to the article, Arthurs had become interested in the Salafist interpretation of Islam, which also forms the theological underpin-ning of groups like ISIS and al-Qaeda, about a year prior to the attack. He remained active in the same neo-Nazi chat rooms but began blending his old views with the new, indicated, for example, by changing his screen name from "weissewolfe" (German for "white wolfs") to "Kekman Al-Amriki" (Reeve, 2017), which includes elements from typical Islamic names or kunyas, often used in jihadist radicalization to signal the transition to a new identity (in this case, Al-Amriki shows the national background as American) and in this case

Kekman builds upon the "Kekistan"/"Kek" theme. Regarding the latter aspect, the satirical religion of "Kekism" with connected attributes such as the imagined country "Kekistan" or the deity "Kek" developed out of the alt-right "Pepe the Frog" meme and utilized the ancient Egyptian god Kek, which was depicted with a frog's face among other animals (Neiwert, 2017).

After his conversion to Islam, Arthurs began defending ISIS online in the extreme-right messaging board he had been active in for years, building support for AWD. The most important online milieu was the neo-Nazi "IronMarch" (IM) forum. Very fittingly, he changed the ideological description of his IM account to "Salafist National Socialism" and the location to "The Land of the Nonbelievers" to express his attempt to reconcile both ideological milieus. Naturally, Arthurs also began to spread his newfound religious faith and attempted to convert others on the platform, which resulted in some backlash and criticism directed at the administrators, calling for the Muslim Arthurs to be removed. One user wrote in November 2016: "why does AW still have that traitor toWeisse? Muslims don't quite count to much" ("Anti-Gay," 2016, spelling as in original) and another one in June 2016 directed at Russell: "yeah but what are you gonna do aboutWeisse?" ("Schmiss," 2016, spelling as in original). Such criticism was rejected by Russell, however, who defended his friend online before the shooting incident happened. Naturally, opinions about Arthurs shifted to almost complete condemnation after the killing. In one post-shooting conversation on IM, one user recounted a story in May 2017 about Arthurs trying to convert a fellow neo-Nazi:

I'm really sorry Alex. For IM and AW. Devon was always a deranged fuck. I am sorry about the two young men who died and I hope Odin [Russell's nickname] gets out well, he didn't do anything wrong. At some point, Devon tried to convert Jake (Über) to Islam and wanted to take him down with him as well, but Jake took his life before that could happen. He was such a fucking freak. He contacted Jake's parents after his death and even called them three months ago and acted like nothing was wrong, whilst he was planning this absolute monstrosity. All I can say is that I hope he gets electrocuted. ("liebling," 2017)

Through his extensive online activities, Arthurs was in touch with many individuals who witnessed his transformation process and developed their own interpretation of the events based on their impressions of him. One such person, for example, is quoted by journalist Elspeth Reeve saying: "He went from communist to national socialism to hyper-pragmatic capitalism to full ISIS . . . and that he found the far-right to be 'soft . . . because groups like ISIS actually do murder homosexuals etc. and take action, while our group had multiple LGBT individuals'" (Reeve, 2017). In addition to mentioning a previous far-left conviction by Arthurs before he entered the extreme right (for which no additional information is available), this quote also highlights more consequent actions against ideologically defined enemies as a potential motive for him to move toward Islamic extremism. Other people who were Arthurs' friends explained his interest in Islam as due to erratic interests and outside manipulation: "I think he was always unstable, and this Salafism shit got to his head more than anything" or "he's always been hopping around ideologies … He wanted to feel like he belonged to something strong … National socialism and Islam both offer a strong worldview – something very masculine, something very optimistic. Conquest and all that" (Reeve, 2017). The issues of masculinity and anti-feminism especially seem to have been a strong push factor for Arthurs toward Islamic extremism. Through an extreme right-wing concept called "white sharia," some far-rightists like Arthurs hoped to implement their version of ultra-conservative role models, male dominance over women, and control over sexuality. Arthurs himself is quoted by Reeve from one of his chat conversations:

Any state that allows adultery or any other form of degeneration is not worth fighting or dying for … See, I wouldn't be so mad, if it wasn't for the fact you literally have millions of western cuckolds ready to defend "freedom." The freedom for their daughters to be pimped out by pornographic distributors, freedom for their wives to be banged by countless guys while they are home, freedom to have their kids innocence be robbed. (Arthurs as cited in Reeve, 2017, spelling as in original)

Salafism might have appealed strongly to Arthurs because of that masculinity and anti-feminism; as one former friend is quoted: "Frustrated young men do crazy stuff. Why do you think ISIS is so popular? … I know testosterone is just a hell of a hormone" (Reeve, 2017). Another potential motivation for developing his own distinct ideology could have been to set himself apart from the rest of the group and to achieve some sort of ideological autonomy. It appears Arthurs was more or less completely dependent on Russel and clearly his subordinate. This should not be misunderstood as a generally hateful relationship between the two or as a toxic climate within the group in general. Even though Arthurs' new faith did cause a lot of surprise and even rejection, "they ignored it because they thought that Devon cared about them and that he wouldn't ever do something like this to them" (Reeve, 2017). However, cutting sarcasm, irony, and mutually derogatory humor was an essential part of the group's culture and the online milieu they lived in. For many members involved in this environment it was simply impossible to tell when joke developed into sincere belief or when sarcastic comments were turning into honest statements of intent. Many persons close to Arthurs simply thought his conversion to Islam and jihadist statements were in fact nothing but an elaborate joke (Reeve, 2017).

After he killed two of his closest friends partially because they had mocked his belief, Arthurs was quickly demonized in far-right online milieus. In a lengthy and detailed official statement by the IronMarch forum administrators three days after the shooting, it was declared that that Arthurs' actions were part of a coordinated Islamic extremist terror attack on the neo-Nazi milieu and that the ranks of the forum had been "purged" of Muslims in reaction. The statement also contains some information on his conversion and jihadist radicalization process, which are naturally to be seen in the light of the extreme-right milieu painting him in the most negative image possible. It is stated that Arthurs' attempts to convert others on the forum caused significant confrontations and intervention by the administrators, which in the aftermath of the shooting is framed as a deliberate attempt to disrupt and harm the far-right community:

The following is an official IM statement on the recent events that we, myself and other IM administrators and coordinators, had compiled after examining the situation. It is very important that you all read this carefully. There are absolutely no words to express what has happened, it was a complete tragedy. Our deepest sympathies are with all Atomwaffen supporters, especially the survivor, Odin, who is currently in police custody, and to the families of the two young men, Jeremy and Andrew who lost their lives ... This was a horrific attack that has left a deep scar on all those concerned in it. Nowhere will this ever be allowed to happen again. No surrender to system tools. You are scum, you are not human, we hate you all, we will detail your disgusting crimes against National Socialists ... The member known as Odin and the two men slain are completely innocent of any accusation that the group conducted or advocated, or planned for terrorist acts – something they all rejected ... IronMarch banned Devon's account when it became known he converted to the terrorist ideology of Islam and we did everything we reasonably could to try and have him removed from the organization. We object in the strongest possible terms that he was in any way "representative" of IM or it's ethos. We have good reason to believe that the attacker, Devon, planned this attack with other fellow coreligionists, and his ambitions to murder AW members far exceeded this tragic event. All Muslims have been isolated and ejected from the group, and appropriate measures taken for the safety of those facing a reasonable threat ... As the older users here are aware, Devon is a former IM user and AtomWaffen member. For the newer users: while Odin was in basic training Devon tried to assert more control in the group and this was around that time he started to obnoxiously annoy people with islamic crap that grew in severity, at first this was ignored as trolling, but then it became so prevalent and with a repeating pattern (trying to "trick" people into saying the shahada for example) that some of us, including myself, had confronted him about it to get a straight answer out of him on his behavior. He said that he was entirely serious and genuine about having converted to Islam and that everything he was saying was serious. He launched into a tirade about how Europe was getting what it deserved, how the mass rape of European women was a good thing and he claimed that he was aiming to turn AW into a muslim organization altogether and would convert Odin to join him and that he would get in contact with ISIS and his bosnian friends would give him a child bride. He was immediately banned from IronMarch after that conversation. He would later try to cover for these statements by claiming that the latter of them were some kind of "joke" or "prank", however at that stage I personally regarded him as absolutely untrustworthy. I contacted some people in AW and advised them to start a separate communication network, one that would exclude Devon and anyone else who were under his thumb, so that they could effectively isolate him and curb any plans he had in mind. He did catch wind of this and convinced most all AW members that this was some attempt by me to divide and conquer AW and take it for myself or some retarded shit like that ... A lot of people who should have known better defended Devon, regurgitating his claim that he was only memeing and pranking us about everything EXCEPT his conversion to Islam ... He [Russell] caved in saying that Devon is his friend from childhood, they're close and that this was just some autistic phase Devon was going through, as he had in the past. Devon had already dabbled in Islam once, but dropped it because he got the hots for some Mexican girl and was obnoxiously autistic about it in conversations with people as well. Then he had returned to Islam, this time, evidently, as a very devout Muslim who prayed five times a day and dedicated himself to thorough study of its history and laws ... In the articles so far released it has been reported that Devon told the police he killed them because they insulted his faith. Myself and others now believe that Devon was, in fact, plotting all along to kill all leading members of the group, and that was the sole reason he was in the organization. He was planning to kill Odin as well. It was an organized plan that included his clique of convert-muslim retards in the AW ranks ... Since Devon was arrested, his clique made statements to the effect of them praying for his well-being and how he did nothing wrong because our two dead brothers were nothing more than "filthy kafirs". After all of this came to light AW had purged Devon's clique of muslim-convert buddies from their ranks. In my personal opinion it makes the most sense that the two dead AW members had discovered Devon's ploy and confronted him about it or were pushing the issue of his expulsion from the movement – feeling cornered he killed them and then surrendered to the police so that he could spin them some tall tales in order to blame all of AW and take it down with him that way ... Let there be no mistake about this: this was not an act of betrayal. We are not talking about traitors, we are talking about a deranged scumbag, whose tendencies were fed and further developed by his conversion to Islam, who had infiltrated a National Socialist group with the explicit purpose of destroying it from within in the name of his heretical "faith". I think I can safely say that this is a unanimous sentiment of every single member of our fraternity, that this deranged scumbag and his little harem of converts deserve death ... The only person in this situation who has been truly betrayed is Odin, who had placed his trust into this person based on their long term familiarity, totally unaware of his "friend's" true intentions ... Personally I am inclined to think the bomb making materials belonged to the fucking Muslim who told the police he had a bomb! ... None of us here on IronMarch knew Jeremy Himmelman and Andrew Oneshuk, however they very well might have saved the lives many more lives from this Muslim terror plot by an unhinged, duplicitous scumbag. This was a tragedy that could have been avoided, but they died as heroes who stood for their brothers – we salute them and honor their memory ... The System and its media lapdogs are actively trying to paint this unpre-cedented event, a Muslim terror attack against National Socialists, as them "exposing" a supposed "neonazi terror ring", staging a witch hunt against the victims of this tragedy. ("Aleksandr-Slavros," 2017, spelling as in original)

Not surprisingly, this narrative caught on and, for example, in June 2017 Arthurs was brought up as the reason for oversensitivity on the side of the regular IronMarch users within a discussion about the potentially negative reaction to one user searching for neo-Nazi chat groups:

assume that people will think you're either trying to expose or infiltrate groups. We take this sort of shit seriously, especially with the recent terrorist infiltrator attack on Atomwaffen Division when Devon Arthurs, an Atomwaffen member, converted to Islam and planned to blow up an Atomwaffen Division meeting. He killed two of his roommates who were also Atomwaffen members. His third roommate, who is a member on this forum (Odin – Brandon Russel), was arrested and is now in police custody. Devon is now telling lies about Odin. Of course the police doesn't believe the lies, but they are pushing them on the media so that the public will believe it and denounce Odin as a terrorist neo-nazi. Be more careful with your posts in the future. ("Tiwaz," 2017, spelling as in original)

Interestingly, even after the shooting incident, voices about Arthurs on IM were not entirely negative. In a lengthy discussion between two openly neo-Nazi users (one of whom had previously voiced support for al-Qaeda) in July 2017, the AWD shooting and the case of Devon Arthurs came up after one asked the other about his opinion on Salafism and the compatibility of Islam with National Socialism. In the conversation, Arthurs was even praised for his fanaticism, which did gain the respect of the two users. Their main point of criticism was not his jihadist ideology or the violence in itself, but rather the fact that he did not attack the US government but his friends instead. Incomprehension about this is increased by the fact that he had access to a functional bomb (for which Brandon Russell was later charged and convicted) and could have easily created a much more meaningful mayhem in the eyes of the two discussants. ISIS and other Islamic extremist groups are partially praised for their radicalism and violence, which one of the users thinks might make them a good ally in bringing down the Western capitalist system. Both recognize that after the killing incident, neo-Nazis and Islamic extremists would become natural enemies but both agree that this fact is subordinated to the destruction of the Western political system. The thread also includes some exchange of thoughts about Arthurs personality and potential warning signs. In one short mention, both users even think about the possibility that their own mocking of him (shitposting) might have backfired and caused the attack. One discussant remembers that Arthurs had spoken negatively about right-wing terrorist Dylann Roof on the day before the shooting but that his main quality was the fanatical radicalism that made him a valid member of Atomwaffen:

USER 1 (U1):   Anyhow what is your opinion on salafism. You seem to sympathize with al-qaeda or at least hold some appreciation of it right? To elaborate on the question you stated fascism and islam are natural allies. Salafism wahhabism whatever you want to call it is very puritan in a sense and I can see your point but from my understanding they aren't racialist and are more than willing in launching jihad against the West. There was also the whole incident with AW. So do you think salafism is well suited for the islamic world and its doctrine makes it the natural ally of fascism and what are your thoughts on salafism in the West?

USER 2 (U2):   I don't know too much about the specific doctrine of salafism, I admire it for it's ability to inspire the Muslim world to reject degeneracy and strike back against the enemies of all humanity, specifically the Zionist and the United States, but Western Europe is also a good place for some remodeling. Our people are just going to have to make sure to be standing when the smoke clears, so that it's our children who'll inherit our traditional lands. In terms of their specific attacks . . . well, some I agree with more than others. I don't know what the point of shooting up a grocery store is, for instance. Like I said, IDK if ISIS forbids rape or not. If they do, it'd be good for those scum in Europe to take up the cause. As long as they keep their targets reasonable, to the extent that it serves a purpose and isn't just pointless slaughter, they can only be an asset in the fight against the system. It's going to be a "death-by-a-thousand-cuts", coming from all enemies of the Zio-Capitalist Regime. If you're asking whether I think Islam is good for white people, the answer is no. We are naturally pagans and I believe we should return our own belief systems . . . And Devon was just a nut, that he claimed to be Muslim had little to do with what he did. Both Islam and National Socialism have had their share of nuts who snap and do stupid things.

U1:   They may be helping in the fight against the system but when the system breaks down the islamists in Europe will be in direct conflict with us. He [Devon Arthurs] was a nut but he was at least fanatical. I'd prefer he had not snapped at his former comrades like a treacherous rat but rather thrown his life away striking at the system. I seriously can't understand why he would just throw his life away like that at 18 and have very little to show for his actions . . .

U2:   Yeah, IDK. Tbh I was pretty cheery when I first heard of what went down, even though it would be a death blow to AW. Of course at the time I hadn't known that the people he'd killed we're National Socialist. It really makes me wonder if things would've been different, had people been more understanding of his viewpoints. Of course there is no excuse for what he did, but it's an interesting thought. But what's more interesting is apparently they had bombs inside the house, along with radioactive materials, yet he didn't think to use them. He didn't even think to use his assault rifle!

. . .

True, but destroying the system takes top priority. If we're destined to die, we should just get it over with, and if our women would be enslaved if we lost . . . many are enslaved already. We've just got to end this hell. We'll worry about what comes after, later . . . I saw a Japanese documentary on ISIS where they showed some Arab guys talking about how they couldn't wait to get the Yazidi women, and that the ones with blue eyes were more expensive. They claimed that these people were ISIS, but they were raggedy and unkempt, and not in uniform. Didn't look like the ISIS troops shown off in their propaganda, but who knows the truth. Devon once said to me that he thought the Yazidis are devil worshipers, and so their slaughter is justified. Of course this is nonsense and I tried to tell him that. Perhaps I should've done it in a better way. I think that he thought I was mocking him, when I was shitposting. For one thing, I said that the devil was based. Lol. He did use his assault rifle to kill our comrades, but not beyond that. He never even intended to hurt anybody else, how fucked up is that?

U I: If he [Devon Arthurs] was planning something it makes what Devon did even worse . . . Couldn't agree more [regarding bringing down the system first before worrying about Muslim enemies], we can worry about cleanup later . . . Oh shit he claimed he did it because people didn't respect his beliefs. Shitposting gone wrong? Nah but seriously how much did you know about him before the incident? Think he gave any signs he was going to do it, and why did Odin tolerate him?

. . .

U2:   There really isn't much to say. I never spoke with him more than a handful of times. He called Dylann Roof a cuck the day before the shooting. Lol I imagine Odin let him stay on because he really wasn't doing anything wrong. Nothing that would be detremental to the group, in terms of getting them in trouble, and he was radical as hell (IM discussion, 2017, spelling as in original).

This exchange shows quite impressively how Arthurs' actions polarized the extreme-right online community, which in part even continued to give him credit for his uncompromising fanaticism. Islamic extremism, in particular Salafism, is seen as a strong ally for achieving the main goal of destroying Western democracy and capitalism, even though a strong consciousness about the mutual hostilities and fundamental differences in moral values (for example) was present. Considering the context of the discussion (the killing of two fellow neo-Nazis by a convert to Islam), the level of pragmatic and ideological differentiation between Arthurs choosing the wrong targets and his alleged ultimate commitment to a cause is remarkable. This indicates that parts of the extreme-right milieu are quite open to Islam as an alternative belief system, as long as the common enemy is still being fought. I will provide further insights into the relationship between the neo-Nazi milieu and Islamic extremists in the Section 4.5, when I will focus on issues related to religious conversion and extremist side-switching.

Of course, reactions to Arthurs' actions in the extreme-right milieu went far beyond the original platform he used (IronMarch) but also came from other prominent far-right venues. Some of these statements included similar references to Arthurs' conversion and proselytizing attempts that allegedly created conflicts. One of the most famous extreme-right online personalities, Andrew Auernheimer (aka "weev"), for example, posted on another large far-right online forum that he had to ban Arthurs from the server for spreading "Muslim terrorist propaganda" and that "he came in to convert people to Islam . . . It didn't work out very well for him" (as cited in Dearen & Kunzelman, 2017b). It also appears that Arthurs' continued attempts to convert his roommates caused increasingly heated and aggressive discussions, especially shortly before the killing (Dearen & Kunzelman, 2017a). Warning signs that some bystanders picked up were not taken seriously:

This is so out-of-leftfield. We all knew he had problems, and in the past six months we tried to get him to seek mental health treatment. He never talked about violence, but talked about killing himself. But he said he couldn't do it because of family . . . He would play with his guns on camera and he pointed it at his roommates one time. Last week, we kind of had a laugh about that, but looking back, you can imagine . . . . (as cited in Altman & Marrero, 2017)

In a sense, Arthurs' side-switching can be seen as a form of predetermined consequence of Atomwaffen Division's particular ideological nature. The group idolized and praised uncompromising fanaticism and radicalism, as well as violence and an all-encompassing nihilism. Especially relevant is the fact that between 2018 and 2019 the group raised international concern by openly celebrating Osama bin Laden, the Taliban, and ISIS in their own channels, including recommendations to read jihadist strategic manuals and theological concepts (Makuch & Lamoureux, 2019). With its own history of a convert killing two founding members, such a development is very noteworthy as it indicates an ideological proximity to the jihadist milieu embedded in the very fabric of AWD's collective identity.

For Arthurs, significant mental health issues appeared to have combined with an ultra-violent ideology and social milieu that was based on dissolving the boundaries between sincerity and sarcasm, which created a toxic spiral toward ever increasing fanaticism. Even though his case offers little information about his own side-switching storyline, the severity of his acts created highly insightful debates and reactions about side-switching in the extreme-right circles. Arthurs was active in before his defection. Although his new faith did raise suspicion and even reactance among many of his neo-Nazi peers, Arthurs was able to remain embedded in the far-right milieu with the support of friends, through a genuine curiosity and even open admiration for Islamic extremists' dedication to their cause. In conclusion, the shift to ultra-radical Salafi-jihadism can be seen as the key link to the far-right milieu, as this allowed for at least some respect and pragmatic recognition of mutually shared enemies and concepts. It is fair to speculate that a conversion to Islam without the jihadist fanaticism would have led to a much more open and immediate rejection of Arthurs.

4.5   Bringing in the Afterworld: Peculiarities of Side-Switching Involving Religion

Since this chapter has presented side-switching storylines that lead to involvement in and commitment to Islamic extremism (mostly Salafi-jihadism), we must acknowledge that these trajectories are inherently different from those connected the far-right and far-left milieus. By definition, a person entering the Islamic extremist milieu will have to enter the religion of Islam as well, even if only on a superficial or phony level (as in the case of David Myatt who claimed a strategic infiltration of Islam at least for some time). Defectors in this category not only switch sides, they convert to a new religion that is the predominant and all-encompassing basis for the new milieu. While the far left is overwhelmingly built on atheism and religion takes a subordinated role for most far-right groups (except Christian fundamentalist and neo-pagan currents), being a Salafi-jihadi without at least claiming to be a Muslim is hardly possible, even though isolated cases might exist.

Obviously, conversion to a new religion is a parallel psychological process next to side-switching and even if the person only attempts to mimic a Muslim appearance and behavior, there is still much more to learn and claim knowledge about beyond the extremist milieu itself (e.g., praying, key terminology, gestures, dietary laws, rituals). We must, however, be careful not to confound conversion to a religion on the outside with developing a real faith inside. The questions of whether or not jihadists actually believe the theological teachings of their leaders, if they truly think they will enter a specific form of paradise after a suicide attack for example, or how much of the religious traditions and reasonings behind the milieu's actions they really know or even care about, are contested.

This academic debate found one of its infamous nuclei in the now legendary conflict between the two formerly friendly and both highly respected scholars Gilles Kepel and Oliver Roy. While Roy argues that theological convictions play only a marginal role in the jihadist radicalization of many teenagers when compared to social and psychological factors, Kepel holds the direct opposite position and sees them as the main driving force in Islamic teachings (Nossiter, 2016). Pointing out two equally obdurate sides in the debate, Dawson (2018) criticized that too often religion is either seen as the sole cause of (jihadist) terrorism or as completely irrelevant (even when clear indications for spiritual motivations of extremists exist). Clearly, many jihadists are religious analphabets and are neither inclined nor capable of accessing the theological and ideological premises of their groups. But not every neo-Nazi has studied Hitler's *Mein Kampf* and not every communist has read Marx's *The Capital*, either. Does the lack of doctrinal or theoretical proficiency make a person necessarily less convinced of the ideology? Arguably, in all extremist environments members with detailed knowledge about the underlying ideologies form the minority, while many others join and remain involved for other reasons. As I have discussed in detail in Chapter 1 (Section 1.3), theoretical knowledge about an ideology does not equal ideological conviction. A person who does not know the first thing about Islam can still be a fiercely convinced jihadist who fights and dies for a cause he or she might only rudimentarily understand or perceive through emotions and social bonds. Here, we must therefore look at the specific psychological process of becoming a member of a religion, namely Islam, in order to meet the functional requirements for achieving an accepted in-group member status in Islamic (extremist) milieus.

The difference between extremist side-switching processes into Islamic extremism and religious conversion is highly important and becomes visible through the fact that one can easily identify many cases of former extremists who have converted to Islam and left radicalism, violence, or extremism behind completely. To be absolutely clear: When extremists convert to Islam, this does not automatically mean they will turn to jihadism or other extremist interpretations of the religion. In fact, research indicates the religious conversions for criminals and many extremists might actually be a source of moderation and positive life change (Hamm, 2013). The overwhelming majority of Muslims from all different schools and traditions reject violence and extremism, so when talking about side-switching converts, we focus on a tiny portion of converts who were extremists before the decision to become a Muslim and who have not moderated their views or actions as a consequence.

For example, many cases of former far-right politicians or activists who converted to Islam are known to not have shifted to radical interpretations. To name only a few prominent examples, the Dutch former far-right and virulently Islamophobic politician Joram Jaron van Klaveren (born 1979, former member of the nationalist and right-wing populist "Party for Freedom" (Partij voor de Vrijheid, or PVV) converted to Islam in October 2018 to the shock of his fellow party members. In his own conversion narrative, van Klaveren discovered Islam while writing a book intended to attack and criticize the religion, but instead convinced himself of the creed (Osborne, 2019). Another PVV politician, Arnoud van Doorn (born 1966), announced his conversion to Islam in April 2012, after the party broke with him in December 2011 (Graham, 2018). A third case would be the former French extreme-right Front National (FN) councilor Maxence Buttey, who publicly announced his conversion to Islam in early 2014, which led to his ousting from the party (F24, 2014). One can also name the Austrian former far-right politician Alfred Wondratsch, who converted to Islam in June 2012 and was able to reconcile as well as defend his membership in and activity for the anti-Islam far-right "Freedom Party of Austria" (Freiheitliche Partei Österreichs, or FPÖ) for a couple of years until he quit and decided to run as a member of the pro-immigration party in 2020 (Ichner, 2020; Natmessnig, 2016). Naturally, one of the largest world religions attracts converts from all kinds of backgrounds, including those with previous extremist involvements. It should therefore not be a surprise that one may find former far-rightists or far-leftists among its fellowship.

There are, of course, also many biographical constellations involving the continuation of radical and extreme views, as we have seen through the case studies presented in this chapter. A special type of such a case is when the conversion to Islam does not lead to involvement in Islamic extremism but instead is seen as independent or complementary to the attempt to remain active in the far right. What might seem highly counterintuitive, has been documented in a couple of instances. The British nobleman and politician Sir Archibald Hamilton (1876–1939), for example, became active in Oswald Mosley's British Union of Fascists in the 1930s after he had converted to Islam in 1924, adding "Abdullah" to the long string of names typical for his status. He seemingly had no issue bringing both his Muslim faith and fascist political activism together (Baxter, 2013).

Another example is the extreme-right "Alternative for Germany" (Alternative für Deutschland, or AfD) party member Arthur Wagner, who publicly announced his conversion to Islam during a press conference in early 2018. Even though his own party quickly moved to dispel him, Wagner stated that he would remain an AfD member, albeit withdrawing from all leading functions. During the announcement, Wagner explained that one of his goals as a Muslim was to reconcile Islam and nationalist conservatism, since he himself would continue to be committed to protect the "German soul" and its national traditions (Metzner, 2018; Strauch, 2018). One can also identify numerous other, oftentimes historic, cases, such as former members of the Nazi party in Germany who converted to Islam and worked with Arab nationalist movements and dictators on the obvious basis of mutually shared anti-Semitism. Thereby these former Nazis retained their far-right activism at least in this sense. As staunch nationalists and anti-Semites, they did not become involved in Islamic extremist milieus like the cases discussed earlier in this chapter. Johann von Leers (1902–1965), for example, became a member of the NSDAP in August 1929 and moved up the ranks to a leading propagandist and ideologue position, including picking up an SS officer career along the way. After the war, von Leers eventually ended up in Egypt, converted to Islam, and changed his name to Omar Amin von Leers in 1957. He continued to be active in the production of anti-Semitic propaganda (Stahl, 2010).

Egypt in particular appears to have been an appealing place for former Nazis after the war. Just as von Leers, Waffen-SS officer Aribert Ferdinand Heim (1914–1992), who was a doctor at the Buchenwald and Mauthausen concentration camps and nicknamed "Dr. Death" or the "butcher of Mauthausen," ended up in Cairo as well. After his conversion he used the name Tarek

Hussein Farid and was exposed only years after his death. It seems that both von Leers and Heim converted out of sincere conviction and became devout Muslims (Mekhennet & Kulish, 2009). A 2015 *New York Times* investigation identified more than 50 Nazi refugees who fled to Syria and over 70 who traveled to Egypt after the war, of which many converted to Islam in their later life (Kulish, 2015). A 1967 Congressional Senate Hearing Record from the USA about the question of US aid to Nasser's Egypt listed many former Nazis who had converted to Islam and were now working for the Egyptian state or with the Algerian rebel government in Cairo. The collection of names includes persons such as former SS Sturmführer Hans Baumann (now Ali ben Khader); former SA leader and Mauthausen concentration camp guard Willi Berner (now Ben Kashir); former Hitler Youth leader Karl Luder (now Abdel Kader); former Gestapo commissioner for Galicia Dr. Erich Alten (now Ali Bella); former chief of Hitler's personal guard and Gestapo security chief in Poland Leopold Gleim (now Ali al-Nahar); and former SS officer Bernhardt Bender (now Ben Salem) (USA, 1967, p. 17436).

Then of course, there are those cases of converts to Islam who developed an interest for far-right extremism afterward and closely collaborated with the milieu, such as Swiss national Ahmed Huber (1927–2008). He was first a member of the Social Democrat Party in Switzerland in the late 1950s and came into contact with Islam through his party's support for the Algerian independence movement. Fascinated with the religion, Huber began to study it in a Swiss Muslim Brotherhood group and converted in 1962, changing his name to Ahmad Abdallah Ramadan al-Swissri. Through his travels to Egypt, he met converts like von Leers and other former Nazis, who introduced him to their ideological mixture of Islam and national socialism. Upon his return to Switzerland, Huber became a close supporter of both neo-Nazi and Islamic extremist groups in secret and was only expelled from the Social Democrat Party in 1994, after journalists had published some of his statements that revealed his ideological positions. One of Huber's main goals was to forge an alliance between neo-Nazis and Islamic extremists against the USA and Israel (Michael, 2006, pp. 148–156).

Finally, one can find (albeit rarely) non-converts who grew up and were raised in a Muslim environment and ended up involved in far-right extremist groups, such as Yousef Omar Barasneh. The 22-year-old man from Milwaukee was arrested and charged in January 2020 with vandalizing a synagogue in September 2019 as part of a neo-Nazi group called The Base (which as its name indicates, was partially inspired by al-Qaeda) (Luthern & Vielmetti, 2020). According to the criminal complaint, Barasneh used the alias "Joseph" in the conversations with other Base members, whom he joined around March 2019, and openly used neo-Nazi language thereby professing his ideological commitment to the group (United States of America vs. Yousef

Omar Barasneh: Criminal Complaint, 2020). According to press reports, Barasneh's father had immigrated from the Jordanian city of Amman and married his mother, a Milwaukee native (Karra, 2020). In July 2020, Barasneh entered a plea agreement, which includes some of his statements to the group that strongly indicate his extreme-right views at the time (e.g., by using the slur "Kikes" or the Nazi salute "Sieg Heil") (Plea Agreement. United States of America v. Yousef O. Barasneh, 2020, pp. 4–5).

In short, conversion to Islam (or any religion for that matter) and the development or continuation of extremist worldviews are two separate psychological processes that can interact on the individual level but very often (arguably even predominantly) do not. Both are very much independent in their basic mechanisms and become part of the highly complex mixture of factors involved in a person's pathway from or to extremist milieus. In any case, to better understand how the psychology of religious conversion might affect side-switching processes and maybe also to understand some peculiarities of switching to Islamic extremist milieus, we must look at what is known about religious conversion first.

The question of why and how humans convert to a religion has been one of the core research themes of the psychology of religion since this research field's founding father made first steps to formalize it. In his famous Gifford Lectures, late nineteenth-century psychologist William James (1842–1910) discussed the process of religious conversion among other topics and set in motion a continuous academic interest in the matter that remains unbroken until this day (James, 1902). Of course, the exploration of the psychology behind conversion processes has advanced a great deal since the time of William James' study, even though many aspects of it are still openly contested and debated. In short, religious conversions are understood to be processes by which a person "commits to the beliefs of a new religious tradition and shifts away from previously held religious beliefs," thereby "involving a series of events rather than a stand-alone experience" (Snook, Williams & Horgan, 2018, p. 224). Much as described in Social Identity Theory (SIT), converts seek meaning and self-identity through active agency in the conversion process. Naturally, external agents such as the religious groups or recruiters exist as well and influence a usually conscious and voluntary decision to join the religion (Snook et al., 2018, p. 224).

In many conceptualizations of religious conversion, personal crises, emotional stress, or traumatic experiences are seen as triggers in a search for meaning that eventually lead converts to their new faith (Snook et al., 2018, p. 224), and some studies estimate the prevalence of stress or conflict-induced conversion at about 80 percent (Rambo, 1993; Ullman, 2013). Another study has found a significant correlation between emotional problems and conversions (Silverstein, 1988). For those converts, the move into a religious community can be seen as the acquisition of intact social relations, which are a fundamental human need. Typically, conversion does involve a change in the individual's identity and self-perception (Machalek & Snow, 1993). This in turn leads to oftentimes radical alterations in the converts' day-to-day lives, for example, "in their mental health and well-being (which, typically, are positive) ... behavior, and ... social contexts and social group memberships" (Snook et al., 2018, p. 227). By now, many different clusters of theories regarding the agency and integration of the convert exist (for an overview and introduction see Snook et al., 2018, pp. 231–233), such as humanistic (convert active agency); psychologically deterministic (converts are passive); interactionist (convert has active agency but is strongly impacted by personal interaction); and social-environmental models (convert is passive and impacted by interpersonal interaction). In addition to the response to a personal crisis, religious conversion has also been found to be driven by intellectual curiosity and experimentation (Richardson, 1978) or social pressure and the need for social integration (Lofland & Skonovd, 1981; Rambo, 1993).

Regarding the persistence of the conversion, it is not surprising that this aspect depends on the original motives (positive agency or forced passive) and the experiences made in the group or milieu. As Snook et al. put it: "such conversions are not once-and-for-all events but are part of a chain of continual spiritual renewals or rebirths. Such a perspective implies that a conversion is never truly 'complete'" (Snook et al., 2018, p. 236). Those studies that look at the potential interaction between certain personality types (e.g., authoritarian) and religious conversion have not come to any conclusive findings (Paloutzian, 1996; Silverstein, 1988). Like any other psychological process, conversion to religion is seen as the outcome of different subsequent steps and phases, for example, context, crisis, search, meeting, interaction, commitment, and consequences (Rambo, 1993).

One of the most important effects of religious conversion processes on our quest to understand extremist side-switching is, that once religion is involved, the defection storylines effectively become religious conversion narratives. These naturally follow their own logic and structure as compared to the nonreligious side-switching accounts. Representative scholars of narrative conversion research argue that by undergoing such a process the "universe of discourse" (Snow & Machalek, 1984) changes for the converts, which leads to distinctive rhetorical indicators for their conversion stories: biographical reconstruction, adoption of a master attribution scheme, suspension of analogical reasoning, and embracement of the convert role (Snow & Machalek, 1984, p. 173).

In the reconstruction step, the convert dismantles his or her past and reconfigures it anew. The adaption of master attribution themes occurs when feelings, behaviors, and events that were formerly interpreted with reference to multiple causal schemes are now seen through one dominant (religious) explanation. Previously inexplicable or ambiguous issues are now clearly understood and framed through single interpretative concepts. In the suspension of analogical reasoning, the convert sees the new faith as unique and so special that he or she refrains from comparing it to anything else. Finally, taking over the role of the convert and fully embracing it means to frame everything of relevance in the life of the convert through that particular identity. A more linguistic-oriented approach to conversion narratives has suggested that converts generally use a language that features one core mechanism: canonical or sacred language is employed to code all individual experiences (Stromberg, 2008). In short, this means that once a religious conversion narrative blends in with an extremist side-switching storyline, an explanation of why the shift from one extremist milieu to the other occurred becomes unnecessary, but not completely useless.

The milieu-specific elements of the storyline (e.g., the neo-Nazi background) might serve the purpose of highlighting a previously sinful life but is clearly subordinated to the overall context of religious conversion language. The switcher might as well speak about drinking, promiscuity, or violent actions, for example, to make the same point without risking alienation of the new milieu. Since the religious conversion is typically presented as an all-encompassing identity reinvention, discussing ideological details of the former milieu to construct rhetorical and ideological bridges to the new environment might quickly turn out to be useless. After all, the key component is to convey the message that one has cut ties with the old bad ways and that one has become a new person on the path to redemption and salvation. In fact, expressing the existence of potential role residuals that might be taken into the new religious life could be counterproductive. After all, the break with the sinful past is usually framed as total as possible. Seen through this perspective, it becomes clear why most side-switcher storylines in this category explain their conversion to Islam instead of the decision to join an Islamic extremist group. Naturally, taking over the faith is a much more significant change for people coming from the far left or far right and their previous milieus. As we have seen in the case of Devon Arthurs, at least in some extreme-right online milieus, understanding and even respect for jihadist groups exists. Historical precedents would make it possible to argue in favor of neo-Nazi activism (for example) and cooperation with Islamic extremist groups. As Arthurs and Falk have experienced, it is the religious conversion that often troubles their former in-groups most.

A good example of such a side-switching and conversion narrative is the British case of Muhammad Islam (formerly John Ord), who in 2005 explained his shift from the extreme-right British National Party (BNP to milieus connected to the Islamic extremist group Hizb ut-Tahrir (HuT) (for an introduction to the British section of the group, see Hamid, 2007; Husain, 2009; Nawaz, 2013) in a *Guardian* newspaper article. Albeit nonviolent in its official tactics, HuT has been linked to numerous terrorist attacks because they facilitated the radicalization process of some of their members who perpetrated acts of violence. It also promotes the reestablishment of the caliphate and holds strongly anti-Semitic, racist, and anti-liberal views. In Muhammad Islam's conversion narrative, two key elements play a central role: buying a Quran without knowing what it was as per divine guidance and personal interactions with other Muslims who he wanted to disprove about their religion. The only explanation he gave for why he chose to be close to HuT is, that members of the group were the persons who helped convert him to Islam. There is no discussion about theological or ideological bridges and similarities (e.g., anti-Semitism). In addition, Muhammad Islam was violent toward Muslims in his BNP time and had a profoundly solidified hatred against them. However, in his narrative the power of personal and spiritual impressions dissolved that hatred against Islam:

Then, one day in 1989, I was walking past a secondhand book stall by the Royal Festival Hall when a cover caught my eye: it was the most beautiful picture, in the most gorgeous colours, of a building. I didn't know what the book was, but it was only 20p so I bought it. I thought I'd buy a cheap frame and have a nice picture for my wall. I had no idea until I got home that I had bought the Qur'an. I was horrified when I found out. My initial reaction was to throw it away. But then I got curious. I started reading it, thinking I would find things to use against Muslims; I thought it would be filled with contradictions ... Now, I would regularly go and debate with Muslims at Speakers' Corner in Hyde Park. As I did so, I started to get a very different picture of Islam. Seeing people pray in unison was such a powerful image. A few years later, I returned to the north-east – I'd got a job as a chef. When I saw a group of Muslims at an Islamic book stall in Newcastle, I thought, "Here's another group I can wind up; I probably know more about Islam than they do." But I was shocked when I approached them; they were very knowledgeable. I kept going back because I enjoyed debating with them, and after four weeks they challenged me. They wanted me to try to disprove the Qur'an and convince them my way of life was better. They said if I succeeded they would become Christians, but if I failed I should become a Muslim. I accepted the challenge. But after months of returning to the stall and debating, I realised I was losing and panicked. I stopped going to the stall. Three years had passed when I bumped into one of the guys from the stall. As I thought about what I wanted to do, I felt as if a big rock were crushing me, but when I told him I wanted to convert, I had a total sense of peace. I made my final decision on Wednesday November 17 1996 and converted the following day. I have been close to the Hizb ut-Tahrir group ever since: I became a Muslim because of them; they were the guys at the stall ... When I look back, I can't believe the things I did; it feels like a different person and a different life. (Islam, 2005)

One can argue that the intended audience for this narrative was neither the far right nor HuT, which could explain the lack of theological or ideological bridging arguments. However, even in dedicated extremist milieus, for example, on the far-right forum IronMarch (IM) (see Section 2.4 for an introduction), some users talk about their conversion to Islam often without getting into the details about potential ideological commonalities. When they do, it usually involves talking about the historical connections between the Nazi Third Reich and parts of the Muslim world, or questions of biological race and kinship. In the following short exchange between a self-professed Muslim woman and a person nick-named "Blackshirt" (in reference to Oswald Mosley's British fascist movement), for example, the discussion evolves around biological race and anti-Islam criticism. Fascinatingly, "Blackshirt" reentered the thread after almost a year-long hiatus (between June 2016 and May 2017), reaching back out after he converted to Islam and began to express his support for Palestinian groups, which might have been extremist since he had his Facebook account suspended (arguably due to pro-terrorist postings):

BLACKSHIRT: Hello, you may be interested in this booklet "Islam and the Reich" written by a Muslim author: ...

VIRALEPISODE: Thank you very much!

BLACKSHIRT: No problem, also Sir Archibald Hamilton a prominent member of the pre-war British Union of Fascists and National Socialists was a Muslim convert: ... The Arab peoples are classed as Caucasian (i.e. white) and the Prophet Muhammad (Peace Be Upon Him) is described in the Hadith as "a white man" who ruled over black slaves, and the Satan is described as a black man! As regards religion I was brought up as a Christian and looked into Paganism, but am now looking at Islam. Regards

VIRALEPISODE: Oh yes I have watched that man's video before. He has an obsession with proving islam wrong. I did hear of Prophet Muhammad (saaw) being white before. I do agree that most Arabs would [be] classified as white. Lol I don't think Satan is the black man, there are some shitty black people and of course whites are superior. I was brought up Muslim but the man I'm with was Catholic (his parents were too but pretty much atheists since they are non practicing). But yes I have seen in a few research that Arabs have the same bone structure (skull) as whites.

Thanks a lot, if you want to stay in contact my Skype is the same username as the other account I have on here that was never confirmed because I wrote I was Muslim ... Thank you a lot sir

BLACKSHIRT: Thanks lady, yes the guy is anti-Islam but the vid is interesting. I'm not on Skype/Facebook yet (I'm a 47 year old dinosaur lol) but let me know if you want to exchange email addresses (I understand if not for security/trust etc). Have you ever visited England? I have cousins in California. Anyway have a nice day.

VIRALEPISODE: I feel like his videos are forced. The arguments are easily about stuff lost in translation. As a native Arabic speaker I think that way too many people don't understand the Quran because of the complex language that needs to be studied and understand. I have never been to England but my father's friend lives in England and some of my bf's family live in California. My email is . . . Thanks a lot for the great conversation. You too, sir!

BLACKSHIRT: As salaam alaikum, Hope you are well Shames. I recently became a Muslim and declared my Shahada at my local mosque and have been warmly welcomed by the local Muslims, as I am the first white man who has joined their Asian mosque for prayers.

. . .   Ramadan Mubarak Take care, Muhammad Amin Best

. . .

BLACKSHIRT: Not yet, but am looking into possibly making a skype account. I was on Facebook but my account got suspended for my posts supporting Palestinian Muslims ("Blackshirt," 2016, spelling as in original).

One can trace the user "Blackshirt" through his activities on IM and follow the development of his positions. It appears that references to British fascist and Muslim convert Sir Archibald Hamilton in the previous thread were an important indication of his ideological inspiration, as he kept the self-description as "Mosleyite" even after the conversion (Hamilton was also a member of Oswald Mosley's British Union of Fascists). In another discussion involving this user from April to early May 2017 (shortly before he became a Muslim), his arguments center around forging an alliance between the far right and Islamic extremists (as many examples in this chapter have). Interestingly, "Blackshirt" and the conversation partner "Eternal Gael" exchange literature recommendations and at the end, "Blackshirt" is apparently moving ahead to read Salafist and Muslim Brotherhood–oriented texts (potentially foreshadowing his theological positions as a Muslim):

BLACKSHIRT: No mate, I didn't convert to Islam . . . However, I still think Fascists/NS could forge an alliance with some Muslims against Jewry.

ETERNAL GAEL: So what do you think of Islam now? I know a lot of white Muslims, what do you think of them? . . .

BLACKSHIRT: Thanks, I think some Islamic ideas are similar to NS and we should co-operate with them – as Hitler met the Grand Mufti of Palestine and they discussed a NS-Islamic Alliance. I have some books on the Bosnian Muslim Handschar SS. Ps. There is an article written by a White British NS Muslim in H & D magazine: . . .

ETERNAL GAEL: Nice, I'll be sure to take a read of it.

BLACKSHIRT: Just been told about this interesting new group. Your white Muslim
                   NS comrades may like to have a look: . . .

ETERNAL GAEL: They sure are interesting, many of them including myself would
                   believe Islam to be an ideology within itself, but I sure do find
                   these guys interesting, they seem a very good option for
                   Britain, sadly they're fairly small in number. They seem to
                   have a view that's aligned completely with the shariah,
                   although some scholars I know of would probably criticise
                   their fiqh in some places. By the way if you are still interested
                   in Islam we have a skype dawah chat, I can link you if you're
                   at all interested.

BLACKSHIRT: Yes comrade, they seem a quite new group so early days yet. I'm
                   not on Skype but may join in the future. I've been to my local
                   mosque (Deobandi) for a discussion. The imam and the
                   secretary said to me as we studied the Holy Qur'an together:
                   "The Jews are the Enemy"! Good stuff!

ETERNAL GAEL: Haha nice, the Deobandi are weird to me, I think they're Sufis but
                   Salafis like them (hence the Taliban, which are Deobandi),
                   they were founded in Delhi to resist British control of the
                   subcontinent but have come to be the dominant ideology of
                   the Taliban, aside from that I don't know much about them,
                   cool that the imam opposed the kikes though. Also the dawah
                   chat . . . is mostly Salafi, as Salafi fiqh seems the most logical
                   to a lot of people including myself, Muhammed ibn Abdul
                   Wahhab is a good place to start reading to get an
                   understanding of this, I'm currently reading Ibn Taymiyyahs
                   book on imaan, which is pretty good so far.

BLACKSHIRT: Thanks for that. I'll have to check out the Salafi books
                   you mention.

. . .

BLACKSHIRT: Nice, I found a UK book store linked on that site . . . They sell a
                   booklet on Imam Shahid Hasan Al-Banna who founded the
                   Muslim Brotherhood, which I will order next week ("Blackshirt,"
                   2017, spelling as in original).

Shortly after this discussion ended, "Blackshirt" announced his conversion
to Islam in various posts on IM, with little visible reaction by the other users.
The group he recommended and was so interested in was called Islamic
Green Shirts Movement of Britain. This short-lived endeavor to promote a
Muslim system of government in the United Kingdom was based on white
British, Irish, and European converts to Islam. The group actively blended
Islamic extremist with neo-Nazi ideologues and their texts, to form what
they dubbed a "white Islam," according to a now defunct blog entry from
2017.

One can find many such discussions regarding ideological or theological
commonalities between the far right and Islam or debates about pragmatic and

strategic reasons for collaboration with jihadist groups. However, this yet again shows how much the overall religious collective identity of Islam supersedes potential group-specific identities and side-switching explanations. This might also be one potential reason (in part) why it is so rare to find former Islamic extremists who have switched to other forms of extremism after leaving this milieu. Sure enough, former Islamic extremists exist who have become critics of certain fundamentalist interpretations of Islam (Husain, 2009; Nawaz, 2013) or even the religion as a whole (especially right after their disengagement from Islamic extremism, for example, the former member of the Dutch jihadist terror cell Hofstad Group Jason Walters), but I was not able to find well-documented cases (including storylines) of such individuals who left the Salafi-jihadist milieu, for example, and moved to the far left or far right in consequence.

One case, however, seems to be moving in that direction. Former German Islamic extremist and intelligence informant Irfan Peci was heavily criticized in October 2019 press reports after racist and anti-immigration related comments in chat conversations became public (Lehberger, 2019). Up until this point, Peci had been involved in high-level governmental and societal advisory positions for countering extremism and anti-Semitism in Germany. Since then, he increasingly radicalized his positions toward immigrants, Muslims, and the far left in particular, through the promotion of far-right conspiracy theories. He began to participate in rallies for conservative-right values in Austria, which at least partially involved extreme-right groups as well and he developed a theory that Islamic extremists would be ideologically related to the far left (Peci, 2019). In a 2019 article that was published on a strongly far-right leaning online blog, Peci points to the anti-capitalist, multicultural, anti-racist, and internationalist elements of jihadist ideology, as well as the politically socialist background of many leading Islamic extremists (for example, former Iraqi Baath party members who joined ISIS). He comes to the conclusion that "today's Islam is thus interspersed with radical left-wing ideas that, coupled with religious promises of salvation, are particularly dangerous" (original in German, translated by author, Peci, 2019). On his personal Telegram channel, Peci called left-wing anti-fascists a threat to cultural values and cowards, after he experienced them as counterprotestors at a right-wing conservative rally in Vienna, Austria, in June 2020. He also voiced support for Martin Sellner, the leader of the Austrian extreme-right Identitarian Movement.

Through such statements he positions himself more and more in the far-right spectrum and seems to be integrating within the anti-immigration counter-jihad current. Albeit he did not provide a side-switching storyline of any kind, his ideological development quite clearly follows strong criticism against Islamic extremism after his disengagement from that environment to anti-Islam positions in general and appears to be focused on opposing political positions in support of immigration, pluralism, and liberal values. This, in combination with the ousting from almost all mainstream society positions after the publication of his racist comments, might have led to the perception that the far-right milieu essentially remains the only place left for his sociopolitical activism.

It must also be noted, that former or still practicing Muslim authors without a previous Islamic extremist background have been partially positively referenced as critical experts on Islam within some extreme-right milieus such as the Identitarian Movement or the far-right wing of the "German Alternative for Germany Party" (Alternative für Deutschland, or AfD). As the work by Göpffarth and Özyürek (2020) has shown, it is possible to identify several different currents and themes of such writers who align with the strategic interest and ideological frameworks of some far-right groups. Among those themes are, for example, claims that Islam is irreformable hostile toward Western culture. In order for Muslim refugees to integrate into Western societies, leaving Islam behind is seen as inevitable.

Other authors in this field have argued that Islam must undergo a fundamental enlightenment type of reform since German (or Western) civilizations are inherently superior. Interestingly, a third exemplary line of reasoning that has found some interest in parts of the extreme right aims to re-spiritualize nationalism using Islam as the role model. This process, it is claimed, would unleash the anti-capitalist, anti-globalist, and anti-liberalist power that is sometimes openly admired by far-rightists, as we have seen in the previous chapters. Such positions can lead to collaboration with the extreme right, for example, in the case of German Muslim convert Andreas Abu Bakr Rieger (born in 1965). The lawyer and publisher converted to Islam in 1990 and followed a Sufi interpretation at first. He quickly developed a notoriety for anti-Semitic views and in 2011 Abu Bakr Rieger became a cofounder of the far-right magazine *Compact* together with Jürgen Elsässer (see Section B1.6). He left the magazine's editorial board in 2014 after the outlet had increasingly developed an anti-Islam position. The partnership with left-wing renegade Elsässer is telling, since Abu Bakr Rieger considers himself to be a Muslim anti-capitalist, calls for the "jihad against the market society" (as cited in Göpffarth & Özyürek, 2020, p. 13), and regularly draws on German far-right or conservative thinkers revered in the extreme right to make his points.

Another example is Muhesir Sebastian Hennig (born in 1972), a German painter and writer who converted to Islam in the 1990s. He developed staunchly critical positions toward immigration that led him to collaborate with many far-right leaders and institutions, such as PEGIDA, the extreme-right wing of the AfD around fascist Björn Höcke (with whom he published a book version of a discussion between the two in 2018), or the "Institute for State Policy" (Institut für Staatspolitik, or IfS) of Götz Kubitschek. Hennig's positions are based on strong criticism of what he claims is a liberalist-induced self-hatred among Germans, which he aims to cure with Islam's spiritual pride (Göpffarth & Özyürek, 2020, p. 13).

Next to Peci, another one of these rare side-switching cases from Islamic extremism to other extremist milieus is the somewhat enigmatic biography of Finnish national Risto Olavi Tammi (born in 1949). Tammi has been active in various political and religious organizations since the 1970s and gained public attention through his profession as a KGB agent infiltrating Finnish neo-Nazi groups (among others). According to his own claims, Tammi served with the KGB from the early 1970s until the mid-1990s and was a convinced communist. However, after the downfall of the Soviet Union and the dissolution of the KGB, Tammi found himself in limbo and with a quest for purpose, which led him to convert to Islam.

Quickly, Tammi established himself as a politically active radical Islamic preacher and founded the Salafist "Finnish Islamic Party" in 2007 (Karagiannis, 2018, p. 39). The organization remained marginal and isolated among the Finnish Islamic community, with only a few hundred members. During his time as the leader of the party, Tammi expressed various Islamic extremist views, such as support for the death penalty for adulterers or critics of Islam, the superiority of Sharia law over democratic societies, portraying the USA and Israel as the "axis of evil," and admiration for the Taliban regime (Peltonen, 2007). In December 2009, Tammi announced his resignation as chairman of the party after disputes between him and other members regarding the organization's position against terrorist groups. According to press reports, Tammi was internally criticized for condemning Chechen terrorist but not Russian crimes in Chechnya, which likely was the result of his own KGB past (STT-Uusi, 2009). In the following years, Tammi moved back to his pre-Salafist far-left ideological convictions and began to shift his political activism into that milieu. In 2011, he was a candidate in the parliamentary elections in the Uusimaa municipality running for the socialist-oriented Finnish Workers' Party, before he moved on to again create a new political party of his own in May that year: the "Marxist-Leninist Red Guard." Based on interviews he gave to the Finnish media during his time as a Salafist and afterward as newborn Marxist-Leninist, it is possible to get a limited glimpse into the narrative of this controversial and certainly highly unusual side-switcher.

While he still chaired the Finnish Islamic Party in 2008, Tammi recounted his communist past for a press portrait about him. According to the journalist who spoke to him, he credits early childhood influences with his integration into the far left and multiple experiences of crises in the early 1990s eventually led to his conversion in August 2001:

Tammi's grandfather had taken part in the October Revolution in St. Petersburg as a young man. Already as a youngster, Risto learned to speak Russian with the help of his grandfather. It was fitting that in the late 1960s, when he was about 20 years old, Risto Tammi finally joined a Finnish communist youth organization. That is where he got his first contacts with the Soviet Union. Tammi trained to be a firefighter, but his real career was somewhere else. He soon officially became a KGB spy. This meant that he was to dedicate his whole life to communism ... The beginning of the 1990s brought troubles for Tammi. First, he suffered a stroke. He was unable to work and went on disability pension ... Nobody had taken care of the company, and Tammi had to deal with the millions in debt that were owed. Wages had been left unpaid, and no bookkeeping was done. Tammi was given a ten-month suspended sentence for aggravated dishonesty by a debtor. At the same time, Tammi was in the midst of a marital crisis. The relationship ended violently. Again Tammi got a suspended sentence for minor assault. "I do not approve of violence, and I am not a violent person. At that time my life was in crisis", he says now. The KGB ceased to exist after the Soviet Union fell apart in 1991 ... Tammi's life was thorough confusion. Tammi hung around the ... shopping mall, and one day he began to chat with a few immigrant men about religion. His new friends suggested that he join them at the modest mosque ... "I had a good feeling, when I returned to Islam, but I did not feel any kind of a religious frenzy". (Hietaneva, 2008)

Interestingly, his Salafist past did not seem to have raised many issues for him as a chairman of the Marxist-Leninist Guard he created in 2011 and as its leader at least until 2014 (when the group seized its activities on social media). In a 2011 interview with Finnish media, it was simply stated that he had previous political experiences with the Islamic Party between 2007 and 2009. While Tammi expressed his goal to achieve a peaceful Marxist-Leninist revolution in Finland, his previous religious background played no role in the narrative whatsoever (Lehto, 2011). One might suspect that the societal problems he chose to highlight in this interview could serve as a potential bridge to his Islamic extremist past (e.g., anti-racism and anti-capitalism), but he does not make that link explicit in the story.

What might explain the apparent lack of side-switching narratives departing from Islamic extremism even remotely as visible and detailed as in the other two milieus discussed in Chapters 2 and 3, as well as the Bonus Chapter? Defectors in the far right overwhelmingly come from the far left (as far as I could establish) and sometimes include former or still practicing Muslims (see for example, the IronMarch discussions presented earlier). The far left in turn most often integrates former right-wing extremists and except for the Tammi case, I could not find any well-documented cases that would fit into the parameters of this book.

Islamic extremists do recruit from all kinds of different biographical backgrounds, with no exception for the far right and far left. But a reverse process of former Islamic extremist fully switching to the far right or far left appears to be exceptionally rare, at least in terms of identifiable narratives and biographies. Of course, this does not mean that such cases do not exist. As Tammi's example shows, they might simply drop all reference to the former Islamic involvement and move on in the new milieu without touching the issue unless absolutely necessary. Due to the lack of such narratives, however, it is only possible to speculate about the potential reasons. One explanation might be that Islam and Islamic extremist groups more specifically are more disliked or seen with suspicion in the far right and far left than is the case with the positions toward each other.

We have seen some discussion about Islam, conversion, and Islamic extremism in the far right that mostly focused on strategic alliances and mutual enemies. Nevertheless, openly expressing Islamic faith in these milieus is definitely not unproblematic. IronMarch barely tolerated Muslims on the forum, expressing a lot of criticism and cutting Islamophobic "humor" throughout. After the Devon Arthurs incident, the forum moved to completely remove all Muslims and actively designated Islam a "terrorist ideology" ("Aleksandr-Slavros," 2017). It should be pointed out again, however, that some militant neo-Nazi groups like Atomwaffen Division have openly expressed their sympathies for Islamic extremism, especially the martyrdom concept (Makuch & Lamoureux, 2019). As the example of Yousef Barasneh indicates, ethnic or religious backgrounds are not insurmountable barriers against involvement in (some) far-right groups and certainly not in far-left ones either. However, it appears that coming from an (extremist) Islamic background would require complete denouncement of all residuals from this previous commitment. Doing so would mean to negate the religious or spiritual importance for the defector's identity altogether

Finally, one can also speculate that the combined psychological processes of religious conversion with extremist radicalization impacts the individual identity more deeply than non-religiously based extremist transitions. Instead of the irreversibility of extremist viewpoints (clearly many former Islamic extremists who have spoken out against their former milieus exist), it could potentially affect the defector's perception of and attraction to alternative extremist milieus. In short, this hypothesis states that Islamic extremism might have on average a higher chance of burning out the defectors' desire for further extremist involvement than the other extremist milieus discussed previously. Leaving Islamic extremism might bring a much more substantial metaphysical crisis with it (if the defector sheds his or her Islamic faith as well) and the far right or far left might simply be unable to fill that search for meaning and purpose on a spiritual level.

One should also be aware that defectors from Islamic extremist groups have a huge fallback milieu to integrate into: non-extremist Islam with all its diversity and currents. This points to a key feature of extremist side-switching, which I will explore in detail in the next chapter: Personal conflicts and ideological arguments in far-left and far-right milieus can lead to side-switching when (among other factors) no alternative milieus providing social identity are perceived to be available to accommodate some of the still active ideological convictions (e.g., anti-Semitism, anti-capitalism). Therefore those persons reintegrating into the mainstream society often do not even consider this to be an option, so they shift sides and adapt their identities. From the perspective of Islamic extremist defectors, leaving Islam and all the personal religious and spiritual convictions behind can be a much more significant and far-reaching step in terms of the psychological consequences. To shift to a non-extremist form of Islam is a much easier and more effective way to avoid cognitive dissonance and other mental consequences of the process (for one example of such inter-Islamic moderation of positions see Anas & Hussein, 2019). If, however, the defectors not only turn their backs on the extremist interpretations of Islam but also on the religion as a whole, identity reconfiguration might be far too substantial as to continue an attraction to other extremist milieus. Again, cases like Irfan Peci or Abdulla Tammi indicate that this is still possible. After all, human attitudes and behavior are so complex that there truly is nothing that does not exist in one way or the other. Nevertheless, the striking "silence" of former Islamic extremists within the far-right or far-left milieus, if they indeed happen to be there, points to Islamic extremism as some form of psychological end stage for extremist side-switchers.

4.6   Conclusion

Extremist side-switching to Islamic extremist milieus overlaps with religious conversion narratives. Many of the case studies presented in this chapter speak of moments of revelation and divine enlightenment, which led individuals on the path of Allah. However, for many who followed extremist interpretations of Islam's theology, this became a matter of continued belief in some very specific ideological core concepts, most importantly strong anti-Semitism, uncompromising violence, or hypermasculinity. The far right, where most of them came from, was too soft on these issues in the eyes of the side-switchers and joining jihadist or other Islamic extremist milieus provided them with a much broader and ideologically more sophisticated legitimization for those core concepts so important to them. Sometimes they had nurtured respect for the fanaticism and militancy of jihadist groups and actors long before they joined them. As shown in some of the online debates, the far right can produce significant admiration for those jihadist milieus and even pragmatically recognize the strong potential for a coalition against common enemies (usually the USA, Israel, and the West in general), as long as one is not attacked by the other side. Islam as a religion is despised in most parts of the extreme right as it is seen to be comprised of "nonwhite" cultures and ethnicities.

Nevertheless, there are some points of contact and attempts to include Islamic perspectives into the far-right discourse, mostly by those currents of the New Right that aim to weaponize every critique against the American-led West or Islam as such for their narrative of racial and cultural clashes of civilizations. It is not surprising that many far-right activists see Islamic extremists with mixed feelings of existential fear (from the perception of Islam as the mortal enemy allegedly working to turn Western countries into a caliphate) and curious respect. After all, Adolf Hitler and the Nazi movement had little reservation about forming an alliance with Muslim countries and created historical and ideological precedents that cannot be ignored easily by the extreme-right milieu. Hence, we can observe somewhat of a split position toward Islam. While the religion and its underlying culture is mostly rejected and attacked, extremist factions are seen in a much more positive light. Shared enemy concepts and militant opposition against the mainstream appears to form the basis of many attempts to walk between the two milieus, oftentimes by not fully giving up on the old far-right environment.

5   Who Are Extremist Side-Switchers and What Drives Them?

Toward a Theory of Motivations and Defector Life Cycles

In August 2019, the United States Federal District Court in Montana ruled that Andrew Anglin (born in 1984), the founder and administrator of the neo-Nazi website The Daily Stormer, must pay more than 14 million dollars in damages for using his website to launch and orchestrate an online harassment campaign (a so-called troll army or shitstorm) against a Jewish woman and her family. The victim received more than 700 threatening and anti-Semitic emails, letters, texts, phone calls, and other messages between December 2016 and April 2017, which left her terrorized and resulted in near complete isolation due to fear of attacks. Anglin's website had posted the victim's name, her address, and contact information, along with photographs of her and her 12-year-old son. The site encouraged people to contact the victim and express outrage over an alleged conflict between her and the mother of another famous right-wing extremist (Richard Spencer). Anglin himself published dozens of articles in which he called upon his followers to attack the victim and falsely accused her of an attempt to extort money from Spencer (Johnson, 2019; SPLC, 2019).

This lawsuit and the underlying troll storm are part of many similar legal actions that followed online harassment campaigns directly involving Anglin and The Daily Stormer. The website has received disproportionate attention within the online and offline far-right due to the combination of its outspoken neo-Nazism and its appeal to teenagers based on technical and stylistic adaption to modern youths' online media consumption. Anglin openly stated in media interviews that "my site is mainly designed to target children ... 11 through teenage years. Young adults, pubescents" (as cited in Edison-Hayden, 2018). However, Anglin and The Daily Stormer were also involved in various feuds within the far right and are seen critically by other members of that milieu who allege that deliberate conflict provocation by Anglin discredits the overall movement (SPLC, n.d.). Interestingly, The Daily Stormer, which was launched in 2013, also managed to inspire the establishment of offline chapters in dozens of locations across the United States, after Anglin called for the creation of "Book Clubs" (modeled after "Fight Clubs" as seen in the Hollywood movie) in 2016, with the goal of preparing for the "coming race war" (as cited in SPLC, n.d.). The Southern Poverty Law Center counted

31 active offline divisions in the same year, which further signals this milieu's importance in mobilizing followers and building a functional collective identity around its own brand and ideological style (SPLC, n.d.). The site was also the main radicalization milieu for right-wing terrorists (O'Brian, 2017) such as Dylann Roof (who killed nine victims in the Charleston attack from June 17, 2015); Thomas Mair (who assassinated British Member of Parliament Jo Cox on June 16, 2016); and James Harris Jackson (who killed one victim on March 20, 2017).

In short, Andrew Anglin managed to become a key online personality in the digital extreme-right landscape with significant influence and reach into the offline world. His own radicalization process and extremist career pathway, however, began on the opposite side. A detailed biographical article about his trajectory into the far right published by the US magazine *The Atlantic* in 2017 notes that he started his political activism as an "antiracist vegan" and that on one of his first webpages "leftist leanings were on full display," mocking the Ku Klux Klan and other racist organization in a way that "wasn't so different, back then, from the antifascist activists who would one day protest outside his dad's office" (O'Brian, 2017). In his sophomore year of high school, Anglin's behavior became more erratic and troublesome, including problems with his girlfriend, self-harming, and violent conflicts (O'Brian, 2017). One consequence of this series of individual crisis moments was that he increasingly engaged in online conspiracy milieus with partial overlap into the digital far-right environment, for example 4chan and Alex Jones' Infowars online radio. The heavy intake of conspiracy theories combined with an overall drifting lifestyle that lacked direction and purpose led to some form of mental breakdown, as Anglin described it: "I just about lost my fucking mind on that conspiracy shit" (as cited in O'Brian, 2017). Anglin created another website that focused on exposing various conspiracies and brought him even deeper into a delusional mindset. This finally resulted in his decision to turn his back on Western civilization and move to South East Asia to live and work closer to nature without what he perceived as cultural-technical burden.

During his time in the Philippines, Anglin developed an outspoken hatred against the "white West" based on its history of colonialism and racism: "You see the way white people—and it is white people—went around the whole world ... and fucked everybody ... I think the white race should be bred out" (as cited in O'Brian, 2017). In 2011, he lived with a Mindanao tribe and thoroughly enjoyed the close connection to nature and technology-free lifestyle. In January 2012, Anglin, somewhat contradictorily, launched a new website documenting his attempts to find and live with his own jungle tribe completely off the grid and outside of "the system." It appears that the conspirational mindset drove him increasingly away from his Western cultural background but Anglin nevertheless expressed a strong desire for community and collective bonds, as well as an ambivalent attraction to presenting himself online (O'Brian, 2017). For roughly six months he was mostly offline and planned to marry a Muslim girl and establish a "rainforest utopia" (O'Brian, 2017). When he reemerged online in late 2012, his views had changed drastically and arguably some negative experiences or failure to integrate with the native tribes caused a reaction based on self-affirmation as a superior white male: "Their minds were as primitive as their mode of living ... It is only they [the "European race"] who share my blood, and can understand my soul ... They're a bunch of idiots ... Monkeys" (as cited in O'Brian, 2017). In December 2012, he launched the precursor website to The Daily Stormer called Total Fascism and went on to promote his brand of "brutal extremism" (O'Brian, 2017) with utmost dedication.

Anglin described his own ideological development process as influenced by reading Noam Chomsky in high school and through the exploration of "all that Communist, Jewish stuff" (as cited in Kavanaugh, 2014). He also studied Islam, Buddhism, and modern French philosophers in his quest to find a system of thought that would help make sense of the world. Eventually, he ended up with Adolf Hitler and Benito Mussolini. In an autobiographical essay published on The Daily Stormer in March 2015, Anglin recounts a twofold maturation process, one ideological and one physical. Both, however, evolved around two themes: the discovery of his racial and cultural roots on the one hand and the recognition of the role of a strong community as counterweight to societies fractured by modern technology:

I started out with normal Alex Jones type conspiracy material, and then moved on to weirder conspiracy material, and then eventually decided Ted Kaczinski [American terrorist born 1942, who became infamous as the so-called Unabomber and argued for a radical anti-technological vision of society achieved through violence in his manifesto] was right with regards to a coming apocalypse due to the rapidity of technological development, read a bunch of stuff from Jaques Ellul and Jean Baudrillard, and went to live in a jungle in Asia for a while ... To be clear, I was actually already living and working in Asia at the time, because it was just so much more sensible economically ... to this day I have little negative to say about Asians, save that I don't think they should be immigrating into Western countries (in any kind of numbers) and I don't think White people should be producing children with them. I will also say that Chinese people don't have souls. Having been raised mostly without exposure to non-Whites, this was when I first started thinking seriously about race as a biological concept. Eventually, I got fed up and realized that I couldn't live in a jungle with a bunch of 80 IQ jungle people. I had always been into 4chan, as I am at heart a troll. This is about the time/new/ [a 4chan board] was going full-Nazi, and so I got into Hitler, and realized that through this type of nationalist system, alienation could be replaced with community in a real sense, while the authoritarianism would allow for technology to develop in a direction that was beneficial rather than destructive to the people. (Anglin, 2015)

Interestingly, Anglin also directly responds to media reporting about his past anti-white statements:

Still, I was definitely confused at the time. I have addressed this recording before by just saying "ah, I was a liberal then and I woke up," but that is an oversimplification. I was not really ever a liberal, in the SJW [far-right online slang and abbreviation for Social Justice Warrior, author' note] sense, as they are fighting for the system which is something I never did. I did for whatever reason at the time think this Black guy had some interesting things to say. This I must admit. But I was also drunk and being stupid ... And that isn't to say I didn't have an issue with White society at the time. I did and still do (at the time I also held on to a bit of White guilt and self-hatred, something which I have fully cleansed myself of). It is merely that when people post these quotes they are out of context from a drunken conversation where I was half making fun of and half seriously engaging a Black conspiracy theorist. The most important point, however, is that I don't agree with these statements now and so the relevance of having said them when I had a different belief system is completely lost on me. If the idea here is that no one who wasn't born into a racist type movement should ever be involved, then I don't know how to respond to that. For me, the purpose of running this site is to change people's views so that they are in-line with my own. Saying "if you didn't already believe this, I want nothing to do with you" strikes me as utterly nonsensical, a type of lunatic raving. (Anglin, 2015)

Anglin uses a rather rare side-switching storyline structure by claiming a complete dissociation from his past views by way of entirely changed world-views. He points out that everyone needs to develop into a fascist identity. Given the stark contrast between his own statements that were brought up against him and the milieu he addresses in the autobiographical essay, any other strategy might have had little chance of success in convincing his followers. Berating himself as drunk and stupid at the time of these anti-white statements further adds to his attempt to present a "newborn" Anglin to the audience. However, he also drops the argument that he never really was a liberal in the "SJW sense," but merely "confused."

Andrew Anglin's biography shows how flexible the development and change of political attitudes can be for some individuals yet again. Table 5.1 gives an overview of the various motives and change in directions we have explored in the detailed case studies. For all of them, a complex interaction between his socioeconomic background, the specific context of his life in each phase of the political development, as well as the shattering of dreams and aspirations due to frustration, conflict, and failure, plays the key role in moving across seemingly hostile milieus and ideologies.

In the next chapter I will explore potential commonalities in the pathways of the defectors we met and learned about through their storylines. The goal is to suggest basic elements for a theory of extremist side-switching life cycles to better understand such processes and recognize the various factors involved. The theoretical components I will present here must be seen as an additional

Table 5.1 *Overview of in-depth side-switching case studies sorted by order of appearance in chapters*

Name	Country	From	To	Stated or Likely Motives
Horst Mahler	Germany	Far Left	Far Right	Anti-Semitism
Iris Niemeyer	Germany	Far Left	Far Right	Anti-Semitism, Anti-Americanism
Julian Fritsch	Germany	Far Left	Far Right	Anti-Semitism, Masculinity, Violence, Camaraderie
Christine Hewicker	Germany	Far Right	Far Left/ Anti-Imperialism	Anti-Imperialism, Palestinian Suffering, Anti-Capitalism, Anti-Americanism
Odfried Hepp	Germany	Far Right	Far Left/ Anti-Imperialism	Anti-Imperialism, Palestinian Suffering, Anti-Capitalism, Anti-Americanism
Ray Hill	United Kingdom	Far Right	Far Left	Disillusionment, Frustration, Conflict, Hate toward Previous Milieu
Tim Hepple	United Kingdom	Far Right	Far Left	Disillusionment, Frustration, Conflict, Hate toward Previous Milieu
Matthew Collins	United Kingdom	Far Right	Far Left	Disillusionment, Frustration, Conflict, Hate toward Previous Milieu
Sascha Lemanski	Germany	Far Right	Islamic Extremism	Anti-Semitism, Violence
Bernhard Falk	Germany	Far Left	Islamic Extremism	Anti-Imperialism, Anti-Zionism, Anti-Americanism, Religious Conviction
David Myatt	United Kingdom	Far Right	Islamic Extremism	Quest for Honor, Masculinity, Violence, Anti-Semitism
Emerson Begolly	United States	Far Right	Islamic Extremism	Anti-Semitism
Nicholas Young	United States	Far Right	Islamic Extremism	Anti-Semitism, Violence
Devon Arthurs	United States	Far Right	Islamic Extremism	Anti-Semitism, Masculinity, Anti-Feminism, Violence
Bonus Chapter Cases				
Armin Mohler	Germany	Far Left	Far Right	Nationalism, Anti-Liberalism, Anti-Americanism
Matthias Matussek	Germany	Far Left	Far Right	Nationalism, Anti-Establishment

Table 5.1 *(cont.)*

Name	Country	From	To	Stated or Likely Motives
Günter Maschke	Germany	Far Left	Far Right	Nationalism, Anti-Modernism, Totalitarianism
Bernd Rabehl	Germany	Far Left	Far Right	Nationalism, Anti-Establishment
Reinhold Oberlercher	Germany	Far Left	Far Right	Learning Process, Nationalism, Conflict with Establishment
Jürgen Elsässer	Germany	Far Left	Far Right	Anti-Establishment, Conflict
Benito Mussolini	Italy	Far Left	Far Right	National Revolution, Elitism, Conflict, Quest for Power
Richard Scheringer	Germany	Far Right	Far Left	National Revolution, Working Class Liberation, Anti-Liberalism, Anti-Democracy, Impressed by Other Side, Lack of Ideological Answers in Own Camp
Joseph Brice	United States	Far Right	Islamic Extremism	Anti-Semitism

piece in the puzzle of extremist radicalization, deradicalization, and the development or change of political attitudes. As I have noted throughout this book, the sample of side-switchers is small and the phenomenon itself is rare as far as we know. Hence, the puzzle piece I am offering is an admittedly modest one without the claim for any general validity. Certainly, extremist side-switchers are unusual and even extraordinary cases in the milieus they left and joined. Their impact in the groups they end up with, however, can be significant and the exploration of the reasons they do not choose to leave extremism behind completely contains important lessons for prevention and counter-radicalization strategies (see Chapter 6).

There is no need to reinvent the wheel when it comes to the development of a theoretical framework around extremist side-switching. Out of the many existing models, I will use the concept of ideological transmission from Knott and Lee as an overarching concept for the following discussion, which defines the process as "the communication, embodiment and practice of socially produced ideas, beliefs, and values for the purposes of generating and expressing shared meanings, traditions and identities, binding communities and legitimizing individual and collective action" (Knott & Lee, 2020, p. 8). The two authors fittingly base their ideological transmission theory on Michael Freeden's understanding of ideology as a socially meaningful practice and communal activity (Knott & Lee, 2020, p. 5), very much in line with the key theoretical basis of this book (see Section 1.3). Side-switcher storylines have provided us with insight into the self-affirmation and narrative explanation strategies employed by defectors who go between hostile extremist milieus. Overwhelmingly, they evolve around claimed ideological commonalities and developments between the milieus each person transitions between. This means that a key question for us at this stage is, what the ideological transmission process for such defectors looks like. To be more specific and to apply Knott and Lee's concept, we need to explore six sides of the phenomenon (Knott & Lee, 2020, p. 6):

- Why did the transmission take place (what were the reasons and motivations)?
- What was transmitted? For our purpose we must ask what the ideological bridges and links were between the milieus?
- How did the transmission take place (through which techniques and practices)?
- Who was involved in the transmission process?
- Where did transmission take place?
- When did the transmission take place?

Such questions might help us to break "ideological transmission down into its constituent dimensions" and to "reveal the linkage between beliefs and behaviour, the processes and people involved, and the underlying conditions" (Knott & Lee, 2020, p. 22).

5.1 The "Why" of Ideological Transmission: Conflicts and Frustration

Understandably, to answer the "why" question lies at the heart of most defector storylines explored in this book. When one enters a certain extremist milieu and comes from its ideologically defined enemy, this naturally raises questions about the trustworthiness and motivations of a person so bold and daring enough to attempt such a move. It is therefore not surprising that the majority of the side-switchers focus on descriptions of deficiencies, conflicts, frustrations, and disappointments in their old groups or environments in order to validate the new milieu's negative stereotypes on the one hand and elicit some form of sympathy on the other.

To name only a couple of examples, Horst Mahler (Section 2.1) clashed so openly with his fellow left-wing terrorist RAF members in prison that they issued an official communiqué expelling him form the organization and denying the later neo-Nazi any importance to the group whatsoever. This came shortly after Mahler had himself voiced cutting ideological criticism against the RAF during his own court proceedings for the public to see. Günter Maschke (see Section B1.3) was shocked by the naiveté of his fellow far-left activists when they visited him in Cuba and simply ignored what he saw as precarious socioeconomic and authoritarian situations in the alleged Communist utopia. Benito Mussolini's (see Section B2.1) clash with the Italian Socialist Party over the question of intervention in the First World War led to a legendary exchange of insults and mutual allegations of corruption and ideological ignorance. Last but not least, Devon Arthurs (Section 4.4.2) was likely driven toward Salafi-jihadism in part by his complete dependency on his neo-Nazi roommate Brendon Russell, who regularly made fun of Arthurs and humiliated him. Finding his own extremist milieu, which would provide autonomy, status, and respect was clearly very appealing to Arthurs in addition to other factors.

Especially strong are the negative sentiments against the old milieu in the ranks of those who defected to the far left (see Chapter 3). In the storylines from that side-switching category, a moral imperative to destroy the far right exists due to the threat it poses and the many "lunatics," "thugs," and "crazy" people within it. Even those who did not move to anti-fascism as their new home but engaged in internationalist and anti-imperialist actions in favor of post-colonialist liberation movements did not spare with hostilities against their former comrades. Christine Hewicker (Section 4.2) and her husband, for example, publicly declared in their trial that the far right mostly consisted of notoriously criminal teenagers with a uniform fetish to brush up their underdeveloped self-esteem. *Searchlight* informant Tim Hepple (Section 3.3) recounted several shocking incidents of betrayal and backstabbing that led him to the brink of quitting a couple of times.

It is fair to say that the motive of "revenge" in combination with "seeking redemption," is a very particular and strong motivational force among the former neo-Nazis who started to engage in anti-fascist or other far-left activities. This is the only category of side-switchers that often includes those willing to issue statements of guilt, shame, and remorse, which would lead to a desire to make good on one's past by helping to contain or even erase some of the threats the defectors were in part responsible for. In addition to a quest for redemption, those individuals often also want to retaliate against the far right, who they blame for lives thoroughly deviant and conflict dominated. This is not to say that all defectors to the far left follow that path, as we have seen in the case of Christine Hewicker and her group (which does not contain strong elements of revenge or even remorse at the time of the side-switching process). Another case of defection to the far left from the far right was described by Sigl (2018, pp. 214–255). Named "Christian Goebel," this side-switcher mainly looked for the most powerful milieu to advance his personal status. Nevertheless, one can say that at least some parts of the far left make the reintegration process of former neo-Nazis conditional to their willingness to assist the fight against the extreme right and recognize this as a moral obligation

We must also highlight the category of defectors to Salafi-jihadist or other Islamic extremist milieus. Here, personal conflicts and frustrations are much less dominant in the storylines and bystander perspectives than among other side-switchers. As I have shown (Section 4.5), religious conversion narratives follow their own logic and style. They are often designed to show the convert's pathway to the "divine light" and therefore include language of exaltation, joy, and peace of mind. Naturally, the previous life is presented as sinful, dark, and bitter but going into detail regarding specific conflicts or moral deficiencies of the far right or far left are oftentimes simply not necessary to make that point. More widely present are story elements that hint at or directly claim divine intervention, for example, by guiding the convert to buy a Quran without their knowledge or making them cross paths with other Muslims who make a deep impact. The answer to the "why" question in religious conversion narratives is not so much based on conscious decisions but rather on a personal quest for deeper meaning and purpose on the one hand, and "fate" or divine guidance on the other.

In addition to these aspects, we have also often seen the notion of remaining "true to one's own beliefs" as a main stated reason to switch sides. Indeed, the need for authenticity and counterculture value persistency have been found elsewhere as a side-switching motive, confirming its power to drive cross-ideological migration. In their study building on subcultural drifting theory, Madfis and Vysotsky looked at a number of former neo-Nazi skinheads who had become anti-racist or anti-fascist activists in the course of their "subcultural trajectories" (Madfis & Vysotsky, 2020, p. 222). Among their sample of former right-wing extremists, the sense of subcultural authenticity and the continued resistance against dominant values were found to be "surprisingly common" (Madfis & Vysotsky, 2020, p. 229), in addition to the effect of peer influence via direct contact with members of the opposing subcultural group.

Especially for many young side-switchers, subcultural change might be seen as a strong if not dominant process along ideological change. As we have seen, for example, in the online discussions of switchers to the far-right in Section 2.4, much of the transition was framed around subcultural aesthetics. For those defectors, finding the one subculture that ultimately represents the most authentic and "true" form of opposition to the mainstream was an essential motivating force. In the perspective of Madfis and Vysotsky this process of shift from racist to anti-racist identity represents the solidity of the subcultural identity for these participants and a direct pathway in their subcultural development. Subcultural participation is not an instant process. Individuals do not simply "drop into" a subculture and attain an identity. Instead, they engage in a process of learning and understanding the beliefs, norms, and values as they increase their participation and solidify their identity. (Madfis & Vysotsky, 2020, p. 231)

5.2   The "What" of Ideological Transmission: Charting Ideological Highways between Milieus

The side-switcher storylines have provided us with the opportunity to explore specific ideological links or, speaking with Michael Freeden (Freeden, 1996), closely related and multidirectional political concepts. I have noted before that we do not currently have anything like a "map" of the ideological DNA underlying the different "families" of extremist milieus. Through side-switcher narratives we can only glimpse at some of the most prominent concepts that allow mental and physical transition between otherwise hostile environments. It is important to point out that each of the concepts that act as bridge between opposing milieus comes with a vast history and complexity of meaning. It is simply not possible to grasp the full breadth behind terms such as "nation" or "race," both within and outside of extremist or non-extremist discourses in the context of a book's chapter. Michael Freeden himself spent a significant amount of time identifying and tracing the evolution of such key concepts for the largest political ideologies in the Western world. In the following sections I can only do so much to highlight those elements most relevant to the side-switcher categories we have identified.

Anti-Semitism is one of the strongest multidirectional ideological concepts used as a linkage between hostile extremist milieus in the side-switching storylines. A fierce hatred of Jews mixed with belief in various anti-Semitic conspiracy theories features very widely among the defectors from the far left to the far right and onward to Islamic extremism. Especially among the violent and militant extremists we looked at, the quest for more radical action against the Jewish communities or Israel as the alleged leader of imperialism (together with the USA) is cited regularly as the main motivation to change milieus. A common strategy used to explain defection to the far right from the left links anti-capitalism and anti-imperialism with a moment of revelation and understanding of the Jews allegedly being the main drivers behind the traditional enemies of the far left (e.g., the big banks, capitalism, and imperialism).

Anti-Semitism, for example, based on the conspiracy theory of global Jewish domination through economic manipulation, also exists within the far left, independent of racist or other extreme-right ideological concepts (e.g., Arnold & Taylor, 2019; Hirsh, 2017; Norwood, 2013; Schapiro, 1979).

Certainly, however, anti-Semitism does not belong to the ideological core of the far left as it does to the far right, even though Karl Marx himself and many of the later leading Marxist-Leninist and communist thinkers or politicians casually expressed partially vile anti-Semitic views (Avineri, 1964; Blanchard, 1984; Fine, 2014; Jacobs, 1992; Wistrich, 1973). It has been convincingly argued, however, that the combination of widespread anti-Semitism being culturally mainstream in Europe at that time and unclear positions on race and nation in the Marxist founding literature (among other socioeconomic details), left interpretation open on many questions unanswered by Marx and Engels (Gregor, 2008; Sternhell et al., 1994). This almost inevitably invited some Marxist intellectuals to marry the emerging orthodoxy of the far left with other concepts, such as Darwinism, in order to claim some form of psychological and biological inferiority of the "Jewish race" as a potential explanation for the postulated economic self-destruction of capitalist societies.

One of those Marxist intellectuals paving the way for later National Socialism, for example, was Ludwig Woltmann (1871–1097), who identified the "Aryan race" as the main power of technological and cultural evolution and declared Jews to be an alien and hostile force (Gregor, 2008, pp. 70–73). In some ideological debates within the far left and far right as well right in between them, the question of difference was boiled down to the mere priority of race or class in the explanation and solution to capitalist forms of society. It is hence not surprising to find anti-Semitism as a strong ideological and rhetorical side-switching strategy, since that particular pathway between the far left and far right has been well-trodden long before. Horst Mahler (Section 2.1), Julian Fritsch (Section 2.3), Sascha Lemanski (Section 4.1), Bernhard Falk (Section 4.2), Nicholas Young (Section B3.2), and Joseph Brice (Section B3.1), for example, all expressed either strong biological racism and anti-Semitism or anti-Semitic critique of the state of Israel.

Anti-Semitism appears to be particularly strong among those who either defected to the far right or to Islamic extremism (from the extreme right), compared to, for example, Bernhard Falk, who became a Salafist straight out of his left-wing past. It is also noteworthy, that anti-Semitism almost completely vanishes among those narratives presented by defectors to the extreme left, even though we can find traces of it, for example, in the courtroom declarations of Christine Hewicker (Section 3.1). In short, anti-Semitism clearly has an exceptionally strong integrative power within the far right and Islamic extremist milieus as it offers multiple links to traditions and well-established ideological teachings in all three of the extremist environments we explored in this book. Despite the fact that anti-Semitism has a strong (albeit not fundamental) root in some parts of the far left, the effect for integrating side-switchers seems not to be completely multidirectional.

Former neo-Nazis or Islamic extremists who base their self-affirmation narratives on anti-Semitism might face much harsher rejection and suspicion regarding their true motives and disengagement from their past milieus. This shows that the direction and background framework matter a great deal for the effect of those multipurpose ideological concepts. Even though they could be used in most extremist milieus theoretically, since relevant traditions and ideological "docking ports" would exist, the combination with adjacent concepts such as biological racism or other neo-Nazi elements might effectively render some of those concepts ineffective for some milieus (i.e., the far left). On the other hand, anti-Semitism can gain significantly more cohesive force when used in the direction of the far-right and Islamic extremism, where the ideological concept is much more central and dominant.

A second ideological multidirection concept is the "nation" or the "national collective" as a counterforce to internationalism. This concept has strong and partially still fluid meaning within the far right, the far left, and in parts of Salafi-jihadist milieus. The extreme left has never truly dissolved the inherent conflict between nationalist vs. internationalist approaches, which essentially has been enshrined in Marx and Engel's writings already. Even in the various Marxist schools of thought that followed, "the issue of the connection of nationalism and revolution had never been resolved" (Gregor, 2008, p. 8). In consequence, many decidedly nationalist variants of Marxism evolved, for example, Maoism, Stalinism, National Bolshevism in general (Brandenberger, 2002; Van Ree, 2001; Von Klemperer, 1951), and the North Korean Juche ideology (Lee, 2003).

As has been shown by Seitenbecher (2013), many German left-wing activists in the 1968 student protest movement and even in the later militant terrorist milieus, were oftentimes thoroughly irritated by the openly nationalist views held by many otherwise orthodox Marxist liberation movements in the post-colonial world. For them, nationalism automatically and inevitably led to fascism and neo-Nazism. Nevertheless, the national question has been a strong ideological highway between the two milieus. Jürgen Elsässer (see Section B1.6), Reinhold Oberlercher (see Section B1.5), Günter Maschke (Section B1.3), and many more in retrospect, claimed nationalist-oriented left-wing convictions to align themselves with their new far-right environments. On the other hand, former neo-Nazis like Christine Hewicker (Section 3.1) or Richard Scheringer (Section B2.2) discovered the ideological breadth of the far-left landscape through nationalist liberation against imperialist occupation and exploitation (in Hewicker's case) or by understanding the utter danger of the Nazi movement for the German working class and the country as a whole (in Scheringer's case).

Even Islamic extremism, which is generally an ideology that transcends national borders and even prides itself as the solution to nationally caused social problems like racism, has an ambivalent relationship to the concept. First, there are of course those Islamic extremist and terrorist groups that are strongly tied to a local, ethnical, or geographical context, such as the Sunni Hamas in Palestine or the Shiite Hezbollah in Lebanon. Second, even Salafi-jihadist or internationalist Islamic extremist groups have embodied two remnants or corresponding ideological concepts that a far-right or far-left understanding of the nation could link up with. There is the sacred goal of the Caliphate's reestablishment as a theocratic form of statehood. In fact, many jihadist writers and thinkers, such as Ahmad ibn Abd al-Halim Ibn Taymiyya (1263–1328) or Muhammad Rashid Rida (Egypt, 1865–1935), have argued that Islam without statehood is "dead" and cannot fulfil its divine purpose. Sayyid Qutb (1906–1966), one of the most influential thinkers for today's Salafi-jihadism, has argued that the so-called Hakimiyyat Allah (the reign of God through state power) is the only way to solve the collective ignorance in the Muslim world (Jahiliyya) (Maher, 2016, pp. 169–185).

In addition to the theocratical concepts of statehood, Islamic extremists and especially Salafi-jihadists have developed a political metanarrative of the Ummah as a spiritual nation based on the shared faith (in its correct form of course) between true Muslims (Egerton, 2011, pp. 8–17). Organizations like ISIS created their own religiously based and post-national state concept, heavily framed around theological concepts such as allegiance, migration, and leadership (Kaneva & Stanton, 2020). In this notion of nationhood, physical boundaries such as geography or ethnicity are declared meaningless and the concept is moved into a metaphysical realm. Nevertheless, secular understandings of nationalism can easily connect to the spiritual version, as there is no contradiction between the two in that particular direction of development. A return to secular nationhood in turn typically means a blasphemous sacrilege and usually evokes mostly radically negative responses from the Salafi-jihadist milieu.

A third highly adaptable ideological concept among side-switchers appears to be anti-capitalism or (in a more comprehensive framing) anti-imperialism. It is no surprise that all extremist milieus we explored here could agree on fundamental hostility toward the Western political and economic ways of organizing human societies as well as their approach to international relations or global and national issues. All of them see an existential threat to their own collective identity and their view of humanity in pluralism, free market economies, and the Western political and economic domination of the world in particular. Naturally, the ideological reasoning for arriving at this threat assessment varies greatly, from a divinely ordained warfare against the infidel forces of evil that use their man-made political concepts to destroy Islam, to capitalism and imperialism as the main driving force behind dialectical materialism.

Even fascism and National Socialism at least claimed some form of anti-bourgeois standpoints, even though the alliances between the Nazis and fascists with entrepreneurs and large companies are well known (e.g., Baker, 2006; Buchheim & Scherner, 2006). Zeev Sternhell (Sternhell et al., 1994) has shown how fascism tried to retain the benefits of market economies while it rejected typical bourgeois values such as humanism, equality, or universalism at the same time. So, at least on paper, the three extremist milieus oppose Western liberalism embodied in capitalism and global domination (imperialism) in their perspective. Hence, many side-switchers have pointed out this shared opposition as their personal ideological bridge between otherwise hostile environments. One of the strongest examples is Bernhard Falk (Section 4.2), who openly states that he wanted to continue his anti-imperialist struggle at a time when his far-left milieu fell apart. In Muslim anti-Western liberation movements (in his view), Falk found a much more determined and promising environment to fight for the same goals and against the same enemies. Even his language still contains many references to his far-left past, which sets him apart from other Salafists without a comparable background.

Anti-imperialism also became the key motive for Christine Hewicker (Section 3.1), her husband, and the small number of like-minded former neo-Nazis, such as Odfried Hepp. They saw the strategic necessity of allying with the militant far left to fight American-led occupation of Germany as part of the global struggle against Western colonialism and imperialism. We have seen how Hepp (Section 3.1), for example, became deeply impressed with Palestinian militancy against Israel and the USA, which eventually led him to join another Arab anti-imperialist terror organization. Interestingly, anti-capitalism and anti-imperialism features not nearly as strong as one might expect among those who shifted to the far left from one of the other two extremist milieus.

Those like Hewicker (Section 3.1) who tried to walk that side-switching pathway largely failed to gain any form of positive resonance in the left. One potential explanation might be the strong suspicion in the extreme left toward the far right, which saw mere strategic and short-term offers in those overtures of collaboration. In addition, the far left had and still has little to gain from such a cooperation, as undisputedly the historical and ideological competency in the fields of anti-capitalist and anti-imperialist activism lies with them. On the contrary even, collaborating with the far right, even though not unheard of, comes with the immense risk of alienating the left's own support base and followers to a substantial degree. Here we see the same mechanism at work as with anti-Semitism that effectively renders ideological bridging narratives ineffective when presented as a key motive for defection from the far right or from Islamic extremists. The mere possibility that the side-switchers might retain some form of mental or physical links into their old milieus is a significant risk for the far left for many reasons. These threats include the potential to be infiltrated for intelligence purposes or to risk losing one's own credibility in the overall environment. Hence, for such a defection to be successful, many far-left groups do require proof beyond a doubt that a full disassociation from the previous milieus, both ideologically and physically, is the fundamental driver behind the transition process.

5.3   The "How" of Ideological Transmission for Extremist Side-Switchers: Activism vs. Learning

After we discussed the "why" and "what" of ideological transmission processes involved in defection between hostile extremist milieus, we must of course also look at how side-switchers accomplish this transition. It is possible to discern two main types of transition pathways: the activist and the learning route. Naturally, the boundaries between the two are fluid and elements from both appear quite often throughout the narratives, regardless of the main thread that runs through a side-switcher's storyline.

The "activist" pathway narrative is typically dominated by emotional elements, such as feelings of betrayal, disappointment, or grievance. Traumatic events or negative push factors that involve the failure of human relations within a given extremist milieu play a significant role. Internal power struggles, backstabbing, conflicts, or open violence between members can quickly lead to the defector's development of a sense of disgust and even hatred against his or her former environment. Ideological disillusionment is still an important factor but this is usually connected to the social-emotional deficiencies of the milieu, which are contrasted with the underlying claims of comradeship and loyalty or other sacred values that focus on building and maintaining a collective identity.

Since extremist and terrorist groups are "normative coercive" (Bates, 2011) and often have to operate under a high level of external pressure (e.g., through law enforcement or military action against them), extremist ideologies typically place great value on higher quality relationships, social bonds, and the personal moral standing of each member. Talking about "elite" or "chosen" brotherhoods and sisterhoods brought together by their "divine" or "sacred" duty and responsibility is therefore quite common in extremist and terrorist milieus. In addition to their function as a potential antidote against negative outside influences, such ideologically enshrined claims of superior morality and community compared to the outside world is also a core mechanism of achieving fused collective and individual identities (for the concept of fused identities, see Atran, 2017; Swann Jr et al., 2012).

Once a member encounters gross misconduct, hypocrisy, or other open violations of the milieu's code of ethics, the ensuing disappointment and frustration can lead to doubt regarding the ideology as a whole. Here, the emotionally based disengagement decision leads to a comparatively swift transition, as the defectors quickly perceive their own identity to be at odds with the collective one. Richard Scheringer (see Section B2.2), for example, was disgusted by Adolf Hitler's public commitment to peaceful means of achieving political power and obey the law during his own trial, something that Scheringer felt was an act of betrayal against everything he believed in. Another case in point is Tim Hepple (Section 3.3) who was nothing short of shocked when a close friend in the extreme-right milieu turned against him and accused Hepple of treason. Bernhard Falk's (Section 4.2) narratives include sadness and disappointment over the rejection of his interest in Islam by his extreme left-wing milieu and the fact that after his conversion none of his former close friends visited him in prison.

There are many more accounts of grievances, conflicts, and emotionally based defusing of the defector's own identity from the group. Side-switchers on this pathway looked for alternatives and prepared the transition in a relatively short time frame. Julian Fritsch (Section 2.3), who claims to have been driven away from the far left in part by the milieu's cowardice and lack of a masculine warrior identity, performed a rapid and fundamental defection. He more or less vanished from all public activities as a left-wing rap musician for about six months and resurfaced through an interview with neo-Nazis in which he announced his defection. A second example is again Richard Scheringer (see Section B2.2), who had his defection declaration read out in the German parliament by a member of the Communist Party, much to the shock of his Nazi milieu. His time frame of initial doubt up until the decision to switch sides was also about six months. Through these two examples, we also see a specific technique of performing the transition. Scheringer and Fritsch used a public declaration designed to achieve a fundamental break with their former milieus (and to shock them at the same time). This coalesces with the emotional reactance to their former milieus and the need to swiftly erase the cognitive dissonance resulting from it. Making a public declaration that recounts all the moral and personal failures of the former in-group is obviously an attempt to damage the previous milieu and "get back" at them. Such a transition strategy is a preliminary stage to more revenge-based pathways, as we have seen with many defectors to the far left who became informants for anti-fascists. Ray Hill (Section 3.2), Time Hepple (Section 3.3), and Matthew Collins (Section 3.4) decided that it was their moral obligation to help destroy the far right, for example.

Next to the emotional activist, we can also identify the intellectual learning pathway that leads to side-switching. Here, the process usually takes much longer, sometimes even decades, and involves intense ideological reflections. Personal conflicts and disappointments also play a role in these narratives of course, but the overall frame and reasoning for the defection is presented as an intellectual maturation and development process. Through their detailed study of an extremist milieu's fundamental texts and philosophies, those persons create an ideological rationale for joining the opposed environment. Typically, they present this process as the natural outcome of an epiphany in which one "truly understands" the teachings and ideological concepts. The language used in these storylines often talks about the previous positions and depicts them as immature, childish, or purely emotional.

Activism in the old in-group is explained by peer pressure or because "everyone did it back then." Aesthetics, thrill, or simple rebellion against authorities are also widely cited. All of this serves the purpose of depreciating the seriousness of the previous commitment. Defection because of personal conflicts and grievances appears to be of lesser quality for those side-switchers, who might fear rejection on the grounds of alleged opportunism. Despite fierce personal conflicts, Horst Mahler (Section 2.1), for example, took years to develop the ideological positions that led him into the extreme right. In retrospect, he credits intensive studies of Hegel's philosophy in prison with the ultimate recognition that Karl Marx fundamentally misunderstood the basic pillars of Hegelianism due to his "Jewish" mind. Another intellectual side-switcher is Reinhold Oberlercher (see Section B1.5), who claims to have made it his life project to finish Karl Marx's *The Capital* and to develop a fundamental philosophy of all academic disciplines he was interested in. Through this process, according to Oberlercher, he gradually moved to the extreme right's positions on national revolution and opposition against the Western capitalist system.

Defections based on religious conversion tend to be swifter and more emotionally framed. However, sometimes they also include elements of ideological learning and reflection over a larger time frame. David Myatt (Section 4.3), for example, sets his defection to Islamic extremism in the context of a lifelong study of religions and philosophies, as well as a quest for spiritual depth and meaning. He quickly advanced to detailed theological reasonings in favor of jihadist leaders, groups, and tactics. He continued his self-professed warrior-philosopher identity through this particular intellectual quest. Another peculiarity of those defectors switching to Islamic extremism is the attempt to argue for the ideological-theological unity between Islam and (mostly) the extreme right. Sascha Lemanski (Section 4.1), Emerson Begolly (Section 5.4.1), and of course David Myatt (Section 4.3) have tried to rationalize the combination of these two milieus based on shared enemies (e.g., the USA and Israel) or moral values.

Even Bernhard Falk (Section 4.2) who entered the Salafist milieu from the far left goes to some length to point out why the Islamic extremist groups are the ultimate anti-imperialists. During his time as a left-wing terrorist, his group was somewhat isolated in the overall milieu due to its repeated calls for collaboration with Islamic terrorist organizations based on ideological and historical reasoning. In Falk's storyline, the act of conversion followed an intense study of Islam to probe whether the worldview behind the religion could fit with his own self-concept.

5.4   The "Who" of Ideological Transmission: Friends, Foes, and Recruiters

Not surprisingly, the main person involved in extremist side-switching is the defector. The storylines evolve around individual push and pull factors behind the decisions to disengage from one extremist milieu and join another. We learned about conflicts and disappointment, ideological or spiritual revelations, and quests for meaning, purpose, or a more honorable life. Other persons, however, were also involved quite often and sometimes are even credited with providing the essential positive or negative impression that tipped the scale toward switching sides. Of course, when we look back to the previous section on the original motives and drivers of defection (the "why"), conflicts and grievances with the old in-group are strongly present throughout the stories we encountered.

Failures of human relationships as a push factor for disengagement requires other human beings who are not living up to the group's standards and ideological code of conduct. Negative examples of someone else's involvement in side-switching process, such as troubled personalities, aggression, hostility toward other members (including the later defectors), or hypocrisy, become embodiments of all that is wrong in the old milieu. Tim Hepple (Section 3.3) talks a lot about his former close friend Eddy Morrison, who struggled with alcoholism and mental health issues. Hepple, according to his own account, supported and cared for him, which is why the shock about Morrison turning on him created a deep shock and perception of betrayal. In Hepple's storyline, Morrison became the archetype of an instable opportunist, and aggressive "lunatic" who inhabited the far right in great numbers. In most cases, however, those negative influences remain hidden behind abstract accounts of arguments and conflicts.

Much more prominent are episodes of individuals who had positive and partially even decisive impacts on the defectors. In many cases, personal conversations with members from the other side, for example, in prison in the case of Richard Scheringer (see Section B2.2), made the difference. Scheringer was deeply impressed by the commitment, integrity, and courage of the communist inmates in his prison, with only rare conflicts between him, the convicted Nazi, and his left-wing enemies. In his autobiography he recounts individual communists who thoroughly impacted him with their character and ideological knowledge. David Myatt (Section 4.3), Bernhard Falk (Section 4.2), and Muhammad Islam (Section 4.5) likewise spoke highly of individual Muslims they met during their travels to the Middle East or at their workplace. Through their devotion and calmness, the narratives claim, Islam as a religion became truly visible and tactile for the defectors. Sometimes, side-switchers were recruited into joining the new environment, for example, in the cases of those former neo-Nazis who became informants for the anti-fascist magazine *Searchlight*.

All storylines by Ray Hill (Section 3.2), Tim Hepple (Section 3.3), and Matthew Collins (Section 3.4) include recollections of the first time they called *Searchlight* and the first time they met their "handlers" in person, during which time they were debriefed and persuaded to continue working for the magazine. These meetings and the actual recruitment were not always friendly and cozy experiences. Collins remembers them as "dreadful" and "intimidating" (Collins, 2012, p. 193). Nevertheless, those individual anti-fascists who worked for *Searchlight* played a major role in bringing the disillusioned neo-Nazis over to their side and making them participate in the magazine's endeavour to destroy as much of the far-right milieu as possible. We can see other forms of recruitment-style influence in attempts to convert other right-wing extremists to Islam on platforms such as IronMarch or Discord. Devon Arthurs (Section 4.4.2), for example, is known to have significantly strained the patience of his fellow neo-Nazis online and offline with his constant proselytizing activities. I found few other cases from IronMarch in which other users converted to Islam and attempted to spread the message with the goal of bringing others to the religion as well (Section 4.5). Also, one must not forget the immense impact individual right-wing conservative or far-right thinkers had on the intellectual side-switching processes of Armin Mohler (see Section B1.1) or Günter Maschke (see Section B1.3). Both were greatly influenced by Carl Schmitt's writings and personal conversations with him.

5.5 The "Where" of Ideological Transmission: Conversations vs. Texts

Transfer of contents that alters ideological concepts from one extremist milieu to the other is a very individual and context-specific process. Sometimes this transmission was mainly driven by the defector, who actively sought out information about the ideology of the other side as part of the constant negative focus on it. The attempt to become better at refuting or outsmarting the opponents can be a very effective pathway for ideological transfer. The negative connotation of the reason for the engagement with the other side's arguments does not always inhibit their persuasive power. Just remember the case of the Dutch far-right politician Joram Jaron van Klaveren (Section 4.5), who wanted to write an anti-Islam book and in the course of researching his critique became convinced that he was wrong and converted. In most defection cases we have seen, the sphere of ideological transmission took the form of written statements, articles, books, or other textual sources. Side-switchers consumed a great deal of such material from the opposing milieu either online or offline.

In a couple of defection stories presented online on IronMarch or Discord (Section 2.4), many users stated, for example, that reading Hitler's *Mein Kampf* was an eye-opener for them. Others traced their ideological develop-ment into the far right on these online platforms to various writers and thinkers on fascist or Nazi ideology, which they recommended to each other. In one case (Section 4.5), a user expressed interest in Islam and Islamic literature, followed by tips regarding Salafist or Muslim Brotherhood texts from another forum member. About a year later, the same user returned to the conversation as a Muslim. Reading the Quran and other Islamic theological material is cited regularly among those who shifted to Islamic extremism, which is not surpris-ing. Sometimes, even those texts that were previously the basis for one's own worldview and actions can fail to answer newly developed questions or doubts. Richard Scheringer (see Section B2.2) was ideologically confused during conversations with communist inmates in prison and actively searched for answers to specific sociopolitical questions in the core Nazi literature. Much to his frustration he did not find any responses and continued to read the far-left material that was available to him.

However important texts in different forms are for defectors to learn about the other side's ideology, a much more effective transmission route for almost all of the cases presented here were personal conversations and interactions. These exchanges were aided by the charisma or impressive biographical background of the respondents in such conversations. In this way, ideas, emotions, connotations of specific concepts, or fundamentally different per-spectives traveled from one person to another and oftentimes fueled lasting changes. Far-right Discord user Kamden Musser (Section 2.4), for example, recounted that experiencing the speeches of and conversations with white nationalist Matthew Heimbach was the game changer for him. More specific-ally, he credits the highly persuasive way Heimbach explained the ideology with the significant impact on himself.

Here we must also remember that side-switching usually is not a straight-forward and linear process. Instead, most defectors actively work hard on their disengagement and reengagement; they learn new terminology and concepts even while the process of integration into the new milieu is not yet complete. Some former far-left users on IronMarch and Discord, for example, apologized for "sounding" like "commies" for a while until they successfully managed to blend in. Especially in those online discussion, the intensive persuasion work that often is part of ideological conversations becomes visible. Users exchange partially detailed views on politicians, socioeconomic policies, or philosophical questions and thereby shape the ideological learning process of each other. Indeed, peer influence through direct contact with members of the opposing group was identified as a major impact factor for former neo-Nazis skinheads joining anti-racist and anti-fascist subcultural groups (Madfis & Vysotsky, 2020, p. 228). Of course, through these interpersonal contacts not only ideology was transmitted but subcultural values, norms, styles, or emotions as well. Nevertheless, through these contacts, conversations, and exchanges, side-switching was significantly facilitated.

5.6 The "When" of Ideological Transmission: Life Stages vs. Symbolic Times

We have already seen that extremist side-switching can happen in a noticeably short time frame, usually as an emotional reaction to feelings of identity friction and incongruency with the milieu or group one is a member in. On the other hand, such transitions can also take years or even decades of ideological learning and development. In order to better understand the "when" of ideological transmission and defection, one must look at *when* in the lives of side-switchers those processes happened. One can argue, for example, that going through such drastic changes in social environments could be a side effect of teenage and adolescent development processes in which humans build and adapt their basic attitudes toward social or political issues. It is well established that the human brain goes through wide-reaching, different developmental stages during adolescence, which oftentimes result in anhedonia, anxiety, and dysphoria that make teenagers not only more susceptible to drug use but also to high-risk behavior in general (Andersen & Teicher, 2009). Extremist milieus have learned to adapt their appearance and recruitment strategies to the psychological needs of youths in different age ranges. For example, the case study of Andrew Anglin at the beginning of this chapter mentioned his own recruitment strategy for The Daily Stormer, which targets children from the age of 11 (Edison-Hayden, 2018).

By no means is Anglin the only extremist who focuses on indoctrinating and recruiting kids into his follower milieu. In fact, most extremist groups and environments predominantly recruit among teenagers and adolescents. As Andrew Silke has found in his sample of jihadist: "Ultimately, most people who join a terrorist group are young – by young here I am referring to teenagers and people in their early twenties" (Silke, 2008, p. 105). Looking at a different extremist milieu, Mark Hamm's sample of 36 US neo-Nazi skinheads had a mean age of 19.6 years and 19 of the sample members had already been involved in the milieu for three or more years (Hamm, 1993, p. 106).

In another study of US right-wing terrorist radicalization and recruitment, Simi et al.'s subsample of 20 former white supremacists reported a mean entry age into the movement of 17.6 years (Simi et al., 2016, p. 34). In the European radical right, this hold true as well: "There is little doubt that the vast majority of new recruits to the various European radical right groups is male, lower class and very young" (Merkl, 1997, p. 36). A German analysis of 1,398 police records for violently criminal extreme right-wing perpetrators between 1991 and 1992 found that more than 75 percent of the investigated suspects were aged 20 or younger and over 35 percent were under 18 (Willems, 1995, p. 168). Another analysis of 255 perpetrators of extreme right-wing arson attacks in Germany between 1990 and 1995 found that 53 percent were between 17 and 19 years old; 19.6 percent of the perpetrators were between 14 and 16 years old (Neubacher, 1998, p. 154).

To find such young age ranges among members of extremist milieus should not surprise. Their mobilization and recruitment strategies usually cater to that particular target group (Bloom & Horgan, 2019; Horgan, Taylor, Bloom & Winter, 2017). They typically do so with specially designed propaganda disseminated on communication channels that are used by teenagers and by promoting specific subcultural products thought to be attractive to younger target groups. Many extremist milieus encourage their members to become parents or even to bring whole families with their children into the milieu. The goal if of course to raise their offspring within the extremist environment. Extremist groups oftentimes present themselves as particularly attractive oppositional countercultures to the mainstream (e.g., Adams & Roscigno, 2005) and thereby appeal to needs for rebellion against the establishment or adult authorities. They regularly use youth-specific social media channels (e.g., Awan, 2017; Ferrara, 2017; Wahlström & Törnberg, 2019) to distribute their youth-oriented propaganda products, such as music (e.g., Conti, 2017; Simi et al., 2016), professionally edited videos (Awan, 2017), fashion (Miller-Idriss, 2018), video games (Lakomy, 2017), subcultural lifestyles (Hamm, 1993), sports, concerts and other attractive leisure activities (Braunthal, 2010), social services (Shelley, 2014), and so on.

The content of these recruitment efforts targeting children and teenagers might be designed to appeal to youth-specific themes, such as offering action and adventure to escape boredom (van der Valk & Wagenaar, 2010), orientation and solutions regarding discontent with social problems (Schils & Verhage, 2017), social networks for friendships, camaraderie, intimate relationships and alternative families (Perešin, 2015; J. Stern, 2010), or glamorization and mystification of violence to portray membership as "cool" (Awan, 2017; Picart, 2015). It is not a coincidence that those mostly emotion-based recruitment efforts fit well with the psychological needs of teenagers. Hence, we can conclude that especially during the formative years of childhood and adolescence, many different extremist milieus compete for attention and membership in these age groups. One can therefore assume that switching sides across ideological boundaries happens more often in younger age, since then the decisions to join or leave an environment might mainly be driven by emotional appeal, thrill, or friendship. While still very much influenced by the milieu's ideology, the perception of the young recruits might be that membership is much more about which group is the most "fun" or "exciting." Indeed, we have found many cases of side-switchers mostly in the far-right online milieu (Section 2.4) who casually mention that they were attracted to the far left in their high school years for many reasons. Aesthetics and the notion of "getting free stuff" seem to have greatly incentivized supporting communism and other far-left ideologies, as it is hinted in some of the discussion threads on IronMarch and Discord. Of course, we need to take into account that many far-right users might see little benefit in disclosing their honest and fully convinced commitment to the far left in their pasts. On the contrary, belittling such a previous involvement as childish and based on a lack of knowledge is likely an effective and easy strategy to avoid suspicion or other negative reactions from the extreme-right environment.

On the other hand, almost all of the detailed side-switching storylines we have studied in this book come from individuals who made the transition between milieus in their twenties or even much later in their lives. The youngest cases in the sample are Devon Arthurs (Section 4.4.2), who was around 17 during his conversion to Islamic extremism; Sascha Lemanski (Section 4.1), who was 18; and Julian Fritsch (Section 2.3), who switched sides around the age of 22. In those rather young defector cases, emotions and the attraction to violence, action, or thrill appears to be a strong factor int the transition process. However, all three also expressed strong interest in the other side's ideology. Arthurs and Lemanski are known to have invested a lot of time in attempts to proselytize their neo-Nazi friends. Even Fritsch's storyline includes strong ideological components, such as the desire to do something good for Germany and helping German youths to rediscover their allegedly lost heritage and patriotism.

A potential source of bias regarding the high age of the defector sample in this book could be that young side-switchers might not have the interest or the platform to express their milieu changes in greater detail. During these phases in their lives, explaining the development of their group affiliations might simply not be a priority or hold any incentive for them. Older defectors in turn might have reached advanced positions in their group's hierarchy and also might be better known in public for their involvement in one extremist group or the other and for a longer time. They also might have the mental maturity and the platforms to express themselves to various audiences and frame their own career pathways.

Whether or not the higher age of the defectors who gave detailed storylines regarding the side-switching (both in terms of the age when they gave the accounts and when they changed milieus) has an impact on the way these processes are presented. Even though it is very difficult to clearly identify the effect of age on side-switching, the indications we can get from the material I was able to collect point to a difference in emotion vs. rational decision-making. In almost all cases, the side-switching is portrayed at least in part as a form of advancement, forward development, or even maturation process. This is understandably an important strategy in maintaining social status and identity-integrity. As we will see in the next chapter, the fact that guilt, remorse, or self-loathing rarely appears among these defectors is something that sets them apart from persons who leave extremism behind altogether.

Only Jürgen Elsässer (see Section B1.6) and Andrew Anglin express some form of shame for their previous positions. Younger defectors in online milieus are typically much more careless in that regard, maybe because they are used to self-ridicule or other forms of ironic and sarcastic humor as a constant part of their communication. Nevertheless, the younger the defectors are (either during the time of their storytelling or the side-switching), the more the importance of highlighting the rational decision to change milieus decreases. In contrast, the older they are, the more this rational reflection becomes stronger in the narratives. This should not be misinterpreted as a juvenile lack of ideological interest or mental capacity to understand the doctrines of the milieus they are active in. The online discussion threads I assessed and partially presented in Section 2.4 very much point to the contrary. Even young extremists of different backgrounds regularly show partially deep knowledge or at least fascination for certain aspects of different ideologies. We have seen throughout this book, that extremist ideologies can transfer their concepts, values, or collective action frames very effectively through emotions, social activities, or aesthetics and subcultural products. At times, lengthy virtual debates among teenage extremists about certain color schemes, music, or clothing styles that would be better or worse in representing the various milieus show this complex relationship between ideology and aesthetics.

For younger generations of defectors, ideology transmission had a sensual and emotional quality that appears to be much stronger and relevant than among the older side-switchers. Again, there is no indication that the younger ones are less interested in the ideology per se, but they do express a strong excitement about how ideological concepts can be presented in an aesthetically appealing (i.e., cool, hip) way. This goes beyond side-switchers of course. Take the example of the 13-year-old Estonian leader of the neo-Nazi group "Feuerkrieg Division" (FKD), who was identified by the authorities in 2020 (Kunzelman & Tanner, 2020). FKD's aesthetics similar to those of the ideologically related "Atomwaffen Division" (AWD) are based on nihilist celebration of the society's ultimate destruction in line with the group's accelerationist philosophy. Graphically very distinct in their appearance, AWD, FKD, and other like-minded groups (e.g., "Sonnenkrieg Division," "Vorherrschaft Division") attract teenagers and adults. They skilfully integrated a partially sophisticated ideological doctrine with highly violent and inciteful aesthetics.

The fact that even the theoretical side of ideology (in the form of doctrinal knowledge and understanding) is not irrelevant for some extremist milieus oriented toward adolescents can be seen through vetting processes used to assure that new recruits show a minimal awareness of the group's worldviews and concepts. The neo-Nazi online chat forum "Fascist Forge," which followed IronMarch after its disbandment has, for example, included a mandatory membership exam with 26 essay questions that needed to be correctly answered before a new user was admitted to the forum (Lamoureux, 2019). Even more advanced ideological vetting was done by the extreme-right group "The Base," which was mostly active in Canada. Young applicants to the group were put through conference call interviews with group leaders and asked "about their personal history, ethnicity, radicalisation journey and experience with weapons, before a panel of senior members posed their own questions. The would-be recruits were quizzed on what books they had read, including Adolf Hitler's Mein Kampf, and were encouraged to familiarise themselves with the group's white supremacist ideology" (De Simone & Winston, 2020). Interestingly, the founder of the group, Rinaldo Nazzaro (born 1973), is a side-switcher too. In the early 1990s, Nazzaro (who used the alias "Norman Spears" for his online neo-Nazi persona) was involved in the anticorporate and left-wing Democratic Socialists of America (DSA) (Wallace, 2020), which is however still part of the democratic and pluralist political spectrum. Why Nazarro decided to leave the left-wing political milieu is unclear. We do know that he dropped out of college in 1994 after his junior year and disappeared from his social environment for a while before resurfacing in governmental and conservative circles 1999 (Wallace, 2020). He still had a long way to go until he started to appear as fully committed and an ideologically well-versed neo-Nazi in far-right online milieus around December 2017 (Wallace, 2020).

Not unlike the IronMarch/Fascist Forge platforms, both of which were founded and administrated by a side-switcher, Nazzaro's The Base also combined ideological indoctrination with youth-centric aesthetics from the first steps of involvement onward. Such ideological vetting for new recruits, however, is quite uncommon, at least among far-right groups that target teenagers and adolescents. The fact that two well-documented and apparently much more serious attempts of such vetting involves side-switchers might be indicative for the importance of knowledge and internalization of ideological concepts in the eyes of the defectors. After all, from all that we now about extremist side-switching so far, transitioning into extremist milieus that are perceived to be hostile works best, according to the storylines, when using the ideological pathway.

5.7   Prevalence and Impact of Side-Switching

Defections between hostile extremist milieus appear to be distributed unevenly when we consider the visibility of side-switchers through their narratives and storylines. It is of course possible that many more such individuals exist across the different milieus, but at least we can say with some certainty that defectors to the far right present themselves significantly more often both in the public and within their extreme-right environment than compared to the other two milieus looked at in this book. This has been noted before by other observers who also commented on the impact of defectors in the US conservative right. As political scientist Cory Robin described in a 2010 *New Yorker* article (Robin, 2019), ex-communists have fundamentally shaped the American neo-conservative and anti-communist political sphere. They brought with them detailed knowledge of the far left and, more importantly, the revolutionary theories and tactics that were developed and refined in this milieu. Those ex-communists were responsible for vitalizing and infusing the conservative right with fresh ideological concepts that renewed their appeal and for mobilizing political power in the American society. This has not been the case vice versa, though:

Curiously, the movement from right to left has never played an equivalent role in modern politics. Not only are there fewer converts in that direction, but those conversions haven't plowed as fertile a field as their counterparts have. Since the end of the Cold War, there have been a handful of notable defections from the right ... They've had virtually no effect on the left. The best the convert from the right can do, it seems, is say goodbye to his comrades and make his way across enemy lines ... This isn't a personal failing that can be explained by some deficit of intelligence or imagination ... Nor can it be chalked up to youth or inexperience ... But perhaps there's a separate insight to be gleaned from the question of age. Counter-revolution critically depends upon revolution. As much as it reacts to the left, so does the right learn from the left. The reason counter-revolutionaries tend to be older than revolutionaries ... is that acquiring an intimacy with revolution takes time. To make that right turn, at least with any precision or efficacy, you have to have been around the block a few times. But that's not true of revolution. Revolutions don't react to or borrow; for better or worse, they create an untried form. They have no need for defectors, no need to turn the other side. (Robin, 2019)

To be clear, those former leftists who presented their storylines in anthologies such as *The God That Failed* (Crossman, 2001) or the influential persons studied by Oppenheimer (2016) did not switch to the extremist far right.

Most of them rather turned to a conservative but anti-communist liberalism and exerted great impact on the American and European publics, politics, and cultural establishments. Nevertheless, almost all became bitterly hostile toward communism and some (e.g., Hungarian British journalist and author Arthur Koestler, 1905–1983) turned out to be quite radical in their views toward the far left. In his foreword to the 2001 edition of *The God That Failed*, historian David Engerman called the book a "political call-to-arms and an opening shot in the cultural Cold War" (Crossman, 2001, p. vii). He also noted that the movement from communism to Cold War anti-communism "was so common in the United States and Western Europe – 'familiar enough to be banal,' in the words of one such apostate" (Crossman, 2001, p. viii).

Common reasons for finding Soviet Communism attractive among the contributors to the book were the appeal of a utopian and technocratic future society without inequality and disorganization, anti-racism, and anti-fascism. National and international events (e.g., the brutality of the cultural revolution in Soviet Russia and the brutal crackdown of protesting workers) forced many to reconsider their initial fascination: "Communism could no longer be seen as the ideology of liberation, of rapid industrialization, of racial tolerance, or of anti-Fascism which had attracted so many believers in the 1930s" (Crossman, 2001, p. xx). The impact of ex-communists went beyond infusing the conservative right with important insights from the other side, new tactics, strategies, and idealism. Their stories also became a "how-to manual for transforming interwar radicals into Cold-War liberals" (Crossman, 2001, p. xxv). As Richard Crossman, the editor of *The God That Failed*, noted:

The only link, indeed, between these six very different personalities is that all of them – after tortured struggles of conscience – chose Communism because they had lost faith in democracy and were willing to sacrifice "bourgeois liberties" in order to defeat Fascism ... The choice seemed to lie between an extreme Right, determined to use power in order to crush human freedom, and a Left which seemed eager to use it in order to free humanity ... The emotional appeal of Communism lay precisely in the sacrifices – both material and spiritual – which it demanded of the convert. (Crossman, 2001, pp. 4–6)

Of course, the global political context at the time those early communists found the far left and then disengaged, matters a lot. The majority of them entered communism and became disillusioned with it in the years between the First and Second World War. The extreme right was mostly dominated by Nazism and fascism during these decades, which did not appeal enough to the ex-communists in the anthology to consider joining them. They in turn took a route we have described as defusing the individual form the collective identity and rediscovering a pluralized view of humanity. Arthur Koestler pointed this out directly in his essay for *The God That Failed*:

The lesson taught by this type of experience, when put into words, always appears under the dowdy guise of perennial commonplaces: that man is a reality, mankind and abstraction; that men cannot be treated as units in operations of political arithmetic because they behave like the symbols for zero and the infinite, which dislocate all mathematical operations; that the end justifies the means only within very narrow limits; that ethics is not a function of social utility, and charity not a petty-bourgeois sentiment but the gravitational force which keeps civilization in orbit. Nothing can sound more flat-footed than such verbalizations of a knowledge which is not of a verbal nature; yet every single one of these trivial statements was incompatible with the Communist faith which I held. (Koestler, 2001, p. 68)

Interestingly, some authors from *The God That Failed* partially recognized a division among their own – the far-left defectors – that in their eyes might explain the difference between the milieus they chose after leaving communism. They could observe that other ex-communists joined the fascists or Nazis and pondered the reasons. Italian political leader and novelist Secondino Tranquilli (1900–1978, using the pseudonym Ignazio Silone), for example, wrote about this crass disparity in dealing with one's exit from communism:

It is not easy to free oneself from an experience as intense as that of the underground organization of the Communist Party. Something of it remains and leaves a mark on the character which lasts all one's life. One can, in fact, notice how recognizable the ex-Communists are. They constitute a category apart, like ex-priests and ex-regular officers. The number of ex-Communists is legion today. "The final struggle" I said jokingly to Togliatti recently "will be between the communists and the ex-Communists." However, I carefully avoided, after I had left the Communist Party, ending up in one of the many groups and splinter-groups of ex-Communists; and I have never regretted this in any way, as I know well the kind of fate which rules over these groups and splinter-groups, and makes little sects of them which have all the defects of official Communism – the fanaticism, the centralization, the abstraction – without the qualities and advantages which the latter derives from its vast working-class following. The logic of opposition at all costs has carried many ex-Communists far from their starting-points, in some cases as far as Fascism. (Silone, 2001, p. 113)

When *The God That Failed* first appeared in 1949, the difference between those defectors who turned to the extreme right and those who rediscovered a pluralist and liberal or democratic anti-communist conservatism was explained by personality variances. Louis Fisher (1896–1970, American journalist who became disillusioned with Stalinism after the Hitler–Stalin pact of 1939) even used the term "authoritarian by inner compulsion" (Fisher, 2001, p. 223), which foreshadowed Theodor Adorno's (1950) immensely influential theory of the authoritarian personality. For Fisher, a "changed outlook or bitter experience may wean him from Stalinism. But he still has the shortcomings which drove him into the Bolshevik camp in the first place. He abandons communism intellectually, yet he needs an emotional substitute for it. Weak within himself, requiring security, a comforting dogma, and a big battalion, he gravitates to a new pole of infallibility, absolutism and doctrinal certainty" (Fisher, 2001, p. 223).

Those ex-communists who turned to other extremist milieus, in Fisher's view, desperately cling to a strong collective identity. In other words, they have failed or were unwilling to defuse their individual identities from a dominant collective one. These side-switchers lack stability out of their own personality and instead derive it from authoritarian unity and overarching enemy concepts. Eventually, "when he finds a new totalitarianism, he fights Communism with Communist-like violence and intolerance. He is an anti-Communist 'Communist'" (Fisher, 2001, pp. 223–224). Somewhat different from Robin's (2019) statement cited earlier, Fisher did see an equally strong move to the far left from the far right: "Similarly, since the war, many Rumanian, Hungarian, and Polish Fascists and German Nazis, many thousands of them, have joined the nationalistic, totalitarian Communist Party of their countries. Totalitarians of all feathers understand each other" (Fisher, 2001, p. 224).

This brings us back to the question of impact and the different roles side-switchers play in their new milieus. Robin (2019) pointed out that defectors to the far right from the far left have had a significantly higher influence than vice versa. We can assume that side-switching as such is not more or less frequent from one milieu to another. At least we have not seen evidence to the contrary. The fact that side-switchers are more visible in the extreme right than in other milieus lends some credibility to Robin's argument. While in the far left and in Islamic extremist milieus defectors can be found, they indeed tend to be of lower status and have a much more reduced variety of explanation frames in their side-switching storylines. There are exceptions of course. Richard Scheringer (see Section B2.2), David Myatt (Section 4.3), Bernhard Falk (Section 4.2), and Risto Tammi (Section 4.5) did reach accentuated and sometimes even leadership positions in their new milieus.

Scheringer (see Section B2.2) became a "poster boy" of sorts for the Communist Party since he willingly engaged the Nazis and tried to convince others to follow his pathway. After the Second World War, he became chairman of the Communist Party in Bavaria and the organization's agricultural expert. When the Communist Party of Germany (Kommunistische Partei Deutschlands, or KPD) was banned in 1958, Scheringer became a member of the national executive board in the newly created subsequent German Communist Party (Deutsche Kommunistische Partei, or DKP). Hence, he is one example of a former Nazi who reached highest hierarchy levels in the far left. Myatt's status and influence within Islamic extremism is difficult to measure. However, at least in the eyes of many Western observers, his fanatical theological support for jihadist tactics, groups, and leaders was seen as a significant threat (Kaplan, 2000; Weitzman, 2010). It is nevertheless fair to say that he did not reach in any way the level of ideological influence and status other converts obtained, such as John Thomas Georgelas (aka Yahya Abu Hassan, 1983–2017, an American convert and leading ISIS figure) (Wood, 2016, pp. 140–176).

Bernhard Falk, in contrast, was able to acquire a certain standing in the German Salafist scene through his relentless and outspoken support for incarcerated jihadists across the country. His organization dedicated to prison support services for "brothers and sisters" as well as his media activities that document judicial actions against the milieu, rallies, or other events of importance, have made him a somewhat dazzling albeit quite untypical Salafist personality. Falk's standing is less of a theological nature, as he never achieved a religious degree that would give him this authority. In his own storylines, he does not claim to aspire to such a position but instead cites a unique source of experiences and skills with immense value for the overall milieu. Nevertheless, his standing and respect in the German Salafist milieu, while far from uncontroversial, has increased over the years since most actors and groups more or less agree on the issue of supporting their imprisoned followers (IM-NRW, 2019, p. 233). Arguably, the defector who reached the highest status in the Islamic extremist environment was Risto Tammi (Section 4.5), who created and chaired the Finish Islamic Party until he left in conflict in December 2009 and moved back to his original far-left milieu.

There is no question that defectors brought valuable information to their new milieus. Just consider the significant damage done to the British far right by those who worked as moles for the anti-fascist magazine *Searchlight*. In these cases, the intimate knowledge about networks, tactics, crimes, or plots in the extreme right was used to great effect by the anti-fascist magazine. The informants were sometimes used to actively stir up conflicts in the far right, erode trust, impede the formation of alliances, and even to avert terrorist attacks (Townsend, 2019). Sometimes, these side-switchers, such as in the case of Matthew Collins, evolve to be handlers of informants themselves and take up leadership positions in organizations (in his case Hope Note Hate). This appears to be very rare, however; even more so in the Islamic extremist milieu, as we have seen. Apart from Myatt and Falk, those defectors I was able to identify and trace through their narratives or the accounts of observers and court records had no significance in the overall extremist milieu except perhaps through their violent acts or terrorist plots. They had no meaningful and influential impact on the groups and environments around them after they had switched. This should nevertheless not be equated with being unimportant or a lack of potential danger. As I have argued throughout this book, technical skills and knowledge transfer can happen without the need for the defector to actually achieve an influential status. On the contrary, oftentimes the new far-left and Islamic extremist milieus will attempt to harness the information and provide the defector with a stable albeit rather limited status. Think about Emerson Begolly (Section 4.4.1) who provided functional and highly detailed instructions for manufacturing explosives to a person he believed was a fellow jihadist.

Of course, the sample is too small to draw robust conclusions about the visibly limited ideological influence and status of side-switchers in far-left and Islamic extremist milieus. It is known, for example, that converts in general are significantly overrepresented among jihadist terrorists (e.g., Azani & Koblentz-Stenzler, 2019; Flower, 2013; Schuurman, Grol & Flower, 2016) and sometimes hold high-ranking positions and influence the birth of new organizations (Berger, 2011). ISIS has been known to specifically target ex-convicts and converts as potential recruits quite heavily, for example (Cottee, 2016), and the strikingly high number of jihadists with previous criminal pasts has led to a research focus on the so-called crime–terror nexus (e.g., Basra & Neumann, 2016; Ilan & Sandberg, 2019).

Additional scholarship on the role of converts in jihadist milieus has revealed that at least in the American and British Islamic extremist environments, those individuals are strongly present but nevertheless marginalized and considered to be somewhat second-class members (Mullins, 2015). They are often strongly disadvantaged in their environments and significantly less capable of performing tasks at a level of sophistication usually found in the milieu around them. Converts still appear to be involved in terrorist acts quite a lot compared to non-converts, which has been explained by some scholars as being due to a strong urge to become active in a group and ideology (Fodeman, Snook & Horgan, 2020). Hence, there is no obvious reason why side-switchers would be treated any different in this environment just because they came from far-right or far-left backgrounds, when ordinary criminals and converts in general can reach influential positions in the jihadist milieu. The fact that there are indications of structural disadvantages for converts in some Islamic extremist environments and that those individuals strive to prove themselves with more extreme actions could explain why those defectors in our sample mostly had only minor roles. Again, this is not to say they had no impact on their groups or society at large, for example, through terrorist attacks or sharing information and skills.

It appears that the far left is the most adversarial milieu for side-switchers who come from the far right or Islamic extremist groups and who aspire to reach influential leadership or ideological positions. The risk of alienating the support and follower base of extreme-left groups once they allow former neo-Nazis or jihadists into higher ranks is arguably more severe when compared to their opposing milieus. While Islamic extremists can rely on a religiously based collective identity of being "reborn" and leaving a previously sinful life behind through conversion to Islam, the extreme right can at least in some parts look back on an ideological development that links its roots to the far left, as well as many defectors who became Nazi, neo-Nazi or fascist leaders, and important thinkers.

While clearly many of today's far-right extremists despise former communists or other side-switchers, the fact that individuals such as "Alexander Slavros," who openly profess their far-left past, are able to establish immensely influential groups or communities such as IronMarch or Fascist Forge shows that generally speaking, their milieu has a much higher integrative power in terms of the availability of high-status positions for defectors. It is difficult to identify equally lasting and significant contributions to the far left or Islamic extremist environments by side-switchers as compared to the extreme right. In Germany, for example, side-switchers such as Hans-Dietrich Sander (see the introduction to the Bonus Chapter), Reinhold Oberlercher (see Section B1.5), or Horst Mahler (Section 2.1) used their legal and political knowledge gained in the far left to create the theoretical foundations of the sovereign citizen movement (Reichsbürgerbewegung), which still widely uses their texts and arguments. Armin Mohler (see Section B1.1) is regarded as one of the founding fathers of Europe's "New Right" and heavily influenced other intellectual leaders in this far-right current, for example, Alain de Benoist. Theories of provocative actions to disrupt public discourses and gain attention for one's own political concepts were translated from the far–left 1968 student protest movement (then called "subversive action") to the extreme right by Reinhold Oberlercher (see Section B1.5). This publicity tactic was continuously developed further and is essential to modern extreme-right groups such as the Generation Identity (also known as the Identitarian Movement) today (Richards, 2019).

One can easily identify other cases of impactful side-switchers in the far right. To name but one, between August 11 and 12, 2017, modern far-right extremists gathered in Charlottesville, Virginia, in the USA. The very heterogenous crowd included members of (among others) the so-called Alt-Right, comprised of white supremacists, neo-Nazis, white nationalists, and right-wing militias. Themed as a "Unite the Right" rally, the organizers' goals were to create a unified American white nationalist movement and to oppose the removal of a local statue in memory of Confederate General Robert E. Lee. On August 12, a white supremacist deliberately drove his car into a crowd of counterprotesters, killing 32-year-old Heather Heyer and injuring 19 other people. One of the rally's featured speakers was 26-year-old Matthew Heimbach, leader of the now dissolved openly neo-Nazi "Traditionalist Workers Party" (TWP). Heimbach, according to a lawsuit against him and others, belonged to a group of people who "conspired to plan, promote and carry out the violent events at Charlottesville" (*Sines* v. *Kessler*, 2019, p. 2).

The Charlottesville rally and the violent as well as nonviolent incidents that occurred during the event became a milestone in white nationalist and right-wing extremist mobilization in the USA and left the nation in shock, as well as deeply polarized over the political and social reactions (Politico, 2018). Matthew Heimbach, who was once a highly prominent leader of the white nationalist movement and now claims to be a deradicalized former extremist, participated in the left–wing Socialist Student Union and actively involved himself in anti-imperialist actions during his time in college (Tenold, 2018, p. 54). During his days as a white nationalist, his youthful and eloquent but nevertheless extremist ideological messaging made him the "Most Important White Supremacist of 2016" (Cain, 2016) and the "the face of a new generation" (as cited in Walker, 2016) of right-wing extremists.

This integrative power of the far right was also noted by one of the leading experts on fascism, Roger Eatwell. In his seminal work "Fascism. A History" (Eatwell, 1997), Eatwell described what he called "syncretic legitimation," which means that fascist movements were often able to profit from conservative political elites who had already nurtured certain important opinions and ideological concepts within their constituency, with the aim to use the extreme right's appeal for their own electoral gain:

Its [fascism] syncretic ideological form meant that it was highly flexible, but in most countries it tended to gather in force where the right was weak. However, space alone was not enough: more importantly, fascism needed a sense of legitimacy, an ability to relate its ideology to what was familiar, respectable: paradoxically, radicalism had to have a familiar face. In particular, it needed to offer the prospect that it could forge some form of national rebirth, which could restore a sense of community and crucial aspects of national identity. In order to do this, shrewd leadership was required by the insurgent forces, particularly by the way in which they managed to combine more affective-traditional and rational-economic appeals and by their ability to hide key aspects of their radicalism. Some form of legitimation by existing mainstream elites, who often sought to turn fascism to their own more conservative purposes, was also important. Yet these decisions too have to be understood within the context of legitimacy and national traditions, for they were taken within a framework of what was considered acceptable, possible – concepts conditioned by history as well as the more immediate force of economic and social circumstance. Put simply, fascism succeeded where it achieved syncretic legitimation, the ability both to appeal to affective and more individualistic voters, and to convince at least a section of the mainstream elites that it could serve their purpose better than existing parties. (Eatwell, 1997, p. 39)

This syncretic flexibility of the far right's ideology might provide it with integrative power, especially for those individuals who already nurtured specific ideological concepts (e.g., anti-Semitism, anti-capitalism) in other extremist milieus.

The examples just given show that defectors from hostile milieus have created numerous and highly influential new ideological variants, tactics, and strategies in the far right, while this is clearly not the case in far-left or Islamic extremist environments. With this strong difference in visibility and the influence of defectors among the three extremist milieus in mind, it is possible to move forward to assess the sources of social status enhancement for side-switchers in order to better understand the observed pathway varieties. Those defectors who joined the far right have the best chances to substantially improve their status and influence within a given extremist environment. Typically, the extreme right offers a broad spectrum of potential routes for integration into the milieu based on anti-Semitism, racism, nationalism, or violent masculinity. We have seen ideological and organizational leaders, subcultural artists (e.g., musicians), or social movement entrepreneurs who created completely new forms of mobilization by actively incorporating their contradictory pasts.

In many cases, the defectors were even able to continue their main type and style of activities, be it rap music (Julian Fritsch, Section 2.3); journalism and writing (Jürgen Elsässer, see Section B1.6); or the fight against their governmental enemy via provocation of endless court trials for publicity (Horst Mahler, Section 2.1). Defectors, as we have seen, were generally welcomed and their knowledge, skills, or insights into the far left were used as an advantage. It is noteworthy that the far-right ideological "DNA" shows significant flexibility and openness to the integration of new concepts or contents around a small rigid core (including, for example, nationalism, anti-Semitism, or racism). The discussions among far-rightists in IronMarch or on Discord that I presented in Section 2.4 display a striking level of active ideological construction and partially detailed debates that weigh many different philosophical, political, social, or economic positions from various ideological backgrounds against established orthodox positions. Such conversations were based on their value for recruiting new followers, reaching the wider society more effectively, or simply the need to update the milieu's theoretical premises to external developments.

Within the far left, the defectors we have studied almost exclusively came from the far right and predominantly framed their decision to switch sides through moral imperatives, a guilty consciousness, and the desire for revenge. As long as they showed their sincere embrace of the new environment, for example, by full disclosure of all information they had on the far right or by doing all in their power to damage the former comrades and in many cases by expressing continued hatred against the authorities, they were generally able to achieve a stable and rewarding social status enhancement. Storylines of far-right side-switchers to the extreme left often talk about the low quality of human relationships in their former groups, which indicates that they might have been looking for more positive and reliable social networks. There is little doubt that once those defectors gained the trust of far-left milieus through their actions, they were swiftly integrated and respected for their decision to make good on their pasts. In this sense, far-right exiters expressed a stronger desire for a moral and ethical social status upgrade by erasing their own perception of guilt and shame. This is something the far left clearly provides in a most effective way, since the ideological core narratives of social justice, equality, and combatting the extreme right (among other enemies) based on a claimed moral superiority allow for individuals to move into that direction and reestablish themselves as someone who has returned to an ethically "good life" and earned the respect of their new social environment.

One example of such a case is the musician Matthew "Matty Blag" Roberts (1964–2000), who was the main vocalist of the British punk rock band Blaggers ITA (formerly The Blaggers), which was founded in 1988. The band became well known for its militant anti-fascist texts and the involvement of its members in the Anti-Fascist Action (AFA). One of the goals of the band was to raise money for AFA and promote its revolutionary anti-fascist ideology. Roberts admitted to an extreme right past during his teenage years and previous links to the far-right "British Movement" (BM). An obituary published by the militant anti-fascist group Red Action explained his decision to switch sides by questioning "his flirtation with fascism" (Red-Action, 2000) while he served a prison sentence. This did not stop him from becoming "regarded with a great deal of affection by his former comrades," which also shown by the "large turnout at Matty's memorial service, which was attended by representatives of both RA and Anti-Fascist Action, [and] demonstrated his lasting popularity with those who had known him both inside and outside of politics" (Red-Action, 2000). In July 1993, Roberts got into a fight with a journalist who claimed that he never actually reformed from his fascist past and the following physical altercation led to a rapid decline of the mainstream music industry's interest in the band, which split as one result. While the band toured Germany in 1995, the left-wing newspaper *taz – Die Tageszeitung* published an article that hinted at controversial views surrounding Roberts' involvement in the far-left milieu and reported that the band was attacked by some because of its stylistic past and changes. Even so, the group enjoyed a steady and enthusiastic fan base. Matthew Roberts, who turned to anti-fascism after reading George Orwell's novel *1984* according to the *taz* newspaper, as an individual, was nevertheless seen as a respected far-left musician (Winkler, 1995).

Islamic extremism in theory allows for a broad integration of defectors via religious conversion mechanisms that facilitate the identity change process and help to establish the convert in the eyes of the new group. However, we have seen that this milieu often treats converts with less respect compared to those who are seen as true Muslims because of their ethnic background or upbringing. One can argue that theological knowledge, proficiency in Arabic language, or cultural skills connected to the historic geographical areas where Islam developed and spread might form barriers between the converts and those "born into" Islam. Indeed, some indication of a clash of cultures among jihadists exists. For example, in 2015 British jihadist and ISIS fighter Omar Hussein (aka Abu Sa'eed al-Britani, 1987–2017) complained about the immense behavioral differences between the Europeans and Arabs within the organization. He expressed his frustration and annoyance about many habits fundamentally at odds with his British socialization, such as casually stealing and using his property or the inability to form queues (Sims, 2015). Europeans or other foreign recruits on the other hand were often seen as undisciplined, physically weak, and tactically worthless by ISIS, which often used them as cannon fodder in the first waves of attacks (Lake, 2015). It has been documented that through their zealotry, Europeans have clashed with locals about their habits and caused alienation from the group they represented (Byman, 2019). This can even cause so many problems for jihadist groups that they need to develop organizational strategies to mitigate overzealous foreign recruits (Mironova, 2019).

5.8   On Gender

When we consider the sample of side-switching storylines I have identified in this book, it becomes immediately clear that male cases overwhelmingly dominate this phenomenon. Only two elaborate narratives come from women (Beate Zschäpe's side-switching is only available from secondary sources): Ires Niemeyer (Section 2.2) and Christine Hewicker (Section 3.1). Of course, we need to apply the same reservation regarding the limitations of the case selection and potential sources of bias. Women could be switching sides equally often but either rarely present their stories in such detail or might receive less interest from their previous and current milieus, as well as the public. When we look at those two female defectors in detail, not much appears to be out of the ordinary compared to the male cases. Iris Niemeyer, for example, bases her complete extremist career narrative on constant unjust treatment and victimization by society (in addition to her increasing fascination with anti-Western conspiracy theories).

Even though one might argue that this particular focus on victimization is less often found among male side-switchers, it is nevertheless not unheard of either. Jürgen Elsässer (see Section B1.6) and Reinhold Oberlercher (see Section B1.5) do not hide their continued grievances over feeling mistreated and victimized by their past milieus, employers, or the mainstream society. Elsässer was repeatedly fired from his jobs as a journalist, which he interpreted as silencing of his controversial opinions. Oberlercher's failure to achieve a professorship position in the 1970s and afterward fueled his grudges against the established academia for decades and remained an influential topic. Niemeyer also does not submit to the claimed role of victim of injustice. On the contrary, her storytelling strategy is to highlight her rebellious, nonconformist, and warrior personality. She chose the name "Jeanne D." (in reference to the French heroine Jeanne d'Arc) for her online blog, which certainly was not a wise decision in terms of the German neo-Nazi milieu's acceptance of the project. It nevertheless reveals much about her self-image.

The "nonconformist rebel" strategy to deal with injustice and victimization is not surprisingly used widely by male defectors as well. Almost all side-switchers want to present their milieu transitions as the outcome of a conscious and deliberate decision, which suggests strong agency and control over their own life courses. The only storyline element that can be seen as somewhat unusual comes from Christine Hewicker, but is part of her retrospective account as someone who has completely disengaged from extremism long after the side-switching took place. Hence, we cannot fully acknowledge this part as a uniquely female defection narrative strategy. Hewicker, in her autobiography, states that the forced separation from her husband when he was in prison at one time put her in a position where she was free to think without (male) influence, and began to develop own ideological interests and concepts (Hewicker, 2001, p. 47). This is certainly (a part of) an explanation for changing viewpoints that we cannot find among the male defector storylines at all. On the contrary, they strongly try to own the side-switching process to avoid being seen as failures in their old groups who merely grasp every straw to find any meaningful position and status.

Terrorism and extremist environments have widely and traditionally been regarded as predominantly male domains. If accurate, a generally higher percentage of men in such milieus would naturally also reduce the chance for female side-switchers to exist. In jihadist environments, studies have consistently shown the overwhelmingly male composition. For example, Bakker's sample of 242 European jihadist terrorists between 2001 and 2006 includes only five women (Bakker, 2006, p. 36). In another study that looks at 784 jihadists who left Germany to join one of the militant opposition or terrorist groups operating in Syria and Iraq by the end of June 2016, 21 percent were female (BKA, BfV & HKE, 2016, p. 11). This is a significantly higher percentage of women among the Syria/Iraq travelers compared to Bakker's findings. A comparable study of American jihadist travelers with a sample of 64 cases by early 2018 identified 11 percent women (Meleagrou-Hitchens & Hughes, 2018, p. 17), and a five-year review of court cases in the USA against extremists from this milieu found the exact same proportion of men vs. women among the 170 individuals charged with criminal offences related to ISIS between March 2014 and January 2019 (GWU-POE, 2019).

The apparent increase of female members in jihadist milieus in recent years can at least partially be explained by ISIS's dedicated efforts to appeal to and recruit women. In fact, this organization's propaganda and mobilization activities directed at female potential recruits has received substantial interest from researchers, who, for example, assessed audio-visual, linguistic, and emotional recruitment strategies (e.g., Brugh, Desmarais, Simons-Rudolph & Zottola, 2019; Gan, Neo, Chin & Khader, 2019; Huey et al., 2017; Musial, 2016; Shapiro & Maras, 2018; Windsor, 2020). ISIS was one of the few jihadist terror organizations that offered a wide range of tasks and positions to female members, including some that are traditionally reserved for men within the Islamic extremist milieu.

The so-called al-Khansaa Brigade created in 2014, for example, performed religious policing duties and allowed women to carry weapons, drive cars, and enforce ISIS regulations (Gilsinan, 2014). Still, women cannot be found among organizational leadership positions in jihadist organizations, with maybe the rare exception of British citizen Samantha Lewthwaite, who reportedly was involved in the leadership of al-Shabaab (de Leede, 2018, p. 7). The almost exclusively male dominance of the top ranks is also codified by some organizations' attempts to frame women's subordination into supportive positions as specifically "female jihad" (Von Knop, 2007). The targeted recruitment of women through ISIS, which used specially designed magazines, article series, or videos to reach a female audience, was unprecedented among jihadist groups (Khelghat-Doost, 2017) and proved effective in increasing appeal. This also led other organizations in that milieu to adopt similar strategies resulting in generally rising numbers of female jihadist recruits (Khelghat-Doost, 2018). However, to name one area of activism forbidden for women, taking part in combat operations (excluding suicide attacks) was reserved for men. This fact actually caused some internal conflict within ISIS, with some female members calling for a full emancipation and the opening of frontline combat for women (Peresin & Cervone, 2015). The group partially gave in to these demands as it produced at least one video in 2018 that appeared to show women who take part in active combat (even though analysts have voiced strong reservations about the accuracy of such claims by ISIS) (Dearden, 2018).

It is also important to point out that with an increasing number of men who were killed or incarcerated, the role of women began to gain significance. "ISIS women" have been seen as the nucleus of an ISIS revival and maintenance of networks, ideological commitment, and reorganization in prisoner camps such as "Al Hol" (Zelin, 2019). Similarly, in Western countries Salafist women networks began to shoulder the major responsibilities for running and maintaining the existing milieus with more and more men ending up in prison (Deutsche-Welle, 2017). However, it is fair to say that the Islamic extremist milieus are far from achieving a gender a balance. According to a 2016 report by the Bavarian state intelligence service, only around 10 percent of the German Salafist milieu were women at the time (Bavaria, 2016, p. 20).

What about far-right and far-left environments? Extreme right-wing environments, such as Islamic extremist milieus, are also not known for their progressive and balanced gender policies. Rough indicators for the gender composition in the far right are studies regarding charged and convicted right-wing terrorists. A sample of 75 individuals indicted for right-wing terrorist-related crimes in the USA between 1980 and 1989 included only 7 percent females (Smith, 1994, p. 49). Only two played a leading role in terrorist violence. Another more recent study from 2016 looks at US far-right terrorist recruitment and radicalization and used a sample of 34 individuals, of which only four were women (Simi et al., 2016, p. 186). Additional accounts from other countries, for example, Germany, estimate the share of women in subcultural extreme-right groups between 10 and 33 percent (Bitzan, 2017, p. 339). Female members of extreme right-wing parties and women who hold elected positions for them equally vary between 10 and 30 percent (Bitzan, 2017, p. 338).

Extreme-right crimes, however, are much more often (over 90 percent) perpetrated by men according to German scholars (Bitzan, 2017, p. 337). In contrast to the Islamic extremist milieu, however, the far right does offer leadership positions to women and includes groups that are either led by or completely composed of female members. In the USA, the Ku Klux Klan and other white supremacist groups, for example, have traditionally featured a strong female component (Blee, 1996, 2002, 2005). The German extreme-right NPD party created its own women's organization, the "Ring Nationaler Frauen" (Association of Nationalist Women, or RNF) in 2006, which is an exclusively female group (Röpke & Speit, 2011). Since the 1980s, female far-right terrorists in Germany are a regular albeit clearly smaller percentage of charged and convicted groups (Manthe, 2019). Curiously, a large German terrorism study that looked at the time before 1980, identified 23 right-wing terrorists who were convicted by 1978, all of them male (Schmidtchen, 1981, p. 23). This likewise indicates a strong male dominance in the far right, but with much more organizational integration potential for women.

Contrary to the far-right and Islamic extremist milieus, the far left is built on a highly egalitarian, anti-sexist, and emancipatory ideology. This does reflect the significantly higher percentages of women involved in this environment. Of 56 left-wing extremists and terrorists indicted in the USA between 1980 and 1981, 27 percent were female (Smith, 1994, p. 49). Women played important roles in the leadership positions in many of the American left-wing terrorist groups in that decade and some even reached a complete gender balance in their membership (Smith, 1994, p. 49). Of 277 convicted left-wing terrorists in Germany up until 1978, 33 percent were female and of those, women even achieved a higher share of leadership positions than men (36 percent female vs. 32 percent male, see Süllwold, 1981, p. 106).

A quite similar situation of female leaders and a higher share of members can be found in other countries with strong militant left-wing milieus, for example, Italy (Cunningham, 2003, p. 157) or Greece (Kassimeris, 2019), and extends to ethno-separatist liberation movements that at least partially base their ideologies on left-wing anti-imperialism and anti-colonialism (Trisko Darden, Henshaw & Szekely, 2019). It is clear that from all the extremist milieus we looked at, the far left provides the most extensive social status enhancement options for women. While still often dominated by men, examples of terror groups founded and led exclusively by women exist, which is unheard of in the other two environments. To name but one, the American Marxist-Leninist "May 19th Communist Organization" (or M19) was active between 1978 and 1985 and committed a series of bombings and robberies to advance its social-revolutionary agenda as an offspring that had evolved out of the Weather Underground. Only two out of 10 members were male and had minor roles in the group (Rosenau, 2020).

In sum, the role of women in extremist milieus is still largely limited but varies sometimes significantly between the different environments. It also appears that, generally speaking, women gained more significance and attention within extremism and terrorism in recent years (Bloom, 2011; Cunningham, 2007). Partially, the overly male domains we looked at here in our attempt to understand extremist side-switching might explain the rarity of female case studies. One can wonder, however, why female defectors to the far left are not much more commonly known, since that milieu clearly provides the best social status enhancement perspectives and is based on an ideology with the greatest integrative power for women (compared to the others). The strong focus on social justice, equality, and anti-sexism (among other topics) might also be a very attractive and convincing set of goals that has the potential to reach a much more diverse audience than, for example, the warrior-centric and hypermasculine far-right and Islamic extremist scenes.

Another possible explanation for the strikingly small number of elaborate female side-switcher storylines might be that women could be generally less likely to tell their stories in these environments and feel less compelled to present their backgrounds in such an exposed manner. It is of course difficult to assess that theory, and one proxy indicator can be the share of women who wrote autobiographical accounts after leaving extremism and terrorism altogether. In their study of 85 such publications, Altier et al. recorded a share of almost 18 percent (15 autobiographies) written by women (online appendix to Altier et al., 2017, p. 20), which is significantly higher than what we have seen here.

There are indications that unreported cases of female side-switching, at least in some extremist milieus, might exist due to a still widespread lack of attention that has been paid to women in these environments. Darby's (2020) presentation of three female right-wing extremists in North America, for example, includes two cases that cannot be categorized as side-switchers between opposed extremist milieus but do involve crossing various ideological boundaries between milieus based on equally strong collective identities. Corinna Olsen, according to Darby, always had a desire for going through extreme experiences of belonging to nonmainstream social milieus or working in jobs that are generally considered to be "extreme" (e.g., the porn or funeral industry). After her defection from the extreme right, she converted to Islam at least partially to embrace "a culture that she knew frightened or enraged many white Americans" and to be "sticking it to the racists she'd once considered friends" (Darby, 2020, pp. 89–90). Ayla, her second case study, entered right-wing extremism from a liberal, New Age, and "anarcho-syndicalist" (Darby, 2020, p. 109) background, which is revealing since we have encountered that particular school of anarchist thought throughout this book, especially among switchers from the extreme left to the extreme right (e.g., see Section B2.1 on Benito Mussolini). Ayla did not transition directly between the two milieus but rather developed her own pathway that first led her to conservative religiosity (by becoming a member of the Church of the Latter Day Saints). Nevertheless, the two cases serve as reminders that we still know far too little about the motives, pathways, and roles of women within extremist milieus.

Naturally, it is much different to present a story to a new and even hostile extremist milieu than to the general public in the form of autobiographies or interviews with journalists, which usually welcomes exiters and stories of positive life change. However, in some environments (e.g., the far left or online far right), where either the ideology or the dominant attitude toward defections is positive, one should expect more female accounts. In short, it appears to be the case that presenting extremist side-switching narratives either to the public or the new environment is an overwhelmingly male phenomenon.

5.9   Conclusion

To conclude this chapter, which brings together various aspects of an extremist side-switching theory, it is important to highlight three main arguments I have tried to make. First, defections between hostile extremist environments are likely to involve significant radicalization boosts via the necessary self-persuasion strategies that are also the key mechanism behind the "choice blindness" phenomenon described in Chapter 1. Persons who transition between opposing political (and other) viewpoints often employ specific strategies to maintain a functional individual identity and integrity. This existential human desire is strengthened by protective psychological barriers such as cognitive dissonance aversion or reactance against forced change.

Switching sides between such fundamentally opposed milieus as we have studied here requires certain efforts to convince oneself and the new group of shared ideological beliefs, goals, or the moral superiority over the group that was left behind. This does not automatically mean that a side-switcher is more likely to engage in escalated forms of criminal activity or violence, but it does significantly decrease the chance of overall disengagement and deradicalization. Successful defectors become exceptionally convinced zealots in most cases. Very few proceed to change sides again or leave behind extremism and terrorism completely. The clear majority of individuals in the cases we looked at provided important knowledge, skills, resources, or ideological legitimacy to their new groups and thereby made themselves more effective in pursuing their goals. In this sense, side-switchers are a seemingly small but potentially very dangerous part of extremist learning and knowledge-sharing processes.

Second, the underlying rationale typically presented by defectors is most often based on the strategy of pointing out that they personally have been committed to the core values all along and that they have been misled, misguided, or simply untruthful to themselves. These narratives are usually enriched with stories of moral degeneration and weakness of the group left behind, as well as unsuccessful attempts to reform or save it. This narrative construct very much aligns with the predictions made in Social Identity Theory (SIT) about the different status enhancement strategies and involved factors. In essence, to successfully "sell" a defection to create sympathy and support in a certain target audience means to create a story of "change without a change." The side-switchers identify key ideological concepts and fuse their identity especially tight to them, while flexibly shedding everything else that might still connect them to their old milieus. "Ideology" becomes a particularly fragmented and highly practical social paradigm for defectors. Activism and milieu involvement are fundamentally connected to a personal identity defined by adherence and commitment to specially selected and partially restructured ideological components (e.g., anti-Semitism, nationalism, anti-imperialism). Extremist side-switching allows us to take a glance at a very dynamic process of reinventing oneself along a thin line of ideological reconstruction, adaption, and adjustment. Defectors present themselves as the masters of their own pathways and point out agency and determination in a process of ideological development that is as much social as it is theoretical.

Third, side-switching is not just an isolated individual psychological process that involves one person who changes social milieus. On the contrary, this phenomenon is very much relational and interactional. Defections such as these are almost always the result of the relationship between a group and a member gone awry. Sometimes negotiation of continued involvement can be observed. Extremist milieus and groups, like any social environment, must face turnover of members but the need to retain members is more often an existential need for them. Through defector storylines, we learn about successful and failed human resource strategies for extremist environments, both on the side being left and the one being joined. In this sense, pathways in and out, and through extremism and terrorism, must be understood as complex spheres of interaction between an individual and multiple, sometimes even competing or hostile, social milieus.

6   Breaking the Cycle
Learning How to Improve Counter-Radicalization, Counterterrorism, and Deradicalization Programs

The small German village of Kirtorf in the state of Hessen has little more than 3,100 inhabitants. One of them is the farmer Bertram Köhler, who is credited with tarnishing the community's public image into a Nazi hotspot (Berghöfer, 2019). Born in 1963, Köhler (who is in no way related to me) has strained the other villagers' patience for decades, for example, by hosting neo-Nazi skinhead concerts on his farm that drew crowds numbering in the hundreds or by spreading the manure of his cows in the form of a giant wolf's angle (a German heraldic charge widely used by neo-Nazis). Only after videos of one of the concerts became public in 2004 did the ensuing outcry cause Köhler to moderate his actions somewhat until 2019, when he again raised public criticism.

Köhler's willingness to give interviews and his open admittance to right-wing extremist views as well as sympathies for the far-right NPD party, of which he is a longtime member, have facilitated reporting about his case. His political biography began in the far left with his involvement in the German Communist Party (Deutsche Kommunistische Partei, or DKP) at the age of 18. In interviews with the press, Köhler explains that his political life has always been impacted by disappointment and chicanery. While being a communist living in West Germany, he observed that close friends lost their jobs and were discriminated against because of their extreme-left views and party affiliation. After the fall of the Berlin Wall and the socialist German Democratic Republic (GDR) in the East, he found that many of the Germans who had lived under socialism were completely disillusioned with it and had no further interest in communism (Eppelsheim, 2019, p. 11).

A second major turning point in his life, according to interviews, was an incident after the German reunification that involved his nephew (at the time a neo-Nazi skinhead) flying a swastika flag in front of a discotheque where Köhler was working as a bouncer. From Köhler's perspective, the following fine (since showing Nazi symbols is illegal in Germany) was a grave injustice and nothing more than another form of political discrimination and harassment (Eppelsheim, 2019, p. 12). Neo-Nazis skinheads were banned from the disco-theque, so Köhler has hosted them on his farm ever since – for more than 15

244

years. In his statements, one can recognize a deeply engrained frustration with what he perceived as bullying by the government, which led him to express sympathies for the left-wing terrorist Red Army Faction (RAF), the GDR, and Adolf Hitler, all at the same time (Eppelsheim, 2019, p. 12).

Since his own biography is filled with many different unskilled jobs and economic problems, social support from the state as well as anti-capitalism feature strongly in his positions. For him, criminal capitalist elites were contained under Hitler and in the GDR, both of which took much greater care of their own people than the current system (Eppelsheim, 2019, p. 12). It appears that Köhler, like so many other side-switchers to the extreme right, felt alienated by society and longed for more social coherency, community, and what he regards as social justice. Why he is allowed to "raise the American flag but not the swastika flag" (original in German, translated by author, as cited in: Eppelsheim, 2019, p. 12) is simply incomprehensible to him. His own attempt to leave extremism by getting married and raising children failed. His wife divorced him because of his alcoholism and other issues. After additional incidents that involved his children talking about their access to guns in school he also lost custody of his two sons (Eppelsheim, 2019, p. 13). As a consequence, he returned to provocative actions and involvement in extremist milieus. The case of Bertram Köhler shows yet again the complex relationship between ideological factors on an emotional level (e.g., grievances over injustice) and lack of socioeconomic success.

Could someone like Bertram Köhler have been supported in his attempt to leave extremism behind or could he even have been diverted away from radicalizing into the far left or far right in the first place? What can we learn from extremist side-switching cases like his for improving our strategies to counter and prevent extremist involvement? In recent years an increasing academic and public interest in preventing and countering violent extremism (P/CVE), counter-radicalization or disengagement, and deradicalization programs has led to some substantial advances in understanding how leaving extremist milieus works on the individual and collective level and how it might be facilitated through external assistance (e.g., Clubb, 2017; Hwang, 2018; Koehler, 2016b; Marsden, 2017). Even though this knowledge lacks far behind our understanding of why individuals enter extremist environments and/or change their behavior to ideologically motivated violence and other extremist activities, it is by now fairly established that locking extremists up indefinitely (which is legally impossible in many countries anyway) or killing them through combat operations will not stop the flow of new recruits into these milieus, and might even fuel grievances and other factors that play into radicalization pathways. Most countries have generally accepted the fact that preventative strategies and reintegration or rehabilitation assistance for those who became involved in extremist milieus and might have turned to crime and violence could be a more effective and cheaper option for fighting terrorism in the long run.

Nevertheless, the evidence base for such programs and strategies, as well as specific methods and tools, is scarce at best. One reason for this is the relatively small number of cases that can be studied and evaluated regarding the potential impact of outsider intervention (i.e., the small base rate problem) and ethical problems involved in testing different approaches using comparison groups in experimental designs (which would mean deliberately risking a group of participants having a higher chance of turning to terrorism). Even though academics and practitioners are increasingly working around these issues and discussing alternative ways to assess the impact of such programs (e.g., Braddock, 2019a; Cherney & Belton, 2019b; Mastroe & Szmania, 2016), there are still many unexplored issues surrounding the P/CVE field.

Seen through the perspective of this book, one of the apparent gaps is that exit processes have been generally regarded as binary in nature: Either a person succeeds in leaving extremist milieus (in many different ways and forms, to be sure) or not (meaning the person remains committed or moves back to the former milieu for various different reasons and in multiple pathways). How, then, can the transition between hostile extremist milieus be understood? Is this a totally new form of exit process in the sense of quitting one extremist milieu? Or rather, is this a failed deradicalization process and should be seen as an instance of recidivism into extremism even though no distance from extremist views per se happened in between? It appears that current P/CVE research has missed a third option for extremists who encounter problems in their milieus: switching sides in addition to remaining or leaving completely. This of course impacts the calculus and underlying premises of many P/CVE approaches and the next chapter will discuss these potential alterations in detail. It is, however, not only the P/CVE side of countering terrorism that we need to look at when we discuss important lessons learned from extremist side-switching. Even so-called hard or kinetic counterterrorism (CT) schools of thought (i.e., repression, containment, and maximum level of penalization or even targeted assassination of extremists) have mostly operated under the assumption that the extremist or terrorist groups and milieus could be destroyed by applying enough outside force, which either leads to the death, imprisonment, or disengagement of the target milieus' members. However, the possibility that such outside pressure might on the contrary result in the dispersal of extremists into completely different milieus has so far not been part of that strategic assessment. What are the lessons extremist side-switching storylines teach us regarding P/CVE and CT?

6.1   What Is Preventing and Countering Violent Extremism?

Countering violent extremism (CVE) is usually understood to be "an approach intended to preclude individuals from engaging in, or materially supporting, ideologically motivated violence" (Williams, 2017, p. 153) or simply as "non-coercive attempts to reduce involvement in terrorism" (Harris-Hogan, Barrelle & Zammit, 2015, p. 6). The term is now widely used in international and national counterterrorism strategies and policies, even though it was criticized as being a "catch-all category that lacks precision and focus" (Heydemann, 2014, p. 1). CVE as a concept was used (albeit rarely) as early as 2005 but became impactful in the USA around 2009/20010 under the Obama administration (2009–2017), which took inspiration from the British "preventing violent extremism" (PVE) approach of their "Counter Terrorism Strategy" (CONTEST) and its pillar "PREVENT." This strategy was developed in 2003 and has been in place since the 7/7 London bombings in 2005. The main goals of PREVENT were set as to: challenge violent extremist ideology and support "mainstream" voices; disrupt those who promote violent extremism and support the institutions where they are active; support individuals who are being targeted and recruited to the cause of violent extremism; increase the resilience of communities to violent extremism; and address the grievances that ideologues are exploiting. One can quickly see that the roots of today's P/CVE strategies and concepts are deliberately broad and vague, which allows practitioners to subsume a wide array of activities, methods, programs, and initiatives under the term. This is both a strength and weakness since there is a risk of P/CVE "meaning everything and nothing" and this could result in an inflationary usage of the label.

What then, are typical activities in the P/CVE field? One widely used classification for understanding the different goals and scope of methods and approaches is the "public health model" from Caplan (Caplan, 1964), which itself comes from clinical psychiatry. "Primary" prevention in this model aims to prevent a deviant behavior from occurring in a "non-infected" system. This includes, for example, activities that aim to raise general awareness, build resilience, or community coherence. Primary prevention addresses societal issues and individuals before extremist groups and ideologies are encountered and potential risk factors manifest themselves. "Secondary" prevention aims to avert solidification of risk factors or a radicalization process in the early stages, for example, through community outreach programs, family counseling, or mental health services directed at individuals and communities thought to be vulnerable. Finally, "tertiary" prevention aims to avoid recidivism into extremism or other risk factors in the future, implying that an initial desistance or disengagement has been achieved.

Naturally, very different methods and programs fall under these three categories because working with long-term members of extremist groups to induce defection is a completely different task than teaching children about the risks posed by extremist groups, for example. One must acknowledge, however, that Caplan's model and other classification schemes are originally based in disease control, which makes the translation to P/CVE problematic. We should be careful not to imply a pathological nature of radicalization and extremism, which sees individuals who undergo this process as "sick" or "spreading a disease." We must also be aware that this approach to understanding what is being done in P/CVE through different types of "prevention" obscures or even leaves out what has been called deradicalization, disengagement, or intervention. As intended by Caplan, everything done in tertiary prevention essentially aims to avoid recidivism and one can find resonance of this in research framing deradicalization programs as methods to reduce risk of terrorist recidivism (Horgan & Altier, 2012). However, preventing recidivism is just one necessary (and subsequent) part of interventions, which must reduce individual physical and psychological commitment to the extremist group and ideology in the first place.

In short, it would be accurate to see P/CVE as an umbrella category under which prevention-oriented initiatives (i.e., before a person radicalizes to the point of using violence) and intervention-oriented initiatives (i.e., deradicalization and disengagement of persons who are already radicalized to the point of using violence) are subsumed. The first is commonly referred to as "counter-radicalization" or "preventing violent extremism" (PVE) programs and the latter as intervention, deradicalization, rehabilitation, or reintegration programs. Of course, there is no clear distinction between prevention or intervention-oriented methods and programs in practice, as it is the nature of radicalization processes, are not linear but dynamic as well as I have discussed in Section 1.2. Hence, most programs and practitioners do not clearly differentiate the various terms and concepts as the academic discourse might suggest. In reality, prevention and intervention-oriented tools form a blend of methods that aim to achieve impact on all levels: preventing further radicalization; decreasing physical and psychological commitment to the radical milieu and ideology; preventing return to violence and extremism; increasing resilience to extremist ideologies or groups; and assisting efforts to build a new self-sustained life and identity. As a consequence, as radicalization is a context-bound phenomenon "par excellence" (Reinares et al., 2008, p. 7), so is countering it.

When looking at side-switchers, we are trying to better understand a psychological process that leads to transitions between groups and milieus that both can be classified as extremist. This means that we focus on a stage in the person's life when they are already involved in one extremist milieu or have radicalized to a certain degree. Quitting such a group or environment is usually described and explored in research on "deradicalization" or "disengagement," and as I have briefly introduced in Section 1.6.3, there are many known push-and-pull factors as well as process steps involved.

Here, I want to go into more detail about this matter as we can see how at least partially, side-switchers overlap with those individuals leaving the extremist milieu completely. "Deradicalization" and "disengagement" are by no means the only terms used to explore exiting from extremism or terrorism, and the conceptual lack of clarity of the terms has been repeatedly noted (Altier et al., 2014). Horgan and Taylor (2011, p. 175), for example, listed "rehabilitation," "reform," "counseling," "reconciliation," "amnesty," "demobilization," "disbandment," "dialogue," and "deprogramming" as alternative and sometimes competing or exchangeable concepts. One could also add "reintegration," "reeducation," "desistance" (primary, secondary, and tertiary), "disaffiliation," and "debiasing" to the list (Koehler, 2016b). All these terms roughly describe a similar process of turning away from a position of perceived deviance or conflict with the surrounding environment toward moderation and equilibrium. This process can take numerous different forms, such as voluntary or involuntary (e.g., through imprisonment), permanent or temporary, individual or collective, and psychological or physical (Koehler, 2016b, p. 14).

We can quickly see that discussing deradicalization (and the related concepts) brings us into similar conceptual troubles as we already encountered in Chapter 1 when looking at what radicalization or extremism means. Essentially, these terms are outside denominators used to describe a psychological and physical process gauged by individuals' or groups' degree of accordance, respectively conflict, with the legal, ideological, or moral views of the surrounding majority (or mainstream) environment. In short, one is considered radical or extremist by their surroundings and typically judged as disengaged or deradicalized based on how far one subscribes to the collective mainstream norms. This leads us directly to Berger's (2018) key argument that being an extremist should not be framed as the adherence to a specific political, philosophical, or religious system that is deemed "normal" by the majority. Equally, leaving such a milieu or attitude cannot be defined solely by returning to said "normal" environment.

Deradicalization and its competing concepts must be understood as terms that describe a specific kind of societal negotiation between a community and perceived deviants and aim to reduce conflict between the two sides. Most of these concepts and terms (including deradicalization) imply that the source of the conflict lies with the "deviant" other, who must be somehow aligned with the position of the mainstream majority or the receiving community, assuming that an increased alignment automatically reduces conflict. Deradicalization, and most of these competing concepts, therefore have to navigate a precarious borderline between reducing the plurality of opinions and convictions on the one hand (in case the end goal of the process is to integrate a person into a democratic society), which sometimes even crosses the threshold into infringing upon central core values of the communities, and on the other, reducing sources of conflict based on the extremist thought patterns, ideologies, or group dynamics of the defector's starting point.

I described this inherent struggle with moral legitimacy of the deradicalization concept in Western democracies (i.e., the attempted change of a person's or group's political or religious opinion, which is oftentimes not illegal) in detail elsewhere (Koehler, 2016b, pp. 201–210), which is why here it must suffice to say that deradicalization cannot mean to make anyone more "democratic" or "tolerant" per se. This would actually be a self-defeating fundamental flaw in the concept. It becomes clear, that the inherent moral legitimacy conflict of deradicalization is tied to the term "ideology," which we already discussed in detail (Section 1.3). This is one of the reasons that the conceptual "Siamese twin" of deradicalization is "disengagement" and both are usually used in combination with each other. Looking at some definitions by leading academic experts, the main difference between deradicalization and disengagement is the focus on ideology, or more precisely the psychological side of exiting a violent extremist milieu. Horgan and Braddock (2010, p. 152), for example, define disengagement as:

the process whereby an individual experiences a change in role or function that is usually associated with a reduction of violent participation. It may not necessarily involve leaving the movement, but is most frequently associated with significant temporary or permanent role change. Additionally, while disengagement may stem from role change, that role change may be influenced by psychological factors such as disillusionment, burnout or the failure to reach the expectations that influenced initial involvement. This can lead to a member seeking out a different role within the movement

and deradicalization as:

the social and psychological process whereby an individual's commitment to, and involvement in, violent radicalization is reduced to the extent that they are no longer at risk of involvement and engagement in violent activity. De-radicalization may also refer to any initiative that tries to achieve a reduction of risk of re-offending through addressing the specific and relevant disengagement issues. (Horgan & Braddock, 2010, p. 153)

More specifically, Braddock points out that deradicalization is a "psychological process through which an individual abandons his extremist ideology and is theoretically rendered a decreased threat for re-engaging in terrorism" (Braddock, 2014, p. 60). Hence, at a first glance, the main difference between disengagement and deradicalization according to this view, is if reduction of the ideological commitment (deradicalization) or physical role change and desistance from illegal behavior (disengagement) is the main outcome of the process.

Research in this area, however, has identified many nuances to the complex process of leaving an extremist milieu. Horgan (2009a, p. 19), for example, noted that even if psychologically reducing commitment to a violent extremist group is the goal, deradicalization (i.e., reduction in ideological commitment) does not have to be part of the process and might not even be a likely outcome. He found with regard to the large sample of interviews with former terrorists he collected between 2006 and 2008 that when using the term "psychological disengagement" as synonymous with "deradicalization" (Horgan, Altier, Shortland & Taylor, 2016, p. 11), "almost all could be described as disengaged, the vast majority of them could not be said to be 'deradicalized'" (2009a, p. 27).

To complicate this even further, the discourse specifically on deradicalization is divided into a "broad" and "narrow" school (Clubb, 2015), with the first aiming to achieve rejection of ideologically based violence and the latter including various other ideological aspects. It has been argued that disengagement, that is, the mere physical role change and desistance from crime, would be more feasible and realistic (e.g., Noricks, 2009), but other scholars have pointed out that in order to reduce recidivism among extremist offenders, it is necessary to address "beliefs and attitudes that drive violent behavior" (Braddock, 2014, p. 60). To not address these underlying beliefs and attitudes, as well as the individual psychological factors of attraction, might increase the chance of a failed exit process and the risk of re-radicalization (Altier, Leonard Boyle & Horgan, 2019; Koehler, 2016b; Rabasa, Pettyjohn, Ghez & Boucek, 2010). As we saw in Chapter 1, attitudes and reasons for attraction to extremism might overlap with the milieu's ideology, but they do not have to be entirely equal. Other parts of the collective identity or oppositional culture within the extremist environment can also provide a pull factor. In that sense, "ideology" is better understood as a dynamic set of political values and ideals, which are constantly renegotiated between the individual and the collective, albeit to a differing degree of involvement from both sides.

It is important to note that the term deradicalization has been used to describe both the process of exiting an extremist environment on the one side, and the wider practical activity of programs or practitioners on the other. Bringing together the terminology of the wider deradicalization field at this point, the different forms of exiting can be defined according to the degree of ideological removal (from the weakest to the strongest): physical disengagement, psychological disengagement or deradicalization (narrow), and deradicalization (broad). These processes can overlap, and an individual might go through all or only one of them in different order. For example, physical disengagement might lead to a narrow deradicalization, which might be broad in the long run (Clubb, 2017). It must also be recognized that these developments are not a one-way process but that they also include setbacks and reversals. Some aspects of the ideology or group might regain attractiveness, for example, in the form of another extremist ideology or group. This essentially means that "deradicalisation should not be considered a psychological return to some pre-radicalised state" (Braddock, 2014, p. 62) but as a new development in itself.

This already points us back to the side-switching phenomenon we have examined in this book. Most of the individuals I have presented would be (and indeed are) very adamant that they have broken with or fully left their old extremist pasts and developed a new identity. Of course, some describe this break more like a gradual maturation and learning process but are still clear about having turned their backs on the old milieus. Few of the defectors to Islamic extremism presented in Chapter 4 have attempted to build some kind of joint identity with active involvement in both sides (e.g., far-right and Islamic extremism). Nevertheless, extremist side-switching seemingly shares an important aspect with deradicalization and disengagement: the exit from an extremist environment as the starting point of the pathway.

6.2   Why Do Defectors Leave Extremist Milieus?

How far can existing knowledge about the root causes of deradicalization and disengagement from extremism and terrorism be applied to side-switching if there is some initial overlap? Or put differently, how much do the different outcomes of the process (one leading to a change of extremist involvement and the other away from any form extremism) impact the individual motives to break with one's milieu initially? One basic but widely established model for shedding more light on individual exits from extremism and terrorism is the so-called push-and-pull framework (Aho, 1988; Bjørgo & Horgan, 2009). Even though it should be seen as a rudimentary explanatory model in need of further development (Altier et al., 2014; Khalil et al., 2019), it nevertheless helps to pinpoint the key influences that set the defection process in motion.

"Push" factors are usually defined as "the negative social incidents and circumstances that make it uncomfortable and unappealing to remain" in the group (Bjørgo, 2016, p. 234). Typically, these include features related to the group's inner workings, such as the quality of relationships, handling of internal conflicts, reactions to new challenges, or the stability of hierarchy and ideological consistency. In short, push factors are those negative experiences inseparably linked with the character of the group. Members might want to quit the group because they suffer from social stigma and sanctions attached to membership in that milieu (e.g., Bjørgo, 2009) or because they are subject to governmental repression including the threat of imprisonment or death (e.g., Kassimeris, 2011; Rosenau, Espach, Ortiz & Herrera, 2014). These and other experiences linked to an extremist or terrorist lifestyle can lead to general exhaustion and burnout (e.g., Bjørgo, 2009; Demant, Slootman, Buijs & Tillie, 2008; Speckhard & Yayla, 2015).

One of the most often cited reasons for leaving are disillusionment with the group and its ideology (Altier et al., 2017; Bjørgo, 2009; Demant et al., 2008; Harris et al., 2017; Horgan et al., 2016; Hwang, 2018; Jacobson, 2010; Latif, Blee, DeMichele, Simi & Alexander, 2019; Reinares, 2011; Rosenau et al., 2014), maybe due to frustration with the hypocritical behavior of other group members or its leadership (Barrelle, 2015; Bjørgo, 2009; Horgan, 2009b; Jacobson, 2010; Reinares, 2011; Speckhard & Yayla, 2015). This might also include excessive substance abuse, violence, and abuse among the in-group or against out-group members (e.g., Jacobson, 2010; Reinares, 2011; Rosenau et al., 2014; Speckhard & Yayla, 2015). Many former terrorists and extremists have reported that at a certain point in their lives they realized that "they had gone too far" and were shocked by the consequences of their own actions. The former high-ranking Jemaah Islamiyah (JI) member Nasir Abas, for example, was shocked about the hundreds of casualties in the October 2002 Bali bombings, which he helped to organize, and subsequently reconsidered his position on the concept of jihad (Abuza, 2008, p. 198). The former high-ranking German neo-Nazi Ingo Hasselbach reconsidered his active involvement during a time of widespread violent attacks against refugee homes in Germany in the early 1990s and after a series of killings of Turkish immigrants (Hasselbach & Reiss, 1996). Equally, defectors from ISIS also reported that they "grew disgusted by the constant stream of executions and the cruel pleasure that some IS cadres appeared to have when beheading and killing others" (Speckhard & Yayla, 2015, p. 114).

Other forms of push factors can be disappointment over the lack of results (e.g., Alonso, 2011; Barrelle, 2015; Demant et al., 2008; Kassimeris, 2011; Reinares, 2011; Rosenau et al., 2014; Speckhard & Yayla, 2015) and different opinions regarding tactics or strategy (e.g., Horgan, 2009b; Hwang, 2015; Jacobson, 2010; Kassimeris, 2011; Reinares, 2011) leading to general disapproval of the group's leadership (e.g., Barrelle, 2015; Horgan, 2009b; Hwang, 2015; Jacobson, 2010; Reinares, 2011). Unmet expectations in general have caused even high ranking al-Qaeda members to leave the group and disengage from the movement (e.g., Jacobson, 2010). This can sometimes be the result of a mismatch between the group's recruitment and propaganda policy as well as the promises made by recruiters about the benefits of membership and lifestyle. Group membership might develop in a very different way than originally envisioned, causing the attempt to readjust among some.

On the other hand, "pull" factors refer to the "positive factors attracting the person to a more rewarding alternative" (Bjørgo, 2016, p. 234), which again reminds us of Social Identity Theory (SIT) and Rusbult's investment model. The desire to live a "normal" life or deeply transforming events resulting in changed priorities, for example, are typically very strong pull factors (e.g., Bjørgo, 2009; Demant et al., 2008; Ferguson, Burgess & Hollywood, 2015; Hwang, 2015; Kassimeris, 2011; Rosenau et al., 2014). Many former extremists and terrorists have described how becoming a parent has altered their priorities and future prospects, reduced the desire for adventure, and raised the perception of responsibility.

In addition, family members and friends might put so much pressure on group members to leave that the emotional cost of continued involvement becomes too large (e.g., Barrelle, 2015; Bjørgo, 2009; Jacobson, 2010; Rosenau et al., 2014). Further, new positive relationships with out-group members have also been mentioned as important pull factor (e.g., Hwang, 2015). Thinking back to SIT in Chapter 1, such relationships can produce a sense of group permeability. Even though one might argue that such milieus are notoriously shielded from the mainstream society via their ideological hatred against it, there is indeed constant and open exchange with the surrounding environment for most of these groups, for example, through recruitment of new members and positive relationships with those members of the society who extremists want to influence in their favor (Koehler, 2015a).

Likewise, we have seen in the case studies in this book that extremist groups and milieus that regard each other as enemies are also not isolated from each other. Many side-switchers have personally encountered the other side, for example, in prison. Richard Scheringer (see Section B2.2) began his defection process during personal conversations and while building friendships with communists he met in custody. David Myatt (Section 4.3) describes in his storyline the deep impression Muslims had on him during his travels to foreign countries. Furthermore, dedicated neo-Nazi forums such as IronMarch (IM) have been a place where users could encounter other individuals with remarkably diverse backgrounds and ideological convictions, including various stages of far-left ideology. Meeting members from the "other side" and having positive experiences also features widely in the slightly more advanced stages of side-switching storylines. Usually, defectors describe the new milieu as much better suited to their needs and moral values, which is not really surprising since the goal is clearly to integrate into that target group as best as possible. Praising the qualities of the new in-group can never be a waste of energy from the perspective of a novice.

In addition to positive outsider contacts with the opposing milieu, one can make a convincing argument that the constant negative focus on the enemy constitutes a form of contact that has the potential to create group permeability in itself. By basing the collective identity on a negative out-group and connecting one's own success to its demise or failure (the key defining feature of extremism according to Berger, 2018), such milieus automatically create a significant and constant mental (through its ideology) and physical (through violent interactions and other activities meant to counter the enemy) contact, albeit fundamentally negative in nature. This dominant psychological and physical occupation with the out-group, for example, through subcultural products (e.g., songs about the enemy, literature disproving their claims, clothing depicting their destruction) and specific behavior (e.g., outing of out-group members, collecting damaging information, counter intelligence), can also create an awareness and even intimate knowledge of the other side, which in turn might create a feeling of permeability. One might simply come to be convinced of the other side's arguments by studying them in detail in an attempt to look for ways to disprove them. In short, outsider contacts in the opposing milieu, whether positive or negative, mentally or physically, appear to be an important overlap with deradicalization and disengagement research. But what about the other push-and-pull factors listed?

Obviously, many of the factors identified as influential in driving the exit processes from extremism and terrorism are irrelevant for side-switchers. They do not long for a "normal" life, are not fed up with violence and hatred, or think that they have "gone too far." On the contrary, in the life stories and narratives of many side-switchers we have looked at, a particularly strong desire to make more of oneself and a notion to have "not gone far enough" are visible. Benito Mussolini's (see Section B2.1) thirst for power was not nearly satisfied with leading the Italian Socialist Party and the former revolutionary leftist Reinhold Oberlercher (see Section B1.5) claimed nothing less than to have completed Karl Marx's *Capital* and Marxism as a whole by solving the role of the nation within its philosophy, for example. For many converts to Islamic extremism, such as Sascha Lemanski (Section 4.1) or Devon Arthurs (Section 4.4.2), their previous far-right environment simply did not do enough to fight the Jews in their view (among other motives to switch sides).

On the other hand, we can quickly recognize that negative in-group characteristics such as power conflicts or disagreements over the milieu's strategy and ideology, as well as overall disillusionment with the milieu, appear often in the side-switching narratives. These push factors were presented as important reasons to leave the former group behind and are very similar to those we know from exit narratives in deradicalization and disengagement research. In both cases we should be aware that the naming of such negative push factors is foremost a rhetorical strategy used to construct meaning around the defection process and elicit sympathy from the audience. Whether or not these factors truly held the importance for the exit later claimed in the storyline is impossible to verify. For both side-switchers and those exiting extremism completely, highlighting negative experiences in the old group to explain the decision to leave and seek out a new social environment makes perfect sense.

Of course, abundant insights into the way extremist and terrorist groups operate have provided us with strong evidence that they are indeed very often socially dysfunctional and dominated by straining toxic stress. However, we should also not ignore that these milieus do possess strategies for mitigating member frustration, for example, positive rewards and problem-solving (Mironova, 2019; Simi & Futrell, 2010). Take the cases of Richard Scheringer in Germany (see Section B2.2) and Devon Arthurs in the USA (Section 4.4.2). Scheringer's public defection from National Socialism to communism prompted intensive attempts by the Nazis to win him back and some of his former comrades remained friends, despite his switching of sides; they even lobbied for his early release from prison. Even before he had made his decision public, he was offered high-ranking positions in the hope of extenuating his growing doubts and criticism. Likewise, Arthurs was deeply embedded in his small neo-Nazi group and even though there was conflict regarding his conversion to Islam, his closest friend and group leader, Brandon Russell, defended him against attacks on the IronMarch forum. Such strong friendships are indicative of the positive sides of membership in some extremist milieus.

In sum, side-switchers share many narrative components with full-fledged exiters from extremism and terrorism. Both point out the negative experience in the old group and the attractive, positive characteristics of the new one. For both types of defectors, disillusionment, conflict with peers, and ideological disagreements play a dominant role in their narratives. The key difference between the two groups regarding the cited push-and-pull factors is, that side-switchers do not question extremist activism and convictions as such. Their ideological and social disillusionment does not lead to a rejection of participation in extremist milieus (full disengagement) or the underlying ideology in total (full deradicalization).

This, of course, is also not regularly the case with individuals reintegrating into a non-extremist environment, but they in contrast stop seeing the commitment to extremist groups and causes as a worthwhile strategy for social status. In essence, they often stop believing that they are able to reach their goals in life or even a basic level of satisfaction inside extremist milieus compared to what the "normal life" has to offer, at least in their narratives. Side-switchers do not perceive or accept non-extremist social environments as viable alternative options to their original group membership. This is overwhelmingly explained in some ideological core convictions that remained active and even increased in importance for the side-switchers (e.g., anti-Semitism, anti-capitalism). I will pick up these issues later on when I discuss the role of ideology for side-switchers compared to complete exiters. To gain further insight into where and how the two groups might differ from each other beyond the mere citation of push-and-pull factors, we must now look at the processes and steps involved in leaving extremist environments with strong role identities intact.

6.3   Process Models for Becoming an Ex

As we saw in my scoping of the research landscape in Chapter 1, significantly more literature focuses on extremism and terrorism entry processes as compared to exit processes. While radicalization process models exist in abundance (for overviews, see Christmann, 2012; Dalgaard-Nielsen, 2010; De Coensel, 2018), equally detailed step-by-step or phase-based accounts of disengagement and deradicalization are very much missing in the current literature. Before discussing the few studies and insights that are helpful in understanding how individuals leave these particular milieus instead of why, we must explore the seminal work of sociologist Helen Ebaugh on the process of changing identity roles (Ebaugh, 1988). Her groundbreaking study is based on 185 interviews with individuals who have experienced role change, such as, ex-convicts, ex-alcoholics, divorcees, mothers without custody of their children, ex-doctors, ex-cops, retirees, ex-nuns, and transsexuals.

Based on her research, Ebaugh identified a unique social process different from those steps involved in entering a role or social milieu attached to it, which contains gradual shifts in the person's self-identification. She describes the process of role change in four major phases: (1) doubt in the role as a result of numerous events (e.g., burnout, changes in organization); (2) seeking of alternatives (a phase during which negative reactions from others can interrupt the process, while positive support can facilitate it); (3) turning point; and (4) creating the ex-role. While the cuing behavior in the first phase is oftentimes picked up by either in-group or out-group members, the second phase (if completed) results in emotional relief and is predominantly based on anticipatory behavior, according to Ebaugh. The turning point phase has three main functions: reduction of cognitive dissonance; opportunity to announce decision to others; and mobilization of resources needed for the exit. This phase is connected to a vacuum experience and personal insecurity, which means social support is required and can act as a bridge.

Ebaugh also identifies a number of problematic issues related to role change of which – among others – "role residuals" (i.e., elements of the former identity that are still in effect during or after the role change) are the most relevant to the study of deradicalization and disengagement from extremist and terrorist milieus, as well as side-switchers. Role residuals refer to the point that a role change can be physically completed (i.e., disengagement from a group has taken place), while parts of the former ideology or social identity are still forcing a psychological connection to the former milieu, movement, or group, which might inhibit a further stabilization of the disengagement or deradica-lization process. These residuals could also become a key factor for recidivism. According to Ebaugh, other major problematic issues (1988, p. 182) include the question of how to signal the role change to others; how to relate to former group members and other defectors; or changes in the friendship network.

In addition to these important aspects, Ebaugh has provided the most detailed and in-depth study on role change so far, which makes it a most valuable resource for comparing side-switchers with other exiters. Reversibility (recidivism) was shown by Ebaugh to be influenced by the duration spent in the former role as well as the positive impact of social support outside of the old role. During the first and second phases, individuals engage in what Ebaugh calls "reality testing," which is essentially a probing process to test for positive or negative reactions that result from the attempted or envisioned role change. If credible alternatives are presented in this phase and individual problems connected to the role become apparent to the defector, this phase might be strengthened – leading to the turning point (Ebaugh, 1988, p. 188).

Ebaugh has also discussed the phenomena of multiple and single exits, individual and group exits, and the degree of control over the turning point and how sequential events impacting the role change process are. In this way, it becomes clear that role change as a process can never be understood from the individual perspective alone, but needs to incorporate the wider social environment, as well as the chronological development and external events. Equally important is the receiving environment, which might expect certain rituals or degree of awareness in order to accept the credibility of the change. This, in turn, seems to be connected to the social desirability (degree of social approval or disapproval of the exit) attached to the role change by the receiving environment (Ebaugh, 1988, p. 197). In addition, the personal impact of role change increases with the importance or "weight" of the former role in that person's life: "when individuals exit a master role, they usually experience a major transformation in self-identity, a fact that makes the exit process a major decision in life with repercussions in terms of adjustment and adaption to a new self" (Ebaugh, 1988, p. 203). At the same time, the former group "simultaneously withdraws from the individual with regard to expectations and social obligations" (Ebaugh, 1988, p. 181).

Some studies have looked at process steps involved in exiting from extremist or other ideologically dominated groups and can help us to refine Ebaugh's general role exit model. We know that leaving extremist milieus can happen either through a gradual and long-term process of disillusionment or through "a moment of reckoning triggered by a specific situation or incident where they feel let down or ill treated by fellow extremists or leaders" (Dalgaard-Nielsen, 2013, p. 104). This clearly is also the case for our side-switchers, many of whom have made transitions between the milieus spanning several years or even decades, such as Horst Mahler (Section 2.1) or Jürgen Elsässer (see Section B1.6), who both shifted from the far left to the far right. We have also encountered storylines that evolved around moments of crisis and wherein defection decisions were made relatively quickly, typically a move from the far right to left-wing (e.g., Ray Hill, see Section 4.2) or Islamic extremism (e.g., Bernhard Falk, see Section 4.2).

In one of the currently most elaborated process models for leaving ideological (including but not limited to extremist) groups, Harris, Gringart, and Drake (2017) identify five key phases: set in motion by an initial trigger (phase one), the defector begins to perceive the group as inconsistent with the self-concept and as conflicted with personally held goals and values (phase two). This might then increase to an actual threat of the exiter's psychological integrity (phase three). Individuals who reach that stage will eventually attempt to dissolve that psychological tension by employing self-concept management strategies (phase four), which finally can lead to the decision to leave and maybe critical reflection on the former group's ideology (phase five). What were the initial triggers stated by the interviewees in this study by Harris, Gringart, and Drake?

Indeed, they all fit perfectly into the push-and-pull factor research we already discussed in detail: failed interpersonal relationships; change in group dynamics; role conflict or performance; leadership's failure to act in accord with expectations and group norms; police pressure; and external family commitments (Harris et al., 2017, p. 98). Very important is this study's finding that disillusionment with the old group was necessary to truly defect. Those who left motivated by external pull factors alone usually maintained positive relationships with the old milieu (Harris et al., 2017, p. 98). This applies in particular to those side-switchers to Islamic extremism who attempted to create some form of dual milieu membership and joint ideology, such as David Myatt (Section 4.3), Sascha Lemanski (Section 4.1), Devon Arthurs (Section 4.4.2), or Nicholas Young (Section B3.2). For them, conversion to Islam and subsequent involvement in Islamic extremist circles was a natural development or addition to their previously held far-right views for several reasons. Myatt, for example, claimed to have investigated the possibility of strategically infiltrating Islam and spreading his National Socialist ideology. For Arthurs, it might have been the particular misogynist and hypermasculine collective identity of jihadists in addition to their uncompromising anti-Semitic hatred. The clear majority of side-switchers, however, describe a certain moment or period of crisis that led to disillusionment and the eventual break with the old milieu.

Harris, Gringart, and Drake furthermore describe how persons perceiving this threat to their concept of self and identity employ methods of self-verification to evaluate their own commitment to the group. Very much as predicted through SIT, many persons first attempt to find reasons justifying their continued involvement, including dialogue with other members, information seeking, and value testing (Harris et al., 2017, pp. 98–99). Since we have seen the power of cognitive dissonance or psychological reactance and biases to change attitudes, it should not surprise that over a period of probing and weighing different options "it was important for participants to feel confident in their attitudes and the validity of any contradicting information" (Harris et al., 2017, p. 99).

In SIT, individuals typically employ various status enhancement strategies at first aimed toward the old group in order to avoid leaving it. Many side-switchers have described how they tried to reform or improve their old group, which mostly resulted in further conflict, rejection, and frustration. Bernhard Falk (Section 4.2), for example, recounts his disappointment about the complete lack of openness toward Islam on the side of his former far-left peers. Devon Arthurs' (Section 4.4.2) repeated attempts to convert other neo-Nazis reportedly resulted in significant conflict with the administrators of the IronMarch forum. Christine and Klaus Dieter Hewicker's (Section 3.1) arguments to develop a more internationalist and anti-capitalist position within the militant far right left them in near complete isolation. One must always acknowledge the duality of the disassociation process, as the milieus and groups themselves fail to adequately respond to their struggling members in these cases. As Harris, Gringart, and Drake put it:

Participants' initial expectations were to reconcile with their group; however, inconsistent responses amplified the initial threat and produced negative affect, which influenced cognitions and social interactions, which when combined, threatened the participants' sense of belonging. These interactions facilitated a feedback loop in terms of interpreting self-relevant information. As the discrepancy between group membership and self-concept increased, participants began reducing psychological dependency on their group as well as increased self-awareness and focus on personal priorities. With the decline in dependency, participants were more receptive to factors that made the exit, or an alternative social group membership, favourable. (Harris et al., 2017, p. 99)

When we look back to the partially severe mutual conflicts many of the side-switchers had with their original milieus, it is easily possible to recognize that often their distancing processes was both a decision to leave on the side of the defector and an expulsion by the group or milieu. Mussolini's (see Section B2.1) conflict with the Italian Socialist Party turned particularly bitter and eventually violent, involving accusations of "moral unworthiness" and "corruption" against the later Fascist dictator during a phase in which he still proclaimed to be a loyal socialist. Also, not to forget Devon Arthurs (Section 4.4.2), who claimed that the mocking of his Islamic faith eventually led him (among other reasons) to shoot and kill his former neo-Nazi friends. A third example is Jürgen Elsässer (see Section B1.6), who recounted multiple incidents of being fired from left-wing newspapers for his controversial positions during his first extremist career.

In Harris, Gringart, and Drake's process model, the defector now begins to develop a perception of certain key differences between the individual and collective identity, essentially defusing his or her own self-concept from the milieu (see the concept of sacred values and identity fusion as part of the Devoted Actor Theory in Section 1.6.2). Defusing one's own identity from a collective one can be done effectively by nurturing the awareness of competency (i.e., not being able or willing to perform according to the group's demands); virtue (i.e., the group is not worthy of participation); power (i.e., lack of status or influence in the group); or significance (i.e., lack of acceptance and respect of others in the group), thereby creating a difference between the group and oneself (Harris et al., 2017, pp. 99–101).

Our side-switchers, especially those who left the far right and joined extreme-left groups or milieus, have pointed out the disgust they developed against their former comrades based on their morally reprehensible behavior and the danger they posed to the society. Ray Hill (Section 3.2), Tim Hepple (Section 3.3), and Matthew Collins (Section 3.4), for example, speak about lunatics and notoriously violent, criminal individuals they found themselves surrounded with in the extreme right. Stopping them and thereby easing their own guilty consciousness became a key driving force behind the collaboration with the anti-fascist magazine *Searchlight*. We can also see clear cases of power and significance differences that were pointed out in the side-switching narratives. Reinhold Oberlercher's (see Section B1.5) narrative connects his failure to attain a professorship position and recognition as a scholar of importance comparable to Hegel and Marx (as he claims for himself) to his far-left commitment.

As I argued in Chapter 1, human beings naturally try to avoid or dissolve any identity conflicts or feelings of misalignment between attitudes, values, and behavior (i.e., cognitive dissonance, reactance). This is the reason why the next stage in Harris, Gringart, and Drake's process model (stage four) focuses on self-management strategies intended to reduce the tension that is the automatic result of highlighting differences between oneself and the group. If one develops a true belief in those differences, the question of how to proceed with group membership must be answered. Some of these management strategies to cope with the inherent contradictions can be, for example, to develop an "atypical identity" (a self-image that contradicts the norms of membership), to adapt one's preferences, or to validate and justify the disillusionments (Harris et al., 2017, p. 111).

These approaches to managing the identity conflict correspond to SIT's status enhancement strategies presented in Section 1.6.1, for example, the social creativity strategy, which seeks to change the parameters of comparison between the in- and out-group. A strongly visible atypical identity approach can be seen in Julian Fritsch's (Section 2.3) storyline, which highlights the fact that due to his values being so fundamentally different from the far-left milieu, he simply "wasn't a good communist" (as cited in Koehler, 2019b, p. 509). Many side-switchers also stayed involved in their original milieu for a while after they first noticed disillusionment or identity conflicts, which led to repeated experiences used in the storylines to confirm the suspicion of them being at odds with the group.

Jürgen Elsässer (see Section B1.6) highlights that again and again he found himself in conflict with the far left over more or less the same issues, which finally convinced him of the environment's ideological stubbornness and the decision to leave. Another important management strategy that appeared in Harris, Gringart, and Drake's process model is to make amends and right wrongs in case the group is perceived as morally corrupt. Mostly we have seen this coping strategy with the side-switchers from the far right to the far left, who presented their support for anti-fascist milieus as their moral duty to destroy what they had helped to build. Ray Hill (Section 3.2), Tim Hepple (Section 3.4), and Matthew Collins (Section 3.4) clearly express their hope to correct at least some of their past errors and erase their feelings of guilt by working against the far right. In fact, no other type of side-switching includes revenge and making amends as key motives in the storylines than those leaving the extreme right for the far left. Richard Scheringer (see Section B2.2) dedicated much of his life to the Third Reich after his defection to Communism to counter the Nazi's with his own insider experience, as he, too, saw the far right as the biggest threat to Germany.

In the final phase of leaving ideological groups (phase five), the physical exit typically comes after another crisis point that acts as the main catalyst for the previous psychological distancing process. Leaving can occur in three different ways: reducing involvement and quietly drifting away; leaving swiftly and quietly; or sudden confrontation (Harris et al., 2017, p. 105). I found the same three exit strategies in a separate study that looks at how neo-Nazi groups react to defectors and how they decide on certain punishment strategies (Koehler, 2015b). Here we can see slight differences to side-switchers in the way they leave their former milieus. Defectors share with general exiters direct confrontation as an exit pathway.

Richard Scheringer (see Section B2.2), Benito Mussolini (see Section B2.1), Horst Mahler (Section 2.1), or Devon Arthurs (Section 4.4.2) approached their former milieus head-on with the decision to switch sides, which often resulted in significant conflict with the old group. In fact, direct confrontation appears to be the predominant strategy for side-switchers trying to break with their old groups, which is the first important difference with defectors leaving extremism behind in general.

Second, we cannot find clearly articulated pathways that involve a quiet drifting away (slow or swift). Since by definition the switchers eventually appear in the milieu hostile to their old one, confrontation is almost inevitable. Sometimes, for example in the case of Julian Fritsch (Section 2.3), the exit is done in a very short period of time and is followed by a public declaration of defection from within the other side. Others, especially in the intellectual defector category (see Bonus Chapter), gradually developed convictions opposed to their old environment through sometimes years of reflection. A special type of side-switching in this regard are those who acted as committed insiders infiltrating their former far-right in-group to gather information for anti-fascist actions, such as Ray Hill (Section 3.2), Tim Hepple (Section 3.3), or Matthew Collins (Section 3.4). For them, leaving the group became a subordinated matter in favor of causing as much damage as possible. Their eventual physical exit usually came when detection as a spy became likely and their final act of revenge was a public outing through press reports or TV documentaries. Side-switchers appear to have much stronger tendencies to foreshadow their defections, usually in the form of ideological or personal conflicts. This is logical to a certain degree, since typically their core convictions did not diminish in the process, making it worthwhile to "fight for what one believes in" (as they portray themselves in the storylines). Quietly drifting away or swiftly quitting without a word (and without a follow-up blow against the former group) makes much more sense for defectors who have lost complete faith in the cause or are otherwise disillusioned with the extremist lifestyle and want to attain a "calm, normal life."

In addition to the steps involved in the process of quitting an extremist groups (the how), we should also compare side-switchers with other exiters in terms of the areas of change (the what) during the disengagement and maybe even partial deradicalization from the old milieu before they entered a new one. One theoretical concept to describe the various aspects of a person's life affected by this change is called "Pro-Integration Model" (PIM) and was developed by Kate Barrelle (2015). PIM is meant to be a "holistic framework of disengagement and reintegration after violent extremism in a Western democratic environment" (Barrelle, 2015, p. 134) and combines individual level "disengagement themes" into five main domains: social relations, coping, identity, ideology, and action orientation.

A key aspect of PIM is understanding leaving extremist milieus as non-linear. "Instead, it involves an interconnected process of change across five key areas of a person's life" (Barrelle, 2015, p. 135). In contrast to other models, PIM does not solely focus on reducing commitment to the extremist in-group in these domains but also involves rebuilding new and positive commitments to the mainstream society as part of the reintegration. Barrelle places often cited push-and-pull factors (or themes) into one of the five domains for mapping disengagement and reengagement (with mainstream society) across psychological needs clusters. It is also important to note that PIM does not stipulate that each and every exiter must necessarily go through full reconstruction of all five domains and achieve a complete fulfillment in all themes in order to be successfully reintegrated. The outcome of a disengagement process is seen as highly individual and flexible, depending on the person's goals and preferences (among other factors). When we apply the PIM concept to our side-switchers, we will notice yet again a striking similarity with those defectors leaving behind extremism for good.

The social relations domain in PIM includes themes such as disillusionment with the group's leadership or other members and with the quality of interpersonal relationship in general. Most side-switchers we have encountered put significant weight on the lack of positive and lasting relations in their old milieus. This can take the form of expressed disgust over cowardice (e.g., Julian Fritsch, Section 2.3); alleged hypocrisy (e.g., Günter Maschke, see Section B1.3); or ideological ignorance (e.g., Horst Mahler, Section 2.1; Christine Hewicker, Section 3.1).

Many of the case studies from the previous chapters include episodes of disappointment and sadness over the shallowness of friendships, backstabbing, power struggles, and petty conflicts (e.g., Tim Hepple, Section 3.3; Bernhard Falk, Section 4.2; Christine Hewicker, Section 3.1). Even though this exit theme does not always directly correspond with motivation to enter the hostile milieu (e.g., explaining the side-switching by finding more stable and trustworthy relationships), it does feature often in these narratives. Bernhard Falk notes that his Muslim brothers and sisters were the only ones visiting him in prison, not his left-wing comrades; and Julian Fritsch praises the manly courage and warrior ethos he found in the far right.

The second category in Barrelle's PIM is coping, which includes themes such as social support, resilience, and psychological issues. To a significant degree, this only appears among side-switchers who left the far right and worked to destroy their former milieus through collaboration with anti-fascist groups. It should not be surprising that only those defectors who express a feeling of guilt and moral responsibility to correct their past errors include statements that fall into this category. In their storylines, coping with their own consciousness and finding social support for redemption is a key thread, while most of the other side-switchers very rarely voice any form of self-criticism about their previous positions. The only notable case here is Jürgen Elsässer (see Section B1.6), who repeatedly calls his old positions foolish or stupid and thereby expresses some form of shame. One can infer from this that he constructs a coping mechanism via his involvement in the far right, now working toward a just and correct cause in his perspective.

However, while one can safely assume that the disengagement themes connected to PIM's coping domain might be more prominent among the side-switchers, they rarely state this as part of the storylines. For them, switching sides is mostly a conscious and self-guided process framed through strength of personal convictions, integrity, and intellectual development rather than the struggle for help to deal with personal problems. Identity-related themes on the other hand (third PIM domain), do appear regularly in the form of an "awakening" of sorts, for example, when the importance of national and racial collective identities is realized (e.g., Benito Mussolini, see Section B2.1; Jürgen Elsässer, see Section B1.6). Of course, most expressively this element appears in storylines that include a religious conversion and subsequent involvement in Islamic extremism. Almost all side-switching narratives that include personal accounts (as opposed to accounts from bystanders) are developed around the moment of "seeing the light of Islam" and recognizing the spiritual truths of the religion.

The last two PIM disengagement domains (ideology and action orientation) can again be found widely among side-switchers. Arguably, the most dominant theme would be disagreement over the group's ideology, as almost all of the defectors presented here describe at least a part of their decision to change milieus with ideological developments (e.g., learning processes) or straightforward rejection of the ignorance and hypocrisy in their original groups. When these milieus do not draw the necessary conclusions from the ideological premises or fail to accept the pressing need to revise their strategies in the light of external significant events, this is often presented as a cause of conflict and disillusionment with the true nature of the milieu. Benito Mussolini (see Section B2.1), to name one example, essentially fell out with the socialist party he led over the question of whether to support Italian intervention in the First World War.

Mussolini's hawkish position was a crass change from his previous pacifism and resulted from many factors, including the decision to seize the moment to gain power in Italy. In another case study, Richard Scheringer's (see Section B2.2) defection from National Socialism was propelled by his outrage over Hitler's vow to abandon illegal means of working within the Weimar system on the one hand, and by the lack of leading Nazis' answers to specific social and economic questions he had on the other. There are many more examples of ideological disillusionment, which appears to be a main driving force of side-switching, albeit in a slightly different way than for those who exited extremism altogether. This is reflected in Barrelle's PIM, which lists "disillusionment with radical ideas" (Barrelle, 2015, p. 134) under this domain.

Clearly, most side-switchers in no way reject radical or extreme methods and ideas in principle. Even those defectors who move from the far right to the far left do so because they either accept that only extreme actions can help destroy their former milieus (e.g., by infiltrating these groups at great personal cost and risk) or because mainstream politics are perceived as incapable of addressing the social and economic issues that became important to them during the process. Similarly, "action orientation" in Barrelle's model involves "disillusionment with radical methods, stop[ping] or reduc[ing] radical methods, prosocial engagement in society" (Barrelle, 2015, p. 134), which is of course usually not what side-switchers have in mind when they shift milieus across hostile ideological boundaries. On the contrary, they often seek more consequent action, more violence, and more radicalism. Julian Fritsch (Section 2.3), for example, explicitly looked for that masculine warrior ethos among his peers that would allow him and his milieu to stand and fight when attacked. In his view, the far left betrayed their own ideological convictions by backing away from fights. Other cases include the defectors to Islamic extremism, who either explicitly stated or left indications to their environment to be driven by the lack of anti-Semitic actions and violence in the far right.

In short, we can see many striking similarities between side-switchers and individuals disengaging and deradicalizing on multiple levels, including the original push-and-pull factors that motivate the initial decision to leave the first extremist group, the process steps involved in making the transition, the domains affected by the disengagement, and reintegration into a new environment. This would suggest that extremist side-switching truly is a form disengagement from (one variant of) extremism, albeit a limited and twisted one. As Madfis and Vysotsky put it:

disengagement and desistance often means moving from one subcultural group to another distinct subcultural group that may lack a racist value system and focus but nevertheless still entails other views and beliefs that are outside of the mainstream, such as anti-capitalist politics, disdain for conventional values, belief in the efficacy of civil disobedience and activism, and acceptance of the use of violence as a means of defending or maintaining cultural space. (Madfis & Vysotsky, 2020, p. 222)

Putting side-switching into the context of deradicalization is a bit more difficult, however. As I discussed in Chapter 1 and early on in this chapter, many different concepts and problems exist around that term. With the key notion of some form of ideological change away from a particular ideological conviction that legitimizes terrorist or extremist behavior, most scholars focus on the support for violence or criminal activities in the name of a specific milieu or worldview. Others (e.g., Clubb, 2015; Tapley & Clubb, 2019), however, have shown that it is much more complicated than that.

To expect complete rejection of violence for a political cause from a fully deradicalized person would create numerous follow-up problems. Is the person expected to reject violence forever and in any circumstance while, for example, the mainstream society contains various positions including support for waging wars (for many different causes); using violence as self-defence; or harsh police measures against criminals? Many of these positions for or against the use of violence align with political attitudes in societies and are mostly part of the accepted societal discourse between conservative and liberal positions. The problem only increases when widening the scope of opinions about violence to include other ideological issues and when looking at the time frame of the expected deradicalization. Is the person only deradicalized when he or she rejects all violence – present, future, and past – which means renouncing the logic behind one's own previous actions? Does it also include the development of positive support for central political features of the main-stream society? In continuation of Berger's (2018) extremism concept, the core of deradicalization would be attaining a psychological and ideological state in which a successful self-identity is decoupled from a negative out-group image or the degradation of an enemy. In that sense, side-switchers clearly do not deradicalize. For them, the awareness of a hostile enemy that needs to be demoted, discriminated against, or even destroyed remains a core feature of their ideological outfit.

6.4   The Role of Ideology

While extremist side-switching appears to be a type of disengagement (at least initially) it certainly does not lead to deradicalization in how we typically use the term. There is no moderation of beliefs or renouncement of radical ideas per se. On the contrary, most side-switchers significantly increase their commitment after having entered their new milieu. I have demonstrated that the initial motivations to leave an extremist group and environment largely overlap with those who turn their backs on extremism altogether, and side-switchers even share most of the process steps involved in doing so.

It must be pointed out that we have encountered cases, for example, Horst Mahler (Section 2.1), who truly reengaged with extremism after a brief but failed period of reintegration into mainstream society. Most side-switchers, however, transitioned directly between the milieus, even if it took them years or decades to complete the process. One key lesson we can learn from how this works for them is the role of ideology. In Section 1.3 I have already discussed some of the peculiarities and conceptional complexities that are deeply engrained in the term. We have also seen, how most radicalization and terrorism research is based on a much too rigid and superficial understanding of ideology as theoretical knowledge about certain ideas and beliefs used to make sense of the world around.

Inevitably, many studies have found extremists and terrorists not to be motivated by ideology in their radicalization processes, as they have shown only a limited if any knowledge and understanding of the political or theological justifications for the milieus' causes (e.g., Borum, 2011a; Laqueur, 2000; Reinares et al., 2008). Furthermore, it has been argued that many if not most extremists and terrorists appear not to show any causal relationship between ideological convictions or exposure to extremist propaganda and violent behavior (Bart Schuurman & Taylor, 2018; Crenshaw, 1988; Sageman, 2004).

On the other side of disengagement and deradicalization, we interestingly can show that disillusionment with the group's ideology ranks high among the typically named reasons for leaving (e.g., Altier et al., 2017; Barrelle, 2015; Dalgaard-Nielsen, 2013; Windisch, Ligon & Simi, 2017). This could mean that ideology might be more important for disengaging than for entering an extremism milieu. Recent scholarship has pointed out the potential misconception behind the term ideology and the consequences for terrorism research (Holbrook & Horgan, 2019; Koehler, 2015a). Donald Holbrook and John Horgan, for example, have highlighted the need to understand much better the social and identity-creating functions of ideology in order to appreciate what the actual effects for people who become involved in terrorism and extremism actually are, namely to provide "collective maps and shared perspectives that help us make sense of the world and define who is or is not part of our community" (Holbrook & Horgan, 2019, p. 7). The cognitive ties between an individual and a milieu's ideology can therefore be emotional and social rather than intellectual, which goes beyond a mere knowledge and understanding of the doctrines and teachings. With that approach, Holbrook and Horgan have moved the concept of ideology in terrorism research significantly closer to Social Identity Theory (SIT) and psychologically nuanced framings of the term.

In the domain of deradicalization and disengagement research, ideology was mostly discussed controversially in terms of the link between attitudes and behavior (e.g., Clubb, 2015; Khalil et al., 2019). This is understandable, since a key question in that field is how much practitioners should focus on dismantling or changing a client's ideological convictions as a necessary precondition for a reduced recidivism risk. While some scholars have opted to abandon deradicalization completely and only focus on disengagement (e.g., Noricks, 2009), meaning to work on the physical reintegration without addressing the beliefs and attitudes behind the extremist involvement, others have voiced concern that this might increase the risk for incomplete and failed exit processes (e.g., Altier et al., 2019; Koehler, 2016b; Rabasa et al., 2010).

Clearly, as with the radicalization debate, a more nuanced understanding of what ideology is and how it effects individual commitment to a milieu or overall behavior is necessary. Even though it seems that most extremists and terrorists do not possess or develop a detailed knowledge about their group's doctrines, they nevertheless can be driven by emotional commitment (e.g., a feeling of responsibility and loyalty or anger and frustration about perceived injustice) and social identity. If these aspects of extremist ideologies are challenged or disturbed, for example, through hypocritical behavior of group leaders, internal power struggles or lack of success as promised, disillusionment with the social identity of member in the milieu can follow.

In order to provide a less rigid understanding of the attitudes and behavior debate in deradicalization and disengagement research, James Khalil, John Horgan, and Martine Zeuthen suggested an "Attitudes-Behaviors Corrective" model (ABC) in 2019 (Khalil et al., 2019). The ABC model is based on two main process streams that dynamically interact in different pathways in and out of extremism: individual attitudes toward ideologically justified violence (opposed vs. sympathy) and the extent of involvement in ideologically justified violence.

While the model does focus on violent extremism, it still leaves ample space for understanding different trajectories in such milieus, for example, persons highly sympathetic toward the ideologically justified violence but without any involvement on their own. Alternatively, a person could be highly violent but motivated mainly by economic gain and power. In this model, structural motivators (e.g., context factors such es inequality, discrimination, corruption); individual incentives (e.g., socioeconomic or psychological benefits); and enabling factors (e.g., radical mentors, recruiters, access to weaponry) are responsible for affecting the attitudes toward violence and/or individual involvement in it (Khalil et al., 2019, pp. 10–12). Conversely, disengagement is seen as reduction in violent behavior and deradicalization as reduction in attitudes supporting ideologically justified violence.

We largely find similar push-and-pull factors in the ABC model, such as disillusionment (structural motivators); longing for a normal and more successful life (individual incentives); or the support of family and friends (enabling factors) (Khalil et al., 2019, pp. 16–17). The ABC model opens up a perception of deradicalization and disengagement as dynamic and multidirectional processes that focus on why and how individuals reduce or retain sympathy for ideological violence, and why and how they reduce involvement in violence or remain engaged. Applying this model to extremist side-switchers, however, means adding another dimension: parallel milieus that each have their own framing of ideological justification for violence and types of behavioral engagements. The ABC model is binary in the sense that it envisions one violent extremist environment and the mainstream non-extremist society as the two poles between individuals moving back and forth on the axes of attitudes and behavior. Hence, the authors of the model speak of reducing, retaining, or increasing either the pro-violent attitudes or the level of violent acts.

We need to add additional extremist milieus to the equation that can appeal to a person via their own behavioral or attitudinal frameworks. A person, for example, might exchange his or her attitudes toward violence or only certain components of them (e.g., from political to religious justification for attacking the same enemy, completely restructuring both justification and enemy frames). This can theoretically have complex effects on the behavioral level as well and vice versa. A person might shift group involvement (behavior) and through that change become more convinced about violence or, the other way around, attitudinal restructuring of ideas, values, and justifications might lead to different forms of involvement.

Take the case of Bernhard Falk (Section 4.2), for example. His first type of involvement in the far left was highly violent and he was subsequently sentenced to prison for explosive attacks he had plotted and perpetrated. From his own narratives and the communiqués of his group at the time, he was a militant and convinced anti-imperialist and anti-capitalist, albeit with partially controversial viewpoints in his milieu. His conversion to Islam and Salafist radicalization substantially rearranged the premises of the socioeconomic, political, and philosophical analysis regarding the problems, solutions, and future visions that drove him forward. Interestingly, this rearrangement of ideological concepts happened around the anti-imperialist and anti-capitalist cores that remained intact. With addition of the global community of Muslims (the Ummah), religious and spiritual fundamentals for individual actions gained utmost importance. Hence, in combination with his own experience of imprisonment, Falk abandoned direct involvement in terrorist acts and shifted to Salafist prison support work for fellow Muslims in order to build the necessary community based on the religiously justified support for actions against the West and Israel (including violence).

One can argue that Falk switched milieus on roughly the same degree of attitudes toward ideologically justified violence (restructuring the basic premises) but in consequence altered the form of involvement completely. Of course, his own trauma from having been put into isolation in prison for a long time should also be taken into account, as this clearly can create a strong motivation to avoid anything that risks repeated imprisonment.

In the previous chapter I explored the theoretical aspects of side-switching and argued that extremist milieus can be linked to each other through single or multiple ideological concepts, or DNA fragments so to speak, for example "justice," "honor," "evil," or "masculinity." Through either slightly different framings of these concepts, almost like evolutionary development of different variants that are nevertheless still related to each other, or through completely different understandings of these concepts, psychological highways or short-cuts between the milieus are opened.

Very much as in the ABC model, there are also links based on behavioral types of engagement, such as more or less brutal violence, more appealing forms of mobilization, or subcultural activities. One must think back to one of the online discussions presented in Section 2.4 that focused on the previously "cool" but now boring and dull aesthetics of the far left in the eyes of the participants. Another example is the biographical case study of a former neo-Nazi skinhead named "Christian Goebel," who was primarily driven by his own status within the social groups he was active in and switched to anti-fascist groups, which he deemed to be superior to the far right (Sigl, 2018, pp. 214–255).

It is therefore necessary to acknowledge that side-switching across the behavioral link between milieus can happen. Nevertheless, in the storylines presented here, using this as an explanation is extremely rare and usually only appears as an additional and marginal aspect. The overwhelming majority of links described in the narratives are ideological in nature and partially even highly detailed and differentiated, for example, through the focus on small nuances of the nation's role in forming a collective identity or specific aspects of social and economic policies tied to certain political philosophies. One might correctly argue that these rhetorical strategies do not represent the reality of side-switchers' motives and pathways, as I have acknowledged throughout this book. We cannot infer any factual reality based solely on those stories.

A key aspect of deradicalization and disengagement from extremism and terrorism, however, is the construction of new meaning-making frameworks in the form of self-redeeming narratives that help the person to cope with the identity reconstruction process, guilt, shame, or stigma, with self-confirmation (e.g., Dalgaard-Nielsen, 2013; Horgan, 2009b; Williams, 2017). Criminological research on desistance processes has confirmed this in a broader sense and highlighted the agency of an exiter in de-labeling and destigmatizing oneself, as well as in building the sense of an earned redemption (Gadd, 2006; Maruna et al., 2006). Such self-narratives can essentially be positive illusions to convince oneself about the success of the change process and more importantly that one deserves it (Maruna, 2004). The side-switching storylines are therefore equally important indications about how the defectors understand, frame, and justify their pathways as they would appear in general deradicalization and disengagement contexts.

Proceeding from these basic assumptions, the role of ideological bridges or channels between the extremist milieus is immense in the self-confirming storylines of defectors. Whatever importance disillusionment with an extremist milieu's ideology truly has for those who fully exit, this unequivocal dominance of ideologically connotated or constructed pathway explanations is the striking and decisive difference between the two groups. Linking this finding back to my understanding of deradicalization as a process of re-pluralization of political concepts and ideas (see Section 1.2), we can begin to understand how side-switchers fail to re-pluralize the core ideological concepts that fuel their meaning-making framework during their disengagement processes (which largely overlaps with those of general exiters).

In other words, side-switchers either consciously or as a result of the specific pathways they travel on, retain rigid, de-contested, and de-pluralized understandings of what matters most to them ideologically. By keeping their ideological core concepts active, they do not even perceive and hence engage with non-extremist milieus and alternative (more pluralized) worldviews. Exchanging peripheral concepts (e.g., the nature of the enemy or most effective solution to the crisis) or altering the essential ones (e.g., justice, honor, other sacred values) appears to be a strategy for avoiding the perceived high costs of fully dismantling the extremist views, taking responsibility for previous actions, facing guilt and shame, or even prosecution and stigma. Side-switching along ideological bridges allows the defector to retain at least a fundamental self-affirmation narrative (e.g., "to have remained true to oneself," "to have found the light," "to have drawn the necessary conclusions"). Indeed, most storylines contain such elements that portray the side-switcher as the one who remained steadfast and loyal to the core beliefs against all odds and against all resistance from the original milieu. This is of course a very powerful self-confirmation strategy and as we have seen through research on the development and change of political attitudes, especially regarding the effects of convincing oneself in the choice blindness phenomenon (see Section 1.6), the consequences can be extremely durable.

6.5   First Lesson Learned from Side-Switchers: Ideology Matters

Our study of extremist side-switchers has revealed that we are looking at a different type of disengagement process, which excludes a re-pluralization of core ideological concepts or values and thereby circumvents the costly and sometimes even painful dismantling of the extremist mindset. In the self-affirmation stories of those defectors to hostile milieus, links between partially isolated ideological concepts (e.g., the nation, race, violence, anti-Semitism) play the most important role. Even though a strong school of thought in deradicalization and disengagement research (as well as practice) that acknowledges the importance of addressing beliefs, attitudes, and the reasons for attraction to extremist environments in one way or the other exists (e.g., Clubb, 2017; Khalil et al., 2019; Koehler, 2016b; Rabasa et al., 2010), side-switchers tell us about the need for a much more nuanced utilization of ideological concepts and values in deradicalization or reintegration work.

First of all, many side-switchers use a detailed and historically informed argumentation to present certain logical consequences from single or small groups of ideological concepts. This indicates that for individuals who disengage from extremist milieus, even and especially if it includes disillusionment with the environment's ideology, certain residual concepts can remain intact and active. Sometimes, they even increase in their importance for the individual since other adjacent concepts connecting the person to the milieu fall apart. Mentors or counselors who assist exiters should therefore be extremely well-versed in the detailed ideological "DNA" of the milieus their clients are attempting to leave (for an overview of the skills such personnel should aquire during dedicated training, see Koehler & Fiebig, 2019). While not every defector will automatically wish to debate ideology as a whole, a nuanced understanding of the term opens up the possibility for practical assistance, namely to focus on those key concepts of high identity-value for the person, for example, "justice" or "honor." These should not be targeted with a strategy of negating or erasing them. On the contrary, an effective approach based on our study of side-switchers must include an affirmation and careful alteration of the components of those ideological concepts that create meaning for those individuals and call for consequences.

This is not fundamentally different from what side-switchers themselves do through their narratives or with the help of their new milieus: They dissect core ideological values and restructure them (ranging from small and detailed changes to fundamental rebuilding) so that they remain intact and effective overall but fit into the new milieu. Programs designed to assist such persons with leaving extremism behind for good with a long-term mitigated risk for reengagement must begin by mapping their clients' ideological "DNA" to identify those concepts that have the highest value and importance. Going in this direction, some scholars have suggested de-idealizing violence or humanizing the enemy (potentially two important concepts) during the deradicalization process (Dalgaard-Nielsen, 2013).

Second, side-switchers point us toward the potential impact of cognitive dissonance, reactance, and the psychological costs of dismantling an extremist worldview altogether. The mental and even physical consequences of a deradicalization process that is too swift or that encompasses the most important ideological core concepts without offering alternatives or careful restructuring might cause the collapse of the person's sense of self and identity construct.

Some exiters have even been shown to suffer from withdrawal symptoms not unlike victims of drug addiction who try to break free with a cold detoxification (Simi, Blee, DeMichele & Windisch, 2017). In another study, I have shown that extremist ideologies typically include traumatizing (e.g., problem focused) and therapeutic (e.g., solution and future vision) elements, which can expose the person who internalizes this system (rationally but also through emotions and social identity) to prolonged levels of toxic stress with severe mental health effects (Koehler, 2020). Deradicalization and disengagement programs must recognize the need for addressing ideological effects of radicalization processes beyond debating the theoretical doctrines of neo-Nazism, Salafi-Jihadism, or violent anti-fascism. Many programs have regarded the ideology as an either-or question depending on the methodological approach that was chosen (Koehler, 2016b). This is mostly due to the fact the "ideology" is still widely equaled to the theoretical doctrines of a group or milieus, instead of the emotional and social effects (Holbrook & Horgan, 2019) or the specific concepts creating meaning, a problem perception, solution strategies, and future vision promises (see Section 1.3 for a detailed discussion).

While knowledge about the theoretical doctrines of an extremist milieu cannot be expected from many members and arguably has only limited impact on the disengagement and deradicalization process for most defectors, the larger and oftentimes even more dominant social and emotional aspects of an ideology are deeply connected to most areas of a person's life. The side-switchers' storylines have shown how much of these individuals' psychological integrity, perception of self-worth, identity coherency, and much more was essentially determined by solving the conflict between milieu membership and their belief in certain ideological core concepts.

In short, side-switchers very often came to the conclusion that staying a member of their groups and environments was "not right" and would compromise their own moral and psychological integrity. This perception as expressed in the storylines was mostly fueled by their strong conviction to some key ideological concepts and the fact that the power of such self-affirmation narratives bridged hostile extremist milieus. It provides us with an insight into the way deradicalization and disengagement programs and practitioners should approach the sometimes sensitive topic of "ideology." One goal in the process should be to construct such a narrative together with the client that includes critical reflection and responsibility taking, but which is also fundamentally constructed around these core concepts most relevant for the client. Social psychologist Michael Williams has shown in his experimental studies that affirmation of the meaning-making system, for example, focusing on respect for the enemy, kindness, or forgiveness (which can be attached to ideological core concepts such as an "honorable" life) can have a significant impact on a persons' pro-social behavior in the P/CVE context (Williams, 2017). Other studies have shown that exercises based on taking the perspective of an ideological enemy can reduce stereotypes and hostility (Noor & Halabi, 2018), which mirrors the side-switching process to a large degree.

Here, too, the defectors began exploring the perspectives of the other side through ideological or personal contact points and reduced their own hostility toward the hostile environment.

In short, ideology in a much more nuanced perspective that takes into account the social, emotional, and detailed concept construction of those affected by it should be a key component in mentoring or counseling designed to help individuals leave extremist milieus and reduce their risk for reengagement (in the same or a different extremist environment) in a safe, effective, and healthy way. Studying side-switcher narratives has helped us to see the power of ideologically based self-affirmation stories in which these individuals actively restructure their lives and find a new identity. Methods in deradicalization and disengagement should neither strive to erase an ideology completely nor ignore it, but attempt to alter and rebuild identity concepts that are essential in order for the exiter to arrive at a new self-perception that is no longer dependent on the exclusive friend–foe differentiation, but is based on re-pluralized values instead.

6.6   Second Lesson Learned from Side-Switchers: Confused Identities

Extremism both on the collective and individual levels is based on the fixed ideological focus on a negative out-group. As Berger (2018) argues, extremist identities can only lead to successful outcomes and satisfaction when the enemy or hostile opponent is discriminated against or destroyed. This inherent link with an ideologically framed foe requires rigid and highly exclusive constructions of collective identities that are fused with the individual self-concept. Such a constant focus on prevailing over the milieu's enemies, as we have seen, can sometimes also open up the pathway for side-switching and intergroup transition. For the purpose of counter-extremism strategies, the existence of such pathways and the storylines of the defectors might open up another angle for targeting the logic and durability of the identity frameworks of certain extremist milieus. In the past, policy makers, counterterrorism professionals, P/CVE practitioners, and researchers have looked at what has been called counter-narrative or counter-messaging campaigns to achieve various degrees of confusion, reduction of commitment, or weakening of extremists' appeal among potential recruits. Side-switcher narratives can add a potentially powerful alternative source for such counter-narrative approaches.

Communication strategies that target members of extremist milieus in an effort to induce disengagement or directed toward at-risk groups in the early stages of recruitment to divert them away from joining, or at the general population to build resilience against the potential attractiveness of extremist messages, have increasingly been integrated into standard counterterrorism tool kits. As a consequence, ways to measure their effectiveness or design such persuasion narratives more systematically grew to be an important part in terrorism and counter-radicalization research (Braddock, 2019b; Braddock & Dillard, 2016; Braddock & Morrison, 2018).

In one of the first structured and evidence-based guidelines for creating such campaigns, Kurt Braddock and John Horgan (2015) suggest first identifying the target themes by studying and understanding the "themes that the group uses as the fundamental tenets of its ideology as communicated in its narratives" (Braddock & Horgan, 2015, p. 388). This ideally should lead to analytic guidelines containing "a general feel for the tone, style, and meaning of the terrorist narratives;" "a preliminary list of codes to identify excerpts that may be related to the terrorist group's ideology;" and the identification of "higher-order concepts within the narratives" (Braddock & Horgan, 2015, pp. 388–389). Counter-narrative campaigns, the authors recommend, should focus on those key themes but avoid reinforcing them.

In order to achieve the desired effects, four key mechanisms need to be utilized: revealing "incongruities and contradictions in both the terrorist narratives and the ways in which the terrorists act with respect to those narratives;" disrupting "analogies that equate aspects of the narrative to real-world events;" disrupting "binary themes of the group's ideology that are communicated through its narrative(s);" and incorporating "themes that advocate an alternative view of the terrorist narrative's target" (Braddock & Horgan, 2015, pp. 390–391). In short, such campaigns should try to disrupt the central meaning-making framework of extremist milieus, diffuse the dichotomous good vs. bad identity construction, and implant alternative concepts.

However, beyond these mechanisms, counter-narrative campaigns must also be adapted to the cultural (including subcultural) environment of the target audience regarding the dissemination strategies, as well as cultivate trust for the sender of the counter-messages. Braddock and Horgan suggest that this could be done by leveraging trusted others, such as peers or former members (Braddock & Horgan, 2015, p. 394). Indeed, former extremists, next to victims of terrorism and family members of extremists, have been seen as a particularly credible source for counter-narratives, which led to multiple campaigns that hoped to dissuade potential and actual followers of extremist milieus (e.g., Clubb, 2016; Hedayah, 2017; Scrivens, Venkatesh, Bérubé & Gaudette, 2019). Involving such persons with their life stories to counter or reduce existing extremist environments' spread has led to an extensive body of autobiographical accounts (Altier et al., 2017) but also to increasing critique based on the lack of proven impact of such methods involving former extremists, as well as significant ethical concerns (e.g., Galloway, 2019; Gilsinan, 2019; Koehler, 2019a; Tapley & Clubb, 2019; Walsh & Gansewig, 2019). Furthermore, the foremost expert on persuasive counterterrorist communication, Kurt Braddock, has shown how extremist milieus have developed their own inoculation strategies against messages from former members, potentially rendering them ineffective (Braddock, 2020, pp. 122–124).

The first important addition to counter-narrative practices and design by side-switchers is the insight into detailed ideological debates and arguments pertaining to identity construction, legitimization, and delegitimization of hostile extremist milieus. Side-switchers offer exemplary narrative strategies employed by these environments against each other and the loopholes that defectors identified for themselves. In short, the storylines we encountered throughout this book allow us to identify much better the key themes and ideological identity-construction mechanisms within and between extremist milieus for the purpose of creating the most effective counter-narratives.

J. M. Berger himself noted in a blog post about the side-switching case of Emerson Begolly (Section 4.4.1) that a theological discussion between the defector and a fellow jihadist (who was actually an FBI informant), as reported through court documents, would be "fodder for those working on deradicalization and narrative-adjustment" (Berger, 2011). These individuals, secondly, also provide us with sources for specific narratives that can be highly credible and confusing to the target audience. Many defectors, even though branded as traitors by their old milieus, remain influential via their previous statements or writings. Take the example of David Myatt, whose texts from his time as a neo-Nazi remained key reading in the far right, even after his conversion to Islam and publicly stated abandonment of extremism following his decision to leave jihadism. The fact that side-switchers often continue to be committed to a radical cause sometimes elicits respect from other extremists, even in the groups they have left.

However, side-switchers provide much more valuable input for the improvement of counter-narratives than studying ideological key themes and finding potentially credible senders of disruptive messages. Based on one of the most advanced theories of counter-narrative design by Haroro Ingram (2016, 2017), the defector storylines we studied here allow us to specifically target the linkages within an extremist milieu's system of meaning. As Ingram explains, such meaning frameworks circle around "bifurcated identity constructs" and involve allocating responsibility for a crisis and its solution to the in- or out-group respectively. Naturally, the in-group receives all the positive values while the enemy is imbued with all the negative ones. Since Ingram's model builds on Berger's extremism concept, the importance of the two identities (in- and out-group) locked into existential rivalry features strongly again. Side-switchers are, by their very biographical characteristics, the embodiment of perforating and dissolving these exclusive and rigid collective identities.

Exiters to the non-extremist world will often be dismissed as weaklings or irrelevant (Koehler, 2015b), thereby protecting the milieu's identity (see also Braddock, 2020, pp. 122–124). It is much more difficult with side-switchers, who can hardly be dismissed as irrelevant or uncommitted. Through their own storylines, these defectors attempt to punch holes into the identity barriers between the hostile milieus for themselves. Through these pathways designers of counter-narrative campaigns might very effectively attempt to erode the exclusiveness of a certain extremist milieu's collective identity and potentially cause the collapse of its system of meaning. This could be done by utilizing either the biographies of the side-switchers against their former and later environments or through repurposing their own arguments of ideological kinship. As the majority of extremists (as far as we know), adhere to the rigid identity and enemy concepts of their milieus, using side-switchers might be the most effective source for denying the de-pluralization of their worldviews and confronting them with impressions that could fundamentally disturb the ideological boundaries of their identities.

6.7   Third Lesson Learned from Side-Switchers: Know the Risks

Next to deradicalization and counter-narrative tools as part of the P/CVE field, extremist side-switchers also provide us with valuable insights for counter-terrorism that are more oriented toward containment and threat mitigation. I argued in Chapter 1 that defectors to hostile extremist milieus might either become a higher risk themselves due to a radicalization boost or that they might make their new groups more effective by providing them with special knowledge and skills. Not all side-switchers we studied in this book have become more violent after their milieu transition. A prime example would be Bernhard Falk (Section 4.2), who changed his personal activities from clandestine terrorist campaigns to Salafist prison counseling and proselytizing. This does not mean, however, that he automatically poses less of a threat. Much like other side-switchers (e.g., Julian Fritsch, Section 2.3), he uses his own biography and skills to be a more effective recruiter than full-fledged terrorist during his far-left time. Fritsch, too, has become a key personality in the German far-right music scene and is credited with establishing a new genre (i.e., rap music) within it (Radke & Staud, 2014).

Examples of extremist milieus that become more effective in their activities as a whole are of course anti-fascists gaining inside intelligence about the extreme right and using it to systematically cause internal turmoil in order to erode trust and disturb the formation of new groups. *Searchlight* magazine and other like-minded initiatives have heavily leaned on their own networks of informants and continue to do so. In 2019, former neo-Nazi Matthew Collins (Section 3.4) used one of the side-switchers who worked for him as an inside informant to uncover a plot to assassinate a British Member of Parliament (Townsend, 2019). On the Salafi-jihadist side, defector from the extreme right David Myatt used his writings to justify the use of suicide terrorism, including against women and children, in what has been described as the most elaborate and detailed theological reasoning for this tactic in the English language (Weitzman, 2010, p. 16).

For counterterrorism purposes, the potential impact of side-switchers has been mostly missed, which is not surprising since the phenomenon is rare from what we know so far. Nevertheless, as the case of Cory Johnson (Section 4.4) tragically shows, risk assessments by law enforcement and intelligence professionals must take into account previous extremist views and involvement when side-switching does occur. Only after Johnson moved toward jihadism were counterterrorism investigations opened and more decisive action taken, including mentoring and counseling attempts before the planned arrest. In the years before, his open support for far-right extremism in combination with violent and overall disturbing behavior in school did not trigger any similar response.

Risk assessment is a contested topic within academia, where the lack of empirical support and evidence that results in questionable predictive validity is usually and correctly pointed out as a key weakness of existing tools (e.g., Sarma, 2017). A 2017 literature review regarding risk factors associated with terrorism concluded that "there is insufficient evidence ... that any of these variables are empirically supported risk factors" and that "some widely accepted 'risk' factors have limited empirical support for their association with terrorism" (Desmarais, Simons-Rudolph, Brugh, Schilling & Hoggan, 2017, p. 180). Despite this rather fragile scientific basis for identifying and assessing such risk factors, many structured professional judgment tools have been developed and put to use due to the strong demand from policy makers, law enforcement, and the intelligence communities. By 2019, the spread of dedicated terrorism and extremism risk assessment tools had increased so much, that directories and comparative overviews were published for this quickly developing field. Between six and seven such tools were identified on the international level (Lloyd, 2019; van der Heide, van der Zwan & van Leyenhorst, 2019).

Some studies have also focused on validating the predictive validity and improvement of specific tools (Hart, Cook, Pressman, Strang & Lim, 2017; Knudsen, 2018). Among those that have been in use for the longest time are the Violent Extremism Risk Assessment (VERA) and the Extremism Risk Guidance (ERG 22+), both of which have also found their way into P/CVE work as well (Knudsen, 2018; Pressman, Duits, Rinne & Flockton, 2016). Beyond the accuracy and scientific support behind such tools, however, it was argued that "one should not 'value' risk assessment solely on its ability to correctly predict those who will and will not become involved in terrorism later. Rather, one should think more broadly about the opportunity to system-atize the collection and processing of information" (Sarma, 2017, p. 283).

In this sense, a structured information assessment regarding individual influences and context factors that might propel a person toward extremism or violence could be a much more realistic goal for such tools. The question of side-switching has so far not featured widely within risk assessment approaches as such. Nevertheless, most risk assessment tools account for previous extremist engagement of the person who being assessed. The VERA tool, for example, which has been revised and restructured multiple times (Lloyd, 2019; Pressman et al., 2016), does include several biographical factors that could be affected by such defection from one extremist milieu to another. However, switching sides per se is not a known risk factor.

Considering our exploration of extremist side-switching and the potential risk for increased threats on individual and collective levels, counterterrorism and intelligence professionals should not underestimate the role previously opposed ideological or physical extremist involvement might play in their assessments of groups and persons. Despite the fact that legally speaking, significant variances between different forms of extremist milieus exist, for example, regarding domestic terrorism vs. international terrorism, I have shown here that defectors rarely break with their pasts completely. Rather, they restructure key ideological concepts and convictions that lead them to the hostile milieus.

Hence, not accounting for the potential extremist convictions that have been nurtured and internalized long before authorities might have picked up a certain person in a later environment can cause significant misconceptions about the degree of radicalization, attitudes toward violence, or personal capabilities for criminal activities. There is of course still a strong need to differentiate between the specific milieus and biographical trajectories. Most former neo-Nazis who ended up in anti-fascist groups in our sample, for example, directed their activities almost completely against the far right and refrained from using violence. It would therefore also be a mistake, to auto-matically regard side-switching as a factor that increases the threat posed by a person. Much like I have demonstrated in this book, effective counterterrorism work needs to individually assess the side-switching pathways and narratives in combination with other factors in order to arrive at a realistic threat scenario and devise the most promising strategy.

6.8   Conclusion

Sadly, one of the most important lessons from extremist side-switching for counterterrorism and P/CVE is that these defectors usually do not perceive the non-extremist society as an alternative social milieu for satisfying their needs or reaching their personal goals. Like other exiters, side-switchers often experience fundamental conflicts in their groups and fall into deep crises; they look for solutions to their grievances, frustrations, or desire for status and recognition. A solidified concept of linked in- and out-group identities that evolved around fundamental conflict seems to deny many defectors the chance to even consider changing course more comprehensively. Others try and fail, which makes them see no other option than extremist activism as a result.

In this sense, side-switching pathways are also in part a failure of non-extremist societies to provide an adequate pull-force for reintegration; to offer meaningful opportunities for social engagement and fulfillment; and targeted help during times of crisis in which even highly committed extremists consider leaving their milieus. Clearly, not every side-switcher from our sample could have been persuaded to leave extremism behind; some defected out of determination to hurt their enemies more instead of less. However, it is also true that none of them ever received any professional prevention or intervention assistance. This is not surprising, since such programs and research about it only existed for a relatively short time. Phases of personal crisis serve as motivation to disengage from extremism for side-switchers as much as for other exiters. Making involvement in other extremist milieus less attractive and providing more appealing alternatives are essential societal protective measures, which must be explored and developed much more in the future.

7   Conclusions

Perhaps because his family background makes the French comedian and political activist Dieudonné M'bala M'bala (born 1966) an unlikely candidate for shifting his positions and allegiances to the extreme right, his case still puzzles many. Known by his stage name "Dieudonné," M'bala began his political career in the anti-racist far left in France. In the 1997 French legislative election, he even ran for office against the extreme-right Front National for the leftist party, "Utopistes," but failed to gain enough votes. He attempted to win a political position again one year later and tried to be listed for the 2002 election, but he could not due to lack of sponsorship (Ball, 2014). Born in Paris, Dieudonné used his early popularity as an artist to speak out against racism and discrimination in his writings and performances. This came to him naturally since his paternal Cameroonian background made him a target for both. While still attempting to run for office in 2002, M'bala gave an interview to the French magazine *Lyon Capitale*, in which he claimed that "the Jews" are nothing but "a sect, a fraud;" that "racism was invented by Abraham;" and anti-Semitism cannot be real because "Jews do not exist" (original in French, translation by author, Lyon-Capitale, 2014). It appears that this was one of the first public instances of a staunchly anti-Semitic and racist conviction that would later lead him to closely ally with the Front National, the very extreme right-wing party he had fought earlier.

In the following years, M'bala continued to cause public outcry and receive fierce criticism for his statements and performances, which, for example, include a 2003 appearance on French TV where he dressed as an orthodox Jewish Rabbi and gave the Nazi salute while shouting "Isra-heil" (Ball, 2014). Since 2006, he has been convicted and fined or sentenced to prison multiple times for (among other crimes) anti-Semitic hate speech, incitement of racial hatred, and support for terrorism. M'bala expressed his admiration for jihadist terrorist Amedy Coulibaly who took hostages and killed four people in eastern Paris as part of the 2015 *Charlie Hebdo* attacks (Lichfield, 2015). His notoriety for anti-Semitism and racism grew to such a degree that he even was barred from entry to the United Kingdom in 2014 (Reuters, 2014) and had his social media accounts banned on Facebook and Instagram in 2020 (Chemla, 2020).

Dieudonné went as far as naming Jean-Marie Le Pen, the founder of the Front National, the godfather of one of his children (Ball, 2014).

There is little concrete evidence as to what exactly motivated M'bala to shift his positions and allegiances so drastically from the far left to the far right. Some speculate that the fact that he remained commercially successful despite his anti-Semitic and racist diatribes indicates a financial motive: cashing in on the image of anti-establishment provocateur. Other commentators think that M'bala's anti-Semitism allows him to bridge the otherwise insurmountable gap between the immigrant community and the extreme right, thereby making it possible for him to reconcile his own background with his desire to belong to French society (Ball, 2014). Whatever his true intentions and beliefs were before and after the side-switching, M'bala's political and artistic positions by now appear solidified in the extreme right.

I have opened every chapter of this book with a brief case study of extreme(ist) side-switching. Even though the phenomenon as such is usually only documented by curious journalists who happen to stumble across a fascinating biography, and not systematically by researchers, one can identify many more examples over the decades than I was able to portray here. Take, for example, one of the founders of the European New Right, Henning Eichberg (1942–2017), who essentially coined the far-right term and concept of ethno-pluralism in the 1970s but ended his political career as a member of the leftist Danish Socialist People's Party (Seitenbecher, 2013, pp. 219–227). Or consider the case of former German far-right terrorist Ernst von Salomon (1902–1072), who helped to plot the assassination of Weimar Republic's Foreign Minister Walther Rathenau on June 24, 1922, by the Organization Consul (on the group see: Stern, 1963). Later he wrote in his post–Second World War autobiographical book *The Questionnaire* (Der Fragebogen) that the communist concept is the "only one on this earth which has the chance to self-actualize" (original in German, translated by author, von Salomon, 1951, p. 402) and professed his deep fascination and admiration for the communists' steadfastness (von Salomon, 1951, p. 356).

In short, I have attempted to show that our understanding and knowledge about extremist radicalization pathways is somewhat limited by our binary approach to the issue. We tend to look at extremist thought and behavior as some form of counterpart opposed to a normal or mainstream position. With Berger's (2018) suggestion to focus on the inherent hostility to an out-group instead, we are able to overcome this problem to a certain degree. Still, most regard extremist radicalization as a process of moving away from something (e.g., moderation in thoughts and action, tolerance for ambiguity and opposing views) and toward something (e.g., ideological convictions in support of violence or a group's cause). Extremist side-switching demonstrates that there are many more psychological and motivational layers to this process, as well as more directions and mutually influencing clusters of emotions, relationships, ideological elements, or social milieus. In that sense, much of our understanding of extremism and radicalization displays a black-and-white thinking that we often ascribe to the extremists themselves.

Naturally, the study of enemy concepts, forms of hostilities, strategies, and tactics of extremist groups and persons has included the analysis of how, why, and when specific forms of action and reaction is directed toward the ideologically defined other. The case studies presented in this book suggest that affiliations with milieus or ideologies can be much more fluid and driven by many other factors that are even considered to be highly counterintuitive. After all, investing heavily in group membership, fighting its enemies, committing crimes, or offering one's own health to advance the cause should logically inhibit acts of "treason." All the cases we studied here involved voluntary involvement in extremist milieus as opposed to, for example, forced brutalization into armed groups as happens with child soldiers in civil wars (Cakaj, 2016). Hence, our defectors made the conscious decision to invest themselves into one milieu and then after a while switch sides to their former enemies. Sometimes they even repeated this process.

In addition to directing us to limitations in our understanding of radicalization processes, we also have to thank extremist side-switchers for pointing us to a much more significant shortcoming in the study of extremism and terrorism: to know when, why, and how a person decides to leave an extremist milieu, as well as where they are heading. I discussed the state of the art in deradicalization and disengagement research in Chapter 6 and devoted an entire book to this field of study and practice (Koehler, 2016b). After diving into the storylines and career pathways of extremist side-switchers, I believe that despite the significant advances in recent years, we have barely scratched the surface of charting the multitudes of mechanisms and factors involved in the decisions and processes that lead to leaving an extremist setting and mindset. I would even venture to suggest that the widespread binary perspective on radicalization and the usually shallow understanding of the complexities of ideologies has blinded us researchers, policy makers, and practitioners in terms of appreciating the immense flexibility of thoughts and action even among the most rigid extremists. For too long, we have regarded (extremist) ideologies as intellectual sets of doctrines without emotional and social aspects or even dismissed internally differentiated layers of components containing varying degrees of importance for the individual believer. For too long, we have quickly judged those who appear to be acting in contradiction to their doctrines (in the way we perceive and understand them) or against their groups' interest in being opportunists, outliers, or simple drifters without any ideological conviction of their own. Extremist side-switchers disturb our compartmentalized vision of radicalization and disengagement.

If we do not want to dismiss all the storylines presented in this book as outright lies designed to mask what are allegedly purely opportunistic motives in reality, we cannot ignore the fact that for many extremists and radicals their journey is much more complex and multifaceted than we often care to admit. As we have seen, one can be a devoted neo-Nazi, anti-fascist, or jihadist right after one another, or even at the same time sometimes, because specific ideological values are so important, not despite ideologically set frameworks and rules. Such shifts occur not because defectors do not care about ideology at all, but in fact because many care so much about (certain parts of) them.

Of course, we have also seen that personal relationships, pure chance, traumatic experiences, or conflicts in the previous milieu play a big role too. Radicalization and allegiance to a certain cause or group are always the outcome of a mixture of different push-and-pull factors. Nevertheless, the defectors presented here generally talk about convictions, values, and causes much more often than about anything else. Their decisions to switch sides might have been caused by conflicts or interpersonal impressions, but in almost all cases they were driven along by fundamental beliefs in doing what they felt was right in order to advance toward an ideological goal. Naturally, these goals adapt along the process. Sometimes, enemies are reframed, core values are refined, or the methods to achieve the envisioned future are altered. To portray side-switchers as individuals who mainly look for better status, friends, or opportunities clearly misses the most important aspect of their journeys. They could have easily found all those things within the extremist ideological family they were active in and spared themselves the struggle of being attacked as traitors or making their former enemies trust them.

Furthermore, we have seen that at least from outside appearances, the extremist milieu that is considered by many to be the most socially dysfunctional – the far right – seems to attract most side-switchers who are identifiable. Without a strong social justice agenda and widespread mainstream support for much of its goals (as in the far left) or an all-encompassing religious community and tradition (as in Islamic extremism), the extreme right has apparently done a much better job to integrate defectors from their enemies than the other two milieus we considered here, while at the same time not hiding the fact. It might very well be that side-switchers are equally distributed or even more common in other milieus in reality. However, they are more visible within the far right. Why is that? Is it because the far-right milieu generally speaking is less ashamed or more welcoming of former enemies converting to their cause? If so, why would a religious community that is based on conversion from previous "false" convictions, such as Islamic extremism, be less forthcoming? To prove their claim of moral superiority, why would far-left circles not celebrate with a lot more enthusiasm each and every neo-Nazi who was won over to fight against his or her former comrades? This is still a mystery to be explored in greater detail.

Our study of extremist side-switchers has taken us deep into a complex web of overlapping factors on the individual and group levels. Most often, radicalization and terrorism researchers have focused on either one. They have rarely considered the mutual influences between these two levels. We have seen how certain extremist milieus and groups react when they are confronted with internal conflicts or discontented members. Sometimes, harsh punishments and repression is used to keep members in line and to warn them of the potentially grave consequences of defection. However, extremist groups are situated within social milieus that are comprised of interpersonal relationships and bonds beyond the mere organizational hierarchy. Even in extremist settings we can find considerable degrees of negotiation and attempts to solve conflicts between individuals and collectives. The outcome of these negotiations or, in other words, human resource management, determines the decision to leave the group and switch to the enemy in many cases. In short, the relationship between an extremist group, milieu, and individual members is highly dynamic and rests on reciprocity.

Naturally, we tend to see extremist groups and milieus as rather normative enforcing. Constructed around highly exclusive collective identity concepts with solidified in-group and out-group definitions, these environments appear to the outside observer as not very flexible when it comes to core values and norms. Side-switchers have alerted us to a very important aspect of this reciprocal relationship, namely the attempt by individual members to shape, develop, and adjust the overall setting, even when this means going to the roots of the very core ideology in order to adapt it to current needs and challenges. One can partially spot the outcome of this, when new clothing or music styles are adopted for the purpose of extremist recruitment, for example (Miller-Idriss, 2018, 2020). One might also think about the use of new technologies (e.g., social media, encrypted messenger apps), attack tactics, or ideological themes (e.g., environmentalism in the far right) as the result of individual members' attempts to import their own visions and interests into the collective mindset.

This realm of social negotiation between an extremist milieu and its members leaves open many possible outcomes. The most widely studied ones are either the full and sustained integration into the extremist setting with advancement in status, position, and conviction on the one hand, and exit with disengagement and deradicalization on the other. A third but much less explored option can be the shift between milieus within the same extremist ideological family, for example, from a neo-Nazi skinhead group to a more elitist and intellectual organization. We can now add a fourth pathway, switching extremist sides without giving up on some of the core ideological values and goals that define a person's extremist thoughts and behavior. In fact, the side-switching process might truly be composed of many different additional pathways. Some might be types of failed disengagement with subsequent reengagement, while others could be considered ideological development and learning or social environment adaption to altered core values. It appears that we have just scratched the surface of understanding the multidirectional relationships and transition possibilities between a mainstream society, an extremist milieu (including many different groups and ideological variants of the same family), and other extremist milieus (which also include various groups and styles). Sometimes, as we have seen, switching sides takes a detour via the mainstream non-extremist society, but it more often involves direct travel between extremist environments.

7.1   What Have We Learned about Extremist Side-Switching?

To summarize the main lessons that we have learned about extremist side-switching and defection across hostile ideologies, we must again revisit the main factors involved in the transmission of specific thought patterns and ideological edifices. Even when some of the main motivations for joining the opposed milieu are based on rather mundane emotions or social networks instead of political or religious convictions, membership in these milieus is defined by the adherence to, and belief in, at least a rudimentary ideological core. Furthermore, we have also seen that the much too widely used understanding of "ideology" as a set of abstract or theoretical doctrines and teachings significantly misses large parts (especially the emotional and social aspects) of how ideology asserts behavioral or attitudinal impact on the individual milieu member. For such a transition between opposed extremist milieus to be successful, certain core values and their framing must first be transported across physical and mental boundaries. Such framing is important because even if the defector does not change his or her actual convictions, it is nevertheless of utmost importance to learn how to express them "correctly" in the new environment without causing suspicion because of "sounding like the enemy." Integrating into an extremist milieu often requires a great deal of learning and adaption to new specialized language, technical knowledge, social norms, accepted and stigmatized behavior, and so on. We must revisit the key questions I asked in the Preface:

How are acts of extremist side-switching across hostile groups possible? How is it, that these individuals not only manage to shift between groups that are actively fighting each other, but to successfully enter the new group, gain trust of the group's members, and even rise to fame and power within them? How is it that they are not branded as traitors, unreliable opportunists, or potential spies? Why are side-switchers between certain milieus and into certain ideological directions seemingly more common than others and what does this reveal about the ideological connections between them? In short, how and why do they do it? I believe that by diving into the various storylines of side-switchers and their biographies as far as I could reconstruct them with publicly available information, we have found at least one key to answering these questions. We have begun to understand the mechanisms involved in the transmission of "ideological DNA" across milieus and between mindsets.

Why do committed and involved members of extremist milieus begin to accept external ideological contents? After all, our understanding of extremism is built around the notion of strictly excluding all outside groups and their opinions. Hence, extremists are trained, forced, and socialized to disregard or even hate and despise everything that does not belong to their trusted inner circle. There are two main reasons setting the side-switching process in motion. One is frustration with deficiencies in the original group or milieu. Members are simply fed up with hypocrisy, double standards, or internal power struggles. Also, they often perceive that they are being pushed aside and ignored in their wishes or visions to improve their extremist environment. This might happen, for example, in the denial to integrate new political themes, recruitment strategies, or aesthetics. On the other hand, a change of course or new strategy put in place by the group leadership could leave some members alienated. Take for example, the New IRA building a relationship with Hezbollah (Mooney, 2020a) to acquire weapons and funding. Even though the two organizations are not direct enemies (neither ideologically nor physically, albeit it might be possible for the Irish to end up as targets for Hezbollah within the Middle East), they do follow extremely different worldviews and goals. Of course, such a collaboration could theoretically lead to the transfer of personnel but it is also possible that some IRA or Hezbollah members perceive such a joint venture as a betrayal of their core values. Another reason to start thinking about the other side in a more positive light is, somewhat ironically, the conflict with the enemy. Of course, this conflict is at the heart of what extremism means but constant mental focus on "the other" might also (consciously or inadvertently) cause a mental convergence.

Next to specific causes for side-switching, we have observed very specific "ideological highways" between different milieus. These highways are themes or core values that are used by defectors to build bridges into the new environment and portray themselves as ideologically more familiar than expected by the new group. Usually, constructing these highways involves picking a certain ideological component that can be claimed to exist on both sides. Furthermore, this core element is then tweaked and twisted into a framing that fits better with the new target milieu. The main goal is basically to convey the message: "I have always been a true believer in [add ideological component of choice most important to the new milieu] and my old group got it wrong or simply lacked knowledge about how essential this really is. Hence, to remain true to myself, I have to go where [ideological value] is practiced." Anti-Semitism, the nation or a national collective, and anti-capitalism or anti-imperialism are among those ideological themes that appear very often in the storylines we have explored are.

Side-switchers often use two main pathways to transition between the opposed milieus. The first one, activism, involves significant activities aimed at the mainstream surrounding the environment or ideological enemy of the new group. The defection in this case is usually presented as a natural outcome of increased desires to "do more" to achieve the ideological goal or as the consequence of personally meeting members of the opposed milieu (e.g., in prison or during rallies or fights). Even though the ideological transmission still is the key mechanism making the side-switching possible in the storylines, presenting oneself as an "activist" and a "hands-on" personality in combination with actually showing behavior (e.g., crimes and violence) that displays a deep commitment to a cause, helps to establish trust and gain respect from the other side. The second extensively used pathway used to frame the change in ideological convictions and milieu affiliations is the "learning process." In it, the defector presents him or herself as someone on an intellectual mission to study and understand the roots or concepts of a certain milieu's philosophy and worldviews. Sometimes via years of exploration, reflection, and learning, the side-switcher actively works through layers of different rationales and eventually ends up with the interpretation of the new environment. Hence, the switching is framed as the necessary outcome of true enlightenment and understanding. This also implies that the extremist milieu to be joined is actively validated in terms of intellectual correctness.

Who do we know plays important roles in the side-switching process other than the defectors themselves? The storylines presented in this book mainly tell us about three types of influencers: friends, foes, and recruiters. It is not uncommon for extremists (at least in our sample here) to form friendships and bonds with members of the opposing environment. Such relationships can form during prison time or even as the result of actively sought discussions and conversations to "convert" the enemy to one's own position. Influencing a side-switching, however, can also happen in hostile relationships. Sometimes, particularly polarizing or intimidating enemies can impact members of the opposed milieu. Charisma or respect for strength or intellectual prowess can effectively create positive perspectives on the previously hated enemy. We have already touched on the mental effects of constantly focusing on hostility toward another group, person, or ideology. This might actually lead to an unwilling adoption of the other side's arguments and positions, or in other words, "one might lose sight of the wood for the trees." Third, recruiters are sometimes responsible for bringing someone over from the enemy camp. We have seen how some extremist milieus spend much time arguing about the best strategies and approaches to convert those deemed to be valuable for one's own cause.

Where does the transmission of ideological concepts between opposed extremist milieus take place according to the side-switchers? They mainly cite two key "places": conversations and textual material. Most importantly, defectors at some point engaged in actual conversation with members from the other side, be it offline or online. These exchanges of opinions, thoughts, and positions are widely presented as the essential way of getting to know the enemy and developing an appreciation for him or her. Second, defectors often cite specific texts written by ideologues, leaders, or simple members from the hostile milieu. The curiosity or even necessity to study the textual basis of the enemy is usually accepted within extremist circles. After all, knowing one's opponent is seen as the key to defeating or learning from him. Especially between extreme right and left environments, partially heated intellectual debates about certain key thinkers and their works can result in someone self-convincing about the previously abhorred positions.

Finally, the storylines of the defectors in this book evolved around certain critical times and situations in their lives, explaining when they made the decision to switch sides. For many, specific life stages that involved much personal change (e.g., teenage years, prison time) became the key frame for their milieu transition. Others, however, used some form of a life-stage explanation to legitimize their departure form the old environment by constructing symbolic times and situations. Meeting certain influential gatekeepers or highly charismatic members of the opposing milieu by chance is sometimes presented as divine intervention or fate, for example.

When we began our exploration of extremist side-switching, we only had a rough impression of how prevalent this phenomenon might be and no insight into how it might affect extremist milieus at all. Data from the PIRUS database in the United States suggests a very small percentage of extremists who have gone through different (arguably mutually exclusive or hostile) ideologies before ending up in their "final" milieu. On the other side, we have found evidence that in countries with much more equally developed extremist milieus in regular contact (e.g., far right and far left in Germany), such side-switching might occur more often. It is also telling that in some virtual extremist environments the casually made statement that one comes more or less directly from the ideological enemy, rarely caused any surprise or criticism. It appears that the extreme right is a lot more open to and welcoming of side-switchers in their ranks, even though this might be a distorted effect based on different communication preferences by members in each milieu. While Islamic extremists can fall back to religious conversion narratives that might overshadow side-switching, far-left activists could fear being stigmatized or marginalized when they talk about an extreme-right past. We saw that known side-switchers very rarely achieve prominent and influential positions in the far left, while this is not at all uncommon in the far right. This could signal to defectors that their far-right past is not necessarily status enhancing. This leads us to the question of impact on the extremist milieu that integrates or receives side-switchers. In the beginning, we speculated that the knowledge, skills, and networks of defectors have the potential to significantly increase the capabilities of the new group or environment. Such effects are most visible in the extreme-right spectrum, which has often benefited enormously from defectors from the far left in many countries. To name but two examples, the creation and establishment of the "New Right" in Europe and highly militant fascist online milieus such as IronMarch or Fascist Forge are mainly the result of work by side-switchers from the extreme left. While there is clear evidence that anti-fascist groups have benefited from defectors and their inside knowledge of extreme-right networks, the impact of defectors appears to be limited to helping target the far right. Side-switchers have had little influence beyond this particular impact in the far left, it seems. Within Islamic extremist groups, defectors' impact is even harder to estimate. We have come across a small number of ideologues or group leaders in the jihadist environment who openly use their former far-right or far-left past to their advantage. Overall, however, this appears to be a rarity. Furthermore, we must acknowledge that women are far less underrepresented among known side-switchers, even when considering the already small number of women in extremist milieus.

7.2   What Comes Next?

This exploration of extremist side-switching is a first peek into a so far mostly ignored aspect of extremists' radicalization careers and pathways. I have shown that behind the curtain separating the mainstream from the extremist milieu, many more different trajectories and movements exist. Unfortunately, we are only at the beginning of understanding the dynamics involved between an extremist environment and its members on the one side and between hostile milieus on the other. We have learned that some core elements of extremist ideological "DNA" are able to provide bridges or even "highways" of mental and physical transition between otherwise opposed groups and environments. Specific ideas and concepts can travel between milieus and in some cases form the basis of significant developments. In short, looking at side-switcher careers within extremism and terrorism provides us with a glimpse at dynamics we currently do not understand well.

Beyond the improvement of our knowledge of radicalization dynamics and extremist milieus' learning, defectors between hostile groups and typically exclusive ideologies also alert us to a significant gap in preventing and countering violent extremism, including deradicalization and disengagement. We do know that extremist and terrorist groups are often socially dysfunctional and put a lot of stress, trauma, and frustration on their members. The fact that many of these environments experience high turnover rates has informed a growing body of research focusing on the exit from extremism and terrorism. So far, practitioners and policy makers (together with researchers) have mostly looked at extremists who suffer from their membership (e.g., through disillusionment, internal power struggles, hypocrisy) as likely "exiters" or "persisters" for their own varying reasons. The option to shift into a different extremist environment as a form of disengagement and "re-radicalization" or "radicalization change" has not been part of P/CVE strategies and programs.

Hence, I want to end this book with a threefold call to action directly taken out of our exploration of extremist side-switchers. First, we need much more extensive research into the dynamics between extremist milieus and their members on "personnel management" strategies in these environments, both on the positive and negative side (e.g., reward systems, conflict solution, sanctions, repression, punishment) and the social and emotional effects of ideology, as well as its components. Following the example of Michael Freeden (1996), we should strive for a form of "ideological mapping" of the extremist landscape to know which "ideological families" exist and the core concepts they are built around. Only in this way we will be able to understand where and into which direction transition pathways are most likely to form. Despite the significant advances in understanding radicalization and deradicalization processes over the last decades, there is still much to learn and study.

Second, counter-extremism strategies and practitioners need to acknowledge that these milieus are living and breathing organisms that undergo constant change and adaption. They exchange ideas, members, and tactics even if they are enemies. This means that effectively assessing the risk or potential future developments within extremist environments also requires holistic approaches that go beyond binary thinking of in or out of (one milieu). Of course, most professionals have largely accepted the significant degree of variance and difference within one extremist milieu. However, we must also not dismiss the possibility of ideological links or personal transitions across ideological boundaries. The import of a certain ideological concept, strategy, or philosophy into one extremist environment has the potential to fundamentally alter the existing landscape or give birth to brand new extremist styles. This highlights the need for much more extensive expertise and knowledge among P/CVE practitioners to better understand the dynamics in the field they are directly working with (Koehler & Fiebig, 2019).

Third and finally, studying side-switcher storylines has brought us in direct touch with the individuals behind these pathways. No matter what the extremist milieu or the behavior resulting from these convictions might entail, we must never forget that we are still dealing with human beings who have their own desires, wishes, fears, frustrations, and goals for their lives. At least in their own narratives, defectors most often expressed the desire to continue some kind of opposition against what they perceived to be evil or unjust, while at the same time solving conflicts or other problems they had in their original group. At its core, fighting extremism and terrorism always means rejecting violence and convictions that arise from hostilities between in- and out-groups while simultaneously accepting and recognizing the individual trapped in this melee. We cannot outrightly ostracize and demonize human beings for being members of a certain group or milieu, as that would be the same behavior we see from the extremists we are trying to weed out from our societies. We must learn to provide societal and individual alternatives that are firmly based in mutual respect, tolerance, and humanity for those caught within extremist circles.

Bibliography

"Aleksandr-Slavros." (2014). Retrieved May 14, 2020 from www.ironmarch.exposed/post/100890.

(2017). IM Statement on the Events of May 2017. Retrieved May 14, 2020 from www.ironmarch.exposed/post/9542.

"Anti-gay." (2016). Reply to Odin's Topic in Urban Exploration Club. Retrieved May 14, 2020 from http://ironmarch.org/index.php?/search/&q=weisse.

"Arnar." (2017). #public-relations in Cascade Thread. Retrieved May 14, 2020 from https://whispers.ddosecrets.com/discord/channel/359509262872870912?page=2.

"Banks=Gay." (2018). /r/SargonOfAkkad (Sparta) #general Thread. Retrieved May 14, 2020 from https://discordleaks.unicornriot.ninja/discord/view/4901399?q=I+was+a+commie#msg.

"Blackshirt." (2016). Islam and the Reich. Retrieved May 14, 2020 from www.ironmarch.exposed/message/19004#msg-19004.

(2017). Islam and the Reich. Retrieved May 14, 2020 from www.ironmarch.exposed/message/24069#msg-24069.

"Clive-Bissel." (2013). Fascism/NS vs Communism/Marxism Thread. Retrieved May 14, 2020 from www.ironmarch.exposed/message/7077#msg-7077.

(2016). Message. Retrieved May 14, 2020 from www.ironmarch.exposed/post/111548.

"Deleted-User." (2013). Post. Retrieved May 14, 2020 from www.ironmarch.exposed/post/135313.

"Faustus." (2018). Retrieved May 14, 2020 from https://whispers.ddosecrets.com/discord/channel/359509262872870912?page=13.

"Hadit." (2014). Hello. Retrieved May 14, 2020 from www.ironmarch.exposed/message/8988#msg-8988.

"John-Q.-Public." (2017). Post. Retrieved May 14, 2020 from www.ironmarch.exposed/post/11145.

"K-Martin." (2018). #tradworker Thread. Retrieved May 14, 2020 from https://discordleaks.unicornriot.ninja/discord/view/464868?q=I+was+a+commie#msg.

"liebling." (2017). X. Retrieved May 14, 2020 from www.ironmarch.exposed/message/24492#msg-24492.

"New-Canadian-Empire." (2013). Post. Retrieved May 14, 2020 from www.ironmarch.exposed/post/139818.

"Peter." (2015). Post. Retrieved May 14, 2020 from www.ironmarch.exposed/post/93566.

294   Bibliography

"Questgiver." (2019). Dank Brigade #general Thread. Retrieved May 14, 2020 from https://discordleaks.unicornriot.ninja/discord/view/7472770?q=I+was+a+commie#msg.

"Raycis." (2014). Post. Retrieved May 14, 2020 from www.ironmarch.exposed/post/116458.

"Ronny-TX." (2017a). Southern Front #general Thread. Retrieved May 14, 2020 from https://discordleaks.unicornriot.ninja/discord/view/207270?q=#msg.

(2017b). Southern Front #general Thread. Retrieved May 14, 2020 from https://discordleaks.unicornriot.ninja/discord/view/197992?q=#msg.

(2017c). Southern Front #general Thread. Retrieved May 14, 2020 from https://discordleaks.unicornriot.ninja/discord/view/203262?q=I+was+a+commie#msg.

"Samus-Aryan." (2017). Post. Retrieved May 14, 2020 from www.ironmarch.exposed/post/194887.

"Schmiss." (2016). Reply to Odin's Topic in Atomwaffen Division. Retrieved May 14, 2020 from http://ironmarch.org/index.php?/search/&q=weisse.

"sporus." (2019). Blue Politics #general-chat Thread. Retrieved May 14, 2020 from https://discordleaks.unicornriot.ninja/discord/view/50957646?q=I+was+a+commie#msg.

"The-Yank." (2014). Same Age, Same State. Retrieved May 14, 2020 from www.ironmarch.exposed/message/8964#msg-8964.

"Tiwaz." (2017). Not a Shill. Just Lost. Retrieved May 14, 2020 from www.ironmarch.exposed/message/25113#msg-25113.

Abuza, Z. (2008). The Rehabilitation of Jemaah Islamiyah Detainees in South East Asia: A Preliminary Assessment. In T. Bjørgo & J. Horgan (eds.), *Leaving Terrorism Behind: Individual and Collective Disengagement* (pp. 193–211). New York: Routledge.

Adams, J. & Roscigno, V. J. (2005). White Supremacists, Oppositional Culture and the World Wide Web. *Social Forces*, 84(2), 759–778. www.jstor.org/stable/3598477.

Adorno, T. W. (1950). *The Authoritarian Personality* (1st ed.). New York: Harper.

Agnew, R. (2006). Storylines as a Neglected Cause of Crime. *Journal of Research in Crime and Delinquency*, 43(2), 119–147.

Aho, J. A. (1988). Out of Hate: A Sociological of Defection from Neo-Nazism. *Current Research on Peace and Violence*, 11(4), 159–168. www.jstor.org/stable/40725104.

AIZ. (1995). AIZ – Erklärung zur Aktion gegen Paul Breuer. Retrieved May 14, 2020 from www.nadir.org/nadir/archiv/PolitischeStroemungen/Stadtguerilla+RAF/Antiimperialistische_Zelle/aiz-breuer.html.

Al-Rawi, A. (2018). Video Games, Terrorism, and ISIS's Jihad 3.0. *Terrorism and Political Violence*, 30(4), 740–760. doi:10.1080/09546553.2016.1207633.

Al-Tamimi, A. J. (2015). Repentance: Financial Income for the Islamic State. Retrieved May 14, 2020 from www.aymennjawad.org/2015/09/repentance-financial-income-for-the-islamic-state.

Alcalde, Á. (2018). Towards Transnational Fascism: German Perceptions of Mussolini's Fascists and the Early NSDAP. *Politics, Religion & Ideology*, 19(2), 176–195. doi:10.1080/21567689.2018.1449109.

Allardyce, G. D. (1966). The Political Transition of Jacques Doriot. *Journal of Contemporary History*, 1(1), 56–74. doi:10.1177/002200946600100105.

Allen, C. (2017). Proscribing National Action: Considering the Impact of Banning the British Far-Right Group. *The Political Quarterly*, 88(4), 652–659.

Allport, G. W. (1958). *The Nature of Prejudice* (abridged ed.). Garden City, NY: Doubleday.

Almohammad, A. & Ingram, H. J. (2019). *Say Upon Them to Strive*. A speech by Abu
Bakr Al-Baghdadi. Retrieved May 14, 2020 from https://extremism.gwu.edu/sites/
g/files/zaxdzs2191/f/Blog%20Post%201.pdf.

Alonso, R. (2011). Why Do Terrorists Stop? Analyzing Why ETA Members Abandon
or Continue with Terrorism. *Studies in Conflict & Terrorism*, *34*(9), 696–716.
doi:10.1080/1057610X.2011.594944.

Altier, M. B., Horgan, J. & Thoroughgood, C. (2012). In Their Own Words? Methodological
Considerations in the Analysis of Terrorist Autobiographies. *Journal of Strategic
Security*, *5*(4), 85–98.

Altier, M. B., Leonard Boyle, E. & Horgan, J. G. (2019). Returning to the Fight: An
Empirical Analysis of Terrorist Reengagement and Recidivism. *Terrorism and
Political Violence*. doi:10.1080/09546553.2019.1679781.

Altier, M. B., Leonard Boyle, E., Shortland, N. D. & Horgan, J. G. (2017). Why They Leave:
An Analysis of Terrorist Disengagement Events from Eighty-Seven Autobiographical
Accounts. *Security Studies*, *26*(2), 305–332. doi:10.1080/09636412.2017.1280307.

Altier, M. B., Thoroughgood, C. N. & Horgan, J. G. (2014). Turning Away from
Terrorism: Lessons from Psychology, Sociology, and Criminology. *Journal of
Peace Research*, *51*(5), 647–661. doi:10.1177/0022343314535946.

Altman, H. & Marrero, T. (2017, May 24). Murder Suspect Claims Valor. *Tampa Bay
Times*.

Amir, Y. (1969). Contact Hypothesis in Ethnic Relations. *Psychological Bulletin*, *71*(5),
319–342.

Anas, A. & Hussein, T. (2019). *To The Mountains: My Life in Jihad, from Algeria to
Afghanistan*. London: Hurst & Company.

Andersen, S. L. & Teicher, M. H. (2009). Desperately Driven and No Brakes: Developmental
Stress Exposure and Subsequent Risk for Substance Abuse. *Neuroscience &
Biobehavioral Reviews*, *33*(4), 516–524. https://doi.org/10.1016/j.neubiorev.2008.09.009.

Andreyev, C. (1989). *Vlasov and the Russian Liberation Movement: Soviet Reality and
Émigré Theories*. Cambridge: Cambridge University Press.

Anglin, A. (2015). Andrew Anglin Exposed! Retrieved May 14, 2020 from http://
dailystormer.name/andrew-anglin-exposed.

Arendt, H. (1973). *The Origins of Totalitarianism*. London: Houghton Mifflin Harcourt.

Ariely, D. & Norton, M. I. (2008). How Actions Create–Not Just Reveal–Preferences.
Trends in Cognitive Sciences, *12*(1), 13–16.

Aristotle. (1999). *Politics. Translated by Benjamin Jowett*. Kitchener: Batoche Books.

Arnold, S. & Taylor, B. (2019). Antisemitism and the Left: Confronting an Invisible
Racism. *Journal of Social Justice*, *9*(2019), 1–33.

Arosoaie, A. (2015). Doctrinal Differences between ISIS and Al Qaeda: An Account of
Ideologues. *Counter Terrorist Trends and Analyses*, *7*(7), 31–37.

Ascher, A. & Lewy, G. (1956). National Bolshevism in Weimar Germany: Alliance of
Political Extremes against Democracy. *Social Research*, *23*(4), 450–480.

Atran, S. (2017). The Role of the Devoted Actor in War, Revolution and Terrorism. In
J. R. Lewis (ed.), *The Cambridge Companion to Religion and Terrorism* (pp.
69–88). New York: Cambridge University Press.

Aust, S. (2009). *Baader-Meinhof: The Inside Story of the RAF*. London: The Bodley Head.

Avineri, S. (1964). Marx and Jewish Emancipation. *Journal of the History of Ideas*, *25*
(3), 445–450.

Awan, I. (2017). Cyber-Extremism: Isis and the Power of Social Media. *Society*, *54*(2), 138–149.

Azani, E. & Koblentz-Stenzler, L. (2019). Muslim Converts Who Turn to Global Jihad: Radicalization Characteristics and Countermeasures. *Studies in Conflict & Terrorism*. doi:10.1080/1057610X.2019.1657304.

Backes, U. (2009). *Political Extremes: A Conceptual History from Antiquity to the Present*. London: Routledge.

Bacon, T. & Arsenault, E. G. (2019). Al Qaeda and the Islamic State's Break: Strategic Strife or Lackluster Leadership? *Studies in Conflict & Terrorism*, *42*(3), 229–263.

Baker, D. (2006). The Political Economy of Fascism: Myth or Reality, or Myth and Reality? *New Political Economy*, *11*(2), 227–250.

Bakker, E. (2006). *Jihadi Terrorists in Europe – Their Characteristics and the Circumstances in Which They Joined the Jihad: An Exploratory Study*. Clingendael Institute. Retrieved May 14, 2020 from www.clingendael.nl/sites/default/files/20061200_cscp_csp_bakker .pdf.

Bale, J. M. (2009). Islamism and Totalitarianism. *Totalitarian Movements and Political Religions*, *10*(2), 73–96.

Ball, S. (2014, January 4). Dieudonné: From Anti-racist to Anti-Semitic zealot. *France 24*. Retrieved May 14, 2020 from www.france24.com/en/20140104-dieudonne-anti-racist-anti-semitic-zealot.

Barrelle, K. (2015). Pro-Integration: Disengagement from and Life after Extremism. *Behavioral Sciences of Terrorism and Political Aggression*, *7*(2), 129–142. doi:10.1080/19434472.2014.988165.

Bartlett, J. & Miller, C. (2012). The Edge of Violence: Towards Telling the Difference between Violent and Non-violent Radicalization. *Terrorism and Political Violence*, *24*(1), 1–21. doi:10.1080/09546553.2011.594923.

Basra, R. & Neumann, P. R. (2016). Criminal Pasts, Terrorist Futures: European Jihadists and the New Crime-Terror Nexus. *Perspectives on Terrorism*, *10*(6), 25–40.

Bates, R. A. (2011). Terrorism within the Community Context. *The Journal of Public and Professional Sociology*, *3*(1), 1–14.

Baumgärtner, M. & Böttcher, M. (2012). *Das Zwickauer Terror-Trio - Ereignisse, Szene, Hintergründe*. Reinbek: Rowohlt.

Bavaria. (2016). *Salafism: Prevention through Information. Questions and Answers*. Munich: Bavarian State Ministry of the Interior, Building and Transport.

Baxter, P. (2013, March 31). Nostalgia: Selsey's Muslim Baronet. *Bognor Regis Observer*. Retrieved May 14, 2020 from https://web.archive.org/web/20171113165537/https:// www.bognor.co.uk/lifestyle/nostalgia/nostalgia-selsey-s-muslim-baronet-1-4948103.

BayObLG. (1983). *Urteil des 3. Strafsenats des Bayerischen Oberlandesgerichts vom 25.11.1983*. (3 St 11/82). Munich.

Beckett, L. & Burke, J. (2017, May 27). Pathway to Extremism: What Neo-Nazis and Jihadis Have in Common. *The Guardian*. Retrieved May 14, 2020 from www.theguardian .com/us-news/2017/may/27/extremism-terrorism-far-right-neo-nazi-devon-arthurs.

Berger, J. M. (2011). *Jihad Joe: Americans Who Go to War in the Name of Islam*. Washington, DC: Potomac Books, Inc.

(2011). A Look into the Troubled Mind of Jihadist Emerson Begolly. Retrieved May 14, 2020 from http://news.intelwire.com/2011/01/look-into-troubled-mind-of-jihadist .html.

(2016). *The Turner Legacy: The Storied Origins and Enduring Impact of White Nationalism's Deadly Bible*. International Centre for Counter-Terrorism in The Hague (ICCT). Retrieved May 14, 2020 from https://icct.nl/wp-content/uploads/2016/09/ICCT-Berger-The-Turner-Legacy-September2016-2.pdf.

(2018). *Extremism*. Cambridge, MA: The MIT Press.

Berghöfer, I. (2019, Februray 20). Kirtorf sieht erneut "braun." *Oberhessische Presse*. Retrieved May 14, 2020 from www.op-marburg.de/Landkreis/Ostkreis/Der-rechtsextreme-Landwirt-Bertram-Koehler-sorgt-in-Kirtorf-fuer-Aerger.

Bernstein, J. (2017, January 23). A Thriving Chat Startup Braces for the Alt-Right. *BuzzFeed*. Retrieved May 14, 2020 from www.buzzfeednews.com/article/josephbernstein/discord-chat-startup-braces-for-the-alt-right.

Bitzan, R. (2017). Geschlechterkonstruktionen und Geschlechterverhältnisse in der extremen Rechten. In F. Virchow, M. Langebach & A. Häusler (eds.), *Handbuch Rechtsextremismus* (pp. 325–374). Wiesbaden: Springer VS.

Bjørgo, T. (1997). *Racist and Right-Wing Violence in Scandinavia: Patterns, Perpetrators, and Responses*. Oslo: Aschehoug.

(2009). Processes of Disengagement from Violent Groups of the Extreme Right. In T. Bjørgo & J. Horgan (eds.), *Leaving Terrorism Behind: Individual and Collective Disengagement* (pp. 30–48). New York: Routledge.

(2016). *Preventing Crime: A Holistic Approach*. New York: Palgrave Macmillan.

Bjørgo, T. & Horgan, J. (2009). *Leaving Terrorism Behind: Individual and Collective Disengagement*. London: Routledge.

BKA, BfV,& HKE. (2016). *Analysis of the Background and Process of Radicalization among Persons Who Left Germany to Travel to Syria or Iraq Based on Islamist Motivations*. Bundeskriminalamt, Berlin. Retrieved May 14, 2020 from www.bka.de/SharedDocs/Downloads/EN/Publications/Other/AnalysisOfTheBackgroundAndProcessOfRadicalization.html.

Blanchard, W. H. (1984). Karl Marx and the Jewish Question. *Political Psychology, 5*(3), 365–374.

Blank, B. (2013). *Deutschland, einig Antifa? Antifaschismus als Agitationsfeld von Linksextremisten*. Baden-Baden: Nomos.

Blee, K. M. (1996). Becoming a Racist: Women in Contemporary Ku Klux Klan and Neo-Nazi Groups. *Gender and Society, 10*(6), 680–702. www.jstor.org/stable/190195.

(2002). *Inside Organized Racism: Women in the Hate Movement*. Berkeley, CA: University of California Press.

(2005). Women and Organized Racial Terrorism in the United States. *Studies in Conflict & Terrorism, 28*(5), 421–433. doi:10.1080/10576100500180303.

Bliuc, A.-M., Betts, J., Vergani, M., Iqbal, M. & Dunn, K. (2019). Collective Identity Changes in Far-Right Online Communities: The Role of Offline Intergroup Conflict. *New Media & Society, 21*(8), 1770–1786. doi:10.1177/1461444819831779.

Bloom, M. (2011). *Bombshell: Women and Terrorism*. Philadelphia, PA: University of Pennsylvania Press.

Bloom, M. & Horgan, J. (2019). *Small Arms: Children and Terrorism*. Ithaca, NY: Cornell University Press.

Blumenau, B. (2020). Unholy Alliance: The Connection between the East German Stasi and the Right-Wing Terrorist Odfried Hepp. *Studies in Conflict & Terrorism, 23* (1), 47–68. doi:10.1080/1057610X.2018.1471969.

BMI. (1982). *betrifft: Verfassungsschutz 1981.* Bonn: Bundesministerium des Innern.
(2000). *Verfassungsschutzbericht 1999.* Berlin: Bundesministerium des Innern.

Boen, F. & Vanbeselaere, N. (2000). Responding to Membership of a Low-Status Group: The Effects of Stability, Permeability and Individual Ability. *Group Processes & Intergroup Relations, 3*(1), 41–62.

Borum, R. (2011a). Radicalization into Violent Extremism I: A Review of Social Science Theories. *Journal of Strategic Security, 4*(4), 7–36.
(2011b). Radicalization into Violent Extremism II: A Review of Conceptual Models and Empirical Research. *Journal of Strategic Security, 4*(4), 37–62.

Bosi, L., Demetriou, C. & Malthaner, S. (2014). A Contentious Politics Approach to the Explanation of Radicalization. In L. Bosi, C. Demetriou & S. Malthaner (eds.), *Dynamics of Political Violence. A Process-Oriented Perspective on Radicalization and the Escalation of Political Conflict* (pp. 1–23). Surrey: Ashgate.

Bovenkerk, F. (2011). On Leaving Criminal Organizations. *Crime, Law and Social Change, 55*(4), 261–276.

Bowman-Grieve, L. (2009). Exploring "Stormfront": A Virtual Community of the Radical Right. *Studies in Conflict & Terrorism, 32*(11), 989–1007.

Boycott, R. (2002, March 10). One Man's War against His Demons. *The Guardian.* Retrieved May 14, 2020 from www.theguardian.com/uk/2002/mar/10/politics.race.

Braddock, K. (2014). The Talking Cure? Communication and Psychological Impact in Prison De-radicalisation Programmes. In A. Silke (ed.), *Prisons, Terrorism and Extremism: Critical Issues in Management, Radicalisation and Reform* (pp. 60–74). London: Routledge.
(2019a). A Brief Primer on Experimental and Quasi-Experimental Methods in the Study of Terrorism. *ICCT Policy Brief, January 2019.* International Centre for Counter-Terrorism in The Hague (ICCT). doi:10.19165/2019.2.01.
(2019b). Vaccinating against Hate: Using Attitudinal Inoculation to Confer Resistance to Persuasion by Extremist Propaganda. *Terrorism and Political Violence.* doi:10.1080/09546553.2019.1693370.
(2020). *Weaponized Words: The Strategic Role of Persuasion in Violent Radicalization and Counter-Radicalization.* Cambridge: Cambridge University Press.

Braddock, K. & Dillard, J. P. (2016). Meta-Analytic Evidence for the Persuasive Effect of Narratives on Beliefs, Attitudes, Intentions, and Behaviors. *Communication Monographs, 83*(4), 446–467. doi:10.1080/03637751.2015.1128555.

Braddock, K. & Horgan, J. (2015). Towards a Guide for Constructing and Disseminating Counter-Narratives to Reduce Support for Terrorism. *Studies in Conflict & Terrorism, 39*(5), 381–404. doi:10.1080/1057610X.2015.1116277.

Braddock, K. & Morrison, J. F. (2018). Cultivating Trust and Perceptions of Source Credibility in Online Counternarratives Intended to Reduce Support for Terrorism. *Studies in Conflict & Terrorism, 43*(6), 468–492. doi:10.1080/1057610X.2018.1452728

Brady, W. J., Wills, J. A., Jost, J. T., Tucker, J. A. & Van Bavel, J. J. (2017). Emotion Shapes the Diffusion of Moralized Content in Social Networks. *Proceedings of the National Academy of Sciences, 114*(28), 7313–7318. doi:10.1073/pnas.1618923114.

Brandenberger, D. (2002). *National Bolshevism: Stalinist Mass Culture and the Formation of Modern Russian National Identity, 1931–1956*. Cambridge, MA: Harvard University Press.

Braunthal, G. (2010). Right-Extremism in Germany: Recruitment of New Members. *German Politics and Society*, 28(4), 41–68.

Brehm, J. (1966). *A Theory of Psychological Reactance*. New York: Academic Press.

Brehm, S. & Brehm, J. (2013). *Psychological Reactance: A Theory of Freedom and Control*. New York: Academic Press.

Brenner, A. D. (2000). Feme Murder: Paramilitary "Self-Justice" in Weimar Germany. In B. B. Campbell & A. D. Brenner (eds.), *Death Squads in Global Perspective* (pp. 57–83). New York: Palgrave Macmillan.

Brewer, M. B. (1979). In-Group bias in the Minimal Intergroup Situation: A Cognitive-Motivational Analysis. *Psychological Bulletin*, 86(2), 307.

   (2010). Intergroup Relations. In *Advanced Social Psychology: The State of the Science* (pp. 535–571). New York: Oxford University Press.

Brown, T. S. (2004). Subcultures, Pop Music and Politics: Skinheads and "Nazi Rock" in England and Germany. *Journal of Social History*, 38(1), 157–178. www.jstor .org/stable/3790031.

   (2009). *Weimar Radicals: Nazis and Communists between Authenticity and Performance*. New York: Berghahn Books.

Brugh, C. S., Desmarais, S. L., Simons-Rudolph, J. & Zottola, S. A. (2019). Gender in the Jihad: Characteristics and Outcomes among Women and Men Involved in Jihadist-Inspired Terrorism. *Journal of Threat Assessment and Management*, 6(2), 76–92. doi:10.1037/tam0000123.

Brunet, J.-P. (1986). *Jacques Doriot*. Paris: FeniXX.

Bubolz, B. F. & Simi, P. (2019). The Problem of Overgeneralization: The Case of Mental Health Problems and U.S. Violent White Supremacists. *American Behavioral Scientist*. doi:10.1177/0002764219831746.

Buchheim, C. & Scherner, J. (2006). The Role of Private Property in the Nazi Economy: The Case of Industry. *The Journal of Economic History*, 66(2), 390–416. www.jstor.org/stable/3874882.

Büchner, T. (2017, August 28). Über "Makss Damage" und seinen Antisemitismus. Retrieved May 14, 2020 from www.belltower.news/ueber-makss-damage-und-seinen-antisemitismus-45238.

Busher, J. & Macklin, G. (2015). Interpreting "Cumulative Extremism": Six Proposals for Enhancing Conceptual Clarity. *Terrorism and Political Violence*, 27(5), 884–905.

Busher, J. & Morrison, J. F. (2018). Micro-Moral Worlds of Contentious Politics: A Reconceptualization of Radical Groups and Their Intersections with One Another and the Mainstream. *Mobilization: An International Quarterly*, 23(2), 219–236. doi:10.17813/1086-671x-23-3-219.

Byman, D. (2019). *Foreign Fighters Are Dangerous – for the Groups They Join*. Brookings Institution. Retrieved May 14, 2020 from www.brookings.edu/blog/order-from-chaos/2019/05/29/foreign-fighters-are-dangerous-for-the-groups-they-join.

Cain, R. (2016, July 3). The Most Important White Supremacist Of 2016. *ThinkProgress*. Retrieved May 14, 2020 from https://archive.thinkprogress.org/the-most-important-white-supremacist-of-2016-a3fa15b9896e.

Cakaj, L. (2016). *When the Walking Defeats You: One Man's Journey as Joseph Kony's Bodyguard*. London: Zed Books Ltd.

CALDT. (n.d.). Milieu. In *Cambridge Advanced Learner's Dictionary & Thesaurus*. Cambridge: Cambridge University Press.

Caplan, G. (1964). *Principles of Preventive Psychiatry*. New York: Basic Books.

Caren, N., Jowers, K. & Gaby, S. (2012). A Social Movement Online Community: Stormfront and the White Nationalist Movement. *Research in Social Movements, Conflicts and Change*, *33*, 163–193.

Carini, M. (1997, May 21). Allein in der Zelle mit Allah. *taz - die Tageszeitung*. Retrieved May 14, 2020 from https://taz.de/!1399933.

Carson, J. V. (2016). Left-Wing Terrorism: From Anarchists to the Radical Environmental Movement and Back. In G. LaFree & J. Freilich (eds.), *The Handbook of the Criminology of Terrorism* (pp. 310–322). Oxford: Wiley and Sons.

Chamberlin, P. (2011). The Struggle against Oppression Everywhere: The Global Politics of Palestinian Liberation. *Middle Eastern Studies*, *47*(1), 25–41. doi:10.1080/00263201003590300.

Chemla, S. (2020, August 5). Antisemitic French Comedian Dieudonne Banned by Facebook and Instagram. *Jerusalem Post*. Retrieved May 14, 2020 from www .jpost.com/diaspora/antisemitism/antisemitic-french-comedian-dieudonne-banned-by-facebook-637340.

Cherney, A. & Belton, E. (2019a). Assessing Intervention Outcomes Targeting Radicalised Offenders: Testing the Pro-integration Model of Extremist Disengagement as an Evaluation Tool. *Dynamics of Asymmetric Conflict*. doi:10.1080/17467586.2019.1680854.

(2019b). Evaluating Case-Managed Approaches to Counter Radicalization and Violent Extremism: An Example of the Proactive Integrated Support Model (PRISM) Intervention. *Studies in Conflict & Terrorism*, 1–21. doi:10.1080/ 1057610X.2019.1577016.

Chidzoy, S. (2008, June 20). Muslim Convert "Recruits" Inmates. *BBC*. Retrieved May 14, 2019 from http://news.bbc.co.uk/2/hi/uk_news/england/cambridgeshire/7464736.stm.

Christmann, K. (2012). *Preventing Religious Radicalisation and Violent Extremism. A Systematic Review of the Research Evidence*. Retrieved May 14, 2020 from www.gov.uk/government/uploads/system/uploads/attachment_data/file/396030/ preventing-violent-extremism-systematic-review.pdf.

Clubb, G. (2015). De-radicalization, Disengagement and the Attitudes–Behavior Debate. In C. Kennedy-Pipe, G. Clubb & S. Mabon (eds.), *Terrorism and Political Violence* (pp. 258–266). London: Sage.

(2016). The Role of Former Combatants in Preventing Youth Involvement in Terrorism in Northern Ireland: A Framework for Assessing Former Islamic State Combatants. *Studies in Conflict & Terrorism*, *39*(9), 842–861. doi:10.1080/ 1057610X.2016.1144917.

(2017). *Social Movement De-radicalisation and the Decline of Terrorism: The Morphogenesis of the Irish Republicanism Movement*. New York: Routledge.

Collins, M. (2012). *Hate: My Life in the British Far Right*. London: Biteback Publishing.

Conti, U. (2017). Between Rap and Jihad: Spectacular Subcultures, Terrorism and Visuality. *Contemporary Social Science*, *12*(3–4), 272–284. doi:10.1080/ 21582041.2017.1385828.

Converse, P. E. (1964). The Nature of Mass Belief Systems in Mass Publics. In
    D. Apter (ed.), *Ideology and Discontent* (pp. 206–261). Glencoe, IL: The Free
    Press.
    (1975). Public Opinion and Voting Behavior. In F. Greenstein & N. Polsby (eds.),
    Handbook of Political Science (vol. 4, pp. 75–171). Reading: Addison Wesley.
Copsey, N. (2016). *Anti-fascism in Britain*. London: Routledge.
Corner, E. & Gill, P. (2018). The Nascent Empirical Literature on Psychopathology
    and Terrorism. *World Psychiatry, 17*(2), 147–148. doi:10.1002/wps.20547.
Corner, E., Gill, P. & Mason, O. (2015). Mental Health Disorders and the
    Terrorist: A Research Note Probing Selection Effects and Disorder
    Prevalence. *Studies in Conflict & Terrorism, 39*(6), 560–568. doi:10.1080/
    1057610X.2015.1120099.
Cottee, S. (2016, January 25). Reborn into Terrorism. Why Are So Many ISIS Recruits
    Ex-cons and Converts? *The Atlantic.* Retrieved May 14, 2020 from www
    .theatlantic.com/international/archive/2016/01/isis-criminals-converts/426822.
Cotter, J. M. (1999). Sounds of Hate: White Power Rock and Roll and the Neo-Nazi
    Skinhead Subculture. *Terrorism and Political Violence, 11*(2), 111–140.
    doi:10.1080/09546559908427509.
Crenshaw, M. (1988). The Subjective Reality of the Terrorist: Ideological and
    Psychological Factors in Terrorism. In R. O. Slater & M. Stohl (eds.),
    Current Perspectives on International Terrorism (pp. 12–46). London:
    Macmillan.
Crossman, R. H. S. (2001). *The God That Failed.* New York: Columbia University Press.
Crüger, H. (1998). *Ein alter Mann erzählt. Lebensbericht eines Kommunisten.*
    Schkeuditz: GNN Verlag.
Cunningham, K. J. (2003). Cross-Regional Trends in Female Terrorism. *Studies in
    Conflict and Terrorism, 26*(3), 171–195.
    (2007). Countering Female Terrorism. *Studies in Conflict & Terrorism, 30*(2),
    113–129.
Dalgaard-Nielsen, A. (2008a). *Studying Violent Radicalization in Europe I: The
    Potential Contribution of Social Movement Theory*: DIIS Working Paper.
    (2008b). *Studying Violent Radicalization in Europe II: The Potential Contribution of
    Socio-psychological and Psychological Approaches*: DIIS Working Paper.
    (2010). Violent Radicalization in Europe: What We Know and What We Do Not
    Know. *Studies in Conflict & Terrorism, 33*, 797–814.
    (2013). Promoting Exit from Violent Extremism: Themes and Approaches.
    Studies in Conflict & Terrorism, 36(2), 99–115. doi:10.1080/
    1057610x.2013.747073.
Daniels, J. (2018). The Algorithmic Rise of the "Alt-Right." *Contexts, 17*(1), 60–65.
Darby, S. (2020). *Sisters in Hate: American Women on the Front Lines of White
    Nationalism.* New York: Little, Brown and Company.
Dawson, L. L. (2018). Challenging the Curious Erasure of Religion from the Study of
    Religious Terrorism. *Numen, 65*(2–3), 141–164. doi:10.1163/15685276-
    12341492.
Daymon, C., van Zuijdewijn, J. D. R. & Malet, D. (2020). *Career Foreign Fighters:
    Expertise Transmission across Insurgencies.* Washington, DC: Resolve
    Network.

De Coensel, S. (2018). Processual Models of Radicalization into Terrorism: A Best Fit Framework Synthesis. *JD Journal for Deradicalization,* Winter 2018/19, (17), 89–127.

De Koster, W. & Houtman, D. (2008). "Stormfront Is Like a Second Home to Me": On Virtual Community Formation by Right-Wing Extremists. *Information, Communication & Society, 11*(8), 1155–1176.

de Leede, S. (2018). Women in Jihad: A Historical Perspective. *ICCT Policy Brief, September 2018.* International Centre for Counter-Terrorism. doi:10.19165/2018.2.06.

De Simone, D. & Winston, A. (2020, June 21). Neo-Nazi Militant Group Grooms Teenagers. *BBC.* Retrieved May 14, 2020 from www.bbc.com/news/amp/uk-53128169.

Dearden, L. (2018, February 18). Isis Propaganda Video Shows Women Fighting for First Time amid "Desperation" to Bolster Ranks. *The Independent.* Retrieved May 14, 2020 from www.independent.co.uk/news/world/middle-east/isis-video-women-jihadis-female-fighters-recruitment-syria-iraq-islamic-state-propaganda-a8200621.html.

Dearen, J. (2017, May 24). Muslim Student Shot Dead Neo-Nazi Roommates "to Prevent Act of Domestic Terrorism." *The Independent.* Retrieved May 14, 2020 from www.independent.co.uk/news/world/americas/florida-muslim-student-kills-neo-nazi-terrorist-bomb-plotters-islam-convert-shoots-dead-roomates-a7753676.html.

Dearen, J. & Kunzelman, M. (2017a, August 22). Deadly Shooting Ends Friendships Forged in Neo-Nazi Group. *Associated Press.* Retrieved May 14, 2020 from https://apnews.com/222eaf9f330e4cdf812634f0baf3d5ca/Deadly-shooting-ends-friendships-forged-in-neo-Nazi-group.

(2017b, May 23). Muslim Student Arrested after Murdering Neo-Nazi Roommates for Disrespecting His Conversion to Islam. *The Independent.* Retrieved May 14, 2020 from www.independent.co.uk/news/world/americas/us-student-devon-arthurs-murders-neo-nazi-roommates-muslim-conversion-tampa-florida-a7750571.html.

Demant, F., Slootman, M., Buijs, F. J. & Tillie, J. (2008). *Decline and Disengagement – An Analysis of Processes of Deradicalisation.* Amsterdam: Institute for Migration and Ethnic Studies (IMES). Retrieved May 14, 2020 from http://dare.uva.nl/document/2/64714.

Desmarais, S. L., Simons-Rudolph, J., Brugh, C. S., Schilling, E. & Hoggan, C. (2017). The State of Scientific Knowledge Regarding Factors Associated with Terrorism. *Journal of Threat Assessment and Management, 4*(4), 180–209. doi:10.1037/tam0000090.

Deutsche-Welle. (2017, December 27). German Authorities Target Islamist Women's Network. *Deutsche Welle.* Retrieved May 14, 2020 from www.dw.com/en/german-authorities-target-islamist-womens-network/a-41939883.

di Scala, S. (2016a). The Battle Within: Benito Mussolini, the Reformists and the Great War. In S. di Scala & E. Gentile (eds.), *Mussolini 1883–1915* (pp. 157–192). New York: Palgrave Macmillan.

(2016b). Making Mussolini. In S. di Scala & E. Gentile (eds.), *Mussolini 1883–1915* (pp. 1–37). New York: Palgrave Macmillan.

Dodd, V., Sabbagh, D. & Syal, R. (2020, February 2). Streatham Attacker Freed from Jail Days Ago after Terror Conviction. *The Guardian.* Retrieved May 14,

2020 from www.theguardian.com/uk-news/2020/feb/02/streatham-attacker-was-released-terror-offender-sudesh-amman.

Dowling, S. (2008, August 7). New Group Helps "Persecuted" Far-Right Women. *Der Spiegel*. Retrieved May 14, 2020 from www.spiegel.de/international/germany/a-shoulder-to-cry-on-new-group-helps-persecuted-far-right-women-a-570229.html.

dpa. (2020, February 21). Salafist attackierte Wärter mit Gabeln – 14 Jahre Haft. *Berliner Morgenpost*. Retrieved May 14, 2020 from www.morgenpost.de/vermischtes/article228491929/Salafist-attackierte-Waerter-mit-Gabeln-14-Jahre-Haft.html.

Eatwell, R. (1997). *Fascism: A History*. Harmondsworth: Penguin Books.

   (2006). Community Cohesion and Cumulative Extremism in Contemporary Britain. *The Political Quarterly, 77*(2), 204–216.

Ebaugh, H. R. F. (1988). *Becoming an Ex: The Process of Role Exit*. Chicago, IL: University of Chicago Press.

Ebner, J. (2017). *The Rage: The Vicious Circle of Islamist and Far-Right Extremism*. New York: I. B. Tauris.

Edison-Hayden, M. (2018, January 16). Neo-Nazi Website Daily Stormer Is "Designed to Target Children" as Young as 11 for Radicalization, Editor Claims. *Newsweek*. Retrieved May 14, 2020 from www.newsweek.com/website-daily-stormer-designed-target-children-editor-claims-782401.

Egerton, F. (2011). *Jihad in The West: The Rise of Militant Salafism*. New York: Cambridge University Press.

El-Said, H. (2015). *New Approaches to Countering Terrorism: Designing and Evaluating Counter Radicalization and De-radicalization Programs*. Basingstoke: Palgrave Macmillan.

Ellemers, N., Spears, R. & Doosje, B. (1997). Sticking Together or Falling Apart: In-Group Identification as a Psychological Determinant of Group Commitment Versus Individual Mobility. *Journal of Personality and Social Psychology, 72*(3), 617–626.

Ellemers, N., van Knippenberg, A., De Vries, N. & Wilke, H. (1988). Social Identification and Permeability of Group Boundaries. *European Journal of Social Psychology, 18*(6), 497–513. doi:10.1002/ejsp.2420180604.

Ellemers, N., van Knippenberg, A. & Wilke, H. (1990). The Influence of Permeability of Group Boundaries and Stability of Group Status on Strategies of Individual Mobility and Social Change. *British Journal of Social Psychology, 29*(3), 233–246. doi:10.1111/j.2044-8309.1990.tb00902.x.

Ellemers, N., Wilke, H. & Van Knippenberg, A. F. M. (1993). Effects of the Legitimacy of Low-Status Group on Individual and Collective Status-Enhancement Strategies. *Journal of Personality and Social Psychology, 64*, 766–778.

Ensor, J. (2016, April 28). Isil "CVs" Reveal British Electronic Engineer, Norwegian Pilot and Turkish Nato Officer. *The Telegraph*. Retrieved May 14, 2020 from www.telegraph.co.uk/news/2016/04/28/isil-cvs-reveal-british-electrical-engineer-norwegian-pilot-and.

Eppelsheim, P. (2019). Sein Reich. *Frankfurter Allgemeine Woche, 8*, 10–13.

Exhibits from the Detention Hearing: United States of America vs. Emerson Begolly, No. Mag. No. 11-4M (United States District Court For The Western District of Pennsylvania 2011).

Eysenck, H. J. (1968). *The Psychology of Politics*. London: Transaction Publishers.

F24. (2014, December 9). France's National Front Sacks Muslim Convert Councillor. *France 24*. Retrieved May 14, 2020 from www.france24.com/en/20141209-france-national-front-sacks-councillor-maxence-buttey-who-converted-islam.

Fabel, P. (1982). Selbstdarstellung Peter Fabel. *Informationen der HNG, August*(1982), 3.

Falk, B. (2012, June 22). Falk blickt zurück (Teil 1 von 2). Retrieved May 14, 2020 from www.youtube.com/watch?v=VJhqcI2UlvI.

FAZ. (2012, March 25). „Die NSU-Morde sind unser 11. September." *Frankfurter Allgemeine Zeitung*. Retrieved May 14, 2020 from www.faz.net/aktuell/politik/inland/generalbundesanwalt-harald-range-die-nsu-morde-sind-unser-11-september-11696086.html.

Feldman, S. (2013). Political Ideology. In L. Huddy, D. O. Sears & J. S. Levy (eds.), *The Oxford Handbook of Political Psychology* (2nd ed.), (pp. 591–626). New York: Oxford University Press.

Ferguson, N., Burgess, M. & Hollywood, I. (2015). Leaving Violence Behind: Disengaging from Politically Motivated Violence in Northern Ireland. *Political Psychology, 36*(2), 199–214.

Ferrara, E. (2017). Contagion Dynamics of Extremist Propaganda in Social Networks. *Information Sciences, 418*–419, 1–12. doi:10.1016/j.ins.2017.07.030.

Festinger, L. (1957). *A Theory of Cognitive Dissonance*. Evanston, IL: Row.

Fine, R. (2014). Rereading Marx on the "Jewish Question" Marx as a Critic of Antisemitism? In M. Stoetzler (ed.), *Antisemitism and the Constitution of Sociology* (pp. 137–159). Lincoln: University of Nebraska Press.

Fischer, M. (2014). *Horst Mahler. Biographische Studie zu Antisemitismus, Antiamerikanismus und Versuchen Deutscher Schuldabwehr*. Karlsruhe: KIT Scientific Publishing.

Fisher, L. (2001). Louis Fisher. In R. H. S. Crossman (ed.), *The God That Failed* (pp. 196–228). New York: Columbia University Press.

Flower, S. (2013). Muslim Converts and Terrorism. *Counter Terrorist Trends and Analyses, 5*(11), 6–9. www.jstor.org/stable/26351197.

Fodeman, A. D., Snook, D. W. & Horgan, J. G. (2020). Picking Up and Defending the Faith: Activism and Radicalism among Muslim Converts in the United States. *Political Psychology, 41*(4), 679–698. doi:10.1111/pops.12645.

Freeden, M. (1994). Political Concepts and Ideological Morphology. *Journal of Political Philosophy, 2*(2), 140–164. doi:10.1111/j.1467-9760.1994.tb00019.x.

(1996). *Ideologies and Political Theory: A Conceptual Approach*. Oxford: Oxford University Press.

Friedrich, C. J. & Brzezinski, Z. K. (1965). *Totalitarian Dictatorship and Autocracy*. Cambridge, MA: Harvard University Press.

Frischlich, L. (2020). Dark Inspiration: Eudaimonic Entertainment in Extremist Instagram Posts. *New Media & Society*. doi:10.1177/1461444819899625.

Fromm, R. (1998). *Die "Wehrsportgruppe Hoffmann." Darstellung, Analyse und Einordnung: ein Beitrag zur Geschichte des deutschen und europäischen Rechtsextremismus*. Frankfurt am Main: P. Lang.

Fuchs, C. (2012, May 31). Beate, die braune Witwe. *Die Zeit*. Retrieved May 14, 2020 from www.zeit.de/2012/23/DOS-Zschaepe/komplettansicht.

Fuchs, C. & Goetz, J. (2012). *Die Zelle: rechter Terror in Deutschland* (1. Aufl. ed.). Reinbek: Rowohlt.

Futrell, R., Simi, P. & Simon, G. (2006). Understanding Music in Movements: The White Power Music Scene. *The Sociological Quarterly*, *47*(2), 275–304. www .jstor.org/stable/4120819.

Gadd, D. (2006). The Role of Recognition in the Desistance Process: A Case Analysis of a Former Far-Right Activist. *Theoretical Criminology*, *10*(2), 179–202. doi:10.1177/1362480606063138.

Galloway, B. (2019, September 5). The Ethics of Engaging Former Extremists to Counter Violent Extremism Online. *Moonshot CVE*. Retrieved May 14, 2020 from http://moonshotcve.com/ethics-of-engaging-formers.

Gambetta, D. & Hertog, S. (2016). *Engineers of Jihad: The Curious Connection between Violent Extremism and Education*. Princeton, NJ: Princeton University Press.

Gan, R., Neo, L. S., Chin, J. & Khader, M. (2019). Change Is the Only Constant: The Evolving Role of Women in the Islamic State in Iraq and Syria (ISIS). *Women & Criminal Justice*, *29*(4–5), 204–220. doi:10.1080/08974454.2018.1547674.

Gartenstein-Ross, D. & Blackman, M. (2019). Fluidity of the Fringes: Prior Extremist Involvement as a Radicalization Pathway. *Studies in Conflict & Terrorism*. doi:10.1080/1057610X.2018.1531545.

Geyer, M. & Fitzpatrick, S. (2009). *Beyond Totalitarianism: Stalinism and Nazism Compared*. Cambridge: Cambridge University Press.

Gilsinan, K. (2014, July 25). The ISIS Crackdown on Women, by Women. *The Atlantic*. Retrieved May 14, 2020 from www.theatlantic.com/international/archive/2014/07/ the-women-of-isis/375047.

(2019, September 9). Should We Listen to Former Extremists? *The Atlantic*. Retrieved October 20, 2020 from www.theatlantic.com/politics/archive/2019/09/ risks-former-extremists-fighting-extremism/597583.

Göpffarth, J. & Özyürek, E. (2020). Spiritualizing Reason, Rationalizing Spirit: Muslim Public Intellectuals in the German Far Right. *Ethnicities*. doi:10.1177/ 1468796820932443.

Gordon, H. J. (2015). *Hitler and the Beer Hall Putsch*. Princeton, NJ: Princeton University Press.

Gøtzsche-Astrup, O. (2018). The Time for Causal Designs: Review and Evaluation of Empirical Support for Mechanisms of Political Radicalisation. *Aggression and Violent Behavior*, *39*, 90–99. doi:10.1016/j.avb.2018.02.003.

Graham, D. A. (2018, January 25). The Strange Cases of Anti-Islam Politicians Turned Muslims. *The Atlantic*. Retrieved May 14, 2019 from www.theatlantic.com/ international/archive/2018/01/far-right-politicians-convert-islam/551438.

Gråtrud, H. (2016). Islamic State Nasheeds as Messaging Tools. *Studies in Conflict & Terrorism*, *39*(12), 1050–1070. doi:10.1080/1057610X.2016.1159429.

Gregor, A. J. (2008). *Marxism, Fascism, and Totalitarianism: Chapters in the Intellectual History of Radicalism*. Stanford, CA: Stanford University Press.

GWU-POE. (2019). *The Islamic State in America 5-Year Review*. Washington, DC: George Washington University Program on Extremism.

Hafez, M. (2020). The Crisis Within Jihadism: The Islamic State's Puritanism vs. al-Qa`ida's Populism. *CTC Sentinel*, *13*(9), 40–46. Retrieved May 14, 2020 from https://ctc.usma.edu/the-crisis-within-jihadism-the-islamic-states-puritanism-vs-al-qaidas-populism/?s=09.

Hagen, T. (1983, April 11). Kühnens Nationale Aktivisten. *taz - Die Tageszeitung*.

Haidt, J. (2001). The Emotional Dog and Its Rational Tail: A Social Intuitionist Approach to Moral Judgment. *Psychological Review*, *108*(4), 814–834.

(2012). *The Righteous Mind: Why Good People Are Divided by Politics and Religion*. New York: Vintage Books.

Hall, E. (2017, May 23). A Neo-Nazi Who Converted to Islam Allegedly Killed His Roommates over Religion. *BuzzFeed*. Retrieved May 14, 2020 from www .buzzfeednews.com/article/ellievhall/former-neo-nazi-allegedly-kills-roommates.

Hall, L., Johansson, P. & Strandberg, T. (2012). Lifting the Veil of Morality: Choice Blindness and Attitude Reversals on a Self-Transforming Survey. *PLOS ONE*, *7* (9), e45457.

Hall, L., Strandberg, T., Pärnamets, P., Lind, A., Tärning, B. & Johansson, P. (2013). How the Polls Can Be Both Spot On and Dead Wrong: Using Choice Blindness to Shift Political Attitudes and Voter Intentions. *PLOS ONE*, *8*(4), e60554.

Hamid, S. (2007). Islamic Political Radicalism in Britain: The Case of Hizb-ut-Tahrir. In T. Abbas (ed.), *Islamic Political Radicalism: A European Perspective* (pp. 145–159). Edinburgh: Edinburgh University Press.

Hamilton, M. B. (1987). The Elements of the Concept of Ideology. *Political Studies*, *35* (1), 18–38.

Hamm, M. (1993). *American Skinheads: The Criminology and Control of Hate Crime*. Westport, CT: Praeger.

(2013). *The Spectacular Few: Prisoner Radicalization and the Evolving Terrorist Threat*. New York: New York University Press.

Harris-Hogan, S., Barrelle, K. & Zammit, A. (2015). What Is Countering Violent Extremism? Exploring CVE Policy and Practice in Australia. *Behavioral Sciences of Terrorism and Political Aggression*, *8*(1), 6–24. doi:10.1080/ 19434472.2015.1104710

Harris, K., Gringart, E. & Drake, D. (2017). Leaving Ideological Groups Behind: A Model of Disengagement. *Behavioral Sciences of Terrorism and Political Aggression*, *10*(2), 91–109. doi:10.1080/19434472.2017.1299782.

Hart, S. D., Cook, A. N., Pressman, D. E., Strang, S. & Lim, Y. L. (2017). *A Concurrent Evaluation of Threat Assessment Tools for the Individual Assessment of Terrorism*. Retrieved May 14, 2020 from http://tsas.ca/wp-content/ uploads/2017/08/2017-01-Hart-WP.pdf.

Haselton, M. G., Nettle, D. & Murray, D. R. (2015). The Evolution of Cognitive Bias. In D. M. Buss (ed.), *The Handbook of Evolutionary Psychology* (2nd ed.), pp. 968–987). Hoboken, NJ: John Wiley & Sons.

Hasselbach, I. & Reiss, T. (1996). *Führer-Ex: Memoirs of a Former Neo-Nazi* (1st ed.). New York: Random House.

Hatemi, P. K., Crabtree, C. & Smith, K. B. (2019). Ideology Justifies Morality: Political Beliefs Predict Moral Foundations. *American Journal of Political Science*, *63*(4), 788–806. doi:10.1111/ajps.12448.

Hatemi, P. K., Funk, C. L., Medland, S. E., Maes, H. M., Silberg, J. L., Martin, N. G. & Eaves, L. J. (2009). Genetic and Environmental Transmission of Political Attitudes over a Lifetime. *The Journal of Politics*, *71*(3), 1141–1156.

Hatemi, P. K. & Verhulst, B. (2015). Political Attitudes Develop Independently of Personality Traits. *PLOS ONE*, *10*(7), e0134072. doi:10.1371/journal.pone.0118106.

Hausken, K. (2000). Migration and Intergroup Conflict. *Economics Letters*, *69*(3), 327–331. doi:10.1016/S0165-1765(00)00326-8.

Hawley, G. (2017). *Making Sense of the Alt-Right*. New York: Columbia University Press.

Hedayah. (2017). *Mapping the Experiences of Formers to Streamline the Process of Engaging in CVE*. Retrieved May 14, 2020 from www.hedayahcenter.org/Admin/Content/File-175201716843.pdf.

Hegghammer, T. (2017). *Jihadi Culture: The Art and Social Practices of Militant Islamists*. Cambridge: Cambridge University Press.

Hepp, O. & Kexel, W. (1983, April 11). Abschied vom Hitlerismus. *taz - Die Tageszeitung*.

Hepple, T. & Gable, G. (1993). *At War with Society*. London: Searchlight.

Hess, R. D. & Torney-Purta, J. V. (2005). *The Development of Political Attitudes in Children*. New Brunswick, NJ: Transaction Publishers.

Hewicker, C. (2001). *Die Aussteigerin. Autobiographie einer ehemaligen Rechtsextremistin*. Oldenburg: Igel.

Heydemann, S. (2014). Countering Violent Extremism as a Field of Practice. *United States Institute of Peace Insights*, *1*(Spring).

Hietaneva, P. (2008, October 31). Leader of Finnish Islamic Party Says He Was a Soviet Spy. *Helsingin Sanomat*. Retrieved May 14, 2020 from https://web.archive.org/web/20140819091524/http://www.hs.fi/english/article/1135240796149.

Hill, R. & Bell, A. (1988). *The Other Face of Terror. Inside Europe's Neo-Nazi Network*. London: Grafton Books.

Hirschi, T. (1969). A Control Theory of Delinquency. In F. P. Williams III & M. D. McShane (eds.), *Criminology Theory: Selected Classic Readings* (pp. 289–305). Abingdon: Routledge.

Hirsh, D. (2017). *Contemporary Left Antisemitism*. New York: Routledge.

Hoffman, B. (1982). *Right-Wing Terrorism in Europe*. Santa Monica, CA: RAND.
  (1984). *Right-Wing Terrorism in Europe since 1980*. Santa Monica, CA: RAND. Retrieved May 14, 2020 from www.rand.org/content/dam/rand/pubs/papers/2005/P7029.pdf.
  (1986). *Right-Wing Terrorism in West Germany*. Santa Monica, CA: RAND. Retrieved May 14, 2020 from www.rand.org/pubs/papers/P7270.html.
  (2006). Inside Terrorism. New York: Columbia University Press.

Hogg, M. A. & Abrams, D. (1988). *Social Identifications: A Social Psychology of Intergroup Relations and Group Processes*. New York: Routledge.

Holbrook, D. & Horgan, J. (2019). Terrorism and Ideology: Cracking the Nut. *Perspectives on Terrorism*, *13*(6), 2–15.

Holt, T. J., Freilich, J. D. & Chermak, S. M. (2020). Examining the Online Expression of Ideology among Far-Right Extremist Forum Users. *Terrorism and Political Violence*, 1–21. doi:10.1080/09546553.2019.1701446.

Horchem, H. J. (1988). *Die verlorene Revolution: Terrorismus in Deutschland*. Herford: Busse Seewald.

Horgan, J. (2005). *The Psychology of Terrorism*. New York: Routledge.
  (2008). From Profiles to Pathways and Roots to Routes: Perspectives from Psychology on Radicalization into Terrorism. *Annals of the American Academy of Political and Social Science*, *618*, 80–94. www.jstor.org/stable/40375777.

(2009a). Individual Disengagement: A Psychological Analysis. In T. Bjørgo & J. Horgan (eds.), *Leaving Terrorism Behind: Individual and Collective Disengagement*. (pp. 17–29). New York: Routledge.

(2009b). *Walking Away from Terrorism: Accounts of Disengagement from Radical and Extremist Movements*. New York: Routledge.

(2017). Psychology of Terrorism: Introduction to the Special Issue. *The American Psychologist*, *72*(3), 199–204.

Horgan, J. & Altier, M. B. (2012). The Future of Terrorist De-radicalization Programs. *Georgetown Journal of International Affairs, Summer/Fall*, 83–90.

Horgan, J., Altier, M. B., Shortland, N. & Taylor, M. (2016). Walking Away: The Disengagement and De-radicalization of a Violent Right-Wing Extremist. *Behavioral Sciences of Terrorism and Political Aggression*, *9*(2), 63–77. doi:10.1080/19434472.2016.1156722.

Horgan, J. & Braddock, K. (2010). Rehabilitating the Terrorists? Challenges in Assessing the Effectiveness of De-radicalization Programs. *Terrorism and Political Violence*, *22*(2), 267–291. doi:10.1080/09546551003594748.

Horgan, J. & Taylor, M. (2011). Disengagement, De-radicalization, and the Arc of Terrorism: Future Directions for Research. In R. Coolsaet (ed.), *Jihadi Terrorism and the Radicalisation Challenge: European and American Experiences* (pp. 173–186). London: Ashgate.

Horgan, J., Taylor, M., Bloom, M. & Winter, C. (2017). From Cubs to Lions: A Six Stage Model of Child Socialization into the Islamic State. *Studies in Conflict & Terrorism*, *40*(7), 645–664. doi:10.1080/1057610X.2016.1221252.

Horkheimer, M. (1939). Die Juden und Europa. *Zeitschrift für Sozialforschung*, *8*(1/2), 115–137.

Huey, L., Inch, R. & Peladeau, H. (2017). "@ Me If You Need Shoutout": Exploring Women's Roles in Islamic State Twitter Networks. *Studies in Conflict & Terrorism*, *42*(5), 445–463. doi:10.1080/1057610X.2017.1393897.

Husain, E. (2009). *The Islamist: Why I Became an Islamic Fundamentalist, What I Saw Inside, and Why I Left* (2009 ed.). New York: Penguin Books USA.

Hwang, C. J. (2015). The Disengagement of Indonesian Jihadists: Understanding the Pathways. *Terrorism and Political Violence*, *29*(2), 277–295. doi:10.1080/09546553.2015.1034855.

(2018). *Why Terrorists Quit. The Disengagement of Indonesian Jihadists*. Ithaca, NY: Cornell University Press.

Hymas, C. (2020, May 1). "High-Risk" Extremist to Be Released from Jail Despite Fears over Copycat Terrorist Attack. *The Telegraph*. Retrieved May 14, 2020 from www.telegraph.co.uk/news/2020/05/01/high-risk-extremist-released-jail-despite-fears-copycat-terrorist.

Ichner, B. (2020, August 27). FPÖ-Bezirksrat konvertierte zum Islam und kandidiert nun für SÖZ. *Der Kurier*. Retrieved May 14, 2020 from https://kurier.at/chronik/wien/fpoe-bezirksrat-konvertierte-zum-islam-und-kandidiert-nun-fuer-soez/401012513.

Ilan, J. & Sandberg, S. (2019). How "Gangsters" Become Jihadists: Bourdieu, Criminology and the Crime–Terrorism Nexus. *European Journal of Criminology*, *16*(3), 278–294. doi:10.1177/1477370819828936.

IM-Discussion. (2017). 🏴? ? Retrieved May 14, 2020 from www.ironmarch.exposed/message/25331#msg-25331.

IM-NRW. (2019). *Verfassungsschutzbericht des Landes Nordrhein-Westfalen über das Jahr 2018*. Düsseldorf: Ministerium des Innern des Landes Nordrhein-Westfalen.

Indictment: United States of America vs. Emerson Winfield Begolly, No. 1:11cr326 (United States District Court For The Eastern District Of Virginia 2011).

Ingram, H. J. (2016). A "Linkage-Based" Approach to Combating Militant Islamist Propaganda: A Two-Tiered Framework for Practitioners. *ICCT Policy Brief, November 2016*. doi:10.19165/2016.2.06.

(2017). The Strategic Logic of the "Linkage-Based" Approach to Combating Militant Islamist Propaganda: Conceptual and Empirical Foundations. *ICCT Policy Brief, April 2017*. doi:10.19165/2017.1.06.

Intelmann, P. (2014, October 3). Ein deutsches Leben. *Lübecker Nachrichten*. Retrieved May 14, 2020 from www.ln-online.de/Nachrichten/Seite-Drei/Ein-deutsches-Leben.

Islam, M. (2005, September 24). I Was a BNP Activist . . . and Converted to Islam. *The Guardian*. Retrieved May 14, 2020 from www.theguardian.com/world/2005/sep/24/religion.uk.

Jackson, L. A., Sullivan, L. A., Harnish, R. & Hodge, C. N. (1996). Achieving Positive Social Identity: Social Mobility, Social Creativity, and Permeability of Group Boundaries. *Journal of Personality and Social Psychology, 70*(2), 241–254. doi:10.1037/0022-3514.70.2.241.

Jackson, P. (2014). #hitlerwasright: National Action and National Socialism for the 21st Century. *Journal of Deradicalisation,* Winter, *14/15*(1), 97–115.

Jacobs, J. (1992). *On Socialists and "the Jewish Question" after Marx*. New York: New York University Press.

Jacobson, M. (2010). Terrorist Dropouts: Learning from Those Who Have Left, vol. 101. Washington, DC: Washington Institute for Near East Policy.

James, W. (1902). *The Varieties of Religious Experience: A Study in Human Nature; Gifford Lectures on Natural Religion Delivered at Edinburgh in 1901–1902*. New York: Longmans, Green and Co.

Jander, M. (2006). Horst Mahler. In W. Kraushaar (ed.), *Die RAF und der linke Terrorismus* (vol. 1, pp. 372–397). Hamburg: Hamburger Edition.

Jaskoski, M., Wilson, M. & Lazareno, B. (2017). Approving of But Not Choosing Violence: Paths of Nonviolent Radicals. *Terrorism and Political Violence, 32*(2), 257–274. doi:10.1080/09546553.2017.1364638.

Johansson, P., Hall, L., Sikström, S. & Olsson, A. (2005). Failure to Detect Mismatches between Intention and Outcome in a Simple Decision Task. *Science, 310*(5745), 116–119.

Johnsen, N. (2019, May 17). IS-kriger Oleg Neganov var nynazist i Norge, nå sitter han fengslet i Syria. *Verdens Gang*. Retrieved May 20, 2020 from www.vg.no/nyheter/utenriks/i/0nW0Ko/is-kriger-oleg-neganov-var-nynazist-i-norge-naa-sitter-han-fengslet-i-syria.

Johnson, A. (2019, July 16). Founder of Neo-Nazi site Daily Stormer Should Pay $14 Million to Victim of "Troll Storm," Judge Says. *NBC News*. Retrieved October 20, 2020 from www.nbcnews.com/tech/tech-news/founder-neo-nazi-site-daily-stormer-should-pay-14-million-n1030211.

Jones, N. P. (2019). Bacterial Conjugation as a Framework for the Homogenization of Tactics in Mexican Organized Crime. *Studies in Conflict & Terrorism*. doi:10.1080/1057610X.2019.1586356.

Jonsson, M. (2015). *Funding the Islamic State: Sources of Revenue, Financing Requirements and Long-Term Vulnerabilities to Counter-Measures*. Stockholm: Swedish Defense Research Agency.

Jüttner, J. (2013, January 18). Rechtsterrorismus: Zschäpes Drogenkonsum verhinderte Karriere als V-Frau. *Der Spiegel*. Retrieved May 20, 2020 from www.spiegel.de/panorama/justiz/beate-zschaepe-drogen-und-anwerbung-des-verfassungsschutzes-a-878377.html.

Kajjo, S. (2016, December 7). 2 Top IS Commanders Reportedly Flee Raqqa. *Voice of America*. Retrieved May 20, 2020 from www.voanews.com/extremism-watch/2-top-commanders-reportedly-flee-raqqa.

Kalmoe, N. P. (2020). Uses and Abuses of Ideology in Political Psychology. *Political Psychology*, *41*(4), 771–793. doi:10.1111/pops.12650.

Kalyvas, S. N. (2008). Ethnic Defection in Civil War. *Comparative Political Studies*, *41*(8), 1043–1068.

Kaneva, N. & Stanton, A. (2020). An Alternative Vision of Statehood: Islamic State's Ideological Challenge to the Nation-State. *Studies in Conflict & Terrorism*, 1–19. doi:10.1080/1057610X.2020.1780030.

Kaplan, J. (2000). David Wulstan Myatt. In J. Kaplan (ed.), *Encyclopedia of White Power: A Sourcebook on the Radical Racist Right* (pp. 216–218). Walnut Creek, CA: AltaMira Press.

Karagiannis, E. (2018). *The New Political Islam: Human Rights, Democracy, and Justice*. Philadelphia: University of Pennsylvania Press.

Karra, Y. (2020, January 19). Neo-Nazi with Jordanian Roots Charged with Vandalizing U.S. Synagogue. *Ynet News*. Retrieved May 20, 2020 from www.ynetnews.com/article/HyFl2o1111I.

Kassimeris, G. (2011). Why Greek Terrorists Give Up: Analyzing Individual Exit from the Revolutionary Organization 17 November. *Studies in Conflict & Terrorism*, *34*(7), 556–571. doi:10.1080/1057610x.2011.578551.

(2019). Greece's Ulrike Meinhof: Pola Roupa and the Revolutionary Struggle. *Studies in Conflict & Terrorism*. doi:10.1080/1057610X.2019.1620470.

Katzman, K. (2002). *The PLO and Its Factions*. Washington, DC: Congressional Research Service.

Kavanaugh, S. D. (2014, March 20). The Man Bringing Back the Nazi Movement in America. *Vocativ*. Retrieved May 20, 2020 from www.vocativ.com/usa/race/man-bringing-back-nazi-movement-america/index.html.

Kellerhoff, S. F. (2012). Neonazi-Spur beim Olympia-Attentat 1972. *Die Welt*. Retrieved May 20, 2020 www.welt.de/politik/deutschland/article106615851/Neonazi-Spur-beim-Olympia-Attentat-1972.html.

Kenney, M. & Clarke, C. P. (2020, June 23). What Antifa Is, What It Isn't, and Why It Matters. *War on the Rocks*. Retrieved May 20, 2020 from https://warontherocks.com/2020/06/what-antifa-is-what-it-isnt-and-why-it-matters.

Kershaw, I. & Lewin, M. (1997). *Stalinism and Nazism: Dictatorships in Comparison*. Cambridge: Cambridge University Press.

Kestel, L. (2012). *La conversion politique. Doriot, le PPF et la question du fascisme français*. Paris: Raisons d'agir.

Khalil, J., Horgan, J. & Zeuthen, M. (2019). The Attitudes-Behaviors Corrective (ABC) Model of Violent Extremism. *Terrorism and Political Violence*, 1–26. doi:10.1080/09546553.2019.1699793.

Khelghat-Doost, H. (2017). Women of the Caliphate: The Mechanism for Women's Incorporation into the Islamic State (IS). *Perspectives on Terrorism*, *11*(1), 17–25.

(2018). The Strategic Logic of Women in Jihadi Organizations. *Studies in Conflict & Terrorism*, *42*(10), 853–877. doi:10.1080/1057610X.2018.1430656.

Killinger, C. (2016). The Enemy of My Enemy: Gaetano Salvemini, Benito Mussolini and the Politics of the Liberal State, 1910–1914. In S. Di Scala & E. Gentile (eds.), *Mussolini 1883–1915. Triumph and Tansformation of a Revolutionary Socialist* (pp. 193–223). New York: Palgrave Macmillan.

Klausen, J. (2016). *A Behavioral Study of the Radicalization Trajectories of American "Homegrown" Al Qaeda-Inspired Terrorist Offenders*. National Criminal Justice Reference Service. Document Number 250417.

Klayman, J. (1995). Varieties of Confirmation Bias. *Psychology of Learning and Motivation*, *32*, 385–418.

Kleinberg, B., van der Vegt, I. & Gill, P. (2020). The Temporal Evolution of a Far-Right Forum. *Journal of Computational Social Science*. doi:10.1007/s42001-020-00064-x.

Kleinberg, E. & Peters, S. (2018, September 28). BallenIsles Stabbing Attack, Boy's Death at Teen's Hands, Detailed in Court Documents *Palm Beach Post*. Retrieved May 20, 2020 from https://web.archive.org/web/20190401105822/https://www.palmbeachpost.com/news/crime–law/teen-charged-with-stabbing-three-one-fatally-fight-for-islam/8zsid6UzhCpvVtPWta80OP.

Knott, K. & Lee, B. J. (2020). Ideological Transmission in Extremist Contexts: Towards a Framework of How Ideas Are Shared. *Politics, Religion & Ideology*, *21*(1), 1–23. doi:10.1080/21567689.2020.1732938.

Knudsen, R. A. (2018). Measuring Radicalisation: Risk Assessment Conceptualisations and Practice in England and Wales. *Behavioral Sciences of Terrorism and Political Aggression*, *12*(1), 37–54. doi:10.1080/19434472.2018.1509105.

Koehler, D. (2014). The Radical Online: Individual Radicalization Processes and the Role of the Internet. *Journal for Deradicalization*, Winter, (2014/15), 116–134.

(2015a). Contrast Societies: Radical Social Movements and Their Relationships with Their Target Societies: A Theoretical Model. *Behavioral Sciences of Terrorism and Political Aggression*, *7*(1), 18–34. doi:10.1080/19434472.2014.977325.

(2015b). Radical Groups' Social Pressure Towards Defectors: The Case of Right-Wing Extremist Groups. *Perspectives on Terrorism*, *IX*(6), 36–50.

(2016a). *Right-Wing Terrorism in the 21st Century: The National Socialist Underground and the History of Terror from the Far-Right in Germany*. New York: Routledge.

(2016b). Understanding Deradicalization: Methods, Tools and Programs for Countering Violent Extremism. New York: Routledge.

(2019a). Involvement of Formers in Countering Violent Extremism: A Critical Perspective on Commonly Held Assumptions. In M. Walsh & A. Gansewig (eds.), *Frühere Extremisten in der Präventionsarbeit. Perspektiven aus Wissenschaft und Praxis* (pp. 15–22). Bonn: Nationales Zentrum Kriminalprävention.

(2019b). Switching Sides: Exploring Violent Extremist Intergroup Migration across Hostile Ideologies. *Political Psychology*, *41*(3), 499–515. doi:10.1111/pops.12633.

(2020). Violent Extremism, Mental Health and Substance Abuse among Adolescents: Towards a Trauma Psychological Perspective on Violent Radicalization and Deradicalization. *The Journal of Forensic Psychiatry and Psychology*, *31*(3), 455–472. doi:10.1080/14789949.2020.1758752.

Koehler, D. & Fiebig, V. (2019). Knowing What to Do: Academic and Practitioner Understanding of How to Counter Violent Radicalization. *Perspectives on Terrorism*, *13*(3), 44–62.

Koestler, A. (2001). Arthur Koestler. In R. H. S. Crossman (ed.), *The God That Failed* (pp. 15–75). New York: Columbia University Press.

Kohler, J. (1918). *Der Prozess gegen die Attentäter von Sarajevo. Aktenmäßig dargestellt von Professor Pharos*. Berlin: R. v. Decker's Verlag.

Kolodziejczyk, M. (2012, December 5). Erst Nazi, dann Antifaschist. *Frankfurter Rundschau*. Retrieved May 20, 2020 from www.fr.de/rhein-main/npd-org27521/erst-nazi-dann-antifaschist-11385818.html.

Kulish, N. (2015, January 11). Old Nazis Never Die. *The New York Times*. Retrieved May 19, 2020 from www.nytimes.com/2015/01/11/sunday-review/old-nazis-never-die.html.

Kunzelman, M. & Tanner, J. (2020, April 11). He Led a Neo-Nazi Group Linked to Bomb Plots: He Was 13. *Associated Press*. Retrieved May 19, 2020 from https://apnews.com/7067c03e1af0b157be7c15888cbe8c27.

LaFree, G. (2018). Is Antifa a Terrorist Group? *Society*, *55*(3), 248–252.

Lake, E. (2015, February 11). Foreign Recruits Are Islamic State's Cannon Fodder. *Bloomberg Opinion*. Retrieved May 19, 2020 from www.bloomberg.com/opinion/articles/2015-02-11/foreign-fighters-are-islamic-state-s-cannon-fodder.

Lakomy, M. (2017). Let's Play a Video Game: Jihadi Propaganda in the World of Electronic Entertainment. *Studies in Conflict & Terrorism*, *42*(4), 383–406. doi:10.1080/1057610X.2017.1385903.

Lalonde, R. N. & Silverman, R. A. (1994). Behavioral Preferences in Response to Social Injustice: The Effects of Group Permeability and Social Identity Salience. *Journal of Personality and Social Psychology*, *66*(1), 78–85. doi:10.1037/0022-3514.66.1.78.

Lamoureux, M. (2019, February 15). Fascist Forge, the Online Neo-Nazi Recruitment Forum, Is Down. *Vice News*. Retrieved May 19, 2020 from www.vice.com/en_ca/article/43zn8j/fascist-forge-the-online-neo-nazi-recruitment-forum-is-down.

Lang, J. (2009). Die sanfte Seite des Rechtsextremismus? *Belltower News*. Retrieved May 19, 2020 from www.belltower.news/die-sanfte-seite-des-rechtsextremismus-2-30352.

Lankford, A. (2018). A Psychological Re-examination of Mental Health Problems among the 9/11 Terrorists. *Studies in Conflict & Terrorism*, *41*(11), 875–898. doi:10.1080/1057610X.2017.1348742.

Laqueur, W. (2000). *The New Terrorism: Fanaticism and the Arms of Mass Destruction.* New York: Oxford University Press.

(2003). *No End to War: Terrorism in the Twenty-First Century.* New York: Bloomsbury Publishing.

Latif, M., Blee, K., DeMichele, M., Simi, P. & Alexander, S. (2019). Why White Supremacist Women Become Disillusioned, and Why They Leave. *The Sociological Quarterly, 61*(3), 367–388. doi:10.1080/00380253.2019.1625733.

Laub, J. H., Nagin, D. S. & Sampson, R. J. (1998). Trajectories of Change in Criminal Offending: Good Marriages and the Desistance Process. *American Sociological Review, 63*(2), 225–238.

Laub, J. H. & Sampson, R. J. (2001). Understanding Desistance from Crime. *Crime and Justice, 28*(2001), 1–69.

Lee, G. (2003). The Political Philosophy of Juche. *Stanford Journal of East Asian Affairs, 3*(1), 105–112.

Lehberger, R. (2019, October 25). Der Vorzeigeaussteiger hetzt über "Dreckszigeuner." *Der Spiegel.* Retrieved October 26, 2020 from www.spiegel.de/politik/irfan-peci-vorzeigeaussteiger-hetzt-gegen-muslime-a-00000000-0002-0001-0000-000166611576.

Lehto, O. (2011, June 15). Abdullah Tammi vaihtoi islamilaisen puolueen puna-aatteeseen. *Länsiväylä.* Retrieved May 19, 2020 from https://web.archive.org/web/20190504211254/https://www.lansivayla.fi/artikkeli/47356-abdullah-tammi-vaihtoi-islamilaisen-puolueen-puna-aatteeseen.

Levine, J. M. & Moreland, R. L. (2002). Group Reactions to Loyalty and Disloyalty. In S. R. Thye (ed.), *Group Cohesion, Trust and Solidarity: Advances in Group Processes* (vol. 19, pp. 203–228). Bingley: Elsevier Science/JAI Press.

Lewandowsky, S., Ecker, U. K. H., Seifert, C. M., Schwarz, N. & Cook, J. (2012). Misinformation and Its Correction: Continued Influence and Successful Debiasing. *Psychological Science in the Public Interest, 13*(3), 106–131. doi:10.1177/1529100612451018.

Lewin, K. (1936). *Principles of Topological Psychology.* London: McGraw-Hill.

Lia, B. (2007). *Architect of Global Jihad: The Life of al-Qaida Strategist Abu Mus' ab al-Suri.* London: Hurst.

Lichfield, J. (2015, January 12). Quenelle Comedian Dieudonné Praises Terrorist Killer: "As Far as I Am Concerned, I Feel I am Charlie Coulibaly." *Independent.* Retrieved May 19, 2020 from www.independent.co.uk/news/people/quenelle-comedian-dieudonne-praises-terrorist-killer-as-far-as-i-am-concerned-i-feel-i-am-charlie-9972035.html.

Ligon, G. S., Simi, P., Harms, M. & Harris, D. J. (2013). Putting the "O" in VEOs: What Makes an Organization? *Dynamics of Asymmetric Conflict, 6*(1–3), 110–134. doi:10.1080/17467586.2013.814069.

Linz, J. J. (2000). *Totalitarian and Authoritarian Regimes.* London: Lynne Rienner Publishers.

Lipset, S. M. (1960). *Political Man: The Social Bases of Politics* (1st ed.). Garden City, NY: Doubleday.

Lloyd, M. (2019). *Extremism Risk Assessment: A Directory.* Centre for Research and Evidence on Security Threats (CREST). Retrieved May 19, 2020 from https://crestresearch.ac.uk/resources/extremism-risk-assessment-directory.

Lofland, J. & Skonovd, N. (1981). Conversion Motifs. *Journal for the Scientific Study of Religion, 20*(4), 373–385.

Logan, M., Ligon, G. & Derrick, D. (2017 October). Applying an Organizational Framework to Examine Jihadi Organizations as an Industry. *Homeland Security Affairs, 13* (Article 6).

Luthern, A. & Vielmetti, B. (2020, January 17). Oak Creek Man, Alleged Member of Neo-Nazi Group "The Base," Charged with Vandalizing Racine Synagogue. *Milwaukee Journal Sentinel.* https://eu.jsonline.com/story/news/crime/2020/01/17/alleged-member-neo-nazi-group-charged-racine-synagogue-vandalism/4505324002.

Lyon-Capitale. (2014, January 8). L'ITW dans Lyon Capitale qui a fait condamner Dieudonné. *Lyon Capitale.* Retrieved May 19, 2020 from www.lyoncapitale.fr/actualite/L-ITW-dans-Lyon-Capitale-qui-a-fait-condamner-Dieudonne.

Lyth, P. J. (1989). Traitor or Patriot? Andrey Vlasov and the Russian Liberation Movement 1942–45. *The Journal of Strategic Studies, 12*(2), 230–238.

Machalek, R. & Snow, D. (1993). Conversion to New Religious Movements. *Religion and the Social Order, 3*, 53–74.

Madfis, E. & Vysotsky, S. (2020). Exploring Subcultural Trajectories: Racist Skinhead Disengagement, Desistance, and Countercultural Value Persistence. *Sociological Focus, 53*(3), 221–235. doi:10.1080/00380237.2020.1782791.

Maher, S. (2016). *Salafi-Jihadism: The History of an Idea.* Oxford: Oxford University Press.

Main, T. J. (2018). *The Rise of the Alt-Right.* Washington, DC: Brookings Institution Press.

Makuch, B. & Lamoureux, M. (2019, September 17). Neo-Nazis Are Glorifying Osama Bin Laden. *Vice.* Retrieved May 19, 2020 from www.vice.com/en_us/article/bjwv4a/neo-nazis-are-glorifying-osama-bin-laden.

Manthe, B. (2019). Germany: The Role of Women in Radical Right Terrorism. www.opendemocracy.net/en/countering-radical-right/germany-role-women-radical-right-terrorism.

Marsden, S. V. (2017). *Reintegrating Extremists. Deradicalisation and Desistance.* London: Palgrave Macmillan.

Marsden, S. V. & Schmid, A. (2011). Typologies of Terrorism and Political Violence. In A. Schmid (ed.), *The Routledge Handbook of Terrorism Research* (pp. 158–200). Oxon, NY: Routledge.

Maruna, S. (2004). Desistance from Crime and Explanatory Style: A New Direction in the Psychology of Reform. *Journal of Contemporary Criminal Justice, 20*(2), 184–200. doi:10.1177/1043986204263778.

Maruna, S., Lebel, T. P., Mitchell, N. & Naples, M. (2006). Pygmalion in the Reintegration Process: Desistance from Crime through the Looking Glass. *Psychology, Crime and Law, 10*(3), 271–281.

Mastroe, C. & Szmania, S. (2016). *Surveying CVE Metrics in Prevention, Disengagement and De-radicalization Programs.* Retrieved May 19, 2020 from College Park, MD: www.start.umd.edu/pubs/START_SurveyingCVEMetrics_March2016.pdf.

Mathias, C. (2017, May 26). The Enemy of My Enemy Is My Friend: What Neo-Nazis Like about ISIS. *Huffington Post.* Retrieved May 19, 2020 from www.huffpost.com/entry/neo-nazis-isis-devon-arthurs_n_5925cd0ae4b00c8df2a13b18?

guccounter=1&guce_referrer=aHR0cHM6Ly93d3cuZ29vZ2xlLmNvbS88&guce_
referrer_sig=AQAAAL6pp_Ok0Yuo3_IdFDD_
mYsZyF8zy9aSBurxotC9UauQKPsMonFPf5u7cI68Iv2MwhgarUKa3iBY__
YRP70vQ8I6ePZ47WCljwqc3mbmlLSDQv_a7ZtcLL-8kDJow_
L6Sitklrvc4ASUawxA6ekiTz-24m35yaukKc5ScV0rxaSr.

McCoy, T. (2018, February 23). "I Don't Know How You Got This Way": A Young
  Neo-Nazi Reveals Himself to His Family. *The Washington Post*. Retrieved May
  19, 2020 from www.washingtonpost.com/news/local/wp/2018/02/23/feature/i-
  dont-know-how-you-got-this-way-a-young-neo-nazi-reveals-himself-to-his-
  family.

Meier, L. D. (2019). The Strategic Use of Emotions in Recruitment Strategies of Armed
  Groups: The Case of the Liberation Tigers of Tamil Eelam. *Studies in Conflict &
  Terrorism*. doi:10.1080/1057610X.2019.1634343.

Mekhennet, S. & Kulish, N. (2009, February 5). Uncovering Lost Path of the Most
  Wanted Nazi (Dr. Death). *The New York Times*. Retrieved May 14, 2020 from
  www.nytimes.com/2009/02/05/world/africa/05nazi.html.

Meleagrou-Hitchens, A. (2017). *Research Perspectives on Online Radicalisation:
  A Literature Review 2006–2016*. Retrieved May 19, 2020 from http://icsr.info/
  2017/05/icsr-vox-pol-paper-research-perspectives-online-radicalisation-literature-
  review-2006-2016.

Meleagrou-Hitchens, A. & Hughes, S. (2018). *The Travelers: American Jihadists in
  Syria and Iraq*. Washington, DC: George Washington University Program on
  Extremism.

Mellor, J. (2020, March 16). Far Right Terrorist Who Became Muslim Extremist behind
  Bars Has Prison Time Extended. *The London Economic*. Retrieved May 14,
  2020 from www.thelondoneconomic.com/news/far-right-terrorist-who-became-
  muslim-extremist-behind-bars-has-prison-time-extended/16/03.

Merkl, P. H. (1982). Approaches to Political Violence: the Stormtroopers, 1925–33. In
  W. J. Mommsen & G. Hirschfeld (eds.), *Social Protest, Violence and Terror in
  Nineteenth-and Twentieth-Century Europe* (pp. 367–383). London: Palgrave
  Macmillan.

  (1997). Why Are They So Strong Now? Comparative Reflections on the Revival of
  the Radical Right in Europe. In P. H. Merkl & L. Weinberg (eds.), *The Revival of
  Right-Wing Extremism in the Nineties* (pp. 17–46). London: Frank Cass.

Metzner, T. (2018, January 31). Warum ein AfD-Politiker zum Islam konvertierte. *Der
  Tagesspiegel*. Retrieved May 14, 2020 from www.tagesspiegel.de/berlin/arthur-
  wagner-warum-ein-afd-politiker-zum-islam-konvertierte/20912342.html.

Michael, G. (2006). *The Enemy of My Enemy: The Alarming Convergence of Militant
  Islam and the Extreme Right*. Lawrence: University of Kansas Press.

  (2009). The Ideological Evolution of Horst Mahler: The Far Left–Extreme Right
  Synthesis. *Studies in Conflict & Terrorism*, 32(4), 346–366. doi:10.1080/
  10576100902743997.

Midlarsky, M. I. (2011). *Origins of Political Extremism: Mass Violence in the
  Twentieth Century and Beyond*. Cambridge: Cambridge University Press.

Mielke, M. (2012, November 1). Wie Thomas U. zum Gotteskrieger wurde. *Die Welt*.
  Retrieved May 14, 2020 from www.welt.de/politik/deutschland/article110501835/
  Wie-Thomas-U-zum-Gotteskrieger-wurde.html.

Miller-Idriss, C. (2018). *The Extreme Gone Mainstream: Commercialization and Far Right Youth Culture in Germany*. Princeton, NJ: Princeton University Press.
(2020). *Hate in the Homeland: The New Global Far Right*. Princeton, NJ: Princeton University Press.
Mironova, V. (2019). *From Freedom Fighters to Jihadists: Human Resources of Non-State Armed Groups*. New York: Oxford University Press.
Misiak, B., Samochowiec, J., Bhui, K., Schouler-Ocak, M., Demunter, H., Kuey, L. & Dom, G. (2019). A Systematic Review on the Relationship between Mental Health, Radicalization and Mass Violence. *European Psychiatry*, 56, 51–59. doi:10.1016/j.eurpsy.2018.11.005.
Moghaddam, F. M. & Perreault, S. (1992). Individual and Collective Mobility Strategies among Minority Group Members. *The Journal of Social Psychology*, 132(3), 343–357. doi:10.1080/00224545.1992.9924710.
Mooney, J. (2020a, September 13). New IRA "Courting Hezbollah" for Weapons. *The Times*. Retrieved May 14, 2020 from www.thetimes.co.uk/article/new-ira-courting-hezbollah-for-weapons-hhp8vnstz.
(2020b, August 16). New IRA Boosted by Defectors after Rival Split. *The Times*. Retrieved May 14, 2020 from www.thetimes.co.uk/article/new-ira-boosted-by-defectors-after-rival-split-v70kp7b9d?s=09.
Moore, M. S. (2020, September 13). Antifa Dust. *Los Angeles Review of Books*. Retrieved October 20, 2020 from https://lareviewofbooks.org/article/antifa-dust.
Morris, N. (2008, June 21). Ex-BNP Activist "Recruiting Prisoners to Join al-Qa'ida." *The Independent*. Retrieved May 14, 2020 from www.independent.co.uk/news/uk/crime/ex-bnp-activist-recruiting-prisoners-to-join-al-qaida-851592.html.
Morris, T. (2014). Networking Vehement Frames: Neo-Nazi and Violent Jihadi Demagoguery. *Behavioral Sciences of Terrorism and Political Aggression*, 6(3), 163–182.
(2016). *Dark Ideas: How Neo-Nazi and Violent Jihadi Ideologues Shaped Modern Terrorism*. New York: Lexington Books.
Morrison, J. F. (2013). *The Origins and Rise of Dissident Irish Republicanism: The Role and Impact of Organizational Splits*: New York: Bloomsbury Publishing.
(2015). Splitting to Survive: Understanding Terrorist Group Fragmentation. *Journal of Criminological Research, Policy and Practice*, 3(3), 222–232. doi:10.1108/JCRPP-07-2016-0013.
Moskalenko, S. & McCauley, C. (2009). Measuring Political Mobilization: The Distinction Between Activism and Radicalism. *Terrorism and Political Violence*, 21(2), 239–260. doi:10.1080/09546550902765508.
Mösken, A. L. (2012a, February 18). Ihr Kampf: Iris Niemeyer ist die Enkeltochter eines Nazigegners und war einmal links. Heute sucht sie ihre politische Heimat bei der NPD und den Holocaustleugnern. Die Geschichte einer Frau am Rand der Gesellschaft. *Berliner Zeitung*.
(2012b, February 2). "Sein Land lieben, das darf man ja wohl." *Frankfurter Rundschau*. Retrieved May 14, 2020 from www.fr.de/panorama/sein-land-lieben-darf-wohl-11346922.html.
Mullen, B., Brown, R. & Smith, C. (1992). Ingroup Bias as a Function of Salience, Relevance, and Status: An Integration. *European Journal of Social Psychology*, 22(2), 103–122.

Mullins, S. (2015). Re-examining the Involvement of Converts in Islamist Terrorism: A Comparison of the US and UK. *Perspectives on Terrorism*, 9(6), 72–84.

Mullins, W. A. (1972). On the Concept of Ideology in Political Science. *American Political Science Review*, 66(2), 498–510.

Munderloh, A. (2018). Vom Neonazi zum Mugahid. *Demokratie-Dialog*, 2(2018), 55–63.

Musial, J. (2016). "My Muslim Sister, Indeed You Are a Mujahidah" – Narratives in the Propaganda of the Islamic State to Address and Radicalize Western Women: An Exemplary Analysis of the Online Magazine Dabiq. *JD Journal for Deradicalization, Winter*, (9), 39–100.

Myatt, D. (1998). My Conversion to Islam. Retrieved May 14, 2020 from http://davidmyatt.portland.co.uk:80/texts/my_conversion_to_islam.htm.

    (2001). A Covert Life: The Fanatical Tale of David Myatt. Retrieved May 14, 2020 from http://davidmyatt.portland.co.uk/texts/a_covert_life.htm.

    (2009). *National-Socialism and Islam: The Case for Co-operation*. Reichsfolk.

    (2013). *Myngath: Some Recollections of a Wyrdful and Extremist Life*. Online: Self Published.

Nagle, A. (2017). *Kill all Normies: Online Culture Wars from 4chan and Tumblr to Trump and the Alt-Right*. Laurel House: John Hunt Publishing.

Natmessnig, E. (2016, June 21). Der FPÖ-Bezirksrat, der nach Mekka pilgern möchte. *Der Kurier*. Retrieved May 14, 2020 from https://kurier.at/chronik/wien/der-fpoe-bezirksrat-der-nach-mekka-pilgern-moechte/205.665.535.

Nawaz, M. (2013). *Radical: My Journey out of Islamist Extremism*. Guilford, CT: Lyons Press.

Neiwert, D. (2017, May 9). What the Kek: Explaining the Alt-Right "Deity" behind Their "Meme Magic." Retrieved May 14, 2020 from www.splcenter.org/hatewatch/2017/05/08/what-kek-explaining-alt-right-deity-behind-their-meme-magic.

Nelson, L. (2011, July 19). Internet Messages Detail "Nazi Jihadist's" Radicalization. *Southern Poverty Law Center (SPLC)*. Retrieved May 14, 2020 from www.splcenter.org/hatewatch/2011/07/19/internet-messages-detail-%E2%80%98nazi-jihadist%E2%80%99s%E2%80%99-radicalization

Neubacher, F. (1998). *Fremdenfeindliche Brandanschläge. Eine kriminologisch-empirische Untersuchuchung von Tätern, Tathintergründen und gerichtlicher Verarbeitung in Jugendstrafverfahren*. Godesberg: Forum.

Neumann, P. (2008). Introduction. In P. Neumann, J. Stoil & D. Esfandiary (eds.), *Perspectives on Radicalisation and Political Violence: Papers from the First International Conference on Radicalisation and Political Violence* (pp. 3–7). London: International Centre for the Study of Radicalisation.

    (2013). The Trouble with Radicalization. *International Affairs*, 89(4), 873–893. doi:10.1111/1468-2346.12049.

Niemann, H. (2017, December 29, 2017). Urteil gegen Northeimer Salafisten ist rechtskräftig. Retrieved May 14, 2020 from www.goettinger-tageblatt.de/Die-Region/Northeim/Urteil-gegen-Northeimer-Salafisten-ist-rechtskraeftig.

Niemi, R. G. & Klingler, J. D. (2012). The Development of Political Attitudes and Behaviour among Young Adults. *Australian Journal of Political Science*, 47(1), 31–54.

Nilsson, A. & Erlandsson, A. (2015). The Moral Foundations Taxonomy: Structural Validity and Relation to Political Ideology in Sweden. *Personality and Individual Differences, 76,* 28–32.

Noor, M. & Halabi, S. (2018). Can We Forgive a Militant Outgroup Member? The Role of Perspective-Taking. *Asian Journal of Social Psychology, 21*(4), 246–255. doi:10.1111/ajsp.12328.

Noricks, D. M. E. (2009). Disengagement and Deradicalization: Processes and Programs. In P. K. Davis & K. Cragin (eds.), *Social Science for Counterterrorism. Putting the Pieces Together* (pp. 299–320). Santa Monica, CA: Rand Corporation.

Norwood, S. H. (2013). *Antisemitism and the American Far Left.* Cambridge: Cambridge University Press.

Nossiter, A. (2016, July 13). "That Ignoramus": 2 French Scholars of Radical Islam Turn Bitter Rivals. *The New York Times.*

Noy, C. (2008). Sampling Knowledge: The Hermeneutics of Snowball Sampling in Qualitative Research. *International Journal of Social Research Methodology, 11* (4), 327–344.

Nyhan, B. & Reifler, J. (2010). When Corrections Fail: The Persistence of Political Misperceptions. *Political Behavior, 32*(2), 303–330.

O'Brian, L. (2017). The Making of an American Nazi. *The Atlantic,* December. Retrieved May 14, 2020 from www.theatlantic.com/magazine/archive/2017/12/the-making-of-an-american-nazi/544119.

O'Hara, L. (1996). *Searchlight for Beginners.* London: Phoenix Press.

Oppenheim, B., Steele, A., Vargas, J. F. & Weintraub, M. (2015). True Believers, Deserters, and Traitors: Who Leaves Insurgent Groups and Why. *Journal of conflict resolution, 59*(5), 794–823.

Oppenheimer, D. (2016). *Exit Right: The People Who Left the Left and Reshaped the American Century.* New York: Simon and Schuster.

Osborne, S. (2019, February 6). Politician Who Said "the Quran Is Poison" Announces He Has Become a Muslim after Trying to Write Anti-Islam Book. *The Independent.* Retrieved May 14, 2020 from www.independent.co.uk/news/world/europe/joram-van-klaveren-islam-muslim-converts-religion-netherlands-geert-wilders-a8765476.html.

Paloutzian, R. F. (1996). *Invitation to the Psychology of Religion.* Boston: Allyn & Bacon.

Patterson, D. (2016). Islamic Jihadism and the Legacy of Nazi Antisemitism. *Journal of Antisemitism, 7,* 189–202.

Peci, I. (2019, April 16). Sind Islamisten Links? *Achgut– Die Achse des Guten.* Retrieved May 14, 2020 from www.achgut.com/artikel/sind_islamisten_links.

Peltonen, A. (2007, October 19). Abdullah Tammi. Kalifiksi Kalifin paikalle. Mistä Suomen islamilaisessa puolueessa on kysymys? *City.* Retrieved May 14, 2020 from www.city.fi/ilmiot/abdullah+tammi/2460.

Perdue, J. B. & Johnson, S. (2012). *The War of All the People: The Nexus of Latin American Radicalism and Middle Eastern Terrorism.* Washington, DC: Potomac Books.

Perešin, A. (2015). Fatal Attraction: Western Muslimas and ISIS. *Perspectives on Terrorism, 9*(3), 21–38.

Peresin, A. & Cervone, A. (2015). The Western Muhajirat of ISIS. *Studies in Conflict & Terrorism*, *38*(7), 495–509. doi:10.1080/1057610x.2015.1025611.

Pettigrew, T. F. & Tropp, L. R. (2000). Does Intergroup Contact Reduce Prejudice? Recent Meta-Analytic Findings. In S. Oskamp (ed.), *Reducing Prejudice and Discrimination* (pp. 93–114). New York: Psychology Press.

Picart, C. (2015). "Jihad Cool/Jihad Chic": The Roles of the Internet and Imagined Relations in the Self-Radicalization of Colleen LaRose (Jihad Jane). *Societies*, *5* (2), 354–383.

Pisoiu, D. (2011). *Islamist Radicalisation in Europe: An Occupational Change Process*. New York: Routledge.

Pisoiu, D. & Lang, F. (2015). The Porous Borders of Extremism: Autonomous Nationalists at the Crossroad with the Extreme Left. *Behavioral Sciences of Terrorism and Political Aggression*, *7*(1), 69–83. doi:10.1080/ 19434472.2014.977327.

Plea Agreement. United States of America v. Yousef O. Barasneh, No. 20-CR-26 (United States District Court Eastern District of Wisconsin 2020).

Politico. (2018, August 12). What Charlottesville Changed. *Politico Magazine*. Retrieved May 14, 2020 from www.politico.com/magazine/story/2018/08/12/ charlottesville-anniversary-supremacists-protests-dc-virginia-219353.

Poulter, J. (2018, March 13). The Obscure Neo-Nazi Forum Linked to a Wave of Terror. *Vice*. Retrieved May 14, 2020 from www.vice.com/en_au/article/437pkd/ the-obscure-neo-nazi-forum-linked-to-a-wave-of-terror.

Pressman, D. E., Duits, N., Rinne, T. & Flockton, J. (2016). *VERA-2R Violent Extremism Risk Assessment-Version 2 Revised*.

Pretus, C., Hamid, N., Sheikh, H., Ginges, J., Tobeña, A., Davis, R. & Atran, S. (2018). Neural and Behavioral Correlates of Sacred Values and Vulnerability to Violent Extremism. *Frontiers in Psychology*, *9* (Article 2462). doi:10.3389/fpsyg.2018.02462.

Rabasa, A., Pettyjohn, S. L., Ghez, J. J. & Boucek, C. (2010). *Deradicalizing Islamist Extremists*. Santa Monica, CA: RAND. Retrieved May 14, 2020 from www.rand .org/content/dam/rand/pubs/monographs/2010/RAND_MG1053.pdf.

Radke, J. & Staud, T. (2014). Neue Töne von Rechtsaußen. Retrieved May 14, 2020 from www.bpb.de/politik/extremismus/rechtsextremismus/185067/neue- toene-von-rechtsaussen.

Rambo, L. R. (1993). *Understanding Religious Conversion*. London: Yale University Press.

Rasch, W. (1979). Psychological Dimensions of Political Terrorism in the Federal Republic of Germany. *International Journal of Law and Psychiatry*, *2*(1), 79–85.

Ray, B. & Marsh, G. E. (2001). Recruitment by Extremist Groups on the Internet. *First Monday*, *6*(2).

Red-Action. (2000). Obituary – Matty "Blag" Roberts. *Red Action*, *4*(6). Retrieved May 14, 2020 from www.redactionarchive.org/2012/03/obituary-matty-blag-roberts .html.

Reeve, E. (2017, May 25). How an 18-Year-Old Gamer Went from Neo-Nazi to Muslim to Alleged Killer. *Vice News*. Retrieved May 14, 2020 from www.vice .com/en_us/article/paz8q7/how-devon-arthurs-went-from-neo-nazi-to-muslim-to- alleged-killer.

Reidy, K. (2018). Radicalization as a Vector: Exploring Non-violent and Benevolent Processes of Radicalization. *Journal for Deradicalization*, (14), 249–294.

Reinares, F. (2011). Exit From Terrorism: A Qualitative Empirical Study on Disengagement and Deradicalization Among Members of ETA. *Terrorism and Political Violence*, *23*(5), 780–803. doi:10.1080/09546553.2011.613307.

Reinares, F., Alonso, R., Bjørgo, T., Della Porta, D., Coolsaet, R., Khosrokhavar, F. &De Vries, G. (2008). *Radicalisation Processes Leading to Acts of Terrorism* Retrieved May 14, 2020 from www.rikcoolsaet.be/files/art_ip_wz/Expert%20Group%20Report%20Violent%20Radicalisation%20FINAL.pdf.

Reuters. (2014, February 3). Britain Bars Entry to French Comedian Accused of Anti-Semitism. *Reuters*. Retrieved May 14, 2020 from https://uk.reuters.com/article/idUKBREA120VZ20140203.

Richards, I. (2019). A Philosophical and Historical Analysis of "Generation Identity": Fascism, Online Media, and the European New Right. *Terrorism and Political Violence*. doi:10.1080/09546553.2019.1662403.

Richardson, J. T. (1978). *Conversion Careers: In and Out of the New Religions*. Beverly Hills, CA: Sage Publications.

Robin, C. (2019, January 23). The Plight of the Political Convert. *The New Yorker*. www.newyorker.com/books/under-review/the-plight-of-the-political-convert.

Rollwage, M., Dolan, R. J. & Fleming, S. M. (2018). Metacognitive Failure as a Feature of Those Holding Radical Beliefs. *Current Biology*, *28*(24), 4014–4021. e4018. doi:10.1016/j.cub.2018.10.053.

Roose, K. (2017, August 15). This Was the Alt-Right's Favorite Chat App. Then Came Charlottesville. *The New York Times*. Retrieved May 14, 2020 from www.nytimes.com/2017/08/15/technology/discord-chat-app-alt-right.html.

Röpke, A. (2012). *Mädelsache! Frauen in der Neonazi-Szene*. Berlin: Christoph Links Verlag.

Röpke, A. & Speit, A. (2011). An der Seite der NPD – der 'Ring Nationaler Frauen' (RNF). In A. Röpke & A. Speit (eds.), *Mädelsache! Frauen in der Neonazi-Szene*. (pp. 23–58). Bonn: Bundeszentrale für politische Bildung.

Rosen, K.-H. (1989). Rechtsterrorismus. Gruppen – Taten – Hintergründe. In G. Paul (ed.), *Hitlers Schatten verblaßt. Die Normalisierung des Rechtsextremismus*. (pp. 49–78). Bonn: Dietz.

Rosenau, W. (2020). *Tonight We Bombed the US Capitol: The Explosive Story of M19, America's First Female Terrorist Group*. New York: Atria Books.

Rosenau, W., Espach, R., Ortiz, R. D. & Herrera, N. (2014). Why They Join, Why They Fight, and Why They Leave: Learning From Colombia's Database of Demobilized Militants. *Terrorism and Political Violence*, *26*(2), 277–285. doi:10.1080/09546553.2012.700658.

Rosenhaft, E. (1983). *Beating the Fascists? The German Communists and Political Violence 1929–1933*. Cambridge: Cambridge University Press.

Ross, G. C. (2000). *The Swastika in Socialism: Right-Wing Extremism in the GDR*. Hamburg: Verlag Dr. Kovac.

Rovenpor, D. R., O'Brien, T. C., Roblain, A., De Guissme, L., Chekroun, P. & Leidner, B. (2019). Intergroup Conflict Self-Perpetuates via Meaning: Exposure to Intergroup Conflict Increases Meaning and Fuels a Desire for Further Conflict.

Journal of Personality and Social Psychology, *116*(1), 119–140. doi:10.1037/pspp0000169.

Ruby, C. L. (2002). Are Terrorists Mentally Deranged? *Analyses of Social Issues and Public Policy*, *2*(1), 15–26. doi:10.1111/j.1530-2415.2002.00022.x.

Rusbult, C. E. (1983). A Longitudinal Test of the Investment Model: The Development (and Deterioration) of Satisfaction and Commitment in Heterosexual Involvements. *Journal of Personality and Social Psychology*, *45*(1), 101–117.

Sacco, V. F. & Kennedy, L. W. (2002). *The Criminal Event: Perspectives in Space and Time*. Belmont, CA: Wadsworth Publishing Company.

Sageman, M. (2004). *Understanding Terror Networks*. Philadelphia: University of Pennsylvania Press.

Said, B. (2012). Hymns (Nasheeds): A Contribution to the Study of the Jihadist Culture. *Studies in Conflict & Terrorism*, *35*(12), 863–879.

Sarma, K. M. (2017). Risk Assessment and the Prevention of Radicalization from Nonviolence into Terrorism. *American Psychologist*, *72*(3), 278–288.

Saucier, G., Akers, L. G., Shen-Miller, S., Kneževié, G. & Stankov, L. (2009). Patterns of Thinking in Militant Extremism. *Perspectives on Psychological Science*, *4*(3), 256–271.

Schapiro, L. B. (1979). Antisemitism in the Communist World. *Soviet Jewish Affairs*, *9*(1), 42–52.

Scheuch, E. K. & Klingermann, H. D. (1967). Theorie des Rechtsradikalismus in westlichen Industriegesellschaften. *Hamburger Jahrbuch für Wirtschafts- und Gesellschaftspolitik*, *12*, 11–29.

Scheurig, B. (1993). *Verräter oder Patrioten: das Nationalkomitee" Freies Deutschland" und der Bund Deutscher Offiziere in der Sowjetunion, 1943–1945*. Berlin: Propyläen.

Schils, N. & Verhage, A. (2017). Understanding How and Why Young People Enter Radical or Violent Extremist Groups. *International Journal of Conflict and Violence (IJCV)*, *11*(2), 1–17.

Schmidtchen, G. (1981). Terroristische Karrieren. Soziologische Analyse anhand von Fahndungsunterlagen und Prozeßakten. In H. Jäger, G. Schmidtchen & L. Süllwold (eds.), *Analysen zum Terrorismus Bd. 2: Lebenslaufanalysen* (pp. 14–77). Opladen: Westdeutscher Verlag.

Schönhuber, F. & Mahler, H. (2000). *Schluss mit deutschem Selbsthass: Plädoyers für ein anderes Deutschland*. Berg: VGB-Verlagsgesellschaft.

Schrock, D., Holden, D. & Reid, L. (2004). Creating Emotional Resonance: Interpersonal Emotion Work and Motivational Framing in a Transgender Community. *Social Problems*, *51*(1), 61–81.

Schüddekopf, O. E. (1960). *Linke Leute von rechts: die national-revolutionären Minderheiten und der Kommunismus in der Weimarer Republik*. Stuttgart: Kohlhammer.

Schulz, B. (2009). Die Anwälte. *Eine deutsche Geschichte*. Retrieved May 14, 2020 from www.youtube.com/watch?v=cnQwU18PqBw&list=PLC45AB48CFEB9840D.

Schuurman, B., Grol, P. & Flower, S. (2016). Converts and Islamist Terrorism: An Introduction. *ICCT Policy Brief*, *7*(3), 1–21.

Schuurman, B. & Taylor, M. (2018). Reconsidering Radicalization: Fanaticism and the Link between Ideas and Violence. *Perspectives on Terrorism*, *12*(1), 3–22.

Scrivens, R. (2020). Exploring Radical Right-Wing Posting Behaviors Online. *Deviant Behavior*, 1–15. doi:10.1080/01639625.2020.1756391.

Scrivens, R., Venkatesh, V., Bérubé, M. & Gaudette, T. (2019). Combating Violent Extremism: Voices of Former Right-Wing Extremists. *Studies in Conflict & Terrorism*. doi:10.1080/1057610X.2019.1686856.

Sears, D. O. & Funk, C. L. (1991). The Role of Self-interest in Social and Political Attitudes. *Advances in Experimental Social Psychology*, *24*, 1–91.

Sedgwick, M. (2010). The Concept of Radicalization as a Source of Confusion. *Terrorism and Political Violence*, *22*(4), 479–494. doi:10.1080/09546553.2010.491009.

Seitenbecher, M. (2013). *Mahler, Maschke & Co. Rechtes Denken in der 68er Bewegung?* Paderborn: Ferdinand Schöningh.

Seliger, M. (1976). *Ideology and Politics*. London: Allen & Unwin.

Seymour, L. J. (2014). Why Factions Switch Sides in Civil Wars: Rivalry, Patronage, and Realignment in Sudan. *International Security*, *39*(2), 92–131.

Shapiro, L. R. & Maras, M.-H. (2018). Women's Radicalization to Religious Terrorism: An Examination of ISIS Cases in the United States. *Studies in Conflict & Terrorism*, 1–32. doi:10.1080/1057610X.2018.1513694.

Shekhovtsov, A. (2018). *Russia and the Western Far Right: Tango Noir*. London: Routledge, Taylor & Francis Group.

Shelley, L. I. (2014). Corruption and Youth's Recruitment into Violent Extremism. In M. Lombardi, E. Ragab, V. Chin, Y. Dandurand, V. D. Divitiis & A. Burato (eds.), *Countering Radicalisation and Violent Extremism among Youth to Prevent Terrorism* (vol. 118, pp. 37–47). Berlin: IOS Press.

Siegel, H. (2011, January 11). Nazi Buff Turned Jihadi Allegedly Bites FBI Agents. *ABC News*. Retrieved May 14, 2020 from https://abcnews.go.com/Blotter/nazi-buff-turned-jihadi-allegedly-bites-fbi-agents/story?id=12557232&tqkw=&tqshow=&nwltr=blotter_featureMore.

Sigl, J. (2018). *Biografische Wandlungen ehemals organisierter Rechtsextremer: Eine biografieanalytische und geschlechterreflektierende Untersuchung*. Wiesbaden: VS Verlag.

Silke, A. (2008). Holy Warriors: Exploring the Psychological Processes of Jihadi Radicalization. *European Journal of Criminology*, *5*(1), 99–123. doi:10.1177/1477370807084226.

Silone, I. (2001). Ignazio Silone. In R. H. S. Crossman (ed.), *The God That Failed* (pp. 76–114). New York: Columbia University Press.

Silverstein, S. M. (1988). A Study of Religious Conversion in North America. *Genetic, Social, and General Psychology Monographs*, *114*(3), 261–305.

Simi, P., Blee, K., DeMichele, M. & Windisch, S. (2017). Addicted to Hate: Identity Residual among Former White Supremacists. *American Sociological Review*, *82*(6), 1167–1187.

Simi, P. & Futrell, R. (2010). *American Swastika. Inside the White Power Movement's Hidden Spaces of Hate*. Lanham, MD: Rowman & Littlefield.

Simi, P., Windisch, S. & Sporer, K. (2016). *Recruitment and Radicalization among US Far-Right Terrorists*. Retrieved May 14, 2020 from www.start.umd.edu/pubs/START_RecruitmentRadicalizationAmongUSFarRightTerrorists_Nov2016.pdf.

Sims, A. (2015, September 16). British Isis Member Complains of "Rude Arabs" Who Steal His Shoes, Eat Like Children and Won't Queue. *The Independent*. Retrieved May 14, 2020 from www.independent.co.uk/news/world/middle-east/british-isis-member-complains-of-rude-arabs-who-steal-his-shoes-eat-like-children-and-wont-queue-10503356.html.

Sines v. Kessler, No. Civil Action No. 3:17-cv-00072-NKM (United States District Court for the Western District of Virginia 2019).

Slovic, P. (1995). The Construction of Preference. *American Psychologist*, *50*(5), 364–371.

Smith, B. L. (1994). *Terrorism in America : Pipe Bombs and Pipe Dreams*. Albany: State University of New York Press.

Smith, K. B., Alford, J. R., Hibbing, J. R., Martin, N. G. & Hatemi, P. K. (2017). Intuitive Ethics and Political Orientations: Testing Moral Foundations as a Theory of Political Ideology. *American Journal of Political Science*, *61*(2), 424–437. doi:10.1111/ajps.12255.

Snook, D. W., Williams, M. J. & Horgan, J. G. (2018). Issues in the Sociology and Psychology of Religious Conversion. *Pastoral Psychology*, *68*, 223–240. doi:10.1007/s11089-018-0841-1.

Snow, D. A. (2004). Framing Processes, Ideology, and Discursive Fields. In D. A. Snow, S. A. Soule & H. Kriesi (eds.), *The Blackwell Companion to Social Movements* (pp. 380–412). Hoboken: Wiley.

Snow, D. A. & Machalek, R. (1984). The Sociology of Conversion. *Annual Review of Sociology*, *10*(1), 167–190.

Southern, D. B. (1982). Anti-democratic Terror in the Weimar Republic: The Black Reichswehr and the Feme-Murders. In W. J. Mommsen & G. Hirschfeld (eds.), *Social Protest, Violence and Terror in Nineteenth-and Twentieth-Century Europe* (pp. 330–341). London: Palgrave Macmillan.

Speckhard, A. & Yayla, A. S. (2015). Eyewitness Accounts from Recent Defectors from Islamic State: Why They Joined, What They Saw, Why They Quit. *Perspectives on Terrorism*, *9*(6), 95–118.

SPLC. (2019, August 10). Weekend Read: Neo-Nazi Leader Must Pay More Than $14 Million in Damages. *Southern Poverty Law Center*. Retrieved May 14, 2020 from www.splcenter.org/news/2019/08/10/weekend-read-neo-nazi-leader-must-pay-more-14-million-damages.

(n.d., n.a.). Andrew Anglin. *Southern Poverty Law Center*. Retrieved May 14, 2020 from www.splcenter.org/fighting-hate/extremist-files/individual/andrew-anglin.

Stahl, K. D. (2010, May 27). Erlösung durch Vernichtung. *Die Zeit*. Retrieved May 14, 2020 from www.zeit.de/2010/22/GES-Johann-von-Leers/komplettansicht.

START. (2018). *Profiles of Individual Radicalization in the United States (PIRUS) Codebook*. College Park, MD: National Consortium for the Study of Terrorism and Responses to Terrorism.

Steinberg, G. (2013). *German Jihad: On the Internationalisation of Islamist Terrorism*. New York: Columbia University Press.

Stern, H. (1963). The Organisation Consul. *The Journal of Modern History*, *35*(1), 20–32.

Stern, J. (2010). Mind over Martyr: How to Deradicalize Islamist Extremists. *Foreign Affairs*, *98*(1), 95–108.

Sternhell, Z., Sznajder, M. & Ashéri, M. (1994). *The Birth of Fascist Ideology: From Cultural Rebellion to Political Revolution*. Princeton, NJ: Princeton University Press.

Strandberg, T., Sivén, D., Hall, L., Johansson, P. & Pärnamets, P. (2018). False Beliefs and Confabulation Can Lead to Lasting Changes in Political Attitudes. *Journal of Experimental Psychology: General, 147*(9), 1382–1400.

Strauch, C. (2018, October 13). Wie Beatrix von Storch um Muslime wirbt. *Frankfurter Allgemeine Zeitung*. Retrieved May 14, 2020 from www.faz.net/aktuell/politik/inland/wie-afd-politikerin-beatrix-von-storch-um-muslime-wirbt-15836366.html.

Stromberg, P. G. (2008). *Language and Self-Transformation: A Study of the Christian Conversion Narrative*. New York: Cambridge University Press.

STT-Uusi. (2009, December 19). Suomen islamilaisen puoleen johtaja erosi: Terrorismikiista. *Uusi Suomi*. Retrieved May 14, 2020 from www.uusisuomi.fi/uutiset/suomen-islamilaisen-puoleen-johtaja-erosi-terrorismikiista/92b8e486-74db-37e2-8b30-cc69c1a642bd.

Sullivan, D. (2018, January 31). Suspect in Neo-Nazi Murders Tells of Anger Problem, Says "I Might Be Kind of Sick." *Tampa Bay Times*. Retrieved May 14, 2020 from www.tampabay.com/news/courts/criminal/Suspect-in-neo-Nazi-murders-tells-of-anger-problem-says-I-might-be-kind-of-sick-w-video-_165018397.

(2019, December 19). Experts: One-Time Neo-Nazi Charged in Double Murder Has Autism, Schizophrenia. *Tampa Bay Times*. Retrieved May 14, 2020 from www.tampabay.com/news/crime/2019/12/19/experts-one-time-neo-nazi-charged-in-double-murder-has-autism-schizophrenia.

(2020, May 18). One-time Neo-Nazi Deemed Unfit for Trial in Tampa Murders. *Tampa Bay Times*. Retrieved May 20, 2020 from www.tampabay.com/news/crime/2020/05/18/one-time-neo-nazi-deemed-unfit-for-trial-in-tampa-murders.

Süllwold, L. (1981). Stationen in der Entwicklung von Terroristen. Psychologische Aspekte biographischer Daten. In H. Jäger, G. Schmidtchen & L. Süllwold (eds.), *Analysen zum Terrorismus Bd. 2: Lebenslaufanalysen*. (pp. 80–116). Opladen: Westdeutscher Verlag.

Svendsen, C. (2019, April 13). De Som Valgte Vold Og Terror. *NRK*. Retrieved May 14, 2020 from www.nrk.no/dette-er-nordmennene-som-valgte-krig-og-terror-i-syria-1.14511716.

Svendsen, C. & Alayoubi, M. (2020, September 29). Oleg (31) var nynazist i Norge – nå er han dømt til åtte års fengsel som IS-medlem i Irak. *Norsk rikskringkasting (NRK)*. Retrieved October 14, 2020 from www.nrk.no/norge/oleg-_31_-var-nynazist-i-norge_-na-er-han-domt-til-atte-ars-fengsel-som-is-medlem-i-irak-1.14800707.

Svendsen, C., Alayoubi, M. & Jentoft, M. (2017, August 29). Sentral i nynazist-miljø i Norge: Ble IS-kriger. *Norsk rikskringkasting (NRK)*. Retrieved May 14, 2020 from www.nrk.no/dokumentar/sentral-i-nynazist-miljo-i-norge_-ble-is-kriger-1.12986425.

Swann Jr, W. B., Jetten, J., Gómez, Á., Whitehouse, H. & Bastian, B. (2012). When Group Membership Gets Personal: A Theory of Identity Fusion. *Psychological Review, 119*(3), 441–456. doi:10.1037/a0028589.

Tajfel, H. (1974). Social Identity and Intergroup Behaviour. *Information (International Social Science Council), 13*(2), 65–93.

(1981). *Human Groups and Social Categories*. Cambridge: Cambridge University Press.

Tajfel, H., Billig, M. G., Bundy, R. P. & Flament, C. (1971). Social Categorization and Intergroup Behavior. *European Journal of Social Psychology*, *1*(2), 149–178.

Tajfel, H. & Turner, J. (1979). An Integrative Theory of Intergroup Conflict. In W. G. Austin & S. Worchel (eds.), *The Social Psychology of Intergroup Relations* (pp. 33–47). Monterey, CA: Brooks/Core Publishing.

Tajfel, H. & Turner, J. C. (2004). *The Social Identity Theory of Intergroup Behavior*. New York: Psychology Press.

Tampa-PD. (2017). *Arrest-Detective Report*. (GO#2017-260921). Tampa, FL.

Tapley, M. & Clubb, G. (2019). *The Role of Formers in Countering Violent Extremism*. International Centre for Counter-Terrorism in the Hague (ICCT). Retrieved May 14, 2020 from https://icct.nl/publication/the-role-of-formers-in-countering-violent-extremism.

Tausch, N., Saguy, T. & Bryson, J. (2015). How Does Intergroup Contact Affect Social Change? Its Impact on Collective Action and Individual Mobility Intentions among Members of a Disadvantaged Group. *Journal of Social Issues*, *71*(3), 536–553. doi:10.1111/josi.12127.

Taylor, D. M. & McKirnan, D. J. (1984). Theoretical Contributions: A Five-Stage Model of Intergroup Relations. *British Journal of Social Psychology*, *23*(4), 291–300.

Taylor, R. (2008, March 25). *Rock against Racism's Thirtieth Anniversary Timeout London*. Retrieved May 14, 2020 from www.timeout.com/london/things-to-do/rock-against-racisma-s-thirtieth-anniversary.

taz. (1983a, April 11). Abschied vom Faschismus? *taz – Die Tageszeitung*.
(1983b, May 3). Alles unwahr? *taz – Die Tageszeitung*.

Team-Ross, Bevenssee & ZC. (2019, December 19). Transnational White Terror: Exposing Atomwaffen and The Iron March Networks. *Bellingcat*. Retrieved May 14, 2020 from www.bellingcat.com/news/2019/12/19/transnational-white-terror-exposing-atomwaffen-and-the-iron-march-networks.

Tenold, V. (2018). *Everything You Love Will Burn: Inside the Rebirth of White Nationalism in America* (1st ed.). New York: Nation Books.

Thompson, K. C. (2001). Watching the Stormfront: White Nationalists and the Building of Community in Cyberspace. *Social Analysis: The International Journal of Social and Cultural Practice*, *45*(1), 32–52.

Thompson-Schill, S. L., D'Esposito, M., Aguirre, G. K. & Farah, M. J. (1997). Role of Left Inferior Prefrontal Cortex in Retrieval of Semantic Knowledge: A Reevaluation. *Proceedings of the National Academy of Sciences of the United States of America*, *94*(26), 14792–14797. doi:10.1073/pnas.94.26.14792.

Townsend, M. (2019, April 21). "It's Ruined My Life," Says Man Who Exposed Plot to Kill MP Rosie Cooper. *The Guardian*. Retrieved May 14, 2020 from www.theguardian.com/uk-news/2019/apr/21/rosie-cooper-murder-plot-whistleblower-robbie-mullen-death-threats.

Trisko Darden, J., Henshaw, A. L. & Szekely, O. (2019). *Insurgent Women: Female Combatants in Civil Wars*. Washington, DC: Georgetown University Press.

Turner, J. (2015). Strategic Differences: Al Qaeda's Split with the Islamic State of Iraq and al-Sham. *Small Wars & Insurgencies*, *26*(2), 208–225.

Ueberschär, G. R. (1996). *Das Nationalkomitee "Freies Deutschland" und der Bund Deutscher Offiziere*. Frankfurt: Fischer.

Ullman, C. (2013). *The Transformed Self: The Psychology of Religious conversion*. New York: Springer Science & Business Media.

United States of America vs. Yousef Omar Barasneh: Criminal Complaint, No. 20m86I (United States District Court For The Eastern District Of Wisconsin 2020).

UNOSAA. (2007). *"Combatants on Foreign Soil": An Assessment of Their Current Status and of Measures to Facilitate Their Disarmament, Repatriation and Inclusion in National Demobilisation and Reintegration Programmes*. Retrieved May 14, 2020 from www.davidmalet.com/uploads/Combatants_on_Foreign_Soil.pdf.

USA. (1967). *Congressional Record: Proceedings and Debates of the 90th Congress. First Session* (vol. 113). Washington, DC: United States Government Printing Office.

Van Bavel, J. J. & Pereira, A. (2018). The Partisan Brain: An Identity-Based Model of Political Belief. *Trends in Cognitive Sciences*, *22*(3), 213–224. doi:10.1016/j. tics.2018.01.004.

van der Heide, L., van der Zwan, M. & van Leyenhorst, M. (2019). The Practitioner's Guide to the Galaxy – A Comparison of Risk Assessment Tools for Violent Extremism. *ICCT Research Paper, September 2019*. doi:10.19165/2019.1.07.

van der Valk, I. & Wagenaar, W. (2010). *The Extreme Right: Entry and Exit*. Retrieved May 14, 2020 from www.annefrank.org/ImageVaultFiles/id_12094/cf_21/ EntryAndExit.PDF.

Van Ree, E. (2001). The Concept of "National Bolshevism": An Interpretative Essay. *Journal of Political Ideologies*, *6*(3), 289–307.

van Stekelenburg, J. (2014). Going All the Way: Politicizing, Polarizing, and Radicalizing Identity Offline and Online. *Sociology Compass*, *8*(5), 540–555.

(2017). Radicalization and Violent Emotions. PS: Political Science & PS: *Political Science & Politics*, *50*(4), 936–939. doi:10.1017/S1049096517001020.

Venkatesh, V., Podoshen, J. S., Wallin, J., Rabah, J. & Glass, D. (2018). Promoting Extreme Violence: Visual and Narrative Analysis of Select Ultraviolent Terror Propaganda Videos Produced by the Islamic State of Iraq and Syria (ISIS) in 2015 and 2016. *Terrorism and Political Violence*, *32*(8), 1753–1775. doi:10.1080/ 09546553.2018.1516209.

Vergara, D. (2020, December 15). Aktiv i VAM på 90-talet - Nu i vänsternationalistiskt nätverk. *Expo*. Retrieved May 14, 2020 from https://expo.se/2020/12/aktiv-i-vam-p%C3%A5–90-talet-nu-i-vansternationalistiskt-natverk.

Vermeulen, F. & Bovenkerk, F. (2012). *Engaging with Violent Islamic Extremism: Local Policies in Western European Cities*. The Hague: Eleven International Publishing.

Von Behr, I., Reding, A., Edwards, C. & Gribbon, L. (2013). *Radicalisation in the Digital Era. The Use of the Internet in 15 Cases of Terrorism and Extremism*. Brussels: RAND Europe.

von Hein, M. & Felden, E. (2018, October 25, 2018). The German Who Went from Left-Wing Terrorist to Salafist Sympathizer. Retrieved May 14, 2020 from www.dw.com/ en/the-german-who-went-from-left-wing-terrorist-to-salafist-sympathizer/a-46011056.

Von Klemperer, K. (1951). Towards a Fourth Reich? The History of National Bolshevism in Germany. *The Review of Politics*, *13*(2), 191–210.

Von Knop, K. (2007). The Female Jihad: Al Qaeda's Women. *Studies in Conflict & Terrorism, 30*(5), 397–414. doi:10.1080/10576100701258585.

von Salomon, E. (1951). *Der Fragebogen*. Hamburg: Rowohlt.

Wahlström, M. & Törnberg, A. (2019). Social Media Mechanisms for Right-Wing Political Violence in the 21st Century: Discursive Opportunities, Group Dynamics, and Co-ordination. *Terrorism and Political Violence*. doi:10.1080/09546553.2019.1586676.

Walker, T. (2016, July 1). Meet the American White Supremacist Who Thinks Brexit Is the Best Thing to Happen to Europe since Hitler. *The Independent*. Retrieved May 14, 2020 from www.independent.co.uk/news/world/americas/white-supremacist-brexit-sacramento-hitler-trump-heimbach-a7112941.html.

Walker, K., Bowen, E. & Brown, S. (2013). Psychological and Criminological Factors Associated with Desistance from Violence: A Review of the Literature. *Aggression and Violent Behavior, 18*(2), 286–299. doi:10.1016/j.avb.2012.11.021.

Wallace, B. (2020, March 30). *The Prep-School Nazi*. *Intelligencer*. Retrieved May 14, 2020 from https://nymag.com/intelligencer/amp/2020/03/rinaldo-nazzaro-the-base-norman-spear.html.

Walsh, M. & Gansewig, A. (2019). A Former Right-Wing Extremist in School-Based Prevention Work: Research Findings from Germany. *JD Journal for Deradicalization, Winter*(21), 1–42.

Wang, A. B. (2018, March 22). A Teen with Former Neo-Nazi Ties Claims His "Muslim Faith" Led Him to Stab Three, Police Say. *The Washington Post*. Retrieved May 14, 2020 from www.washingtonpost.com/news/acts-of-faith/wp/2018/03/22/a-teen-with-former-neo-nazi-ties-claims-his-muslim-faith-led-him-to-stab-three-police-say.

Ware, J. (2019). Siege: The Atomwaffen Division and Rising Far-Right Terrorism in the United States. *ICCT Policy Brief, July 2019*. Retrieved May 14, 2020 from https://icct.nl/wp-content/uploads/2019/07/ICCT-Ware-Siege-July2019.pdf.

Warren, C., McGraw, A. P. & Van Boven, L. (2011). Values and Preferences: Defining Preference Construction. *Wiley Interdisciplinary Reviews: Cognitive Science, 2*(2), 193–205.

Weatherston, D. & Moran, J. (2003). Terrorism and Mental Illness: Is There a Relationship? *International Journal of Offender Therapy and Comparative Criminology, 47*(6), 698–713.

Weitzman, M. (2010). Anti-Semitism and Terrorism. In H.-L. Dienel, Y. Sharan, C. Rapp & N. Ahituv (eds.), *Terrorism and the Internet: Threats, Target Groups, Deradicalisation Strategies* (pp. 7–26). Amsterdam: IOS Press.

Willems, H. (1995). Development, Patterns and Causes of Violence against Foreigners in Germany: Social and Biographical Characteristics of Perpetrators and the Process of Escalation. In T. Bjørgo (ed.), *Terror from the Extreme Right* (pp. 162–181). London: Frank Cass.

Williams, M. J. (2017). Prosocial Behavior Following Immortality Priming: Experimental Tests of Factors with Implications for CVE Interventions. *Behavioral Sciences of Terrorism and Political Aggression, 9*(3), 153–190. doi:10.1080/19434472.2016.1186718.

Windisch, S., Ligon, G. S. & Simi, P. (2017). Organizational [Dis]trust: Comparing Disengagement among Former Left-Wing and Right-Wing Violent Extremists.

Studies in Conflict & Terrorism, *42*(6), 559–580. doi:10.1080/1057610X.2017.1404000.

Windsor, L. (2020). The Language of Radicalization: Female Internet Recruitment to Participation in ISIS Activities. *Terrorism and Political Violence*, *32*(3), 506–538. doi:10.1080/09546553.2017.1385457.

Winkler, T. (1995, August 18). Durchs Droehnland; Doppelter Elvis. Die wichtigsten und ueberfluessigsten Konzerte der kommenden Woche. *Die Tageszeitung*.

Winterberg, Y. & Peter, J. (2004). *Der Rebell. Odfried Hepp: Neonazi, Terrorist, Aussteiger*: Bergisch Gladbach: Verlagsgruppe Lübbe.

Wistrich, R. S. (1973). Karl Marx, German Socialists and the Jewish Question, 1880–1914. *East European Jewish Affairs*, *3*(1), 92–97.

Wood, G. (2016). The Way of the Strangers: Encounters with the Islamic State. New York: Random House.

Wright, S. C., Taylor, D. M. & Moghaddam, F. M. (1990). Responding to Membership in a Disadvantaged Group: From Acceptance to Collective Protest. *Journal of Personality and Social Psychology*, *58*, 994–1003.

Wynne-Jones, R. (2011, August 9). Back from the Front: Inside the Mind of a Reformed UK Far-Right Extremist. *The Independent*. Retrieved May 14, 2020 from www.independent.co.uk/arts-entertainment/books/features/back-from-the-front-inside-the-mind-of-a-reformed-uk-far-right-extremist-2334059.html.

Zaller, J. R. (1992). *The Nature and Origins of Mass Opinion*. Cambridge: Cambridge University Press.

Zannettou, S., Bradlyn, B., De Cristofaro, E., Kwak, H., Sirivianos, M., Stringini, G. & Blackburn, J. (2018). *What Is Gab: A Bastion of Free Speech or an Alt-Right Echo Chamber*. Paper presented at the Companion Proceedings of the Web Conference 2018.

Zelin, A. (2014). The War between ISIS and al-Qaeda for Supremacy of the Global Jihadist Movement. *The Washington Institute for Near East Policy*, *20*(1), 1–11.

Zelin, A. (2019). *Wilayat al-Hawl: "Remaining" and Incubating the Next Islamic State Generation*. Retrieved May 14, 2020 from www.washingtoninstitute.org/uploads/Documents/pubs/PolicyNote70-Zelin.pdf.

Index